The Black Metropolis in the Twenty-First Century

The Black Metropolis in the Twenty-First Century

Race, Power, and Politics of Place

Robert D. Bullard

ROWMAN & LITTLEFIELD PUBLISHERS, INC.
Lanham • Boulder • New York • Toronto • Plymouth, UK

ROWMAN & LITTLEFIELD PUBLISHERS, INC.

Published in the United States of America
by Rowman & Littlefield Publishers, Inc.
A wholly owned subsidary of The Rowman & Littlefield Publishing Group, Inc.
4501 Forbes Boulevard, Suite 200, Lanham, Maryland 20706
www.rowmanlittlefield.com

Estover Road
Plymouth PL6 7PY
United Kingdom

British Library Cataloguing in Publication Information Available

Library of Congress Cataloging-in-Publication Data

The Black metropolis in the twenty-first century : race, power, and politics of place /
   [edited by] Robert D. Bullard.
     p. cm.
   Includes bibliographical references.
   ISBN-13: 978-0-7425-4329-4 (pbk. : alk. paper)
   ISBN-10: 0-7425-4329-3 (pbk. : alk. paper)
   ISBN-13: 978-0-7425-4328-7 (cloth : alk. paper)
   ISBN-10: 0-7425-4328-5 (cloth : alk. paper)
    1. City dwellers—United States. 2. African Americans—Social conditions.
   3. Blacks—Segregation—United States. 4. Sociology, Urban—United States.
   5. Urban geography—United States. 6. Human geography—United States.
   I. Bullard, Robert D. (Robert Doyle), 1946-
   HT221.B53 2007
   305.896'073—dc22   2006038128

Printed in the United States of America

♾™ The paper used in this publication meets the minimum requirements of
American National Standard for Information Sciences—Permanence of Paper
for Printed Library Materials, ANSI/NISO Z39.48-1992.

Contents

Foreword

This book brings together key essays that seek to make visible and expand our understanding of the role of government (policies, programs, and investments) in shaping cities and metropolitan regions; the costs and consequences of uneven urban and regional growth patterns; suburban sprawl and public health, transportation, and economic development; and the enduring connection of place, space, and race in the era of increased globalization. Whether intended or unintended, many government policies (housing, transportation, land use, environmental, economic development, education, etc.) have aided and in some cases subsidized suburban sprawl, job flight, and spatial mismatch; concentrated urban poverty; and heightened racial and economic disparities.

This book is the outgrowth of a series of meetings that began in 2003 cosponsored by the Ford Foundation. We began this collaboration with several gatherings—two at the Kirwan Institute for the Study of Race and Ethnicity at Ohio State University in Columbus, Ohio, and a final one at the Environmental Justice Resource Center at Clark Atlanta University in Atlanta—that brought together several dozen of the nation's leading African American scholars, social scientists, educators, lawyers, urban planners, environmentalists, and activists to discuss alternative strategies and action plans to solve urban and metropolitan problems.

Having spent more than two decades studying and participating in real-world efforts to address inequality in America, the authors tackle the difficult issue of race head-on—with emphasis on the African American experience—and provide a context for assessing black progress and prospects in the post–civil rights era. The chapters are interdisciplinary and written in a readable style suitable for undergraduate and graduate students in the various

social and behavioral sciences, education, urban and regional planning, ethnic studies, urban studies, American studies, law and legal studies, and public health. The content also has appeal to individuals and organizations that
are concerned about equal opportunity, social justice, civil and human
rights, and racial and ethnic disparities in the United States.

The chapters in this book, written mostly by African American scholars,
capture the dynamism of these meetings, describing the challenges facing
cities, suburbs, and metropolitan regions as they seek to address continuing
and emerging patterns of racial polarization in the twenty-first century. The
book clearly shows that the United States entered the new millennium as
one of the wealthiest and most powerful nations on earth. Yet amid this
prosperity, our nation is faced with some of the same challenges that confronted it at the beginning of the twentieth century—including rising inequality in income, wealth, and opportunity; economic restructuring; immigration pressures and ethnic tension; and a widening gap between
"haves" and "have-nots."

Nowhere is the gulf between haves and have-nots more pronounced than
in Metropolitan America. Many of our central cities and inner-ring suburbs
are in worse shape today than they were two decades ago. Sociologist W. E.
B. Du Bois wrote his prophetic prediction in 1903, saying that "the problem
of the twentieth century is the color line." While different in degree and context, the "color line" persists as a key problem of the twenty-first century.

Race matters. Place also matters. Place (cities, suburbs, and rural areas) is
unequal. Where we live impacts the quality of our lives and chances for the
"good life." We understand that race in contemporary America is much
more complex than the black-white prism, because of changing demographics that shaped much of the nation's thinking about race and ethnic
relations over the last century. While there is no scientific basis for race—
since race is a social construct, a human invention—the color line is no
imaginary line; it is real and has real consequences. Similarly, white privilege is real. It is the "other side of racism."

Today, people of color (African Americans, Latino Americans, Native
Americans, and Asian and Pacific Islander Americans) make up just under
a third of the total U.S. population. In 2004, the Census Bureau predicted
that in the year 2050 people of color would comprise one-half of the total
American population of 420 million people. Hispanics, who can be of any
race, will comprise roughly one-quarter of the U.S. population, blacks 15
percent, and Asians 8 percent.

Color even divides Hispanics. Black and white Hispanics (and Hispanics
who say they are "some other race") work in different jobs, earn different
levels of pay, have different poverty rates, and reside in segregated neighborhoods. Although black Hispanics are better educated (an average of
twelve years of education, compared with eleven for white Hispanics and

ten for the "other race" group), black Hispanics have 12 percent unemployment, compared with 8 percent for white Hispanics and 10 percent for Hispanics who report they are neither race. Still, the old adage holds true, "if you are white you are right, if you are brown stick around, but if you are black get back."

The Ford Foundation has been engaged in efforts to address the challenges of urban poverty and racial isolation since the 1950s. Much has changed since those early days. In 1950, 70 percent of the American people lived in 157 cities. Most of the remaining population lived in rural areas. Very few people lived in the suburbs. The majority of 15 million African Americans resided in the South. The Hispanic population was mostly concentrated in small towns and cities of the Southwest. The heavily urbanized Asian American population was settled in a few cities on the West Coast.

Today, we are a suburban nation. Over 60 percent of Americans live in the suburbs in almost 30,000 jurisdictions, and 40 percent of the African American population now lives there as well. Forty-six percent of people below the poverty line also live in suburbs, many in pockets of poverty that have formed in the last two decades. Many of the older, inner-ring suburbs, those contiguous to the core cities, are losing population at an alarming rate and exhibit declining incomes relative to their surroundings, while new developments farther out are booming with jobs and economic opportunity for their privileged residents. Instead of addressing these urban ills, an increasing number of communities are fortifying with gates, "walling in" and "walling out."

For more than a third of a century, African American scholars and other advocates for racial justice have documented metropolitan racial polarization, much of it lamenting the racism endemic in society, without hope of a progressive coalition within the larger society to implement change. The modern civil rights movement made a difference in the lives of millions of African Americans. Black America made gains in education, employment, home and business ownership, and wealth creation. They also used the vote to increase the number of black elected officials. For nearly a quarter century, we have had a sizable number of black congresspersons, black mayors, black state representatives, black city council members, black superintendents, and black judges. Yet despite incremental change, equality has eluded most African Americans. Today, we find more black males in prison than enrolled in college. Racial segregation exists in housing and schools, and income disparities persist despite African American movement to the suburbs. More important, racial discrimination in the real estate, mortgage, and insurance industries continues to deny millions of African Americans wealth accumulation through home ownership. The wealth gap is actually widening because of the informal "tax" levied for being black in America.

During the past decade, however, there are reasons to be cautiously hopeful that a progressive coalition may be possible at the metropolitan level.

The negative dimensions of rapidly expanding suburbs affecting other groups have led to a potent environmental, economic, and fiscal critique of the dominant paradigm of metropolitan development. Environmentalists have mounted a powerful case that sprawl squanders energy resources and contributes mightily to land, air, and water pollution; global warming; and loss of biodiversity.

Business coalitions across the country, finding common ground with environmental groups and advocates of economic justice, are recognizing that the fragmented political boundaries of individual cities and suburbs do not encompass the operative economies in an increasingly globalizing world. These economies require coordinated approaches to transportation, a high-quality workforce, and greater corporate involvement in issues concerning the metropolitan area. A number of elected officials have argued that their jurisdictions in older, inner-ring suburbs and declining rural areas have a self-interest in promoting greater regional coordination of land-use fiscal planning. Taken together these actors potentially represent new allies for metropolitan regional equity.

This book takes an uncompromising look at the threats and promises of the quest for regional equity at the beginning of a new century. It examines the places where African Americans now live, the historic and continuing patterns of racial segregation in housing, schools, jobs, health, and governance. And the authors have set out an agenda for the future, which to be successful, they argue, must incorporate the voices and leadership of African Americans.

To this end, a second outgrowth of the collaboration that led to this publication has been the formation of the African American Forum on Race and Regionalism (AAFRR), with its secretariat at Global Environmental Resources, Inc., supported by the Ford Foundation. Its goal is to serve as a clearinghouse and to promote widespread public discourse of the topics discussed in this volume. The cochairs of the forum are Angela Glover Blackwell of PolicyLink, john a. powell of the Kirwan Institute for the Study of Race and Ethnicity, and Robert D. Bullard of the Clark Atlanta University Environmental Justice Resource Center, each of whom, along with their colleagues, continue to build, strengthen, and broaden the network of African American scholars, analysts, policy makers, and elected officials who are working on equity and regional growth issues.

Carl Anthony
Deputy Director
Community and Resource Unit
The Ford Foundation

Acknowledgments

There are a number of persons and organizations we wish to thank for making this book possible. We are especially grateful to Carl Anthony of the Ford Foundation, which provided financial support for the Environmental Justice Resource Center's race, smart growth, and regional equity work. A hearty thanks is extended to Deeohn Ferris, executive director of Global Environmental Resources, Inc., who assisted in organizing the hectic schedules of some extremely busy people, numerous conference calls, and face-to-face meetings of the African American Forum on Race and Regionalism (AAFRR).

I want to thank my staff at the Environmental Justice Resource Center, Lisa Sutton, and Michele Dawkins, for their assistance in organizing the authors/scholars roundtable and making sure the authors received their honoraria in a reasonable time. Thanks go out to my colleagues Glenn S. Johnson and Angel O. Torres, who read the manuscript and assisted in editing. I am also grateful for the contributions of my colleagues from across the country who took time out of their busy schedules to participate in the meetings, prepare and present their papers, and endure the constant nagging about deadlines. Finally, our hats go off to Alan McClare at Rowman & Littlefield for his patience and hard work in bringing this project to completion.

Introduction:
The Significance of
Race and Place

Robert D. Bullard

Over 150 years after the infamous Dred Scott U.S. Supreme Court Decision in 1857, some people and entire communities still feel that "no black man [or woman] has any rights that any white man is bound to respect."[1] Some six decades ago, in 1944, Swedish sociologist Gunnar Myrdal published his classic study, *An American Dilemma*,[2] and in 1945 St. Claire Drake and Horace R. Clayton wrote their groundbreaking *Black Metropolis*, documenting the role racism played in creating racial inequality and the black ghetto.[3]

In 1965, psychologist Kenneth Clark proclaimed that racism created our nation's "dark ghettos."[4] In 1968, the National Advisory Commission on Civil Disorders (Kerner Commission) reported that "white society is deeply implicated in the ghetto" and that "white institutions created it, white institutions maintain it, and white society condones it."[5]

This introductory chapter provides the sociohistorical framework for the book and examines the progress African Americans have made over the past four decades and the barriers they still must overcome. It also lays the foundations for understanding the interconnections between race, class, and space in shaping our nation's metropolitan regions. While the physical signs of "Jim Crow" have come down, invisible walls still limit access to opportunity and maintain social inequality between black life and white life in the United States.

The black population in the United States grew from 20.7 million in 1964 to over 39.7 million (13.4 percent of the population) by July 1, 2005. The Hispanic population (who may be of any race) swelled to over 42.7 million (14.4 percent of the population), becoming the largest ethnic minority group in the nation.[6] The United States is no longer a biracial society of blacks and whites exclusively. But even though the "browning" of the

nation—rapid growth in Hispanic population—is changing the racial relations landscape, black-white disparities are for the most part still the greatest of all racial challenges in the country.

Much progress has been made since the passage of the Civil Rights Act of
1964 and the Voting Rights Act of 1965. As a group, the African American
population is larger, richer, wiser, and politically more powerful than it was
when those laws were enacted. A growing number of African Americans complete high school, go to college, increase their incomes and buying power, buy
homes, open businesses, win elections to political offices, join the middle
class, and move to the suburbs. Yet four decades later, America has yet to
achieve a color-blind status. The nation is closer to achieving *equality of opportunity* than it is achieving *equality of condition* for African Americans.[7]

RACE, PLACE, AND OPPORTUNITY

In this volume we are especially interested in the way the metropolitan pie
is sliced and the impact of suburbanization and sprawl-driven development
on African Americans within metropolitan regions. Clearly, suburbanization does not automatically translate into racially and ethnically diverse
neighborhoods for African Americans. In cities or suburbs and across regions, African Americans remain the most segregated racial/ethnic group in
the United States.[8]

Majority-black communities are not created by random chance. There is
considerable evidence that real estate brokers still "steer" prospective home
buyers to certain neighborhoods based on race, despite laws that ban such
practices.[9] Racial steering, a form of housing discrimination in which minority home buyers are shown houses in neighborhoods less desirable than
those shown to comparable whites, can prevent even middle-class African
Americans from purchasing property. Racial steering lowers the demand for
housing in predominantly African American areas.

The National Fair Housing Alliance (NFHA) study, *Unequal Opportunity:
Perpetuating Housing Segregation in America*, discovered that in targeted underserved areas, properties are marketed to whites as affordable, solid, long-term
investments in up-and-coming communities.[10] But African Americans are often steered from these communities, told that property prices are overinflated.
The study found that the quality of a neighborhood's school district was often used as a proxy for the racial composition of a neighborhood. Whites are
told to steer clear of certain neighborhoods because of "bad schools."[11] The
NFHA estimates that the 26,092 complaints it received last year represent less
than one percent of 3.7 million violations of the FHA nationwide.

There is mounting evidence that some businesses systematically avoid
(redlining) African American areas of all class levels and selectively target

white areas for their operations—creating "opportunity-poor" communities (mostly black) and "opportunity-rich" communities (mostly white). Racial redlining, a form of credit discrimination based on the characteristics of the neighborhood surrounding the would-be borrower's dwelling or business, denies residents of mostly African American communities equal access to residential, consumer, and small business credit.

Similarly, "reverse redlining," the extension of credit on unfair terms to particular geographic areas because of the race or national origin of their residents, also hits African Americans especially hard. The absence of mainstream banking institutions and their services in African American neighborhoods helps create market conditions in which reverse redlining thrives. Redlining and reverse redlining are opposite sides of the same coin. Both have negative consequences for black wealth creation in cities and suburbs. These patterns are institutionalized by lending practices and reproduced again and again by subsequent generations.[12]

Today, 71 percent of whites, 58 percent of Asians, 49 percent of Hispanics, and 39 percent of African Americans live in the suburbs.[13] Many African Americans choose suburbs that already have large black populations. For example, the average African American lives in a majority-black suburb in Newark and Miami (60 percent), Atlanta and Cleveland (56 percent), St. Louis (55 percent), Chicago and Washington, D.C. (51 percent), and Fort Lauderdale (50 percent).[14] But majority-black suburban neighborhoods generally provide fewer economic opportunities in terms of rising home values and access to good schools and jobs, making it harder for them to catch up and keep up, financially, with whites. A recent study by the Leadership Council found that 94 percent of African Americans in Chicago live in "low-opportunity" (rated on factors such as strength of tax base, quality of schools, and availability of employment) suburbs, compared with 44 percent of whites.[15]

Generally, African Americans' housing patterns have little to do with choice or preference but are outcomes of centuries of housing discrimination that gives them no choice. Similarly, those African Americans who prefer majority-black neighborhoods and are successful in making this choice happen do so to avoid discrimination or social isolation in a predominately white environment. Clearly, there are benefits and penalties of living in black suburbia and majority-black central cities.

The costly downside is that homes in black suburbia appreciate in value more slowly than comparable homes in majority-white suburbs with similar median incomes. Black flight to the majority-black suburbs does not insulate middle-class residents from poverty. In Chicago, African Americans with household incomes over $60,000 are more likely to have neighbors in poverty than whites with household incomes below $30,000.[16] Suburban poverty is on the rise. Suburban poverty increased by 9.9 percent from 2001 to 2002.[17] Clearly, new solutions to inequitable regional development patterns are needed to create opportunity and build strong, healthy communities where all residents can participate and prosper.[18]

In the early years of the twenty-first century, race still matters. Place also matters. All cities, suburbs, and metropolitan regions are not created equal. Some regions are declining, offering less opportunity for African Americans, while others are growing, which may offer more opportunity. If a community happens to be poor, working class, or black, its residents generally have fewer choices and opportunities—on a range of residential amenities such as housing, schools, jobs, shopping, parks, green space, hospitals, police, and fire protection—than affluent, middle-class, or white residents.[19]

Race and place in America are interconnected.[20] Race continues to polarize and spatially divide cities.[21] Racialized place creates perpetual demarcations and provides advantage, privilege, and an "edge" for whites, while penalizing black home owners for living in all-black segregated neighborhoods.[22] It also affects access to jobs, education and public services, culture, medical services, level of personal security, and shopping.[23]

It is far easier to find fast-food outlets and payday loan stores than sit-down restaurants and commercial banks in middle-income black neighborhoods. Generally, stricter zoning ordinances ban locally unwanted land uses (LULUs) from white neighborhoods. Developers also build in amenities that most middle-income whites take as a given. These amenities go in before the new housing development is finished since all residents don't move in at the same time. Residents of new African American subdivisions have to wait, sometimes years, after construction is over.[24]

In the United States, place is racialized with benefits, resources, and opportunities unevenly distributed across the urban landscape.[25] Redlining practices used by insurance companies, banks, and mortgage companies are built largely around racialized zip codes. Although illegal, redlining is still practiced—even by pizza companies and taxi services. Some pizza companies won't deliver to some black inner-city neighborhoods.

The color of your skin and your destination does matter to some cab drivers. Many black men, including myself, have had problems with Washington, D.C., cab drivers who pass them up or refuse to take them to mostly black neighborhoods such as Anacostia or even to Howard University. Some of my African American friends and I have even resorted to letting our white and Asian colleagues hail taxis, and we later hop in after the taxi stops. An elaborate "jitney" cab system was established in Harlem to counter this problem.

ENDANGERED SPACE

Racialized place even affects the air African Americans breathe.[26] Living in "endangered space" can be hazardous to you health. Locally unwanted land uses and polluting facilities are not randomly scattered across the urban landscape. African Americans and other people of color are more likely than whites to live in communities with dirty air and dangerous polluting facilities.[27] For example, according to National Argonne Laboratory researchers, 57 percent of whites, 65 percent of African Americans, and 80 percent of Hispanics live in 437 counties with substandard air quality.[28] In the heavily populated Los Angeles basin, the South Coast Air Quality Management District estimates that 71 percent of African Americans and 50 percent of Latinos live in areas with the most polluted air, compared to 34 percent of whites. Air pollution costs Americans $10 to $200 billion a year.[29]

In December 2005, the Associated Press released results from its analysis of an EPA research project showing that African Americans are 79 percent more likely than whites to live in neighborhoods where industrial pollution is suspected of posing the greatest health danger. Using the EPA's own data and government scientists, the Associated Press's *More Blacks Live with Pollution* study revealed that in nineteen states, blacks were more than twice as likely as whites to live in neighborhoods where air pollution seems to pose the greatest health danger.[30]

The AP analyzed the health risk posed by industrial air pollution using toxic chemical air releases reported by factories to calculate a health risk score for each square kilometer of the United States. The scores can be used to compare risks from long-term exposure to factory pollution from one area to another. The scores are based on the amount of toxic pollution released by each factory, the path the pollution takes as it spreads through the air, the level of danger to humans posed by each different chemical released, and the number of males and females of different ages who live in the exposure paths.

Although the AP findings are important headline-grabbing news, they are not news to millions of African American residents and activists who have labored on the frontline for equal enforcement of the nation's environmental laws. The AP study results confirm a long string of reports that show race maps closely with the geography of pollution and unequal protection. For decades, African Americans and other communities of people of color have borne a disproportionate burden of pollution from incinerators, smelters, sewage treatment plants, chemical factories, and a host of other polluting facilities. And for decades government regulators have largely ignored these compelling facts.[31]

Race also maps closely with economic and environmental vulnerability— as seen in the aftermath of Hurricane Katrina and the devastation of New Orleans. It is no mystery which racial group was the most vulnerable and which groups were most likely to be physically left behind in a hurricane, flood, or a man-made disaster: blacks, the poor, homeless, elderly, disabled, nondriver and carless, and sick people.[32] For decades, black poverty was hidden from sight. Katrina brought the "dirty little secret" of urban poverty and vulnerability to light in living color. The storm also served as a wake-up call to other black communities across the country—where concentrated poverty, lack of transportation, racial segregation, economic isolation, and environmental vulnerability persist as real threats.

Businesses and employers are keenly aware of and contribute to racialized place.[33] Some employers use space as a "signal" associated with perceptions about race, class, worker skills, and attitudes.[34] Using these signals, many employers often recruit white suburban workers while avoiding central black workers. In metropolitan Atlanta, for example, space "inside" and "outside" of I-285 (a perimeter highway that encircles the city) has become racialized. A business location advertised as "inner-city and inside the perimeter" is code for black, while a location defined as "outside the perimeter" connotes suburban and whites.

Middle-income home owners in black neighborhoods have fewer services, retail shopping, banking, good schools, and other residential amenities— amenities that are commonplace in most middle-class neighborhoods that white home owners take for granted.[35] One can easily observe "commercial" redlining of black communities in Prince George's County, Maryland, and South DeKalb, Georgia—two affluent and mostly African American enclaves—outside Washington, D.C., and Atlanta.[36]

BLACK WEALTH AND THE COLOR LINE

The 100th anniversary of W. E. B. Du Bois's classic *The Souls of Black Folk* was celebrated in 2003. Writing from his home in Atlanta, Du Bois predicted that "the problem of the twentieth century is the problem of the color-line."[37] Du Bois wrote his classic book just seven years after the infamous *Plessy v. Ferguson* ruling.

The color line was not an imaginary line when Du Bois made his profound statement in 1903. It is not imaginary today for Black America in 2006—though it may be less rigid. African Americans have shattered "glass ceilings" and moved well beyond becoming the "first" in many fields. However, social equality has remained elusive. Whether embedded in "racial stigma"[38] or institutionalized discrimination, it is a stark reality for millions of poor and middle-class blacks.[39] America has never been color-blind when it pertains to blacks.[40]

Housing is a critical example of where the color line dynamics operate. Home ownership is still the cornerstone of the American dream. Today, African Americans are denied mortgages and home improvement loans at twice the rate of whites. Housing segregation and institutional racism in the real estate market render black homes, on average, $42,800 less than white homes. Government housing policies, according to the Federal Housing Administration, have contributed to residential segregation and subsidized inequities between black and white neighborhoods.[41] Discrimination in real estate and mortgage markets and educational environments robs the current and future generations of African Americans of important wealth-creating opportunities.

Home ownership is the largest investment most families will make in their lifetime. Home ownership is a cushion against inflation, the cornerstone of wealth creation, and a long-term asset that can secure advantages that transfer across generations. Home ownership is the "most critical pathway for transformative assets."[42] Thomas Shapiro defines transformative assets as "inherited wealth lifting a family beyond their own achievement."[43]

When President Lincoln signed the Emancipation Proclamation in 1865, blacks owned 0.5 percent of the total wealth of the United States. By 1990, 135 years after the abolition of slavery, African Americans owned only 1 percent of total wealth.[44] In 2001, the nation's 13.2 million African American households constituted 12.4 percent of all households, earned 7.1 percent of aggregate household income, and owned 2.5 percent of the aggregate wealth in the United States.[45]

About 60 percent of America's middle-class families' wealth is derived from their homes.[46] Much of the increase in black wealth is due to rising home ownership, which increased from 42 percent in 1990 to 48 percent in 2003—still far behind the nationwide home-ownership rate of 68 percent. Sadly, the American dream is beyond the reach of millions of Americans because of closed home ownership opportunities.

African Americans and other minority families experienced a major increase in their income between 1996 and 2003, helping narrow the income inequality gap. About half of the progress in median income for these groups was wiped out in the following three years. African Americans finally broke the $30,000 barrier in 2000, with a household income of $31,690, but then lost more than $2,000 by 2003. Latinos and Asians lost even more; about $2,500 and $4,000 respectively (all numbers are inflation adjusted for 2003). The typical white household lost less than $1,000 in income from 2000 to 2003.[47]

Racial segregation exacerbates black poverty.[48] Children represent a disproportionate share of the poor in the United States; they are 25 percent of the total population, but 35 percent of the poor population. The number of black children who live in deep poverty has risen sharply since 2000 and is at its highest level since the federal government began collecting such figures in 1980.

In 2004, 17.8 percent of the nation's children lived in poverty, compared with 10.5 percent of white children, 9.8 percent of Asian children, 28.9 percent of Hispanic children, and 33.2 percent of black children.[49] In 2004,

Atlanta led the nation in child poverty (48.1 percent), followed by Detroit (47.8 percent), Long Beach, California (45.2 percent), Miami (41.3 percent), Milwaukee (41.3 percent), El Paso (40.7 percent), Memphis (38.5 percent), New Orleans (38.1 percent), Philadelphia (35.7 percent), and Baltimore (34.6 percent).[50]

The national poverty rate jumped from 12.1 percent in 2002 to 12.5 percent in 2003 to 12.7 percent in 2004.[51] The national poverty rate was essentially unchanged in 2005, the first year it hasn't increased since President George W. Bush took office.[52] More than 37 million Americans were living under the poverty line in 2004, about 12.6 percent of the population. In 2004, the poverty rate declined for Asians (9.8 percent in 2004, down from 11.8 percent in 2003), remained unchanged for Hispanics (21.9 percent) and blacks (24.7 percent), and rose for non-Hispanic whites (8.6 percent in 2004, up from 8.2 percent in 2003). The poverty rate remained statistically unchanged for blacks (24.9 percent) and Hispanics (21.8 percent). In 2005, the poverty rate decreased for non-Hispanic whites (8.3 percent in 2005, down from 8.7 percent in 2004) and increased for Asians (11.1 percent in 2005, up from 9.8 percent in 2004).[53]

Rising personal income and education attainment have not erased the black-white wealth gap.[54] During the economic boom years of the 1990s, black income gains had little or no impact in narrowing the wealth-gap between blacks and whites. The wealth gap actually widened.[55] The number of blacks holding middle-class occupations increased in the 1980s and 1990s. There were nearly 3.3 million blacks in middle-class jobs in 1980 and nearly seven million in 1995.[56] Black families have had to work harder than their white counterparts to achieve and keep their middle-class status. In 2000, black middle-income families worked about twelve more weeks than white families to earn the same money.[57]

The 1990s was one of the most sustained periods of economic prosperity in the twentieth century. Black household incomes soared, black-white wage disparities narrowed somewhat, and black unemployment rates reached historic lows. Yet, despite these gains, the National Urban League *State of Black America 2004* report described black progress as precarious at best.[58]

In 2001, the median income in the United States dropped 1.1 percent. This drop was twice as great for African Americans. The total drop in median household income since 2000 was 6.3 percent for African Americans, 4.4 percent for Hispanics, and 1.6 percent for non-Hispanic whites. Real median household income remained statistically unchanged between 2004 and 2005 for whites, non-Hispanic whites, African Americans and Asians, and for Hispanic households. African American households had the lowest median income in 2005 ($30,858) among race groups. Asian households had the highest median income ($61,094). The median income for non-Hispanic white households was $50,784. Median income for Hispanic households was $35,967.[59]

A great deal of research and attention is given to black-white income disparities. However, the black-white income gap is small compared to the staggering and persistent chasm in wealth ownership.[60] While income is an important dimension of understanding racial inequality, the correlation between income and wealth is weak. Wealth is what families own (often passed down from generation to generation), combined with income and other financial assets that families have at their disposal to use in the short term and the long term for securing opportunities and a desired standard of living and pursuing the "good life."

Although African American households benefited from the expanding economy and boom years of the 1990s, these gains did not readily translate into a sizable change in permanent assets or narrow the black-white wealth gap.[61] The black-white wealth gap widened while the income gap narrowed. For millions of middle-class blacks, hard work, college education, good-paying jobs, and owning homes have done little to narrow the wealth gap.

Melvin Oliver and Thomas Shapiro, in their book *Black Wealth/White Wealth*, show that the average black family held only ten cents of wealth for every dollar that whites possess.[62] The typical white family is worth $81,000 compared to only $8,000 for a typical black family.[63] In his book *The Hidden Cost of Being African American*, Thomas Shapiro says the penalty in net worth for being black amounts to $136,173, and the net financial asset penalty is $94,426.[64]

The wealth gap holds true for otherwise equally achieving blacks and whites. Net worth is all a family owns minus total amount of outstanding debt. Nationally, 17.6 percent of households had zero or negative net wealth in 2001. However, 13.1 percent of white households versus 30.9 percent of African American households have zero or negative net wealth. African American families saw virtually no change in their median net worth from 2001 ($20,300) to 2004 ($20,400), but their mean net worth rose 37.1 percent, from $80,700 to $110,600.[65]

Wealth, unlike income, is usually passed along to one's children. In 2001, the net worth of African American households reached $1 trillion (in 2003 dollars) after a decade of steady growth. Yet, the African American share of total household net worth fell because the wealth of other households grew more rapidly. Researchers at the Boston College Center on Wealth and Philanthropy (CWP) estimate that the total amount of wealth to be transferred from African American households via estates from 2001 through 2055 will range between $1.1 trillion and $3.4 trillion (in 2003 dollars).[66]

ORGANIZATION OF THE BOOK

This book is a follow-up to two books that I edited in the early and mid-1990s. They are *In Search of the New South: The Black Urban Experience in the 1970s and 1980s*, published in 1991, and *Residential Apartheid: The American Legacy*, published in 1994. Both of these books examined the continuing significance of race in shaping the lives and livelihoods of urban African Americans. A decade later, this book builds on this work and extends the analysis into the early years of the twenty-first century. There is no way that one book can reflect the complex life experiences of all African Americans. Our analysis only touches the surface of the many complexities that make the black urban experience the unique experience that it is.

The chapters were written specifically for this book under a grant from the Ford Foundation's Sustainable Metropolitan Communities Initiative (SMCI). The contributors include a team of social scientists, urban planners, educators, lawyers, and environmentalists. Our core analysis examines the impact of uneven growth patterns, sprawl, spatial mismatch between blacks and jobs, and enduring segregation of and racial discrimination against African Americans.

There are dozens of books out today that address urbanism, regionalism, and smart growth. However, few place race at the center of their analysis or examine the urban African American experience in the context of smart growth, social justice, and regional equity.

This book was not conceived or written in a vacuum. A conscious effort was made to assemble a multidisciplinary team of scholars who would blend their work into a coherent and readable book. We do not always agree. Universal consensus was not our goal. Nevertheless, we did reach some common ground on interpretation of problems, solutions, and plans of action for addressing the many challenges facing the African American community today and beyond.

In eleven chapters, the authors cover a wide range of topics and lay out a framework for a better understanding of factors that continue to shape black life in our nation's cities, suburbs, and metropolitan regions. The authors examine the role of government in promoting equal opportunity and civil rights laws without regard to race, color, or national origin. They examine the economic progress blacks made in the 1990s and the changes in the early years of the twenty-first century.

In chapter 1, I focus on a range of issues, including metropolitan growth and regional disparities, smart growth, environmental justice, housing, economic opportunity, metropolitan development, health, community development, sustainability, transportation, land use, politics, civil rights, and related quality-of-life issues.

In chapter 2, Ohio State University law professor john a. powell offers a structural framework from which to interpret lingering racial disparities. The author uses a structural racism approach to examine how space and resource allocation function as a broad illustration of racial inequalities in the United States. He also discusses strategies and solutions to address inequalities by expanding opportunity structures under a general perspective called "federated regionalism."

Chapter 3, written by Michigan State University geographer Joe T. Darden, examines the most recent research and 2000 census data to determine the status of African Americans in the areas of home ownership, residential segregation, and suburbanization. These three indicators are examined within the theoretical frameworks of "spatial assimilation" and "place stratification." The former model is employed to determine whether black socioeconomic mobility through increased home ownership, income, education, and occupation are strongly linked to increased black suburbanization. The latter model is employed to determine whether the spatial mobility of blacks continues to be limited to segregated neighborhoods within metropolitan areas despite increases in socioeconomic status.

Georgetown University law professor Sheryll Cashin wrote chapter 4. She addresses the timely and difficult question of whether the middle-class black suburb is a new utopia, or merely a separate but unequal community. In weighing the benefits of the middle-class black suburb, she raises the even larger issue of whether the advantages of not feeling outnumbered by the white community are worth the costs of segregation.

In chapter 5, Edward J. Blakely and Thomas W. Sanchez examine the emerging trend of the private gated community. Americans are electing to live behind walls with active security mechanisms to prevent intrusion into their private domains. Their analysis examines where these places are and outlines the dynamics that lead to a fortress mentality and culminate in physical walls and gates. Since September 11, 2001, many more people feel vulnerable in the face of rapid change and the real or imagined threats of urban terrorism. Gated communities are a response to the rising tide of fear. They are residential areas with restricted access such that normally public spaces have been privatized.

Chapter 6, written by UCLA professor Michael A. Stoll, analyzes the "spatial mismatch" model in examining where African Americans live and where the jobs are concentrated. He reports that African Americans continue to be the group most physically isolated from jobs in 2000. During the 1990s, blacks' overall proximity to jobs improved slightly, narrowing the gap in "spatial mismatch" between blacks and whites by 13 percent. Metropolitan areas with higher levels of black-white residential segregation exhibit a higher degree of spatial mismatch between blacks and jobs. The residential movement of black households within metropolitan areas drove most of the overall decline in spatial mismatch for blacks in the 1990s.

In chapter 7, Glenn S. Johnson, Angel O. Torres, and I explore metropolitan Atlanta as the "Black Mecca." Our analysis shows that sprawl-fueled growth is widening the gap between the region's haves and have-nots. The bulk of the housing and job growth in metropolitan Atlanta occurred in the mostly white northern suburban counties. Yet the authors report that Atlanta is still viewed as the "Black Mecca," for its continued attractiveness for African Americans. Metropolitan Atlanta is an attractive destination for middle-class African Americans because of its large black population, its black-owned businesses, and its many colleges, including the five historically black colleges and universities (HBCUs) that are part of the Atlanta University Center (AUC)—the largest concentration of black college students in the United States.

Chapter 8, written by sociologists Beverly Wright, a Hurricane Katrina evacuee, and me, examines social and environmental vulnerability of Black New Orleans before and after Hurricane Katrina. On August 29, 2005, Hurricane Katrina made landfall near New Orleans, leaving death and destruction across the Louisiana, Mississippi, and Alabama Gulf Coast counties. The authors delineate the role race and class is playing in environmental cleanup, repopulation, reconstruction, rebuilding, recovery, and rebirth of the rich black culture that gave New Orleans its flavor.

Chapter 9, written by sociologist J. Eugene Grigsby III, explores the question of how well the health needs of the African American population have been served over the past thirty years, particularly in light of the fact that during this time many African Americans have moved to the "suburbs." Census data are used to identify key suburban locations for African American residential growth. He also examines some of the proposed contemporary solutions for addressing these disparities to better understand the health status of Los Angeles's African Americans in the twenty-first century.

In chapter 10, David A. Bositis examines black political power subsequent to the passage of the Voting Rights Act in 1965. He asks the question: Have African American leaders made a difference in the lives of urban African Americans? The number of black elected officials has increased steadily since the passage of the Voting Rights Act, with more than 9,100 black elected officials in January 2001. Cities such as Chicago, Houston, Dallas, Seattle, Los Angeles, Washington, New York, Philadelphia, Baltimore, Birmingham, Memphis, Detroit, and Cleveland have all had black mayors. A number of cities, such as Atlanta and New Orleans, have had a quarter century of successive black mayors.

In chapter 11, Angela Glover Blackwell discusses why the inequity that affects African Americans must also be understood—and solved—in a multiracial context. The equitable development lens helps to name issues and frame strategies for solutions. As with other efforts to achieve greater equity and improved lives, equitable development promotes people and place solutions; double bottom-line investments; and meaningful community participation, leadership, and ownership. The author uses cases studies from the San Francisco Bay Area, Boston, Washington, D.C., Portland, New York City, and Atlanta as a basis for understanding the challenges and successes of multiethnic cooperation.

Finally, the authors assembled in this volume clearly illustrate that African Americans have made advancements and that equal opportunity laws when enforced provide benefits for millions who were formally locked out because of the color of their skin. They also show that some government policies—including housing, land use, transportation, environment, economic development, and education—may have unintended consequences that subsidize black-white inequality and heighten the wealth gap. It is within this context that we explore the African American population and metropolitan regional equity issues.

NOTES

1. "Scott v. Sandford," *Wikipedia: The Free Encyclopedia*, http://en.wikipedia.org/wiki/Dred_Scott_v._Sandford (accessed December 22, 2006).

2. Gunnar Myrdal, *An American Dilemma: The Negro Problem and Modern Democracy* (New York: McGraw-Hill, 1944).

3. St. Claire Drake and Horace R. Clayton, *Black Metropolis* (Chicago: University of Chicago Press, reprint, 1993).

4. Kenneth B. Clark, *Dark Ghetto: Dilemmas of Social Power* (New York: Harper & Row, 1965), 11.

5. Kerner Commission, *Report of the National Advisory Commission on Civil Disorder* (New York: Viking Press, 1969), 1.

6. See U.S. Bureau of the Census, Table 3: "Annual Estimates of the Population by Sex, Race and Hispanic or Latino Origin for the United States: April 1, 2000 to July 1, 2005," (NC-EST2005-03), Population Division, U.S. Census Bureau, http://www.census.gov/popest/national/asrh/NC-EST2005/NC-EST2005-03.xls (accessed May 10, 2006).

7. Dalton Conley, *Being Black, Living in the Red: Race, Wealth, and Social Policy in America* (Berkeley: University of California Press, 1999), 8.

8. Andrew Wiese, *Places of Their Own: African American Suburbanization in the Twentieth Century* (Chicago: University of Chicago Press, 2004).

9. John W. Frazier, Florence M. Margai, and Eugene Tettey-Fio, *Race and Place* (Boulder, CO: Westview Press, 2003).

10. National Fair Housing Alliance, *Unequal Opportunity: Perpetuating Housing Segregation in America* (Washington, DC: NFHA, April 5, 2006), 6–7.

11. Ibid., 11.

12. Stephen Ross and John Yinger, *The Color of Money: Mortgage Discrimination, Research Methodology and Fair-Lending Enforcement* (Cambridge, MA: MIT Press, 2002).

13. John R. Logan, *The New Ethnic Enclaves in American Suburbs* (Albany, NY: Lewis Mumford Center for Comparative Urban and Regional Research, 2001), 2.

14. Ibid., 10.

15. Monifa A. Thomas, "Slighted in the Suburbs," *Chicago Sun Times*, November 15, 2005.

16. Logan, *The New Ethnic Enclaves in American Suburbs*, 10.

17. Carmen DeNavas-Walt, Robert W. Cleveland, and Bruce H. Webster Jr., *Income in the United States: 2000* (Washington, DC: U.S. Census Bureau, September 2003), http://www.census.gov/prod/2003pubs/p60-221.pdf. (accessed February 5, 2005).

18. Radhika K. Fox, Sarah Treuhaft, and Regan Douglas, *Shared Opportunity, Stronger Regions: An Agenda for Rebuilding America's Older Core Cities* (Oakland, CA: PolicyLink, Inc., 2005), 14.

19. Robert D. Bullard, Glenn S. Johnson, and Angel O. Torres, *Sprawl City: Race, Politics and Planning in Atlanta* (Washington, DC: Island Press, 2000).

20. Frazier, Margai, and Tettey-Fio, *Race and Place*.

21. Reynolds Farley, Sheldon Danziger, and Harry J. Holzer, *Detroit Divided* (New York: Russell Sage Foundation, 2002).

22. David Rusk, *The Segregation Tax: The Cost of Racial Segregation on Black Homeowners* (Washington, DC: Brookings Institution Center on Urban and Metropolitan Policy, 2001).

23. Peter Dreier, John Mollenkopf, and Todd Swanstrom, *Place Matters: Metropolitics for the Twenty-First Century* (Lawrence: University Press of Kansas, 2001).

24. Bullard, Johnson, and Torres, *Sprawl City*, 89–110.

25. Ibid.

26. Robert D. Bullard, *Unequal Protection: Environmental Justice and Communities of Color* (San Francisco: Sierra Club Books, 1996).

27. Robert D. Bullard, *The Quest for Environmental Justice: Human Rights and the Politics of Pollution* (San Francisco: Sierra Club Books, 2005).

28. D. R. Wernett and L. A. Nieves, "Breathing Polluted Air: Minorities Are Disproportionately Exposed," *EPA Journal* 18 (1992): 16–17.

29. Robert D. Bullard, "Climate Justice and People of Color," http://www.ejrc.cau.edu/climatechgpoc.htm (accessed March 1, 2006).

30. David Pace, "AP: More Blacks Live with Pollution," ABC News, December 13, 2005, available at http://abcnews.go.com/Health/wireStory?id=1402790&CMP=OTC-RSSFeeds0312 (accessed December 14, 2005).

31. Bullard, *The Quest for Environmental Justice*.

32. Manuel Pastor, Robert D. Bullard, James K. Boyce, Alice Fothergill, Rachel Morello-Frosch, and Beverly Wright, *In the Wake of the Storm: Environment, Disaster, and Race after Katrina* (New York: Russell Sage Foundation, 2006).

33. Ibid., 313.

34. Chris Tilly, Phillip Moss, Joleen Kirscheman, and Ivy Kennelly, in *Urban Inequality: Evidence from Four Cities*, ed. Alice O'Connor, Chris Tilly, and Lawrence D. Bobo (New York: Russell Sage Foundation, 2003), 306.

35. Sheryll Cashin, *The Failures of Integration: How Race and Class Are Undermining the American Dream* (New York: Public Affairs, 2004).

36. Ibid.

37. W. E. B. Du Bois, *The Souls of Black Folk* (New York: Penguin Books, 1903, reprint edition, 1996), 46–47.

38. Glenn C. Loury, *The Anatomy of Racial Inequality* (Cambridge, MA: Harvard University Press, 2003).

39. Mary Waters, *Black Identities* (Cambridge, MA: Harvard University Press, 1999).

40. Michael K. Brown, Martin Carnoy, Elliot Currie, Troy Duster, David B. Oppenheimer, Marjorie M. Schultz, and David Wellman, *Whitewashing Racism: The Myth of a Color-Blind Society* (Berkeley: University of California Press, 2003).

41. Douglas Massey and Nancy A. Denton, *American Apartheid* (Cambridge, MA: Harvard University Press, 1993).

42. Thomas M. Shapiro, *The Hidden Cost of Being African American: How Wealth Perpetuates Inequality* (New York: Oxford, 2004), 3.

43. Ibid., 10.

44. Claud Anderson, *Black Labor, White Wealth: The Search for Power and Economic Justice* (Edgewood, MD: Duncan and Duncan, 1994).

45. John F. Havens and Paul G. Schervish, "Wealth Transfer Estimates for African American Households," *New Directions for Philanthropic Fundraising* 48 (Summer 2005): 47–55.

46. Shapiro, *The Hidden Cost of Being African American*, 107.

47. United for a Fair Economy, *State of the Dream 2005 Report* (Boston, 2005), 9, available at http://www.faireconomy.org/press/2005/StateoftheDream2005.pdf (accessed June 12, 2006).

48. Paul Jargowsky, *Poverty and Place* (New York: Russell Sage Foundation, 1997).

49. U.S. Bureau of the Census, *Income, Poverty, and Health Insurance Coverage in the United States: 2004*, Report P60, n. 229, Table B-2 (Washington, DC: U.S. Bureau of the Census), 52–57.

50. U.S. Bureau of the Census, "Percent of Children Under 18 Years Below Poverty Level in the Past 12 Months (For Whom Poverty Status Is Determined): 2004," Table R1704 in *American Community Survey* (Washington, DC: U.S. Bureau of the Census, 2004).

51. Jonathan Weisman and Ceci Connolly, "Poverty Rate Continues to Climb: 2004 Census Data Show Labor Market Is Still Struggling," *Washington Post*, August 31, 2005, A03.

52. Carmen DeNavas-Walt, Bernadette D. Proctor, and Cheryl Hill Lee, *Income, Poverty, and Health Insurance Coverage in the United States: 2005*, Current Population Reports P6-231 (Washington, DC: U.S. Bureau of the Census, August 2006).

53. National Poverty Center, *Poverty in the United States* (Ann Arbor: University of Michigan, n.d.). Available at http://www.npc.umich.edu/poverty/ (accessed June 14, 2006).

54. Conley, *Being Black, Living in the Red*.

55. Samuel L. Myers Jr., "African American Economic Well-Being During the Boom and Bust," in *State of Black America 2004*, National Urban League, 4–5, abstract found at http://www.nul.org/pdf/sobaabstracts.pdf (accessed March 11, 2005).

56. Mary Pattillo-McCoy, *Black Picket Fences* (Chicago: University of Chicago Press, 1999), 8.

57. Lawrence Mishe, Jared Bernstein, and Heather Boushey, *The State of Working America, 2002–2003* (Ithaca, NY: Cornell University Press, 2003), 11.

58. Marc H. Morial, "African Americans' Status Is 73% of Whites Says New 'State of America' 2004 Report," press release, National Urban League (March 24, 2004), found at http://www.nul.org/news/2004/soba.html (accessed March 15, 2005).

59. DeNavas-Walt, Proctor, and Lee, *Income, Poverty, and Health Insurance Coverage in the United States: 2005*, 56.

60. See Melvin O. Oliver and Thomas M. Shapiro, *Black Wealth/White Wealth: A New Perspective on Racial Inequality* (New York: Routledge, 1995); Conley, *Being Black, Living in the Red*; Lisa Keister, *Wealth in America* (New York: Cambridge University Press, 2000); Edward N. Wolff, *Top Heavy* (New York: New Press, 2002); Shapiro, *The Hidden Cost of Being African American*.

61. Myers, "African-American Economic Well-Being During the Boom and Bust," 53–54.

62. Oliver and Shapiro, *Black Wealth/White Wealth*, 100.

63. Shapiro, *The Hidden Cost of Being African American*, 47.

64. Ibid., 56.

65. Brian K. Bucks, Arthur B. Kennickell, and Kevin B. Moore, *Recent Changes in U.S. Family Finances: Evidence from the 2001 and 2004 Survey of Consumer Finances*, Federal Reserve Bulletin 2006 (Washington, DC: The Federal Reserve Board, 2006), A9, available at http://www.federalreserve.gov/pubs/bulletin/2006/financesurvey.pdf (accessed June 12, 2006).

66. Havens and Schervish, "Wealth Transfer Estimates for African American Households," 52.

1

The Black Metropolis in the Era of Sprawl

Robert D. Bullard

Five decades after *Brown v. Board of Education* outlawed Jim Crow, black equality remains elusive.[1] Race and class are still underlying factors that explain the sociospatial layout of most of our cities, suburbs, and metropolitan regions, including quality of schools, location of job centers, housing patterns, environmental quality, commercial and business development, access to health care, and a host of other quality-of-life indicators for African Americans.

This chapter examines the impact of race and class factors in shaping urban and regional growth patterns. It also discusses why African Americans should be concerned about sprawl and the emerging metropolitan and regional equity movement. Americans are spreading out residentially. Opportunity is shifting to the suburbs and beyond. As opportunity—housing, jobs, and other amenities—shifts to outlying suburbs, where are African Americans settling? How are African Americans adapting to the shift in metropolitan investments, resources, and opportunity? Are they being left out and left behind? These are some of the questions explored in this chapter.

WHY METROPOLITAN REGIONS? WHY RACIAL EQUITY?

Many of the nation's large metropolitan areas have become ethnic melting pots with new ethnic immigrant enclaves dotting the urban and suburban landscape. A new wave of ethnic segregation dominates many large central-city neighborhoods, inner-ring suburbs, deep suburbs, and some rural communities in metropolitan regions that attract low-wage laborers. In nearly a third of all metropolitan areas, including Washington, D.C., Chicago,

Phoenix, and Atlanta, fewer than one-half of all people under age fifteen are white.[2]

In 2002, over one-half (52 percent) of all African Americans lived in a central city within a metropolitan area, compared with 21 percent of non-Hispanic whites. In contrast, 57 percent of non-Hispanic whites lived outside the central city but within the metropolitan area, compared with 36 percent of blacks. Only 13 percent of blacks and 22 percent of non-Hispanic whites lived in nonmetropolitan areas.[3]

About 60 percent of the African American population lived in ten metropolitan areas. In 2004, the metropolitan areas with the largest black population included New York (2.3 million), Chicago (1.7 million), Atlanta (1.4 million), Washington, D.C. (1.3 million), Philadelphia (1.1 million), Miami (1.0 million), Detroit (1.0 million), Los Angeles (0.9 million), Houston (0.8 million), and Dallas (0.8 million).[4] The largest black population gains during 2000–2004 were in large southern metropolitan statistical areas (MSAs), those with populations greater than 500,000 (table 1.1). Eight of the ten metropolitan areas with the largest population gains between 2000 and 2004 were located in the South (table 1.2). Over 56 percent of the nation's blacks now live in the South, up from 54 percent in 1990.[5]

The Atlanta metropolitan area added over 183,000 blacks during the 2000–2004 period. Atlanta moved from having the seventh-largest population in 1990 to having the third-largest in 2004. If current trends continue Atlanta will soon overtake Chicago in total black population. The Miami metropolitan area was second, adding nearly 97,000 blacks during the five-year period. Miami rose from having the eighth-largest black population in 2000 to sixth in 2004.

The 1990s saw an increasing number of jobs flee to the suburbs. Social scientists refer to this phenomenon as "job sprawl."[6] Higher percentages of a metropolitan area's employment located outside a five-mile ring around the central business district (CBD) imply higher job sprawl, while lower percentages of employment outside the five-mile ring indicate lower job sprawl. In an analysis of office space in thirteen of the nation's largest metropolitan commercial real estate markets, the Brookings Institution's *Office Sprawl* study found that central cities' share of office space dropped from 74 percent in 1979 to 58 percent in 1999.[7] Nearly an equal share of office space is found in traditional downtowns (38 percent) and "edgeless" cities that often extend over hundreds of square miles. They are generally not mixed use, pedestrian friendly, or accessible by transit.

Nationally, the job sprawl rate stood at 64.7 for all metropolitan areas in 2000, indicating that on average 64.7 percent of jobs in metropolitan areas are located at least five miles outside of CBDs. The job sprawl rate was 92.4 percent in Detroit, 84.6 percent in Atlanta and St. Louis, 80.9 percent in Philadelphia, and 75.5 percent in Cleveland.

Table 1.1. Metropolitan Statistical Areas with Largest Black Populations, 2004

Rank			Metro Area	Population 2004	Share of the Metro Area Population (%)
2004	2000	1990			
1	1	1	New York-Northern New Jersey-Long Island, NY-NJ-PA	3,202,808	17.1
2	2	2	Chicago-Naperville-Joliet, IL-IN-WI	1,694,518	18.0
3	4	7	Atlanta-Sandy Springs-Marietta, GA	1,406,290	29.9
4	3	3	Washington-Arlington-Alexandria, DC-VA-MD-WV	1,335,823	26.0
5	5	4	Philadelphia-Camden-Wilmington, PA-NJ-DE-MD	1,162,847	20.0
6	8	8	Miami-Fort Lauderdale-Miami Beach, FL	1,044,406	19.5
7	6	6	Detroit-Warren-Livonia, MI	1,026,048	22.8
8	7	5	Los Angeles-Long Beach-Santa Ana, CA	947,351	7.3
9	9	9	Houston-Baytown-Sugar Land, TX	848,221	16.4
10	10	11	Dallas-Fort Worth-Arlington, TX	789,807	13.9

Source: William H. Frey, *Diversity Spreads Out: Metropolitan Shifts in Hispanic, Asian, and Black Populations Since 2000* (Washington, DC: The Brookings Institution, 2006), p. 5.

Table 1.2. Metropolitan Statistical Areas with Largest Black Population Gains, 2000–2004

Rank 2000–2004	Rank 1990–2000	Metro Area	Population Change 2000–2004	Black Share of Total Population[1] (%) 2000	Black Share of Total Population (%) 2004
1	1	Atlanta-Sandy Springs-Marietta, GA	183,817	29	30
2	3	Miami-Fort Lauderdale-Miami Beach, FL	96,934	20	19
3	5	Dallas-Fort Worth-Arlington, TX	74,562	14	14
4	4	Washington-Arlington-Alexandria, DC-VA-MD-WV*	64,439	26	26
5	7	Houston-Baytown-Sugar Land, TX*	56,694	17	16
6	8	Philadelphia-Camden-Wilmington, PA-NJ-DE-MD	42,997	19	20
7	11	Orlando, FL	41,729	14	14
8	14	Charlotte-Gastonia-Concord, NC-SC*	40,703	21	23
9	9	Baltimore-Towson, MD*	38,759	26	28
10	15	Riverside-San Bernardino-Ontario, CA	35,292	8	7

Source: William H. Frey, *Diversity Spreads Out: Metropolitan Shifts in Hispanic, Asian, and Black Populations Since 2000* (Washington, DC: The Brookings Institution, 2006), 6, 22–24; U.S. Census Bureau, *Census 2000 SF3*, available at http://factfinder.census.gov/servlet/DatasetMainPageServlet?_program=DEC&_submenuId=datasets_1&_lang=en&_ts= (accessed June 19, 2006).

[1] In 2003, the Office of Management and Budget (OMB) redefined the metropolitan area definitions. As a result, some of the MSAs included in this table changed; affected MSAs are identified by an asterisk (*). The Black Share of Total Population 2000 was calculated using the previous (2000) MSA's definition. For more information about the definition changes please see OMB Bulletin No. 06-01, *Update of Statistical Area Definitions and Guidance on Their Uses*, located at http://www.whitehouse.gov/omb/bulletins/fy2006/b06-01.pdf (accessed June 19, 2006).

Urban jobs are not randomly distributed across neighborhoods in metropolitan areas. Sociologist William Julius Wilson, in his book *When Work Disappears*, contends that black unemployment is aggravated by the transition from a manufacturing to a service economy and the removal of jobs from cities to suburbs.[8] In general, central cities in the United States have lost out in this new economy, with African Americans hit especially hard, while newer suburbs have benefited. New job growth and economic activity centers are now concentrated on the fringe of the metropolitan areas and often beyond the reach of public transportation.

The absence of a national urban policy has left hundreds of financially strapped cities and their aging first-ring suburbs in a sink-or-swim posture. This scenario does not only apply to the reconstruction of storm-damaged New Orleans but to nearly every major city in the nation where the slow-moving disasters called urban neglect, abandonment, and racism have taken their toll. Generally, central cities and their older inner-ring suburbs are increasingly resource poor, while developing and sprawling suburbs are resource rich.

Chicago's south-side suburbs mirror this pattern. The sociospatial layout and negative relations between cities, older suburbs, and newer suburbs resulted from decades of policies and practices to isolate poor people of color.[9] Over the years, central cities and inner-ring suburbs have become more alike. Many of the social ills such as poverty, unemployment, infrastructure decline, environmental degradation, crime, and drugs, once associated with big cities, now are commonplace in many older suburbs.[10]

Reducing inequities within metropolitan regions makes economic, social, environmental, and health sense since the future of cities and suburbs is inextricably interdependent. The fate of business is linked with the workforce, and that of the middle class with the poor.[11] Central city poverty and inequality (education, income, employment, housing, environment, land use, transportation, taxes, etc.) across a region can stifle the whole region's development. Problem-ridden cities and declining suburbs are two sides of the same coin. They are interconnected across the metropolitan landscape because of region-level economic restructuring.[12]

GROWING SMARTER AND FAIRER

The politics of race and metropolitan development are intertwined. Race is a major component in white flight, residential segregation, urban infrastructure decline, and the recent "rediscovery" of urban neighborhoods and the "back-to-the-city" migration. Fair growth means dismantling artificial barriers that limit the social and economic mobility of African Americans and other racial and ethnic groups and expanding opportunities (i.e., housing, employment, education, transportation, land use and zoning, health and safety, public investments, etc.) for those groups.[13]

Smart-growth advocates are just beginning to address equitable development issues. Much of the core of the movement involves choices, protection of the environment, using resources wisely, investing in and rebuilding our inner cities, regionalism, cooperation, families, neighborhoods, and communities.[14] But some smart-growth initiatives in sprawl-threatened regions will not work if the interests of African Americans and low-income community residents are not protected. African American communities have been redlined, abandoned, and targeted for locally unwanted land uses, or LULUs. Moreover, many in-town African American neighborhoods have also been "rediscovered," accelerating gentrification and displacement of incumbent residents. New waves of housing gentrification are a by-product of "mixed-income" housing plans designed to break up "concentrated poverty." But quite often these government-subsidized programs also displace a disproportionately large share of African American families. From Bayview-Hunters Point in San Francisco to West Harlem, black renters and home owners are being pushed out and priced out of their homes and neighborhoods.

The American Planning Association (APA), in its *Policy Guide on Smart Growth*, states that

> smart growth means using comprehensive planning to guide, design, develop, revitalize and build communities for all that: have a unique sense of community and place; preserve and enhance valuable natural and cultural resources; equitably distribute the costs and benefits of development; expand the range of transportation, employment and housing choices in a fiscally responsible manner; value long-range, regional considerations of sustainability over short-term incremental geographically isolated actions; and promote public health and healthy communities.[15]

They add that smart growth should not be limited to combating the symptoms of sprawl, but should "promote fairness in rebuilding inner city and inner suburban areas, in the development of suburban communities, and in the growth of small towns and rural areas."[16]

The fate of many metropolitan regions is intricately tied to how the issues of race and social equity are handled. African Americans are often underrepresented in the decision-making arena that affects their quality of life and their livelihood. With few exceptions, smart-growth conferences and meetings are mostly white and dominated by environmental and business interests.

Sprawl means different things to different people.[17] Suburban sprawl is an extension of long-established patterns of suburbanization, decentralization, and low-density development. Sprawl-driven development has "literally sucked population, jobs, investment capital, and tax base from the urban core."[18] Growth and sprawl are not synonymous. Nevertheless, suburban sprawl has been the dominant growth pattern for nearly all metropolitan regions in the United States for the past five decades.[19] Historically, the decentralization of employment centers has had a major role in shaping metropolitan growth patterns and the location of people, housing, and jobs. Government policies buttressed and tax dollars subsidized suburban sprawl through new roads and highways at the expense of public transit.[20] Tax subsidies made it possible for new suburban employment centers to become dominant outside of cities and to pull middle-income workers and home owners from the urban core.

The smart-growth movement—like its environmental movement counterpart—has been slow to address race, equity, and social justice issues. Many white environmental and smart-growth groups run from race. On the other hand, most African American smart-growth advocates tend to place racial justice and equity at the forefront of their analysis of metropolitan regional issues. This causes problems when others tend to tag on equity as an afterthought or when they marginalize the regressive impacts of smart-growth initiatives on African Americans and the poor.

When smart-growth initiatives incorporate "fair growth" elements—elements that build in strategies to address long-standing issues such as fair housing, redlining, abandonment and economic disinvestments, poverty, gentrification, transportation, and public schools—then one can expect an entirely different turnout among African Americans and other victims of institutional and government-subsidized racism.

Where money and investments flow has a lot to do with where opportunities flow. In most sprawl-threatened areas of the United States the politics of race and place are prevalent.[21] First, it is clear that sprawl-fueled growth is widening the gap between the haves and have-nots. Moreover, suburban sprawl has significant social, economic, environmental, and health effects.[22] Suburban sprawl impacts the daily lives of rich and poor as well as blacks and whites.

A handful of blacks have taken up this issue. William Johnson, former mayor of Rochester, New York, even defined it as a fundamental civil rights issue.[23] If this is the case, then why are there so few organizations of color leading the charge to ensure that fairness and equity principles are imbedded in the smart-growth debate? In 2005, the African American Forum on Race and Regionalism (AAFRR) forced the issue onto the NAACP national agenda in Philadelphia. The AAFRR has also conducted workshops at several NAACP chapter events, including the Detroit chapter—the largest in the country.

METROPOLITAN APARTHEID

Suburban sprawl represents the dominant growth pattern in the United States. It would be a mistake to lay all of the nation's urban ills at the doorstep of sprawl. However, there is growing evidence that suburban sprawl concentrates urban core poverty, closes economic opportunity, limits mobility, accelerates urban disinvestment, fosters social isolation, and increases urban-suburban disparities that closely mirror racial inequities.[24] Some of the other negative effects of suburban sprawl include urban infrastructure decline; increased energy consumption; automobile dependency; and threats to public health and the environment such as air pollution, flooding, climate change, and encroachment on farmland and wildlife habitat.

Metropolitan apartheid is exhibited in urban labor markets, the spatial location of jobs, and the extent to which jobs and economic activity centers are accessible to urban blacks. Globalization pressures pose special challenges to closing racial inequities in the United States. In the twenty-first century, economic development in our cities and metropolitan regions will be increasingly driven by global forces "marked by increasing international trade and investments, growing transnational communication, and expanding cross-border alliances, businesses, and industries."[25]

Apartheid-type employment, housing, and development policies have resulted in limited mobility, reduced neighborhood options, decreased residential choices, and diminished job opportunities for African Americans and other people of color. Residential apartheid is the dominant housing pattern for most African Americans—the most racially segregated group in America.[26] Residential apartheid did not result from some impersonal superstructural process. It is part of the national heritage.[27]

Studies over the past three decades clearly document the relationship between redlining and disinvestment decisions and neighborhood decline.[28] Redlining accelerates the flight of full-service banks, food stores, restaurants, and other shopping centers from inner-city neighborhoods. In their place, inner-city neighborhoods are left with only check-cashing operations, small grocery and liquor stores, and fast-food outlets.

In April 2006, a group in Detroit sued National City Bank of the Midwest for discriminatory lending practices based on race. In 2004, National City Bank originated 339 small-business guaranteed loans in the state of Michigan.[29] Of those SBA-guaranteed loans 13, or 3.8 percent, were originated for businesses in the city of Detroit, according to the suit. The city of Detroit is located in Wayne County and has a population of 951,270, of whom 81.6 percent are African American. Michigan has a population of 9,938,444, of whom 14.1 percent are African American. More than half (55 percent) of the African Americans in Michigan live in Detroit.

Redlining is not limited to insurance companies, banks, and lending institutions. Retail redlining also denies millions of African Americans basic goods and services that most people take for granted. African Americans who are segregated in black neighborhoods have difficulty accessing something as basic as a full-service supermarket. Studies show that wealthier neighborhoods have more than three times as many supermarkets as poor neighborhoods.[30]

When broken down by race, not just wealth, predominately white neighborhoods in Maryland, Minnesota, Mississippi, and North Carolina have four times as many supermarkets as predominantly black neighborhoods.[31] In many black neighborhoods it is far easier to get an artery-clogging box of fried chicken or slice of pizza than it is to get a bag of fresh apples or a bunch of fresh grapes.

Supermarkets are more likely to offer a wide selection of food at affordable prices. More important, medical research shows that eating lots of fruits and vegetables can lower blood pressure, reduce the risk of heart disease and stroke, and help prevent bone loss. Not having a supermarket nearby severely limits African Americans' access to the basic elements of a healthy diet, thereby placing them at greater risk of chronic diseases such as diabetes and congestive heart failure. The more supermarkets a neighborhood has, the more fruits and vegetables its residents eat. For example, the presence of at least one supermarket in a black neighborhood was associated with a 25 percent increase in the number of residents who limited the amount of fat in their diets, as compared with people in neighborhoods with no supermarket.[32]

While urban black neighborhoods may have a shortage of supermarkets and sit-down restaurants, many have an overabundance of fast-food outlets. Fast foods add to this health crisis, crowding out access to healthier foods, contributing to overweight and obesity among the low income and people of color residents. The U.S. Surgeon General reports that over 60 percent of American adults are overweight or obese, as are nearly 13 percent of children.[33] Children are the special targets of saturation marketing by the junk food industry. The death toll from obesity is expected to soon exceed deaths from smoking. Annual U.S. obesity-attributable medical expenditures are estimated at $75 billion in 2003 dollars.

In addition to the lack of availability of healthy foods, poor black neighborhood residents end up paying more for lower-quality foods at the nearby "mom and pop" stores, corner markets, liquor stores, and small ethnic groceries—few of these establishments offering fresh fruits and vegetables. Most black inner-city residents have no choice because of limited transportation options—few have private automobiles. In New York City, Los Angeles, Hartford, Knoxville, and Minneapolis, low-income residents pay 10 to 40 percent more for food than higher-income residents. Urban residents are fighting back and demanding "food justice," involving local people from seed to sale.[34] Food justice advocates view access to healthy food as a human rights issue and that "lack of access to food in a community is an indicator of material deprivation."[35]

Even without supermarkets and residential amenities, some black urban core neighborhoods are attracting a clientele of in-migrants—largely white, childless, and home owners. Every decade or so people "rediscover" the city and close-in neighborhoods. They soon discover that living in the city has many advantages. Over the past five decades, government-subsidized initiatives have cleared "blighted" neighborhoods and slums under various urban renewal programs. Successive waves of urban revitalization programs all resulted in "urban removal" of large numbers of renters, poor, and black residents, that is, gentrification.

African Americans tend to live away from where the jobs are found. This separation of African Americans in segregated neighborhoods away from job growth negatively impacts their workforce participation. The "spatial mismatch" hypothesis was first proposed by John Kain in the late 1960s.[36] Mounting evidence shows that spatial mismatches produce negative labor market outcomes for black and other people of color.

Where business firms locate is not accidental.[37] Roadblocks to spatial mobility are roadblocks to social mobility. According to UCLA economist Michael Stoll, in 2000, no other group was more physically isolated from jobs and employment centers than African Americans. The exodus of entry-level jobs to the suburbs hits African Americans especially hard.[38] Even with job flight to the suburbs, most job opportunities for low-income workers are still located in central cities.[39]

The spatial mismatch index can be interpreted as the percentage of either population or jobs that would have to relocate to different areas to completely eliminate any geographic imbalance. In 2000, the spatial mismatch for blacks was 53.5 percent for all metropolitan areas, indicating that a little over half of all blacks would have had to relocate within metropolitan areas to be geographically distributed in the same way as jobs.

The gap in spatial mismatch for blacks between high and low job-sprawl areas is wider in the Midwest, in metropolitan areas with a larger black share of the population, and in small- to medium-sized metropolitan areas. The top ten cities where the black spatial mismatch was greatest were: Detroit (71.4 percent), Chicago (69.5 percent), Newark (65.2 percent), Philadelphia (64.2 percent), St. Louis (62.6 percent), Cleveland (62.0 percent), Los Angeles (61.6 percent), Cincinnati (58.8 percent), San Diego (58.6 percent), and Indianapolis (58.3 percent).[40]

Suburbs now contain the majority of the office space in many of the country's top metropolitan office markets.[41] As jobs have migrated out of the central city into suburban and edge-city locations, it has become increasingly difficult for African Americans to get to work. This is a big problem in cities nationwide, perhaps exemplified by Cleveland, where 90 percent of new entry-level jobs are located outside of the city.

CLOSED DOORS AND BLOCKED OPPORTUNITIES

Racial segregation in housing, as well as schools and jobs, is fundamental to the geography of the modern American city.[42] Housing discrimination is still rampant in America.[43] Fair housing testing is the most widely used tool for gathering evidence of housing discrimination.[44] Test audits conducted in the mid-1990s in two dozen large metropolitan areas found that black testers seeking to rent apartments faced discrimination by landlords 53 percent of the time, while black testers seeking to buy a home faced discriminatory treatment by real estate persons 59 percent of the time.[45] A 2002 Urban Institute study revealed that African Americans in Los Angeles were offered less coaching than comparable white home buyers, and were more likely to be encouraged to consider an FHA loan.[46] In Chicago, African Americans were denied basic information about loan amount and house price, told about fewer products, offered less coaching, and given less follow-up than comparable white home buyers. Clearly, African Americans in Los Angeles and Chicago face a significant risk of unequal treatment from mortgage lending institutions.

Decades of empirical studies show that some banks and lending institutions avoid making loans in heavily black and low-income areas that they serve. In 1977, Congress passed the Community Reinvestment Act (CRA) to encourage depository institutions to help meet the credit needs of the communities in which they operate, including low- and moderate-income neighborhoods. Despite the law, some lenders still discriminate against entire neighborhoods.[47]

Other lenders use predatory lending practices to target black neighborhoods for the sale of high-rate loans. This practice is also referred to as "reverse redlining."

High-cost lenders target minority, especially African American, borrowers and communities. Predatory lending hits African Americans especially hard.[48] Even high-income African Americans are hurt by these practices. In 2001, prime loans accounted for about 71 percent of home refinancing for African Americans who live in African American high-income neighborhoods. In contrast, over 83 percent of white lower-income borrowers living in predominately white lower-income neighborhoods received prime loans.[49] The gap between prime conventional loans to African Americans and those to whites is wide. Prime conventional lenders accounted for nearly three-quarters of all home purchases to whites but less than 50 percent of lending to Hispanics and only 40 percent of lending to African Americans.[50]

Risk factors alone do not explain racial differences in subprime lending.[51] Predatory lending creates separate and unequal housing opportunities.[52] Predatory practices by some subprime lenders have resulted in extremely high foreclosures in once stable neighborhoods.[53] A 2005 study from the Association of Community Organizations for Reform Now (ACORN) found that African Americans and Latinos tend to get more than their fair share of high-interest subprime mortgages compared with whites.[54]

Nationally, for conventional first-lien home-purchase loans (which excludes government-backed loans like FHA and VA), 32.4 percent of the loans to African Americans were high-cost loans compared to 8.7 percent of the loans to whites. In comparative terms, African Americans were 4.1 times more likely to receive a high-cost loan than whites when buying a house. Out of the home purchase loans to Latinos, 16.8 percent were high-cost loans, meaning that Latino home buyers were 1.6 times more likely to receive a high-cost loan than white home buyers.

In Miami, for example, Wells Fargo dispersed high-cost loans to 11.2 percent of African Americans compared to 1.2 percent of whites. In Philadelphia, the "city of brotherly love," African Americans are 7.8 times more likely to receive high-interest loans than whites; in Chicago, 7.2 times more likely, and six times more likely in New York and Washington, D.C. A June 2006 study from the Center for Responsible Lending observed similar racial lending disparities even when the borrowers have the same qualifications as whites.

Lenders usually say they charge more because African Americans and Latinos tend to have shakier credit histories, which makes lending to them riskier. However, Center for Responsible Lending researchers dispute this claim. They show that even after controlling for differences such as credit scores and the amount of the downpayment, African Americans and Latinos still wind up with a disproportionate share of expensive loans. Examining 50,000 subprime loans, the Center's researchers found these groups were almost a third more likely to get a high-priced loan than white borrowers with the same credit profile. Moreover, the findings show that decades of work by the civil rights movement to bring fairness and opportunity to all home buyers are still unfinished.[55]

Disparate lending treatment against African Americans persists in good times and bad times and even after natural and man-made disasters. For example, African Americans in pre-Katrina New Orleans were more than three times as likely as white borrowers to get high-interest loans. The ACORN report found that African American applicants for conventional loans were two and one-third times more likely to be turned down for a mortgage than white applicants. One of every three African American applicants, 29.83 percent, were denied conventional home purchase loans in 2002, down from 39.73 percent in 2001 and down from 56.6 percent in 1997.[56] In 2004, African

Americans in New Orleans were twice as likely as their white counterparts to have their loans rejected—20.41 percent and 10.5 percent, respectively.[57]

In December 2005, the National Fair Housing Alliance (NFHA) released a report, *No Home for the Holidays: Report on Housing Discrimination Against Hurricane Katrina Survivors*, documenting high rates of housing discrimination against African Americans displaced by Hurricane Katrina.[58] NFHA conducted tests over the telephone to determine what both African American and white home seekers were told about unit availability, rent, discounts, and other terms and conditions of apartment leasing.

In 66 percent of these tests—43 of 65 instances—white callers were favored over African American callers. NFHA also conducted five matched-pair tests in which persons visited apartment complexes. In those five tests, whites were favored over African Americans three times. NFHA conducted an investigation of rental housing practices in five states to determine whether victims of Katrina would be treated unfairly based on their race.[59] Based on the evidence uncovered by testing conducted in seventeen cities, the NFHA filed five race-based housing discrimination complaints against rental housing complexes located in Dallas, Texas; Birmingham, Alabama; and Gainesville, Florida.[60]

The percentage of conventional loans made to African Americans nationwide also lags far behind the percentage of the population that they make up. For example, African Americans make up almost 13 percent of the country's population but receive just 5.1 percent of the conventional loans. Lenders also fail to adequately serve low- and moderate-income communities. Low- and moderate-income neighborhoods comprise 26 percent of the population, yet they receive just 11 percent of the conventional loans.[61]

Many real estate and insurance agents respond to the fears and biases of whites. Syracuse University professor John Yinger describes the consequences of this "tax" on black and Latino households:

> The base-case results reveal that when an event, such as a new child or an increase in income, induces a Black or Hispanic household to search for a house or to buy, it must pay, on average, a discrimination "tax" of roughly $3,700. A cost of this magnitude implies that a total cost of current discrimination amounts to about $3 billion per year for all Black households, owners and renters, and to almost $2 billion per year for Hispanic households.[62]

Discrimination lowers the nation's gross national product by almost 2 percent a year.[63] A large share of this loss is a result of housing discrimination. Sociologists Melvin O. Oliver and Thomas M. Shapiro estimate that the current generation of African Americans has lost $82 billion due to discrimination. Of this total, $58 billion was lost as a result of lack of housing appreciation, $10.5 billion from paying higher mortgage rates, and $13.5 billion from the denial of mortgages. Real estate agents, brokers, and mortgage lenders cater to the racist attitudes of some of their clients—and in effect determine the racial neighborhoods, cities, suburbs, and metropolitan regions.

Housing discrimination has changed over the past three decades. No overt signs are posted indicating "white only" or "blacks need not apply." Nevertheless, discrimination is just as real. Ownership of property, land, and businesses is still a central part of the American dream of success—a dream that has eluded millions of Americans.[64] The home ownership rate for African American households has grown significantly, from 43 percent in 1994 to 48.8 percent in 2005. That amounts to more than 1.5 million new African American home owner households.[65] About 50 percent of Hispanics owned their homes, compared with a 69 percent overall home ownership rate in the nation in 2005.

Discrimination denies a substantial segment of the African American community a basic form of wealth accumulation and investment through home ownership. Only about 59 percent of the nation's middle-class African Americans own their homes, compared with 74 percent of whites. On the other hand, some $50 billion to $90 billion dollars a year in tax subsidies underwrite suburban home owners. This middle-class entitlement is by far "the broadest and most expensive welfare program in the U.S.A."[66]

Although the nation has come a long way in race relations and civil rights, race still matters in twenty-first-century America.[67] Law professor and civil rights activist Derek Bell, in *Faces at the Bottom of the Well*, insists that "racism is an integral, permanent, and indestructible component of this society."[68] Race is not based on scientific fact, but a "social construct," with racial categories emerging out of a "sociohistoric process,"[69] yet it is realized as political power and the power to define "insiders" and "outsiders" and to redefine "who is white."[70]

There is no country in world history in which racism has been more important, for so long a time, as the United States.[71] With few exceptions, most Americans do not wish to see themselves as racist or want to be called a racist. Sociologist Eduardo Bonilla-Silva describes the current period we are living in as the era of "racism without racists" and "color-blind racism." Yet racism persists and shades everything in America.[72] Writing in *American Apartheid*, Douglas S. Massey and Nancy A. Denton summed up race and residence in the United States:

> A racially segregated society cannot be a color-blind society; as long as U.S. cities remain segregated—indeed, hypersegregated—the United States cannot claim to have equalized opportunities for blacks and whites. In a segregated world, the deck is stacked against black socioeconomic progress, political empowerment, and full participation in the mainstream of American life.[73]

Race is still an important factor in explaining social inequality, political exploitation, social isolation, and the health and well-being of people of color in the United States. Many of our central cities are "invisible" places where the quality of life for millions of low-income African Americans is worse today than it was during the turbulent 1960s. The growing economic disparity between racial/ethnic groups has a direct correlation to institutional barriers in health, education, housing, lending, and employment.

African American urban unemployment is worsened by persistent racial discrimination, inadequate public transportation, and a breakdown in the informal job information network among low-income black workers. Over the past three decades, low-income and affluent African Americans have become more isolated from the larger society, "creating bastions of privilege and pockets of distress in America."[74] Poor African Americans and poor whites live worlds apart. In 2000, over 60.6 percent of poor African Americans lived in central cities, 24.0 percent lived in the suburbs, and 15.4 percent lived in rural areas. For poor whites, only 27.0 percent lived in central cities, 41.3 percent lived in the suburbs, and 31.7 percent lived in rural areas.[75]

Black America is experiencing an employment crisis. The economic recession of 2000–2003 took its largest toll on African American males. In 2003, for example, barely half (51.8 percent) of the African American males in New York City were employed, compared with 75.7 percent of New York's white men.[76] In 1989, New York City's African American male employment-population ratio was 16.6 percentage points below the white male ratio and 8.3 percentage points below the ratio of Hispanic men. By 2003, the black-white gap grew to 23.9 percentage points and the black/Hispanic gap increased to 13.9 percentage points.[77]

In 1954, at the time of *Brown v. Board of Education*, over 52 percent of African American male teens worked, a rate slightly higher than their white peers.[78] By 2003, only 19.9 percent of African American male teens were employed in a typical month, nearly 20 percentage points below that of white male teens and well below that of Hispanic male teens.[79] Among twenty- to twenty-four-year-old African American men, employment rates averaged only 57 percent during the 2001–2003 period, compared with an average of 80 percent employment in the late 1960s. These unattached youth are out of both school and the labor market.

In 2002, one-quarter of all African American men were not employed at any point during the year. In May 2006, African American teen unemployment was a whopping 31.4 percent compared to a 13.3 percent overall teen unemployment rate. The 2006 African American teen jobless rate was nearly seven times the national unemployment rate of 4.7 percent.

GROWING APART IN PUBLIC SCHOOLS

Housing and schools are intricately linked. Generally, families with children weigh the quality of local schools in assessing their housing and residential priorities. In 2000, the average white American lived in a neighborhood that was 80 percent white, 8 percent Hispanic, 7 percent black, and 4 percent Asian. Similarly, the typical African American lived in a neighborhood that was 51 percent black, 33 percent white, 12 percent Hispanic, and 3 percent Asian.[80] In the major metropolitan areas where most African Americans, Latinos, and Asians live, segregation levels changed little between 1990 and 2000.

The top three most segregated cities for African Americans in 2000 were Detroit, Memphis, and Chicago. In addition to being the *most* segregated big city for blacks, Detroit also led the nation in office sprawl (percent of office space located outside the central city), and it falls at the bottom of the list of metropolitan areas whose workers use public transit. Detroit received its international fame as the "Motor City."

Schools are a powerful perpetrator of metropolitan polarization.[81] The drift toward racially segmented metropolitan areas is most pronounced in public education. A 2002 Harvard Civil Rights Project study, *Race in American Public Schools: Rapidly Resegregating School Districts*, reports that the nation's school districts are becoming more diverse and more segregated.[82] In 2000, over 70 percent of African American students attended schools where students of color were in the majority; 40 percent of African American students attended schools that were 90 to 100 percent black.

In 2003–2004, African Americans comprised a majority of the students enrolled in nine of the sixteen "most sprawl-threatened" large cities.[83] These cities include Detroit (90.8 percent), Baltimore (88.6 percent), Atlanta (88.2 percent), St. Louis (80.4 percent), Washington, D.C. (83.6 percent), Cleveland (70.6 percent), Cincinnati (70.3 percent), Kansas City (69.8 percent), Chicago (50.3 percent), Minneapolis (42.1 percent), Fort Lauderdale (36.7 percent), Dallas (31.3 percent), St. Paul (28.1 percent), Seattle (22.8 percent), Tampa (23.6 percent), and Denver (18.8 percent).

The Latino share of the nation's students has almost tripled since 1968. The black student enrollment increased by 30 percent and the white student enrollment decreased by 17 percent over the same period.[84] Over 37 percent of Latino students attend schools where 90 to 100 percent of the students are students of color. The average Latino student is enrolled in a school that is less than 30 percent white. Generally, over 80 percent of white students attend schools where more than 80 percent of the students are white.[85] Gary Orfield and Susan E. Eaton, two leading authors on schools desegregation, write:

Segregation is so deeply sewn into America's social fabric that the media rarely see it. And policy-makers, thinkers, pundits and "education reformers" steer around the gross fact of segregation as if it were heaven ordained, without insidious causes or acceptable cure.[86]

Huge disparities still exist between the education quality and funding of suburbs and inner-city schools. These disparities are buttressed by the archaic school property tax financing method. Funding schools is an investment in the future. Failure to invest in education ends up costing the nation more tax dollars for youth detention centers, jails, and prisons.

INVESTMENT IN SCHOOLS VERSUS PRISONS

The rate of incarceration in prison and jail in 2005 was 738 inmates per 100,000 U.S. residents, or 1 in every 136 U.S. residents.[87] At midyear 2005, the nation's prisons and jails incarcerated 2,186,230 persons. Prisoners in the custody of the state and federal systems accounted for two-thirds of the incarcerated population (1,438,701 inmates). The other third were held in local jails (747,529), not including persons in community-based programs.[88]

Incarceration rates climbed in the United States during the 1990s and reached record highs in the past few years. In 1995, 16 percent of African American men in their twenties who did not attend college were in jail or prison. By 2004, this number had climbed to 21 percent. By their midthirties, six in ten African American men who had dropped out of school had spent time in prison. More African American men earn their high school equivalency diplomas in prison each year than graduate from college.[89]

At the end of 2000, 791,600 African American men were behind bars and 603,032 were enrolled in colleges or universities. By contrast, in 1980—before the prison boom—African American men in college outnumbered African American men behind bars by a ratio of more than 3 to 1. In 2001, 179,500 African American men ages eighteen to twenty-four were in prison and jail. The college/imprisoned ratio for African American males eighteen to twenty-four was 2.6 to 1. For their white male counterparts, the ratio was 28 to 1. In 2000, there were 3.5 million white men ages eighteen to twenty-four enrolled in college, which represents 32.8 percent of that age group, while 125,700 were in prison in 2001.

The United States operates the largest prison system on the planet. The nation added over a thousand new prisons and jails during the past two decades.[90] Keeping prisoners behind bars is not cheap. On average, spending on corrections alone amounts to $23,406 per inmate; correctional, judicial, and legal costs total $39,201 per inmate; and corrections, judicial, legal, and police costs add up to a staggering $71,465 per inmate. The total expenditure in the United States on prisons is $35 billion a year. States now spend more on building prisons than on colleges and universities.[91]

The United States jails African American men at four times the rate of incarceration of black men in South Africa.[92] Nearly six in ten persons in local jails were racial or ethnic minorities. At midyear 2005, whites made up 44.3 percent of the jail population; blacks, 38.9 percent; Hispanics, 15.0 percent; and other races (American Indians, Alaska Natives, Asians, Native Hawaiians, and other Pacific Islanders), 1.7 percent.[93] Private companies reap hefty profits from the $35 billion-a-year spending on prisons.[94] For them, crime pays and prisons are good for business.

An estimated 12 percent of African American males in their late twenties were in prison or jail in 2005.[95] According to U.S. Department of Justice research, African American males in their twenties and thirties have higher rates relative to other groups. Among the nearly 2.2 million offenders incarcerated on June 30, 2005, an estimated 548,300 were African American males between the ages of twenty and thirty-nine. Of black non-Hispanic males age twenty-five to twenty-nine, 11.9 percent were in prison or jail, compared to 3.9 percent of Hispanic males and about 1.7 percent of white males in the same age group. In general, the incarceration rates for African American males of all ages were five to seven times greater than those for white males in the same age groups.[96]

The proliferation of prisons in the United States is an integral part of the globalization of capital. The federal "War on Drugs" fueled the prison industrial complex—now big business and rapidly becoming an essential component of the U.S. economy. The Federal Bureau of Prisons (BOP) budget increased from $220 million in 1986 to $3.19 billion in 1997. The 2007 budget provides $5 billion for the BOP and $1.3 billion for the Office of the Federal Detention Trustee (OFDT).[97] Many impoverished rural areas now use prisons as economic development. Crime also "pays" for these communities.

The federal "War on Drugs," launched under the Reagan administration in the mid-1980s, was in effect a "war on blacks, Hispanics, and the poor." A federal survey estimated some 9.9 million whites (72 percent of all drug users), 2.0 million African Americans (15 percent), and 1.4 million Hispanics (10 percent) were current illegal drug users in 1998. Yet African Americans constitute 36.8 percent of the drug arrests and over 42 percent of those in federal prison on drug violations. African Americans make up almost 58 percent of the inmates in state prisons for drug felonies and Hispanics account for 20.7 percent.[98]

Whether locked in prisons, confined to poorly performing public schools, or trapped in opportunity-poor communities, the fate of millions of African Americans is shaped by the politics of place and race. Those who have the economic means continue to leave. Higher-income African American households are leading this flight to "opportunity."

Some African Americans are moving into black suburbia in record numbers. However, the majority of African Americans still live in central cities. Only 19 percent of African Americans lived in the suburbs in 1970. Today, nearly 35 percent of African Americans are suburbanites. We now see "two separate realities in Black America, those who have benefited from opportunities created by the civil rights movement, and those whose economic position has slipped further and further behind."[99]

NOTES

1. Derek Bell, *Silent Covenants: Brown v. Board of Education and the Unfulfilled Hope of Racial Reform* (New York: Oxford University Press, 2004).

2. William H. Frey, *Diversity Spreads Out: Metropolitan Shifts in Hispanic, Asian, and Black Population Since 2000* (Washington, DC: The Brookings Institution, March 2006), 10.

3. Jesse McKinnon, *The Black Population in the United States: March 2002*, Publication P20-541 (Washington, DC: U.S. Bureau of the Census, April 2003), 2.

4. Frey, *Diversity Spreads Out*, 11.

5. Ibid., 7.

6. Michael A. Stoll, *Job Sprawl and the Spatial Mismatch Between Blacks and Jobs* (Washington, DC: The Brookings Institution, February 2005).

7. Robert E. Lang, *Office Sprawl: The Evolving Geography of Business* (Washington, DC: The Brookings Institution, 2000), 3.

8. William Julius Wilson, *When Work Disappears: The World of the New Urban Poor* (New York: Alfred A. Knopf, 1996), 567–95.

9. Paul Jargowsky, *Poverty and Place: Ghettos, Barrios, and the American City* (New York: Russell Sage Foundation, 1997), 193.

10. Myron Orfield, *Metropolitics: A Regional Agenda for Community and Stability* (Washington, DC: Brookings Institution Press, 1997).

11. Manuel Pastor Jr., Peter J. Dreier, J. Eugene Grigsby III, and Marta Lopez, *Regions That Work: How Cities and Suburbs Can Grow Together* (Minneapolis: University of Minnesota Press, 2000), 157.

12. Ibid., 3.

13. Robert D. Bullard, Glenn S. Johnson, and Angel O. Torres, "Atlanta: Megasprawl," *Forum: Applied Research and Public Policy* 14, no. 3 (1999): 17–23.

14. Bank of America, Greenbelt Alliance, California Resource Agency, and Low-Income Housing Fund, *Beyond Sprawl: New Patterns of Growth to Fit the New California*, Executive Summary (San Francisco, CA, 1995).

15. American Planning Association, *Policy Guide on Smart Growth*, adopted by Chapter Delegate Assembly, Chicago, IL, April 14, 2002, 1.

16. Ibid., 6.

17. See Robert D. Bullard, Glenn S. Johnson, and Angel Torres, *Sprawl City: Race, Politics, and Planning in Atlanta* (Washington, DC: Island Press, 2000).

18. Carl Anthony, *Suburbs Are Making Us Sick: Health Implications of Suburban Sprawl and Inner City Abandonment on Communities of Color*, Environmental Justice

Health Research Needs Report Series (Atlanta: Environmental Justice Resource Center, 1998), 3.

19. Orfield, *Metropolitics*, 11.

20. Robert D. Bullard and Glenn S. Johnson, eds., *Just Transportation: Dismantling Race and Class Barriers to Mobility* (Gabriola Island, BC: New Society Publishers, 1997), 8.

21. Bullard, Johnson, and Torres, *Sprawl City*.

22. Howard Frumkin, Lawrence Frank, and Richard Jackson, *Urban Sprawl and Public Health: Designing, Planning, and Building Healthy Communities* (Washington, DC: Island Press, 2004).

23. William A. Johnson Jr., "Sprawl as a Civil Right: A Mayor's Reflection," a discussion paper presented at the George Washington University Center on Sustainable Growth, Washington, DC (March, 2002), 1.

24. Bullard, Johnson, and Torres, *Sprawl City*.

25. Dennis A. Rondinelli, James H. Johnson, and John D. Karsada, "The Changing Forces of Urban Economic Development: Globalization and City Competitiveness in the 21st Century," *Cityscape: A Journal of Policy Development and Research* 3 (1998): 71–105.

26. Robert D. Bullard, J. Eugene Grigsby III, and Charles Lee, eds., *Residential Apartheid: The American Legacy* (Los Angeles: UCLA Center for African American Studies, 1994), chapter 1; Douglas S. Massey and Nancy A. Denton, eds., *American Apartheid and the Making of the Underclass* (Cambridge, MA: Harvard University Press, 1993), 83–114.

27. Joe R. Feagin and Clairece B. Feagin, *Racial and Ethnic Relations* (Upper Saddle River, NJ: Prentice-Hall, 1999), chapter 1.

28. Gary A. Dymski and John M. Veitch, "Taking It to the Bank: Race, Credit, and Income in Los Angeles," in *Residential Apartheid: The American Legacy*, ed. Robert D. Bullard, J. Eugene Grigsby III, and Charles Lee (Los Angeles: UCLA Center for African Studies Publication, 1994), 150–79; G. Squires, "Forgoing a Tradition of Redlining for a Future of Reinvestment," *Business Journal Serving Greater Milwaukee* (July 24, 1998): 50.

29. *St. Louis Business Journal*, "National City Sued Over Racial Discrimination," April 26, 2006.

30. See Ronald Cotterill and Andrew Franklin, "The Urban Grocery Store Gap," Food Marketing Policy Center, University of Connecticut, April 1995; Amanda Shaffer, "The Persistence of Los Angeles' Grocery Store Gap," Urban and Environmental Policy Institute, May 31, 2002; Kimberly Morland et al., "Access to Healthy Foods Limited in Poor Neighborhoods," *American Journal of Preventive Health*, January 2002.

31. Morland et al., "Access to Healthy Foods Limited in Poor Neighborhoods," 20.

32. Ibid.

33. See "Surgeon General: Obesity Rivals Tobacco as Health Ill," *USA Today*, December 13, 2001, also found at http://www.usatoday.com/news/health/diet/2001-12-12-obesity.htm (accessed April 1, 2005).

34. Mark Winston Griffith, "The 'Food Justice' Movement: Trying to Break the Food Chains," *Gotham Gazette*, December 2003, also found at http://www.gothamgazette.com/article/communitydevelopment/20031218/20/808 (accessed March 30, 2005).

35. Ibid.

36. John F. Kain, "Housing Segregation, Negro Employment, and Metropolitan Decentralization," *The Quarterly Journal of Economics* 82 (1968): 175–77.

37. Paul D. Gottlieb, "Residential Amenities, Firm Location and Economic Development," *Urban Studies* 32 (1995): 1413–36.

38. Robert D. Bullard et al., *Race, Equity, and Smart Growth: Why People of Color Must Speak for Themselves*, available at http://socialclass.org/modules.php?op=modload&name=News&file=article&sid=211&mode=thread&order=0&thold=0 (posted April 9, 2004).

39. Qin Shen, "Location Characteristics of Inner-City Neighborhoods and Employment Accessibility of Low-Wage Workers," *Environment and Planning B: Planning and Design* 25 (1998): 345–65.

40. Stoll, *Job Sprawl and the Spatial Mismatch Between Blacks and Jobs*, 5.

41. Lang, *Office Sprawl*, 25.

42. Ibid.

43. Joe R. Feagin, "Excluding Black and Others from Housing: The Foundations of White Racism," *Cityscape: A Journal of Policy Development and Research* 4 (1999): 79–91.

44. Bill Lann Lee, "An Issue of Public Importance: The Justice Department's Enforcement of the Fair Housing Act," *Cityscape: A Journal of Policy Development and Research* 4 (1999): 35–56.

45. Margery Austin Turner, Raymond J. Struyk, and John Yinger, *Housing Discrimination Study: Synthesis* (Washington, DC: U.S. Government Printing Office, 1996), 50.

46. Margery Austin Turner, Fred Freiberg, Erin Godfrey, Carla Herbig, Diane K. Levy, and Robin Smith, *All Other Things Being Equal: A Paired Testing Study of Mortgage Lending Institutions* (Washington, DC: The Urban Institute, April 2002), iv.

47. Bullard, Johnson, and Torres, eds., *Sprawl City*; Joe R. Feagin, *Racist America: Roots, Current Realities and Future Reparations* (New York: Routledge, 2001).

48. See CNN Money, "Subprime Lenders Target Minorities: Study Finds African-Americans, Hispanics Pay Higher Loan Rates Than Whites with Similar Incomes," May 1, 2002, http://money.cnn.com/2002/05/01/pf/banking/subprime (accessed April 5, 2005).

49. William C. Apgar and Allegra Calder, "The Dual Mortgage Market: The Persistence of Discrimination in Mortgage Lending," in *The Geography of Opportunity: Race and Housing Choice in Metropolitan America*, ed. Xavier de Souza (Washington, DC: Brookings Institution Press, 2005), 101–25.

50. Ibid., 10.

51. Calvin Bradford, *Risk or Race? Racial Disparities and the Subprime Refinance Market* (Washington, DC: The Neighborhood Revitalization Project, May 2002).

52. ACORN, *Separate and Unequal: Predatory Lending in America* (Washington, DC: Association of Community Organizations for Reform Now, February 2004).

53. See Glenn Canner, "The Role of Specialized Lenders in Extending Mortgages to Low-Income and Minority Homebuyers," *Federal Reserve Bulletin* 85 (November 1999): 709–23; U.S. Department of Housing and Urban Development and U.S. Department of Treasury Joint Task Force, *Curbing Predatory Home Mortgage Lending* (Washington, DC: U.S. Department of HUD and U.S. Department of Treasury, 2000); Bullard, Johnson, and Torres, *Race, Equity, and Smart Growth*.

54. ACORN, *The High Cost of Credit: Disparities in High-Priced Refinancing Loans to Minority Homeowners in 125 American Cities* (Washington, DC: Association of Community Organizations for Reform Now, September 27, 2005), 17.

55. Debbie Gruenstein Bacian, Keith S. Ernst, and Wei Lu, *Unfair Lending: The Effect of Race and Ethnicity on the Price of Subprime Lending* (Center for Responsible Lending, May 31, 2006).

56. Ibid., 5.

57. See Federal Financial Institutions Examination Council (FFIEC), *Home Mortgage Disclosure Act, Aggregate Report Search by State*, Washington, DC, 2004, found at http://www.ffiec.gov/hmdaadwebreport/aggwelcome.aspx (accessed January 30, 2005).

58. National Fair Housing Alliance, *No Home for the Holidays: Report on Housing Discrimination Against Hurricane Katrina Survivors*, Executive Summary (Washington, DC: NFHA, December 20, 2005), available at http://www.nationalfairhousing.org/html/Press%20Releases/Katrina/Hurricane%20Katrina%20Survivors%20-%20Report.pdf (accessed January 15, 2006).

59. Ibid. From mid-September through mid-December 2005, the NFHA conducted telephone tests of rental housing providers in seventeen cities in five states: Alabama (Birmingham, Mobile, Huntsville, and Montgomery); Florida (Gainesville, Tallahassee, and Pensacola); Georgia (Atlanta, Columbus, Macon, and Savannah); Tennessee (Nashville, Chattanooga, and Memphis); and Texas (Houston, Dallas, and Waco).

60. Ibid., 2.

61. Ibid., 1–3.

62. John Yinger, "Sustaining the Fair Housing Act," *Cityscape: A Journal of Policy Development and Research* 4 (1999): 97.

63. Walter L. Updegrade, "Race and Money," *Money* 18 (1989): 152–72.

64. Donald R. Haurin and Stuart S. Rosenthal, *The Influence of Household Formation on Homeownership Rates Across Time and Race* (Washington, DC: U.S. Department of Housing and Urban Development, October 2004).

65. Danilo Pelletiere, "House of Cards: The State of Black Housing," *The Crisis* (May/June 2005): 30.

66. Douglas Kelbaugh, *Common Place: Toward Neighborhood and Regional Design* (Seattle: University of Washington Press, 1997), 31.

67. Cornel West, *Race Matters* (New York: Vintage Books, 1994).

68. Derek Bell, *Faces at the Bottom of the Well* (New York: Basic Books, 1993), ix.

69. Michael Omi and Howard Winant, eds., *Racial Formation in the United States*, 2nd ed. (New York: Routledge, 1996), 3–13.

70. Andrew Hacker, *Two Nations: Black and White, Separate, Hostile, Unequal* (New York: Scribner's, 1992), 13.

71. Howard Zinn, *A People's History of the United States* (New York: Harper-Collins, 1980), 60.

72. Eduardo Bonilla-Silva, *Racism without Racists: Color-Blind Racism and the Persistence of Racial Inequality in the United States* (Lanham, MD: Rowman & Littlefield, 2003), 1.

73. Douglas S. Massey and Nancy A. Denton, *American Apartheid: Segregation and the Making of the Underclass* (Cambridge, MA: Harvard University Press, 1994), 137–70.

74. Sheryll Cashin, *The Failures of Integration: How Race and Class Are Undermining the American Dream* (New York: Public Affairs, 2004), 83.

75. Hacker, *Two Nations*, 117.

76. Mark Levitan, *A Crisis of Black Male Employment: Unemployment and Joblessness in New York City, 2003* (New York: Community Service Society, February 2004), 2.

77. Ibid., 15.

78. Andrew Sum, *Trends in Black Male Joblessness and Year-Round Idleness: An Employment Crisis Ignored* (Chicago: Alternative Schools Network, June 2004), also found at http://www.nupr.neu.edu/7-04/Black%20males%20report.pdf (accessed May 5, 2005).

79. Ibid., 6.

80. John R. Logan, *Separate and Unequal: The Neighborhood Gap of Blacks and Hispanics in Metropolitan America* (Albany, NY: Lewis Mumford Center for Comparative Urban and Regional Research, University of Albany, October 13, 2002), 45.

81. Orfield, *Metropolitics*.

82. Erica Frankenberg and Chungmei Lee, *Race in American Public Schools: Rapidly Resegregating School Districts* (Cambridge, MA: Harvard Civil Rights Project, August 2002).

83. U.S. Department of Education, The National Center for Education Statistics (NCES), *Information on Public Elementary/Secondary School Universe Survey Data 2003–2004*, available at http://nces.ed.gov/ccd/bat/ (accessed April 30, 2005).

84. Ibid., 2.

85. Gary Orfield, "Back to Segregation," *Nation* (March 3, 2003): 27–30.

86. Ibid.

87. Paige M. Harrison and Allen J. Beck, U.S. Department of Justice, Office of Justice Programs, *Prison and Jail Inmates at Midyear 2005*, 2, available at http://www.ojp.usdoj.gov/bjs/pub/pdf/pjim05.pdf (accessed June 7, 2006).

88. Ibid.

89. Michael A. Fletcher, "At the Corner of Progress and Peril," *Washington Post*, June 6, 2006, A01.

90. Eric Schlosser, "The Prison Industrial Complex," *Atlantic Monthly* (December 1998): 51–77.

91. Vincent Scheraldi and Jason Ziedenberg, *Cellblocks or Classrooms? The Funding of Higher Education and Corrections and Its Impact on African American Men* (Washington, DC: Justice Policy Institute, 2002), 4.

92. Craig Haney and Phillip Zimbardo, "The Past and Future of U.S. Prison Policy: Twenty-Five Years After the Stanford Prison Experiment," *American Psychologist* 53 (July 1998): 714.

93. Harrison and Beck, *Prison and Jail Inmates at Midyear 2005*, 8.

94. Schlosser, "The Prison Industrial Complex," 51–77.

95. Harrison and Beck, *Prison and Jail Inmates at Midyear 2005*, 10.

96. Ibid.

97. Office of Management and Budget, *Budget of the United States Government FY 2007* (Washington, DC: OMB, 2006).

98. Substance Abuse and Mental Health Services Administration, *National Household Survey on Drug Abuse: Summary Report 1998* (Rockville, MD: Substance Abuse and Mental Health Services Administration, 1999), 13; Bureau of Justice Statistics,

Sourcebook of Criminal Justice Statistics 1998 (Washington, DC: U.S. Department of Justice, August 1999), 75; Allen J. Beck and Christopher J. Mumola, *Bureau of Justice Statistics, Prisoners in 1998* (Washington, DC: U.S. Department of Justice, August 1999), 31.; Allen J. Beck and Paige M. Harrison, U.S. Department of Justice, *Bureau of Justice Statistics, Prisoners in 2000* (Washington, DC: U.S. Department of Justice, August 2001), 20.

99. Nicholas A. Jones and James S. Jackson, "The Demographic Profile of African Americans, 1970–1971 to 2000–2001," *The Black Collegian Online* (2001), found at http://www.black-collegian.com/issues/30thAnn/demographic2001-30th.shtml (accessed June 1, 2005).

2

Structural Racism and Spatial Jim Crow

john a. powell[1]

Despite more than fifty years of civil rights law aimed at dismantling racial subordination and a culture that purports to be more racially tolerant than ever before, "the elimination of Jim Crow did not really occur."[2] Clearly, the United States has undergone a shift away from the formalized, official, overt racism that characterized the Jim Crow South. However, more subtle and insidious forms of racism continue to shape American culture despite post–civil rights policies that ostensibly seek egalitarianism.

In his book *The World Is a Ghetto*, Howard Winant argues that contemporary policy remains "largely symbolic" due in part to a disjuncture between the "apparent intent" of usually color-blind initiatives and their "practical implementation" in an already racially stratified and hierarchical culture. Primarily, civil rights law fails to "address the deeper logic of race in U.S. history and culture."[3]

Similarly, in *Whitewashing Racism* the authors challenge the normative conception that racial attitudes have improved since the 1950s.[4] While acknowledging that an increasing number of whites profess to have more enlightened racial views, the book argues that this improvement must be understood within the context of current arrangements that maintain racial hierarchy even without any explicit racial hostility. Whites maintain privilege and "hoard opportunities" today without the stigma of being called racist. When one looks at the persistent racial disparities, or what sociologist Charles Tilly identifies as "durable inequality,"[5] there is a need to explain them in the face of the civil rights movement, which has been rightfully called one of the most important movements in American history. How then are we to make sense of this powerful movement and the lasting racial hierarchy that besets American society?

41

This chapter uses a structural framework to interpret historical events and continued racial disparities embedded in American society. The analysis traces the history of racist practices exercised through space and explores how space and resource allocation function as a broad illustration of racial inequalities in the United States.

THE ILLUSION OF PROGRESS

In 1968, the typical black family had 60 percent[6] as much income as a white family.[7] Today it has only 58 percent as much.[8] In 1968, for every dollar of white per-capita income, African Americans earned fifty-five cents.[9] Today they earn only fifty-seven cents.[10] At this pace, it would take blacks 580 years to make up the remaining forty-three cents.[11] Similarly, at the slow rate that the black-white poverty gap has been narrowing since 1968, it would take approximately 150 years to close.[12]

Black unemployment is more than twice the white rate—a wider gap than in 1972. This means that one in nine African Americans cannot find a job. In terms of home ownership, the rate for whites has jumped from 65 percent to 75 percent since 1970. Black home ownership has only risen from 42 percent to 48 percent. At this rate, it would take approximately 1,660 years to close the home ownership gap, which amounts to about fifty-five generations. Health disparities also persist. Black infants are almost two-and-a-half times as likely as white infants to die before age one— a greater gap than in 1970.

These disparities in life opportunities are compounded by separatism and entrenched by residential segregation. Our nation is growing in ethnic diversity and residential separation. The average white person within our metropolitan areas lives in a neighborhood that is 80 percent white and only 7 percent black. Despite a substantial migration of nonwhites to the suburbs, nonwhites have not gained access to largely white, opportunity-rich neighborhoods. The average black person lives in a neighborhood that is only 33 percent white and as much as 51 percent black.

Although there was some progress in the 1980s, with a five-point drop in the segregation index (from 73.8 to 68.8), the drop continued at a slower rate in the 1990s (a decline of just under four points). At this pace it would take forty more years for black-white segregation to come down even to the current level of Latino/a-white segregation. Hispanics and Asians, although considerably less segregated than blacks, have been growing more populous in the last twenty years without a decrease in their level of segregation. This means that these groups now live in more isolated settings than they did in 1980, with a smaller proportion of white residents in their neighborhoods both in the cities and in the suburbs.[13]

Historically, three explanations have been advanced to clarify the production of this enduring racial disparity. The first argues that people of color are inherently biologically inferior. A second, distinguishing itself from the biological explanation, argues that the ill success of African Americans and Latino/as emerges from their specific cultural attitudes and practices. A third perspective suggests that external societal forces and arrangements, present and past, produce these disparities. The first explanation, while common throughout the eighteenth, nineteenth, and early twentieth centuries in the United States, is no longer a frequently deployed discourse.

There is a growing consensus that no biological basis for race exists, but rather that race is a social construct. This entails that a biological explanation for racial disparities must also be rejected and that only the second and third explanations remain. In *The Anatomy of Racial Inequality*, economist Glenn Loury asserts that a democratic society committed to equality among its members must seriously consider the external structural explanation before asserting that some group of members is failing because of its culture.[14] Loury argues that it is the racial stigma that makes us all too eager to find the explanation in the internal cultural dynamics of the black community without seriously considering other alternatives.

STRUCTURAL RACISM

A structural racism approach examines racist ideologies and practices embedded in structures and institutional arrangements, focusing on the interrelated, dynamic nature of social opportunity structures. Rather than looking at singular institutional or individual actions, a more accurate gauge of equitable structures and institutional arrangements is access to opportunity. Because structural racism is relational, it is also dynamic. A set of institutional relationships can change because of new technology or a shift in what appears to be a distant institution.

A structural racism approach argues that intent and individual-focused analysis is only a small part of changing dynamic structures. Therefore, racialized processes often produce racist effects without any racist actor. In particular, this approach exposes the contemporary effects of historical forms of discrimination in institutions and structures.

In *Making Race and Nation*, Anthony Marx argues that the early arrangement of state power, along with a weak federal government, was in part designed to protect the institution of slavery and reinforce the subordination of blacks.[15] Marx further argues that the Civil War amendments to the Constitution were about restructuring the relationship between state and federal power. Without the weakening of states' rights and the restructuring and strengthening of the federal government, Marx asserts, the civil rights movement as we experienced it could not have occurred.

Examining the institutional arrangements that were reshaped during the beginning of the civil rights movement illuminates some of the limitations of the movement's reach. Blacks were moving from rural areas to urbanized areas throughout the country, especially in the Midwest and Northeast. This migration was fueled by increasing opportunities in the robust industrial areas flourishing from the demands of war and by the southern style of racism that subordinated blacks in all areas of life.

Changes in technology diminished the need for field labor, an occupation that concentrated blacks in the rural south. At the same time, over a million black soldiers were returning home from fighting white supremacy in Europe. Together these forces precipitated a racially charged arrangement of the institutions and structures that regulate opportunity and racial boundaries.

In the North, whites demanded a continued or new set of arrangements to protect their investment in whiteness in an imminent post–Jim Crow era, while blacks and others in the South worked to promote arrangements that would support equity and inclusion. This effort is now known as the civil rights movement. The conflicting demands of both groups have not been resolved and continue to shape institutions and structures to this day.

The demise of formal Jim Crow altered the arrangements that regulated housing, public accommodation, voting, and schools and assisted blacks in moving to urbanized areas and accessing lower-level industrial jobs. At the same time, the federal government was creating new programs and resources for whites and jobs to leave the central cities. These competing structural measures embodied in the civil rights and suburbanization movements, had and continue to have a powerful impact on each other that the court system and advocates often overlook. These new arrangements limited many of the promises of nonwhite inclusion and opportunity that were at the heart of the civil rights movement

Although de jure Jim Crow ended, de facto Jim Crow was reinscribed spatially. As blacks poured into industrialized cities looking for opportunity and inclusion, opportunity was being relocated to emerging suburban white enclaves with new forms of legal protection. In city after city, blacks sued and won the right to desegregate schools only to watch whites and resources move to areas where new forms of segregation were emerging. While the federal courts were willing to desegregate singular municipalities, they were also willing to tolerate entire fragmented segregated regions.

Indeed, in an important U.S. Supreme Court case, *Milliken v. Bradley*, the Court rejected a remedy for intentional segregation within the Detroit schools that would have involved the surrounding suburbs. As Justice Marshall, the lead attorney in *Brown v. Board of Education*, noted, this new arrangement would further encourage whites to flee to the suburbs and undermine deseg-regation efforts. In a beguiling twist, the Court attributed the problems of seg-regated housing patterns in the Detroit area to choice and natural market forces. The Court ignored the role of the government, including the courts, in creating, subsidizing, and maintaining this segregation.[16]

In another important shift, the Court in *Milliken* moved to constitution-alize localism and regional fragmentation. While there had been a long his-tory, legal and otherwise, recognizing that localities were fictions and crea-tures of the state, the Court raised the right to control local boundaries beyond the imperative of *Brown* and the aspiration of racial justice. The point is not that the Court was wrong, but that it reinforced and redefined local control in such a way as to retrench and eventually undermine the scope and promise of civil rights.[17] The limitations of the civil rights prom-ise are mysterious only if one focuses narrowly at one institution at a time.

When one looks, however, at the shift in institutional arrangements in the Detroit area, it is clear that what was given in one sphere was taken away in another. While one may assert that this shift was predictable and inten-tional, this argument is largely irrelevant from the analytics of structural racism. The focus instead should address modes of collective response shaped by an understanding of the consequences of these institutional arrangements.

Loury asserts that American culture would not be sanguine with contem-porary arrangements that so powerfully impact blacks in a negative way were it not for racist ideologies. His important insight suggests that how we understand and respond to these changes is affected by our racial under-standing. Complementing Loury's assertions, in his text *The Possessive In-vestment of Whiteness*, George Lipsitz claims that it is not merely a lack of re-sponse to institutional racism that is defined by racial understanding, but that it is the desire to protect white privilege that is generative of the set of arrangements that are installed in the first place.[18]

The creation of the suburbs was designed specifically to protect white privilege in a changing world with new racialized arrangements put in place as the old ones decayed. His argument is credible but incomplete, for not only does white privilege and interest produce the arrangements of institu-tions, but white interest and privilege is produced through institutional arrangements. Correspondingly, racism both produces and is produced by the organization of institutions.

From the structural racism framework it is logical to conclude that the or-ganization and location of housing is directly related to, and therefore an important response to, education. Educational opportunities are still grossly unequal for city and suburban residents.[19] And housing choices con-tinue to shrink as existing affordable housing is being demolished or up-graded out of reach of lower- and middle-income residents without being replaced.[20] Yet, an important rejoinder to this relationship is that schools cannot address housing issues. Rather than throwing up our hands, it is essential to recognize that this may be an example of racialized institutional arrangements. Structural racism requires that we examine these arrangements relationally and accept the existing and emerging coherency of institutions to address the issues at hand.

Moreover, because institutional functions and capacities are dynamic in these relationships, one must consider how capacities and coherencies are constantly shifting. Consider the role and capacities of the federal government from the 1930s to the 1970s or 1980s. The government was in a period of growth in terms of power and resources. In some respects, the civil rights movement involved redefining and wresting power away from the states, at times directly and at others, through money. Within the contemporary context, we must also consider the increasingly significant role of globalization in shaping the power and effectiveness of the federal government to create social change in relationship to the local, state, and global regions.

Globalization, an economic phenomenon where the traditional borders of trade and financial transactions have become less rigid and more permeable, is increasingly connecting and integrating formerly distinct political units through a "global economy." As the global economy grows, the economic costs of racially disparate outcomes will become more evident and significant for everyone in nations like Brazil, South Africa, and the United States.

Based on a past model developed by the President's Council of Economic Advisors, economist Jonas Zoninsein estimates that all three nations (Brazil, South Africa, and the United States) could gain a combined increase in economic productivity equal to the Gross Domestic Product (GDP) of the world's fifteenth-largest economy by uprooting racial discrimination.[21] Because of global competition, people of all "races" in Brazil, South Africa, and the United States will increasingly suffer the economic costs of exclusion when people of African descent remain poor, unemployed, underemployed, and undereducated. Equitable social and human development should be a basic standard for future human progress and increasingly an essential strategy for long-term economic development.

While intensifying global disparities along racial lines, globalization also diminishes the power of the federal government to correct inequities as it did through civil rights legislation in earlier periods of capitalist development. Globalization causes the federal government to disperse power transnationally, while at the same time globalization's derivative, devolution, works within the U.S. context to diminish federal power. Devolution is the transfer of responsibilities, revenues, and taxing powers from the federal and state governments to local governments.

Because of globalization and devolution in the United States the state and regional levels of government are increasingly important, yet incoherent for global problems. Furthermore, due to the increased fragmentation and incoherency, coordination becomes more difficult, which also makes addressing racial and social inequality more difficult. These two processes have exacted power and resources from the federal government, which we must consider in order to delineate our strategies for action.

Our idea of development cannot be economic growth without racial and social justice. Rather, development should be measured in terms of the quality of human life.[22] Joseph Stiglitz argues that "globalization, by increasing the interdependence among the people of the world, has enhanced the need for global collective action and the importance of global public goods" and created new institutional arrangements and incoherencies.[23] This is important from the point of view of coordinating efforts and applying pressure.

Rather than merely critiquing and demonizing the processes of globalization and devolution, we must strategize within the range of possibilities and restrictions created by the global and interconnected context that exists. This is the reason for advocating for a federated regionalism with a racial content. It is a strategy embedded within the reality of devolution and globalization and a restructuring of our civil rights movement's strategies and conceptualization of the federal government.

CONSTRUCTION OF RACIALIZED SPACE

Spatial racism produces inequality. According to Richard Thompson Ford, "[s]pace as we experience it, is in many ways the product, and not the fixed context, of social interactions, ideological conceptions and of course, legal doctrine and public policy."[24] Indeed, the use of space to both control and racialize different populations has a long history in this country and internationally. In *The World Is a Ghetto*, Winant argues that the emergence of nation-states and national identities in modernity, which clearly serve to demarcate (and occupy and colonize) space, was organized according to processes of racial signification.[25]

The construction of nation-states required a unified and homogeneous identity from which to differentiate the "Other." Such differentiation in turn provided the justification for the usurpation of the labor and resources of racially "Other" nations for capitalist advancement. Winant draws a direct correlation between spatial divisions of racialized imperialist conquest and contemporary organization of American culture noting that the "ex-colonials, descendants of slaves, and indigenes" "are long gone from the hinterlands" but have been relocated "today in the metropolitan centers."[26]

The use of space for the maintenance of racial homogeneity has indeed been central in the construction of American national identity. The white inhabitants of the "new world" have constricted Native Americans in their movement, location, and access to opportunity since precolonial times. During the Civil War, Congress moved the eastern tribes west of the Mississippi, but as settlers pushed farther on, a policy of assimilation soon predominated.[27] It wasn't until the Citizenship Act of 1924 that Native Americans were granted citizenship.[28]

Immigration laws have also controlled who and how one could share the space of an emerging nation. In 1875, Congress passed legislation barring the entrance of Chinese prostitutes into the United States. This bias culminated with the wholesale exclusion of Chinese immigrant laborers through the Chinese Exclusion Act of 1882, the first exclusively racial immigration law.[29] It wasn't until we became allies with China during World War II that these types of restrictions were lifted.[30] The nineteenth-century "sovereignty cases"—*Johnson v. McIntosh, Cherokee Nation v. Georgia*, and *Worcester v. Georgia*[31]—also gave Congress plenary power to construct the American state and its membership, largely immune from judicial review. As a result, nonwhites, including Native Americans, Chinese, Japanese, and Mexicans, suffered exploitation and discrimination similar to black experiences.[32] Behind these policies lay a conception of the United States as a white, Anglo-Saxon nation-state. Nonwhites who were allowed to settle in this country were excluded through arbitrary racial constructs.

The history of space in relationship to civil rights and urbanized minorities, particularly blacks, however, manifests itself quite differently and is important to our understanding of today's institutions and regional dynamics. Unlike other racial groups who were denied access to space through formal exclusion, blacks and whites initially lived in close proximity to one another, primarily in the South, prior to and after emancipation. The status of black slaves in the United States, however, was less about racialized space and more about control through explicit and formal means. Yet the issue did not stray far from the concept of membership and opportunity associated with belonging and space.

The *Dred Scott* case[33] set clear parameters around who could access membership and opportunity. There, the Supreme Court concluded that because Scott, a runaway slave, was not a citizen, he could be excluded from being a member of the imagined society. Not only were blacks denied the rights, privileges, and immunities of citizenship granted under the Constitution, they were deemed "a subordinate inferior class of beings" subject to the authority of the dominant white race. This was, and is possibly, the most defining case in United States history. Segregation under Jim Crow, and later as embraced in *Plessy v. Ferguson*,[34] is an extension of the same issue.

It is important to note that in *Dred Scott* the Supreme Court asserted that only the federal government could confer citizenship, not the states. After the Civil War, the privilege and immunities clause of the Fourteenth Amendment attempted to correct *Dred Scott* and confer citizenship on blacks. But the Supreme Court substantially undermined the citizenship implication of the privilege and immunities clause.

In the *Slaughterhouse Case*, which was about the right to work as an incident of national citizenship, however, the Supreme Court rendered this clause virtually meaningless, as most of the privileges associated with citizenship were offered by the state.[35] This reinforcement of states' rights has led some to call this one of the worst cases in U.S. history.[36]

Like many monumental events, the Civil War was about many things. One of those things enshrined in the Civil War amendments was a restructuring of federal and states' powers. But significant shift to federal power was both delayed and undermined by the Supreme Court until the 1930s and the New Deal. Even then, the Court attempted to limit the federal government, and capitulated only when threatened with court packing.

It was critical to have a strong federal government for the civil rights movement to succeed. It is not surprising that many of those who oppose civil rights also argued and continue to argue in favor of states' rights. But the new localism arrangement that grew up after the civil rights movement, as many scholars have demonstrated, is similar to the states' rights movement. One will notice that neither of these movements is explicitly about race.

The arrangement of space has been one of the most important ways to distribute and retard opportunity along racial lines. Jim Crow emerged in the South as the dominant form of spatial apartheid, segregating public accommodations and transportation, clearly demarcating the spaces occupied by whites and blacks, and reinforcing the highly visible and powerful racial hierarchy. In the Northeast and Midwest, where many blacks relocated, the use of space was intensified, segregating blacks by neighborhood and jurisdiction.

Whites fled to the suburbs, while those left behind faced displacement through urban renewal and removal. These two migrations—blacks to and whites away from city centers—led to a dearth of opportunity on the one hand and opportunity-rich subsidized spatial enclaves on the other, respectively. These inequitable spatial arrangements, both in the South and the North, created further demands for inclusion and citizenship.

As such, the civil rights movement was more about *Dred Scott* than about *Plessy*. It was about the claim of full membership and full opportunity associated with being a full partner in the imagined community. Despite the demise of Jim Crow, the movement came up short. Communities of color remain isolated from essential life opportunities in the impoverished city and inner-ring suburbs, while whites continue to sprawl into the opportunity-rich outer suburbs or return to the city to gentrify it.

It is important to acknowledge the role the federal government has played and continues to play in distributing opportunities spatially. The departure of whites from the central city was no accident, nor was the isolation of people of color in central cities. As Kenneth Jackson and others have described, the government first opened up the suburbs to whites through the National Housing Act of 1934.[37] This law created the Home Owners' Loan Corporation, later called the Federal Housing Administration, which subsidized home mortgages for whites in the suburbs.

Before this time, home ownership was beyond the reach of many families because of the requirement that one-third or even more of the purchase price be paid down. The federal government changed this by making it affordable to buy a home, enabling millions of families to purchase and build equity in their homes. But the government explicitly offered these subsidies only to whites. It funded houses in racially homogeneous white neighborhoods, and favored the purchase of homes in the suburbs. The underwriting manual for home mortgage insurance disseminated by the federal government was explicitly racist.[38]

The federal government pushed home purchasers to adopt covenants that would restrict the future sale of these government-subsidized homes to non-whites.[39] While both the racist practice of lending support only to whites as well as the covenants that emerged from these practices were declared unconstitutional in 1948, the legacy prompted private companies to engage in racialized practices of redlining, which continue to shape the industry.[40]

This denial of home ownership to people of color has had devastating intergenerational effects because home ownership is the primary source of wealth accumulation in this nation. If we could end all discrimination and racial animus today, racial disparity would persist indefinitely without correcting the racial disparities in wealth. Wealth derived from home ownership accounts for 60 percent of the total wealth among America's middle class.[41]

According to an analysis by Dalton Conley, African Americans could claim 0.5 percent of the wealth in the United States at the time of the Emancipation Proclamation in 1865. By 1990, 125 years later, African Americans' share of the nation's wealth had risen to only 1.0 percent.[42] A disparity of 900 percent exists between the median assets (wealth) of black householders and white householders.

There is an obvious correlation between this deficit in home ownership and disparities in education, health, and employment. The relationship between economic wealth and education, health, and employment determines our ability to live as we would like to live in this society. The modern world denies basic elementary freedoms to a majority of us in this world. Amartya Sen stated in *Development as Freedom*, "We generally have excellent reasons for wanting more income or wealth. This is not because income and wealth are desirable for their own sake, but because, typically, they are admirable generable-purpose means for having more freedom and to lead the kind of lives we have reason to value."[43]

The government also facilitated racialized space by funding "the largest public works program in the history of the world"—a highway system to the white suburbs.[44] With the Federal Aid Highway Act of 1956, the federal government became the largest subsidizer of the interstate highway system. These highways were intended for long-distance travel, but over half of the funding had gone to highways within metropolitan regions as of the mid-1990s. The highway system walled-in black communities, using the highways to clearly demarcate "bad" black from "good" white neighborhoods. It also frequently tore through "vibrant black commercial corridors," clearing out inner-city "blight."[45]

While the funding and construction of highways demarcated and destroyed black neighborhoods, it also forestalled the development of the kind of public transportation that metropolitan people of color were more likely to use. Highway spending has eclipsed transit spending by a five-to-one margin over the past half-dozen decades.[46] Simultaneously, the federal government bankrolled white flight not only through the construction of the highway system, but through federal subsidies of gasoline, suburban sewage-treatment plants (infrastructure that supports suburban living), and other policies that have made possible further abandonment of the central city and the inner-ring suburbs.

While suburbs are intentionally distanced and segregated from the city, they draw on, but do not replenish, its resources. Residents of the suburbs frequently work in and enjoy the services of the city, but, except in a few cases, do not pay taxes for it.[47] The increasing segregation of cities and suburbs via the highway system has contributed to a lack of opportunities, including stable housing, wealth creation, educational opportunities, and jobs. As jobs have moved away from the labor pool in many metropolitan areas, connecting job seekers with jobs became a challenge: 70 percent of all new jobs are in the suburbs; 40 percent of all suburban jobs cannot be reached by public transportation; 58 percent of all welfare participants in the nation live in central cities.

At the same time that the federal government was shaping racial and economically inequitable regions, the federal courts made it very difficult for racial justice advocates to obtain regional remedies for matters such as school desegregation. The victory of *Brown* was tempered considerably by court decisions such as *Milliken* that restricted regional remedies to those instances where it could be proved that suburban jurisdictions intended to cause harm to communities of color.

The federal government also engaged in a number of programs and practices that decimated the neighborhoods of people of color. The so-called urban-renewal policies initiated in the late 1940s are a chief example. The federal government directed funding to revitalize central-city neighborhoods in economic decline. Some $13.5 billion went to urban redevelopment between 1953 and 1986. Local governmental officials used the funds to demolish housing and black businesses, displacing and dislocating entire communities.[48]

From the 1930s to today, the federal government has shifted its approach from an explicitly racist program to one that has failed to confront structural racism in metropolitan dynamics—the dynamics it helped to engineer. State governments also played a substantial role in constructing the spatial and structural inequities present in metropolitan regions by granting executive power for residential zoning to local municipalities.

In her text *The Failures of Integration*, Sheryll Cashin explains that zoning functions as a means of "social control" wherein local municipalities can exclude "unfavored" communities, "shaping their economic and social destiny" and maintaining their homogeneity.[49] Such ordinances, for example, have adjoined affordable rental housing and other "nuisances," creating upper-class neighborhoods whose resources benefit only those within their boundaries.

The empowerment of local governments in this area has had detrimental effects on low-income communities of color, contributing overwhelmingly to the affordable housing crisis, the jobs and housing mismatch, and inequitable educational funding. Indeed, Cashin notes that researchers have revealed that two primary reasons for the foundation of local governments by middle- and upper-class subjects are "to escape financing public services for low-income citizens of older cities and the desire for racial exclusion."[50]

Because of the power to preserve resources and opportunities within racialized neighborhood boundaries, governmental fragmentation has actually increased over time. In 1942, we had 24,500 municipalities and special districts in the United States. By 2002, that number had more than doubled, to 54,481. Metropolitan regions are now governed by an average of 360 local governments and special districts. Racial and economically isolated municipalities retain few opportunities while affluent largely white municipalities attract and subsidize a disproportionate amount of them. Throughout this balkanization process, local governmental control over such matters as zoning, planning, public services, and public education has perpetuated the disparities between the high-need sectors and the "favored quarters."[51] These powers have had important ramifications for racial justice.

Rolf Pendall recently analyzed zoning in 1,000 jurisdictions in the 25 largest metropolitan areas and found that low-density zoning—the zoning commonly found in newer suburbs—has limited the total supply of multi-family housing and excluded people of color who need more affordable housing.[52] But we must remember that it wasn't always the case that local control was the "law of the land" and localities could embrace exclusionary policies; the states only began this delegation in the 1920s.[53]

Even today, governmental policies continue to organize space in racially restrictive forms. Gentrification and low-income housing provide two examples. Local governmental entities may promote gentrification through policies that encourage home purchasing in the city. In areas with tight housing markets the influx of higher-income residents displaces people of color from their neighborhoods, forcing them to seek housing in other, often economically struggling, parts of the metropolitan region. The Mission District in San Francisco is one notorious example of this trend.

We might consider our nation's racially polarized situation as a contemporary form of spatial Jim Crow. Francis Cardinal George, archbishop of the diocese of Chicago, writes: "Spatial racism refers to patterns of metropolitan development in which some affluent whites create racially and economically segregated suburbs or gentrified areas of cities, leaving the poor—mainly African Americans, Hispanics and some newly arrived immigrants—isolated in deteriorating areas of the cities and older suburbs."[54] Metropolitan equity calls for the equalization of opportunities through regional strategies that transform spatial and structural arrangements to benefit all persons within a region.

REGIONALISM: A RESPONSE TO SPATIAL RACISM

Over the last three decades there has been a substantial restructuring of institutional arrangements that has changed the role of the federal, state, and local government. The role of the economy on a global scale has become increasingly important, and regions in the United States compete with regions throughout the world. Shifts in populations, new technology, highway infrastructure, and globalization have converged to make regions the loci of business activity.

While individuals, businesses, and capital move across jurisdictional boundaries at the regional level and across national boundaries at the global level, our schools, housing, and fiscal capacity remains fragmented and tied largely to single jurisdictions. Local jurisdictions, like nations, try to capture business and other attractive institutions while sorting people to keep down demands for cost and benefit. This sorting process is very much racialized. More important, racialized metropolitan space creates racialized opportunity.

Because of the racist effects of this spatial organization, metropolitan equity should be perceived as the civil rights issue of the twenty-first century. Recognizing that space and other infrastructure-related allocations are the main purveyors of continued racial stratification, metropolitan equity calls for the equalization of opportunities through regional strategies. These strategies attempt to transform spatial and structural arrangements to benefit all persons within a region, taking into consideration the demarcation of possibilities presented by the two intertwined phenomena of globalization and devolution.

Throughout the past ten years, I have proposed that a regional analysis is necessary to any systemic rectification of racist structures under the current arrangement. Such an analysis reconceptualizes a metropolitan area as an organic whole functioning for the common good of all residents, rather than as a collection of increasingly fragmented and conflicted municipalities fighting over scarce resources. It offers, at its heart, a vision of cooperation rather than competition. This vision is neither inherently "good" nor "bad." However, it allows us to better understand how institutional arrangements and practices are interactive within a regional context and how to respond accordingly.

If the fragmentation is allowed to persist undisturbed, it will continue to produce racially inequitable outcomes. The scope and power of the federal government will increasingly be altered and limited and will no longer be adequate to regulate such practices. Even the state, and certainly the city, acting alone, will be unable to create effective solutions. Together, they will produce institutional incoherence.

A region is an amalgam of geographically connected local governments, which have been institutionally fragmented over time. Once single political entities, regions are now commonly divided into many autonomous local governments whose leaders advocate for insular policies that affect their residents. Rather than conceptualizing neighborhoods as regions and acting in holistic terms, citizens delineate the limits of "their" communities, squabbling over resources and constructing problems (and solutions) in dualistic "us vs. them" terms. This has grave consequences for not only our losers—impoverished urban people of color—but our regions as a whole.

If we let our core cities deteriorate beyond recuperation, the entire metropolitan area suffers the loss. In an increasingly globalized economy, it is regions (or "city-states") that are increasingly the units of competition in trade and commerce, yet we are still loath to think of them in unified terms. I am not calling for centralization or power usurpation from localities, but for an institutionally coordinated effort to promote what is most productive for the region as a whole.

Some scholars have argued that the solution to spatial racism is democratized, decentralized local government that allows small municipalities to maintain autonomous control of commercial and financial entities within their borders.[55] It is clear, however, that unequal power differentials in localities have contributed greatly to segregation and economic and educational disparities. Moreover, localized community and advocacy organizations cannot adequately respond to problems that span over and are interconnected with multiple spaces.

A single community, even a single municipality, faces obstacles when trying to link low-income workers of color in the city with jobs emerging in the metropolitan periphery, particularly when transit and low-income housing availability hinder the linkage. A single community organization or advocacy group can be frustrated trying to improve schools in a high-poverty, racially segregated district as "racially neutral" taxation and other policies continue to privilege schools in affluent, majority-white districts. The work undertaken by individual communities is essential, but the dynamics of inequality are regional.

Equalizing opportunities is best effected at the regional level through "federated regionalism." Federated regionalism is a model in which a regional authority controls access to opportunities while local authorities regulate issues of local identity, governmental responsiveness, and community—much as the states and the federal government interrelate. To fit within the model of racially just federated regionalism, regional structures should: explicitly address racial inequity; distribute opportunities in all key areas equitably across regions, addressing their interconnected nature; have a representative regional body with power over these distribution matters; incorporate racially inclusive and genuinely participatory decision making; respect the importance of local issues like community strength and decision-making power; and allow local authorities to retain control over matters of community identity and local governmental responsiveness.

Regional strategies in the areas of affordable housing, transit, revenue, business location, and educational policies must complement the work being undertaken at the organizational, community, and municipal level. Work must also be done to make public decision-making processes inclusive, to protect and expand the political power bases of communities of color, to preserve and strengthen social institutions, and to shield established communities from displacement and dispersal.

Regional strategies have at times hindered or limited work toward attainment of this set of goals. They have at times damaged the political power bases of communities of color. They have destroyed neighborhoods physically and have broken down important social networks and institutions. Regional programs have dispersed families and disrupted community. Unfortunately, racial justice advocates and communities of color have been given "either-or" propositions by policy makers and social scientists. You can have affordable housing in middle-class areas *or* the preservation of a community, few employment opportunities *or* assimilation into majority-white suburbs, high-achieving schools *or* meaningful participation in decision-making processes.

These "either-or" propositions are unacceptable and derive from the current structures in place. Communities of color must be able to access the full spectrum of rights and opportunities or racism will continue to reconfigure and reproduce itself. And this is what I am proposing, a reorientation of regional strategies with the expansion of and access to essential opportunity structures for people of color as central to them. Nevertheless, these strategies are embedded within known institutions and with potential benefit to all groups within these regional arrangements.

In a racially just region, resources of all varieties would not flood the suburban periphery where whites predominate. Instead, resources and development would be distributed fairly throughout the region. Each municipality would have adequate revenue to provide public services, an adequate supply of affordable housing, homes that can appreciate without restraint from forces like segregation, high-performing schools not marked by disproportionately high levels of students with special needs, effective transit infrastructure, and equitable economic development.

If resources and opportunities were fairly distributed and racial discrimination did not limit genuine access to people of color, a given metropolitan region would be more racially just. There is no need for a city to be responsible for raising its own fiscal resources. Consider tax base sharing similar to what exists in Minnesota. Or consider when states raise and allocate funds for schools. No community should be able to opt out of its responsibilities for its fair share of affordable housing built with a focus on opportunity.

New roads and infrastructure should be conditioned on fair participation. Municipalities should not be able to use tax relief to "steal" business from one part of a region to another without any net increase in jobs or benefits for the region or the state. If opportunity and people are fairly arranged, it is likely that racial disparities in life chances would be diminished.[56] As Pastor has demonstrated, racial equity is more likely to occur if there is an explicit part of regional planning.[57]

Regional Inclusionary Zoning

Zoning, while ostensibly a tool for separating land for different usable purposes (industrial, residential, commercial, etc.), has often been used as an exclusionary tool to keep affordable housing out of wealthy suburbs. The end result has been a profound segregation by income and race, often keeping low-income people of color outside of areas with amenities such as job growth and well-funded school systems.

Regional inclusionary zoning provides one approach to the problem of this imbalance. Inclusionary zoning is a method of equitably distributing affordable housing throughout a region—either by offering incentives for

developers, or by making the inclusion of affordable housing units mandatory. Recently, inclusionary zoning has grown exponentially among cities
such as Boston, Denver, Sacramento, San Diego, and San Francisco, and in
over one hundred communities in California. Montgomery County, Maryland, employs the most renowned and successful inclusionary zoning ordinance.[58]

Land Bank Programs

Vacant land and abandoned buildings remain persistent problems in
many of our cities. A preponderance of these properties encourages blight,
disinvestment, and crime; they also diminish tax revenue and burden taxpayers in already struggling cities. Surveys by the Brookings Institution
found that on average major cities in America had 15 percent of their land
deemed vacant.[59] Land bank programs have been established in many cities
across the nation to tap the potential of these vacant properties for urban
redevelopment. A land bank authority is a public entity granted specific
powers with the goal of facilitating the reuse and redevelopment of vacant
and foreclosed properties.

A land bank authority can provide the legal and administrative framework
to efficiently acquire and redevelop vacant land. The specialized function of
a land bank allows a prolonged commitment of resources to redevelop properties. The land bank authority is also capable of comprehensively looking
at the city's vacant land and adopting strategies for reuse that best fit community needs.

By working with planners, community development groups, and for-
profit developers land bank authorities have an opportunity to spur major
reinvestment and revitalization of urban cores. With an equitable development vision, land bank authorities can make properties available at a nom-
inal fee for needed projects: affordable housing, new employment centers,
and recreation facilities. Land banks have been set up in various cities in the
United States with varying degrees of success. As with most programs, if it
is unattached to a larger regional strategy and instead used to turn over
properties to developers as quickly as possible, it will provide only short-
term benefits. It is best employed as a tool within a larger regional vision,
and not a solution in and of itself, having always present the goal of equalizing opportunity structures within an interrelated web.

The land bank is a redevelopment tool to assist the city in meeting its
other community development needs, such as housing, job growth, and
public safety. Land bank programs should be targeted to meet these other
goals and interlinked with additional planning initiatives of the city such as
comprehensive planning or neighborhood development plans. Land bank
programs should also be aligned with existing development initiatives and

development incentive programs to maximize the potential for redevelopment.[60]

Educational Strategies

When schools are built at the edges of regions, residential development and resources tend to follow. This process becomes racialized as it pulls resources from the central city and inner-ring suburbs. School districts located in wealthy white suburban enclaves are awash in funds, while their inner-city counterparts have crumbling infrastructure. Most state funding formulas promote new school development rather than rehabilitation of schools in the central city, but Maryland does it differently. In 1995, only 34 percent of the funding for school facilities went to improving existing buildings. By 1998, 84 percent of school construction funding went to rehabilitation of existing facilities rather than to schools at the metropolitan periphery.

In addition to funding equalization, desegregating schools at a regional level has benefits of all kinds, not least the enhancement of educational opportunity. There can be legal, social, and economic limitations to desegregating schools. With the recent anniversary of *Brown v. Board of Education*, we can look back at its charge that "separate is inherently unequal" and recognize that many, if not most, of our school districts are still unequal, and therefore, unlawful. A litigation strategy that ties together school segregation and residential segregation has the potential of effecting remedies on a regional scale that has effects on both housing and education. By using the right to an adequate education found in most state constitutions, and tying adequacy to equitable funding and desegregation, litigation using state constitutions is a promising new strategy for effecting regional educational change.

In Hartford, Connecticut, school district lines followed city lines and reproduced in the classroom the racial and economic segregation found in municipalities. A lawsuit was brought under the state constitution, which promises all students "substantially equal educational opportunity." The courts agreed that the district boundaries created a serious problem and ordered a set of regional remedies.

Another innovative approach is under way in Chattanooga, Tennessee. There, local communities, developers, and city planners are building two new schools downtown that will educate nearby residents (predominantly low-income and students of color) and set aside seats for the children of downtown employees (tending to be more middle-income and white students). This approach considers the regional employment market and matches it with a regional educational approach, targeted to produce integration.[61]

Recognizing that urban sprawl and fragmentation have contributed to an America where educational segregation has been almost constant, a racially just regionalism will look hard at the links between education segregation and housing segregation and seek solutions that will affect change in both. It will seek true integration and equity, not just desegregation; a positive creative vision rather than just an eliminative one.

Transportation Strategies

A regional approach to transportation already has been created by federal legislation, the Intermodal Surface Transportation Efficiency Act (ISTEA), which requires that areas of 50,000 or more residents have in place a metropolitan planning organization that plots out transportation development after considering land use, environmental impact, and other factors.[62] Of central significance to racial and economic equity work, these organizations must include public participation and consider the needs of economically and racially marginalized communities when making decisions.[63] Under federal regulations, these organizations must seek out and consider the needs of those traditionally underserved by existing transportation systems, including but not limited to low-income and minority households.

In 1999, when a metropolitan planning organization in Indiana was seeking triennial renewal of its federal funding, a faith-based coalition, the Interfaith Federation of Northwest Indiana, challenged the planning process. The process had not included the voices of people of color and had not responded to their needs. As a result of this grassroots challenge, the planning organization was only conditionally recertified for federal funding and must alter its processes and planning. The federation continues to closely monitor the planning organization to ensure that federal regulations are complied with and that the needs of low-income families and people of color are genuinely met.[64]

A regional transportation policy must address the imbalance between highway spending and mass transit funding, recognizing that highways are not only built as a result of urban sprawl, but also to foster it.[65] It must take into consideration the jobs-housing mismatch. It must seek to improve existing transportation infrastructure before building new infrastructure. However, without a regional transportation policy linked to housing and employment policies we run the risk of legitimizing our patterns of urban sprawl and segregation by simply accommodating the infrastructure and transit needs of wealthy suburbs.

Opportunity-Based Housing

A model that holds out great promise in eradicating spatial racism is "opportunity-based housing." The central principle of opportunity-based housing is that residents of metropolitan regions are situated within a complex,

interconnected web of opportunity structures (or lack thereof) that significantly shape their quality of life. Opportunity structures are the vehicles for
racial and economic fairness (or oppression) for all residents of the region
and are tied to metropolitan space. That is, the geographical distribution of
these structures within a metropolitan region is strongly linked to the degree to which residents can access them. An analysis of opportunities must
therefore recognize the reality of economic and racial segregation and how
it functions differently for different communities of color.

Opportunity-based housing suggests that the creation and preservation
of affordable housing must be deliberate and intelligently connected on a
regional scale to high-performing schools, meaningful employment opportunities, transportation, child care, health care, and other institutions that
facilitate civic and political activity. Policies should increase the ability of
low-income people to live near existing opportunity, as well as tie opportunity creation in other areas to existing and potential affordable housing.
Important to note is that creating opportunity-based housing is not a static
task, but must be assessed and tracked over time and space.

The past few years have seen more communities moving toward thinking
more holistically about housing. The state of Illinois is in the second year of
its "live near work" program for low-income housing tax-credit projects, and
their qualified allocation plan states that "projects located within an appropriate distance of employer(s) . . . who have difficulty attracting a quality
workforce due to the lack of affordable housing within that radius" will be
preferred to those that don't.[66] Other states are moving in the same direction. Both California and Minnesota have implemented initiatives pushing
toward the placement of low-income housing in higher-income areas.[67]

Distributing Municipal Revenue Regionally

Municipalities in most metropolitan regions rely on local taxes to provide essential services, including police protection, fire safety, and public
education. Because municipalities differ in terms of their economic status
and home values, revenues available to municipalities are disparate—often
along racial lines. Revenue sharing offers a way to offset these disparities
and to encourage regional planning and cooperation. However, while revenue sharing is an important part of most smart growth plans, its actual use
has been fairly limited to one large metropolitan area (the Twin Cities) and
smaller cities and counties.

The Minneapolis/St. Paul region has the most comprehensive revenue
sharing plan, which was accomplished through the state legislature in the
1970s, and is titled the *Twin Cities Fiscal Disparities Plan*. Under the plan,
municipalities in the multicounty region contribute 40 percent of gains in
commercial and industrial property revenue into a pool. These funds are

then distributed back to the municipalities based on their property value, or their fiscal needs. Among the fifty-six communities of three thousand or more households, the ratio of fiscal capacity of richest-to-poorest community is four to one under the plan. According to David Rusk, without the plan, the ratio would be seventeen to one.[68]

Coordinating Development and Promoting Environmental Justice

Environmental advocates are strong allies in pushing for regional development strategies, mixed-density housing, and antisprawl measures. Environmental racism is also a strong concern of any development plan that promotes racial justice. Poor communities of color are often located near the heaviest polluters, the region's landfills, and traffic-choked streets.[69] However, metropolitan growth policies focused on environmental concerns have not always incorporated racial justice concerns and have even harmed the interests of communities of color. For example, antisprawl measures implemented in the Portland, Oregon, region are successful in restricting growth, but may be causing people of color to be "priced out" of their housing due to increases in rents and home values. There can be tensions between strategies that restrict development and those that actually open access to opportunities for people of color. One approach to this is to analyze in advance the potential impact of growth policies on communities of color and make regional policy adjustments to prevent harm.

Maryland has been a leader in the nation in terms of regional coordination and development over the past several years. In March 2001, Governor Parris Glendening signed an executive order establishing the Commission on Environmental Justice and Sustainable Communities. The governor declared that environmental justice considerations would be integrated into the state's revitalization initiatives for reducing sprawl, encouraging redevelopment, and enhancing community life. Maryland's new commitment to ensuring that growth control does not come at the expense of communities of color merits consideration by those in other regions because it considers, up front, the implications of regional policies on communities of color and seeks to avoid negative impacts.[70]

CONCLUSION

The goal of this chapter has been to help social justice advocates, especially those who focus on race, to better understand the need for a structural racism framework. This framework draws our attention to the interrelated and dynamic nature of the structures and institutions that powerfully impact the work and the lives of people throughout the United States and the world.

There is little doubt that many of our institutions are now arranged to hoard opportunity for certain groups at the expense of others. Space and regional equity together make up one of the best prisms with which to look at some of these arrangements. Metropolitan equity is a movement that begins to recognize this interrelationship between structures and institutional arrangements. But it should be seen as a particular expression of a general proposition, that is, that institutional arrangements matter. How those arrangements matter and what should be done to produce the desired outcome must be carefully studied and monitored.

Shifts in technology, laws, and private business arrangements, and the involvement of community groups and individuals matter. It is very seductive to focus on a single neighborhood, institution, or issue and to work solely at that location. It can also be daunting to think about how institutions are interrelated in a complex web. This insight, even if accepted, can seem overpowering and too complex. It need not. Because things are related, changes across sectors can occur by strategically focusing on one critical site. There is also the need for some division of labor and knowledge, but it must be coordinated.

NOTES

1. Research assistance for this chapter was provided by Melanie Maltry, Hiram Irizarry-Osorio, Marguerite Spencer, and Eric Stiens.

2. Howard Winant, *The World Is a Ghetto* (New York: Basic Books, 2001), 168.

3. Ibid., 167.

4. Michael K. Brown, Martin Carnoy, Elliott Currie, Troy Duster, David B. Oppenheimer, Marjorie M. Shultz, and David Wellman, *Whitewashing Racism: The Myth of a Color-Blind Society* (Berkeley: University of California Press, 2003), 17.

5. Charles Tilly, *Durable Inequality* (Berkeley: University of California Press, 1998).

6. Resource Generation, "Resources: Relationship to Money, Class, Giving, Financial, Undoing Oppression, and Fundraising," http://www.resourcegeneration .org/Resources/class.html (accessed January 15, 2005).

7. United for a Fair Economy, "The State of the Dream: Black-White Gaps Still Wide—Some Even Widening—Since Dr. King's Death," http://www.faireconomy.org/ 0115/ (accessed January 20, 2005); *Real Change News*, "A Dream Deferred—Some More," http://www.realchangenews.org/pastissuesupgrade/2004_22_04/current/ features/news_you_cn_use.html (accessed January 15, 2005).

8. Ibid.

9. See Johanna Thatch-Briggs, "Study: African Americans Still Have a Long Way to Go," *Wilmington Journal*, February 20, 2004, http://www.wilmingtonjournal.com/ News/article/article.asp?NewsID=39128&sID=12 (accessed January 20, 2005).

10. *Real Change News*, "A Dream Deferred—Some More."

11. United for a Fair Economy, "The State of the Dream."

12. Ibid.

13. Lewis Mumford Center, "Ethnic Diversity Grows, Neighborhood Integration Lags Behind," Albany, NY, 2001, http://mumford1.dyndns.org/cen2000/WholePop/WPreport/MumfordReport.pdf, 1 (accessed August 1, 2004).

14. Glenn C. Loury, *The Anatomy of Racial Inequality* (Cambridge, MA: Harvard University Press, 2002).

15. Anthony Marx, *Making Race and Nation: A Comparison of South Africa, the United States, and Brazil* (Cambridge: Cambridge University Press, 1998).

16. Thomas J. Sugrue, *The Origins of the Urban Crisis: Race and Inequality in Post-War Detroit* (Princeton, NJ: Princeton University Press, 1996), 268, 270.

17. john a. powell, Gavin Kearny, and Vina Kay, eds., *In Pursuit of a Dream Deferred: Linking Housing and Education Policy* (New York: Peter Lang, 2001).

18. George Lipsitz, *The Possessive Investment of Whiteness* (Philadelphia: Temple University Press, 1998).

19. Myron Orfield, *Metropolitics: A Regional Agenda for Community and Stability* (Washington, DC: Brookings Institution Press, 1997), 39–54.

20. Ramon G. McLeod, "Rental Housing Crunch Hits Poor Hardest," *San Francisco Chronicle*, June 16, 1998, 1A.

21. International Working and Advisory Group, *Overview Report: Beyond Racism: Embracing an Interdependent Future—Brazil, South Africa, and the United States*, The Comparative Human Relations Initiative (Atlanta, GA: The Southern Education Foundation, 1999), 40.

22. Amartya Sen, *Development as Freedom* (New York: Anchor Books, 2000), 297–98.

23. Joseph E. Stiglitz, *Globalization and Its Discontents* (New York: W. W. Norton, 2002), 224.

24. Richard Thompson Ford, "The Boundaries of Race: Political Geography in Legal Analysis," *Harvard Law Review* 107 (1994): 1841–59.

25. Winant, *The World Is a Ghetto*.

26. Ibid., 34.

27. Derrick Bell, *Race, Racism, and American Law* (New York: Aspen Law and Business, 2000), 87.

28. *Citizenship Act of 1924*, ch. 233, 43 Stat. 253 (current version at 8 U.S.C. §1401(b) (1982).

29. Bill Ong Hing, *Making and Remaking Asian America Through Immigration Policy, 1850–1990* (Palo Alto, CA: Stanford University Press, 1994), 23.

30. Bell, *Race, Racism, and American Law*, 118.

31. *Johnson v. McIntosh*, 21 U.S. 543, 8 Wheat. 543 (1823); *Cherokee Nation v. Georgia*, 30 U.S. 5, Pet. 1 (1831); *Worcester v. Georgia*, 31 U.S. 6, Pet. 515 (1832).

32. Bell, *Race, Racism, and American Law*, 81–129.

33. *Scott v. Sandford*, 60 U.S. 393 (1865).

34. *Plessy v. Ferguson*, 163 U.S. 537 (1896).

35. Slaughterhouse Cases, 83 U.S. (16 Wall.) 36 (1873).

36. Charles L. Black, *A New Birth of Freedom: Human Rights, Named and Unnamed* (New Haven, CT: Yale University Press, 1997).

37. Kenneth T. Jackson, *Crabgrass Frontier: The Suburbanization of the United States* (New York: Oxford University Press, 1985).

38. Institute on Race & Poverty, *Racism and Metropolitan Dynamics: The Civil Rights Challenge of the 21st Century* (Minneapolis: Commissioned for the Ford Foundation, 2002) http://www1.umn.edu/irp/fordinfo.html, 9 (accessed August 10, 2004).

39. Ibid., 9–10.

40. Sheryll Cashin, *The Failures of Integration* (New York: Public Affairs, 2004), 112.

41. Thomas Shapiro, *The Hidden Cost of Being African American* (Oxford: Oxford University Press, 2004).

42. Dalton Conley, *Being Black, Living in the Red: Race, Wealth, and Social Policy in America* (Berkeley: University of California Press, 1999), 25.

43. Sen, *Development as Freedom*, 14.

44. Cashin, *The Failures of Integration*, 113.

45. Ibid., 114.

46. Institute on Race & Poverty, *Racism and Metropolitan Dynamics*, 10.

47. Iris Marion Young, *Justice and the Politics of Difference* (Princeton, NJ: Princeton University Press, 1990), 247.

48. Institute on Race & Poverty, *Racism and Metropolitan Dynamics*, 11; powell, Kearney, and Kay, eds., *In Pursuit of a Dream Deferred*; john a. powell, Karen B. Brown, and Mary Louise Fellows, eds., "How Government Tax and Housing Policies Have Racially Segregated Americans," in *Taxing America* (New York: New York University Press, 1997); john a. powell, "Living and Learning: Linking Housing and Education," *Minnesota Law Review* 80 (1996): 749.

49. Cashin, *The Failures of Integration*, 108.

50. Ibid., 109.

51. Institute on Race & Poverty, *Racism and Metropolitan Dynamics*, 7; john a. powell, "Sprawl, Fragmentation, and the Persistence of Racial Inequality," in *Urban Sprawl: Causes, Consequences and Policy Responses*, ed. Gregory D. Squires (Washington, DC: Urban Institute Press, 2002); john a powell, "Race, Poverty, and Urban Sprawl: Access to Opportunities Through Regional Strategies," *Forum of Social Economics*, Spring 1999: 1–20; john a. powell, "Race and Space: What Really Drives Metropolitan Growth," *Brookings Review* 16 (Fall 1998): 20–22.

52. Rolf Pendall, "Local Land Use Regulation and the Chain of Exclusion," *Journal of the American Planning Association* 66, no. 2: 125–42.

53. See Nancy Burns, *The Formation of American Local Governments: Private Values in Public Institutions* (New York: Oxford University Press, 1994).

54. Francis Cardinal George, OMI, *Dwell in My Love: A Pastoral Letter on Racism* (Chicago: Archdiocese of Chicago, 2001).

55. Young, *Justice and the Politics of Difference*, 248.

56. Institute on Race & Poverty, *Racism and Metropolitan Dynamics*, 16.

57. Manuel Pastor Jr., *Regions That Work: How Cities and Suburbs Can Grow Together* (Minneapolis: University of Minnesota Press, 2000).

58. Nick Brunick, Lauren Goldberg, and Susannah Levine, *Large Cities and Inclusionary Zoning* (Chicago: Business and Professional People for the Public Interest, 2003), http://www.bpichicago.org/rah/pubs/large_cities_iz.pdf (accessed August 10, 2004).

59. Paul C. Brophy and Jennifer S. Vey, *Seizing City Assets: Ten Steps to Urban Land Reform* (Washington, DC: The Brookings Institution, 2002).

60. Currently, the Kirwan Institute for the Study of Race and Ethnicity is in the process of consulting with MOSES, a faith-based organization in Detroit, about how a land bank could be used to promote racial justice and to access opportunities in a city that contains some of the highest concentrations of vacant and underutilized land in the nation.

61. Institute on Race & Poverty, *Racism and Metropolitan Dynamics*.

62. U.S. Department of Transportation, *A Guide to Metropolitan Transportation Planning Under ISTEA: How the Pieces Fit Together* (Washington, DC: U.S. Department of Transportation, 1995), http://www.itsdocs.fhwa.dot.gov//JPODOCS/REPT_MIS/KL01!.PDF (accessed August 10, 2004).

63. Robert D. Bullard and Glenn S. Johnson, eds., *Just Transportation: Dismantling Race and Class Barriers to Mobility* (Gabriola Island, BC: New Society Publishers, 1997).

64. Institute on Race & Poverty, *Racism and Metropolitan Dynamics*, 19.

65. Robert D. Bullard, Glenn S. Johnson, and Angel O. Torres, eds., *Highway Robbery: Transportation Racism and New Routes to Equity* (Boston: South End Press, 2004).

66. Illinois Housing Development Agency (IHD), *Draft State of Illinois Consolidated Plan of Action* (Chicago: State of Illinois, 2004).

67. The Kirwan Institute for the Study of Race and Ethnicity is currently helping the Wisconsin Housing and Economic Development Authority redesign its housing allocation plan to take opportunity structures—specifically job growth—into account.

68. Institute on Race & Poverty, *Racism and Metropolitan Dynamics*, 20.

69. Robert D. Bullard, *Unequal Protection: Environmental Justice and Communities of Color* (San Francisco: Sierra Club Books, 1996).

70. Institute on Race & Poverty, *Racism and Metropolitan Dynamics*, 20.

3

Residential Apartheid American Style

Joe T. Darden

As America enters the twenty-first century, several demographic changes impacting black Americans continue to deserve attention. This chapter examines both the most recent demographic studies and the 2000 population and housing census data to determine the status of black Americans, using the indicators of residential segregation, suburbanization, and home ownership. These three indicators are examined within the theoretical framework of spatial assimilation and place stratification. The former model is employed to determine whether black socioeconomic mobility, via increase in home ownership, income, education, and occupation, has been strongly linked to increased black suburbanization. The latter model is employed to determine whether the spatial mobility of blacks continues to be limited to segregated neighborhoods within metropolitan areas despite increases in their socioeconomic status.

At the beginning of the twenty-first century, blacks are still not able to convert their socioeconomic gains into integrated suburban residences because of continued discrimination in housing.

THEORETICAL FRAMEWORK

Several researchers have attempted to explain the high level of residential segregation and the low level of suburbanization of the black population by using the ecological theory and the concepts of spatial assimilation and place stratification.[1] Spatial assimilation is a process whereby a group attains residential propinquity with members of the host society.[2] In the United States, it generally involves the spatial movement outward of minority groups from established inner-city racial and ethnic neighborhoods to the suburbs. According to the concept of spatial assimilation, the urbanization of blacks is an important step toward residential integration within mainstream American society.[3]

Because blacks have been historically concentrated in central cities and excluded from suburbs, black suburbanization is, theoretically, an indicator that blacks are leaving their lower-status, black-concentrated, residential neighborhoods and achieving residential integration in higher-status suburbs. In this sense, black suburbanization can be viewed within the context of the ecological theory. Implicit in the ecological theory is the idea that a group's social and economic status strongly influences its ability to obtain access to housing within the suburbs of metropolitan areas.[4] Since home ownership is positively correlated with suburbanization, increased black home ownership can be viewed, theoretically, as an indicator of increasing social and spatial mobility that leads to greater racial residential integration.[5]

Some researchers have found limitations with the class-based spatial assimilation concept when applied to certain racial groups. This has led to the introduction of the place stratification concept.[6] According to this concept, movement to the suburbs does not necessarily lead to residential integration, equal access to resources, or racial equality. This is because the more powerful, white-majority group maintains its advantaged position by keeping less advantaged minority groups out of the most desired municipalities. This behavior results in racial and ethnic groups being sorted by each group's relative standing in society. The outcome is a hierarchy of places within metropolitan areas, including places within the suburbs. Disadvantaged groups may remain segregated in undesirable neighborhoods or entire places even within the suburbs.

This structural inequality in residential locations occurs through public and private discrimination in the housing market.[7] Thus, a minority group may attain income, education, and occupational status equal to that attained by the white-majority group and still face difficulties in purchasing a suburban home in certain places. The place stratification concept implies that some groups, especially blacks, may not be able to fully convert socioeconomic gains into the quality of suburban neighborhoods occupied by whites who have comparable socioeconomic status.[8]

In other words, regardless of their socioeconomic status, blacks may be steered away from certain suburban places or neighborhoods or face discrimination in obtaining mortgages from financial institutions.[9] Therefore, because of racial steering and limited mortgage financing, blacks in the suburbs may experience as much residential segregation as blacks in the city.[10] Moreover, greater black movement to the suburbs may not necessarily reduce racial residential segregation within the metropolitan areas.

THE BLACK POPULATION AND
RESIDENTIAL SEGREGATION

As America entered the twenty-first century, the black population in the United States stood at 36.4 million. This figure includes blacks or African Americans alone or in combination with another race. The number of people who identified themselves as black or African American alone in the 2000 census was 34.7 million.[11] Blacks comprised 13 percent of the population in 2000 and 86.5 percent lived in metropolitan areas.

The 2000 census revealed that the black population in the United States has become more diverse. Blacks who consider themselves African American constituted 33,048,095. However, Afro-Caribbeans numbered more than 1.5 million, and there were more than 600,000 who identified themselves as Africans. Nationally, nearly 25 percent of the growth of the black population between 1990 and 2000 was due to immigration of people from Africa and the Caribbean.[12]

There is also geographic variation within America's diverse black population. Afro-Caribbeans are located, disproportionately, in the three metropolitan areas of New York, Miami, and Fort Lauderdale. They consist mainly of Haitians and Jamaicans. Americans of African origin who came primarily from Ghana, Nigeria, Ethiopia, and Somalia are more geographically dispersed over regions of the United States.

To determine the extent to which blacks share neighborhood space with whites, researchers most often use the index of dissimilarity (*D*). The index measures residential segregation that is defined as the overall unevenness in the spatial distribution of two racial groups. The index of dissimilarity can be stated mathematically as:

$$D = 100 \left(1/2 \sum_{i=1}^{k} |x_i - y_i| \right)$$

where x_i = the percentage of a metropolitan area's white population living in a given census tract (neighborhood)

y_i = the percentage of a metropolitan area's black population living in the same census tract (neighborhood)

k = the number of census tracts

D = the index of dissimilarity. It is ? the sum of the absolute differences (positive and negative) between the percentage distributions of the black population and white population in the metropolitan area.[13]

The index value may range from 0, indicating no residential segregation, to 100, indicating complete residential segregation. The higher the index, the greater is the degree of residential segregation.

Logan and Deane[14] analyzed all 331 metropolitan areas and found a common residential pattern when African Americans, Afro-Caribbeans, and Africans are compared to whites. The level of residential segregation from whites is high (above 60 percent). The index of dissimilarity is highest between Afro-Caribbeans and whites (71.8 percent), and lowest between African Americans and whites (65 percent). The index of dissimilarity between African-born blacks and whites was 67.8 percent.[15] Thus, regardless of the country of origin of blacks, there is little sharing of residential neighborhoods with whites in metropolitan areas of the United States.

At the turn of the century, blacks remained the most racially segregated group in the United States. Whereas the level of black-white segregation is 64 percent, the levels of segregation between Asians and whites, Hispanics and whites, and American Indians and whites ranged from 33 to 50.9 percent.

When the neighborhood diversity experience of blacks is compared to that of other minority groups, blacks have a higher probability of living in a neighborhood that is majority black. Hispanics are more likely to live in a neighborhood that is 45.5 percent Hispanic and 36.5 percent white. Asians are more likely to reside in a neighborhood that is 17.9 percent Asian and 54 percent white. However, since whites are more likely to reside in a neighborhood that is 80.2 percent white, it appears that whites avoid racial minority neighborhoods generally, but avoid black neighborhoods more often.[16]

VARIATION IN LEVELS OF
BLACK RESIDENTIAL SEGREGATION

The level of residential segregation varied by the *size* of the metropolitan area. The largest metropolitan areas (one million or more population) had higher residential segregation than did middle-sized areas (500,000 to 999,999 population) and the smallest metropolitan areas (less than 500,000 population) had the lowest segregation. Regardless of size, however, the level of black residential segregation on average exceeded 50 percent. This meant that more than a majority of blacks in those metropolitan areas would have to change neighborhoods (census tracts) in order for the neighborhoods to become completely nonsegregated.

The level of residential segregation also varied by region. It was highest in the Midwest (74.1 percent) followed by the Northeast (73.9 percent). The South, with levels of black-white residential segregation of 58.1 percent, and the West, with levels of 55.9 percent, showed substantial differences.[17] However, no region had mean levels of black residential segregation below 50 percent. Levels of residential segregation above 50 percent are still considered high. Residential segregation varied by percent black population.

The higher the percentage of blacks, the higher the level of residential segregation.

Iceland, Weinberg, and Steinmetz examined the percentage of blacks in 220 metropolitan areas by quartiles and found that metropolitan areas under 6.2 percent black had an average level of segregation of 53.1 percent.[18] On the other hand, metropolitan areas that were more than 19.1 percent black had an average level of segregation of 69.6 percent.

Residential segregation also varied by the black-white gap in household income. The authors found that the racial disparity gap was highest in the Midwest ($19,639) and so was the black-white residential segregation level (74.1 percent).[19] The Northeast also had a high racial gap in median household income ($17,399) and the second-highest level of black-white residential segregation (73.9 percent).

The South and West had the smallest racial gap in median household income ($16,740 and $16,231, respectively), and the lowest black-white levels of residential segregation. The index of dissimilarity in the South was 58.1 percent, and 55.9 percent in the West. The West also experienced the greatest decline in black-white residential segregation (-6.6 percentage points) over the decade (table 3.1).

Despite the variation in black residential segregation and variation in the racial household income gap, differences in black and white educational attainment, occupation, or income cannot explain the high level of black-white residential segregation. Studies published prior to 2000 indicated that, contrary to ecological theory, rising black socioeconomic status has not resulted in a higher degree of racial residential integration.[20] Blacks have continued to live in different neighborhoods from whites, regardless of their having similar income, education, and occupations. Thus, previous studies have concluded that race and not class is the most important factor explaining the residential location of blacks.[21]

Iceland, Sharpe, and Steinmetz updated previous studies on blacks, class, and residential segregation from whites using 2000 census data.[22] Using the index of dissimilarity and socioeconomic data from Summary File 3[23] of the U.S. Census, the authors analyzed residential patterns of blacks and non-Hispanic whites of similar and different levels of income, education, and occupation in 331 metropolitan areas. The results revealed that the residential patterns of blacks still differed from the residential patterns of whites even when the two groups were similar in socioeconomic status (SES).

Although higher SES blacks were generally moderately less segregated than lower SES blacks, overall class differences appear to explain only a modest amount of the difference in black-white residential segregation. Thus, in 2000, as in the past, race matters more than class in explaining black residential segregation from whites.[24] Such segregation because of race has consequences for the black population.

Table 3.1. Black-White Household Income Disparity and Levels of Residential Segregation by Region

	Income		Differences	Mean Index of Dissimilarity	1990 to 2000 Index Change
	White	*Black*			
National (220 MSAs)	$49,997	$31,885	−$18,112	64.5	−3.7
Absolute Change 1990–2000	$4,511	$4,077	−$434		
Percentage Change 1990–2000	9.9%	14.7%	+4.8%		
Northeast (31 MSAs)	$52,435.0%	$35,036.0%	−$17,399	73.9	−2.7
Absolute Change 1990–2000	$2,977	$2,695	−$282		
Percentage Change	6.0%	8.3%	+2.3%		
Midwest (53 MSAs)	$48,880	$29,241	−$19,639	74.1	−4.7
Absolute Change 1990–2000	$5,385	$4,391	−$994		
Percentage Change	12.4%	17.7%	+5.3%		
South (114 MSAs)	$47,743	$31,003	−$16,740	58.1	−2.4
Absolute Change 1990–2000	$5,030	$5,008	−$22		
Percentage Change	11.8%	19.3%	+7.5%		
West (22 MSAs)	$52,096	$35,865	−$16,231	55.9	−6.6
Absolute Change 1990–2000	$4,791	$2,814	−$1,977		
Percentage Change	10.1%	8.5%	−1.6%		

Source: John Iceland, Daniel Weinberg, and Erika Steinmetz, U.S. Census Bureau, Series CENSR-3, *Racial and Ethnic Residential Segregation in the United States: 1980–2000* (Washington, DC: U.S. Government Printing Office, 2002).

CONSEQUENCES OF RESIDENTIAL SEGREGATION

Residential segregation reduces the options of blacks to live in better quality neighborhoods based on income earned comparable to that earned by whites.[25] In many metropolitan areas, blacks with incomes of more than $60,000 live in lower quality neighborhoods than whites earning less than $30,000.[26] This phenomenon is related to the concept of place stratification in which whites, using discriminatory means, exclude blacks from places that whites consider to be more desirable.[27]

Furthermore, over the latter part of the twentieth century, blacks have remained at a significant disadvantage in their proximity to jobs compared to other racial groups. In 2000, no group was more physically isolated from jobs than blacks. In nearly all metropolitan areas with significant black populations, the separation between residences and jobs was much greater for blacks than for whites.[28]

This separation of blacks from jobs has been called "spatial mismatch."[29] The extent of spatial mismatch was measured by Raphael and Stoll,[30] who used the index of dissimilarity. The index of dissimilarity is employed elsewhere in this chapter to measure residential segregation by race. Here the analysis substitutes one of the racial groups for jobs. This allows for a measure of the unevenness between the residential distribution of the black population and the spatial distribution of jobs. The index ranges from 0 to 100. The higher values indicate a greater spatial mismatch between the black population and jobs. The value of the index can be interpreted as the percentage of either jobs or black people that would have to relocate to different neighborhoods to eliminate the spatial mismatch. Given the variety of employment data, one can also measure the spatial mismatch between blacks and certain types of jobs, in particular, manufacturing or retail. In an analysis by Raphael and Stoll, however, total employment was used.

There is a positive relationship between the spatial mismatch for blacks and black-white residential segregation. There is also a positive relationship between black spatial mismatch and the black-white median household income gap. There is a negative relationship between black suburbanization and spatial mismatch. Where the average level of black residential segregation is lowest (66.8 percent), black suburbanization is highest (17.5 percent), the black-white household income ratio is highest (.632) and spatial mismatch is lowest (54.2 percent). On the other hand, where average black residential segregation is highest (72.1 percent), black suburbanization is lowest (8.7 percent), the black-white household income ratio is lowest (.576) and spatial mismatch is highest (63 percent).

Research by Raphael and Stoll of fifty metropolitan areas revealed that nearly 50 percent of the variation in the mismatch index across metropolitan areas in 2000 could be explained by variation in the degree of black-white residential segregation.[31] Blacks residing in metropolitan areas of the Northeast and Midwest were the most physically isolated from employment opportunities. These two regions also had the highest black-white household income gap and the highest levels of black-white residential segregation.[32] Because of the high level of black residential segregation, and low level of black suburbanization, blacks have the highest level of spatial mismatch of any racial group. The spatial mismatch index for blacks in 2000 was 53.3, based on zip codes. The index was only 33.3 for whites, 43.3 for Asians, and 44.0 for Hispanics.[33]

TRENDS IN BLACK RESIDENTIAL SEGREGATION, 1980–2000

Although black residential segregation at the turn of the century remained high, black-white residential segregation actually declined over the previous decade in most metropolitan areas.[34] However, there was little change in the high levels of segregation in the larger northern metropolitan areas, where a high percentage of blacks continue to reside.[35]

Cutler, Glaeser, and Vigdor[36] note that the decline in black segregation started in 1970. In fact, during every decade from 1890 to 1970, black-white residential segregation increased. Also, the authors note that overall levels of black residential segregation are at their lowest levels since 1920.[37] Segregation declined most sharply in metropolitan areas that were, first, growing fast; second, where the percentage of blacks in the population was changing (either growing or declining), and third, where blacks made up a small portion of the population in 1990.[38]

From 1980 to 2000, black-white residential segregation declined by more than twelve percentage points in metropolitan areas with fewer than 5 percent black and nearly ten percentage points in areas that are 10–20 percent black. However, in areas that were more than 20 percent black, the decline was only six percentage points. Thus, in areas where the black population is greatest, residential segregation decreased the least.[39]

The decline was a result of the movement of blacks into formerly all-white neighborhoods, rather than the movement of whites into majority-black neighborhoods. It has been this trend toward the integration of white neighborhoods that has brought the decline in black-white segregation levels.[40] Since white neighborhoods are most often located in the suburbs, there is the expectation that an increase in black suburbanization may bring about a decline in black residential segregation followed by a decline in black spatial mismatch. Mere black suburbanization, however, does not necessarily result in a decline in segregation.

TRENDS IN SPATIAL MISMATCH AND
BLACK SUBURBANIZATION

Analyses by Raphael and Stoll have led to the conclusion that changes in spatial mismatch conditions are positively associated with changes in residential segregation between blacks and whites.[41] It was the general trend of decreasing black-white residential segregation in metropolitan areas during the 1990s that contributed to the modest decline in spatial mismatch between blacks and jobs over the decade. I should also add that the decline in black segregation and spatial mismatch was aided by the increase in black suburbanization.

During the 1990s, blacks' overall proximity to jobs improved slightly, narrowing the gap in spatial mismatch between blacks and whites by 13 percent. The decline in spatial mismatch varied by region. It was smallest in metropolitan areas in the Northeast and in metropolitan areas where blacks represent a relatively large share of the population.[42]

In the year 2000, the percentage of blacks living in the suburbs remained low compared to other racial groups. Whites remain the most suburbanized racial group, followed by Asians. Nationally, 71 percent of the white population lived in the suburbs. For Asians, the percentage was 58 percent. Nearly half of all Hispanics (49 percent) lived in the suburbs, but only 39 percent of all blacks resided there.[43]

It is worth repeating that black suburbanization does not necessarily result in black residential integration. Based on data from the Mumford Center on metropolitan areas with large black populations, the average level of residential segregation was 65.1 percent in metropolitan areas where more than 20 percent of blacks resided in the suburbs.

In metropolitan areas where blacks were more than 10 percent, but less than 20 percent, blacks, on average, were almost equally as segregated, with a mean index of 66.3 percent. Moreover, in those metropolitan areas where blacks were less than 10 percent, their average level of segregation in the metropolitan areas was 68 percent (table 3.2).

The figures in table 3.1 suggest only a slight difference (2.9 percentage points) in the average level of segregation where blacks have a greater than 20 percent representation in the suburbs and where blacks have less than 10 percent representation. Also, like some central cities, a number of suburbs have become predominantly black. Among the fifty largest suburbs of metropolitan areas, there are eight where the average black person actually lives in a majority-black suburban neighborhood. These are: Newark and Miami (60 percent); Atlanta and Cleveland (56 percent); St. Louis (55 percent); Chicago and Washington, D.C. (51 percent), and Fort Lauderdale (50 percent).[44]

The 2000 census data suggest that the average residential segregation of blacks in the suburbs exceeds 50 percent in the fifty largest suburban areas

Table 3.2. The Relationship between Blacks in the Suburbs and Black Residential Segregation in Selected Metropolitan Areas, 2000

Suburbs More Than 20 Percent Black and Levels of Residential Segregation in Metropolitan Areas	Percent Black	Suburban Area Dissimilarity Index	Metropolitan Area Dissimilarity Index
Atlanta	25.6	61.8	66
Washington, D.C.	22.9	57.8	63
Richmond	21.3	46.5	57
New Orleans	21.0	57.5	69
Fort Lauderdale	20.6	59.8	62
Miami	20.4	72.4	74
Mean	26.5	59.3	65.1

Suburbs More Than 10 Percent Black but Less Than 20 Percent Black and Levels of Residential Segregation in Metropolitan Areas			
Newark	17.8	77.1	80
Baltimore	14.9	56.6	68
Greenville	14.6	40.4	46
West Palm Beach	13.7	65.9	67
New York	12.6	66.6	82
St. Louis	12.5	71.7	74
Orlando	12.4	53.7	57
Charlotte	10.9	42.5	55
Houston	10.7	56.5	68
Mean	13.3	59.0	66.3

Suburbs Less Than 10 Percent Black and Levels of Residential Segregation in Metropolitan Areas			
Cleveland	9.7	74.9	77
Philadelphia	9.7	58.1	72
Dallas	9.7	46.3	59
Chicago	8.8	73.4	81
Nassau-Suffolk	8.7	74.4	74
Oakland	8.4	56.8	63
Los Angeles	8.2	67.7	68
Riverside	7.9	46.2	46
Detroit	6.6	65.4	85
Tampa	5.8	54.9	65
Cincinnati	5.7	68.4	75
Pittsburgh	5.3	61.4	67
San Diego	4.6	47.4	54
Fort Worth	4.5	53.2	60
Kansas City	3.7	40.9	69
Minneapolis-St. Paul	2.9	44.6	58
Boston	2.8	45.3	66
Indianapolis	2.2	60.7	71
Milwaukee	1.6	46.4	82
Mean	6.6	57.1	68

Source: Computed by the author from data obtained from Mumford Center, www.albany.edu/mumford/census.

in the country.[45] Moreover, there is only a slight difference in the level of suburban segregation where there are few blacks in the suburbs (fewer than 10 percent) and in suburbs where blacks exceed 20 percent. Table 3.2 shows that where the average level of black suburbanization is 26.5 percent, the mean level of black suburban residential segregation is 59.3 percent. On the other hand, where the average level of black suburbanization is 6.6 percent, the mean suburban index of dissimilarity is 57.1 percent, a difference of only 2.2 percentage points. Whether blacks live in central cities or the suburbs, they are highly segregated residentially. However, black suburban segregation varies by region. Black suburbanites are least segregated in the South and West, where their numbers are few.

Nationally, there has been a change in the level of black suburban residential segregation over the last decade.[46] In suburbs with more than 20 percent black population, there was a decrease on average of about 3.4 percentage points. The change ranged from a decline of 8.8 percentage points in the suburb of Fort Lauderdale to an increase of 1.2 percentage points in suburban Miami (table 3.3).

In suburbs that were more than 10 percent but less than 20 percent black, the average decline in black suburban segregation was 2.2 percentage points. The change in segregation ranged from an 11.1 percentage point decline in suburban West Palm Beach to an increase of 1.3 percentage points in suburban Baltimore and Houston. The largest decline in black suburban residential segregation occurred in suburbs with small percentages of blacks (i.e., fewer than 10 percent). In these suburbs, the average decrease in segregation between 1990 and 2000 was 4.7 percentage points. The change in segregation ranged from a decrease of 20.3 percentage points in suburban Milwaukee to an increase of 2.2 percentage points in suburban Dallas.[47] In sum, residence in the suburbs does not necessarily mean a substantial reduction in residential segregation. The next section shows, however, that suburbanization facilitates black home ownership.

BLACK HOME OWNERSHIP TRENDS

When blacks buy a home, it is an important indicator of black socioeconomic achievement. For example, buying a home is the most expensive purchase ever made by most households. Thus, narrowing the home ownership rate gap between blacks and whites would be one indicator of progress toward racial equality.[48]

Any increases in black home ownership rates also would reflect a degree of socioeconomic mobility of the group. The equity in the home, for example, provides an opportunity to build wealth.[49] Such equity is the largest single asset held by most households.[50]

Table 3.3.   Changes in Black Suburban Segregation, 1990–2000

Mean Changes in Black Suburban Residential Segregation in Suburbs with Various Percentage Black Populations

Greater Than 20 Percent Black

Atlanta	+0.4
Washington, D.C.	+1.1
Richmond	−2.9
New Orleans	−1.5
Fort Lauderdale	−8.8
Miami	+1.2

Greater Than 10 Percent Black but Less Than 20 Percent Black

Newark	−2.2
Baltimore	+1.3
Greenville	−1.7
West Palm Beach	−11.1
New York	−1.6
St. Louis	−0.7
Orlando	−3.2
Charlotte	−4.6
Houston	+1.3

Less Than 10 Percent Black

Cleveland	−4.8
Philadelphia	−2.8
Dallas	+2.2
Chicago	−3.6
Nassau-Suffolk	−3.6
Oakland	−1.8
Los Angeles	−4.1
Riverside	+0.5
Detroit	−12.3
Tampa	−7.2
Cincinnati	−5.2
Pittsburgh	−1.9
San Diego	−2.9
Fort Worth	−5.9
Kansas City	−6.5
Minneapolis-St. Paul	−3.5
Boston	−2.0
Indianapolis	−15.4
Milwaukee	−20.3

Source: Computed from data in John Logan, "The New Ethnic Enclaves in America's Suburbs," http://www.albany.eau/mumford/census.

Home owners accumulate assets through home ownership in two ways. First, home owners reap the full return (or loss) associated with the home's price appreciation. Second, as their mortgage is amortized through repayment, a household builds equity, that is, the difference between the value of the home and what is owed on it.[51] Furthermore, equity in the home is an important source of intergenerational mobility.[52]

Home ownership also provides increased satisfaction and improved outcomes for children.[53] Moreover, home owners, compared to renters, are more likely to invest in their property and neighborhood. They also have a higher participation in local political activities and organizations, relatively high rates of voting, and participate more in local school parent-teacher organizations.[54] It has been found that increased home ownership rates in a metropolitan area also reduce some types of crime.[55]

The purchase of a home has a special significance in the establishment of a family. Apart from its importance as a symbol of status and security, home ownership also hastens considerable financial benefits. These financial benefits are particularly important to people with low and middle incomes.[56] Blacks are disproportionately represented in these income categories. Given the importance of home ownership, the key is to determine the trends in black home ownership as reflected in the 2000 census.

Based on the 2000 census,[57] the home ownership gap between blacks and whites widened slightly despite the fact that home ownership rates increased for all racial/ethnic groups during the 1990s. The home ownership rate for non-Hispanic whites was 72.4 percent, compared to a rate of 46.3 percent for blacks, a difference of 26.1 percentage points. While almost three-quarters of white households owned their homes at the beginning of the century, less than half of black households were owners.[58] Moreover, the increase in white home ownership over the decade was slightly greater (3.4 percentage points) than the increase in black home ownership (2.9 percentage points).

Thus, the gap in home ownership rates between blacks and whites widened. The increase in the home ownership gap could be explained in part by changes in the age structures between whites and blacks. The white population shifted more rapidly into the older age groups where home ownership rates are higher.[59] Black households tend to be younger.

The difference in marital status also partially explains the difference in home ownership rates. A lower proportion of black households, compared to white households, consists of married couples. Married families have higher home ownership rates.

Socioeconomic differences (e.g., income, education, and occupation) also help explain the racial differences in home ownership rates. Median incomes, educational attainment, and occupational status tend to be lower for blacks compared to whites. These socioeconomic factors are important to home ownership in that the rates of home ownership rise with increasing socioeconomic status.[60]

In addition to socioeconomic status differences, home ownership rates between blacks and whites can also be partly explained by differences in wealth or assets to cover the downpayment and closing costs.[61] Blacks, compared to whites, have, on average, fewer assets, and blacks are disadvantaged relative to whites in terms of rising intergenerational wealth transfers to finance a home purchase. For example, whites are three times more likely than blacks to receive assets from their parents to purchase a home.[62] Where blacks reside also plays a role in lower black home ownership rates. Blacks continue to live, disproportionately, in central cities, compared to whites. In central cities, home ownership rates are lower.[63]

Finally, all of the factors mentioned do not completely explain the gap in home ownership rates between black and white households. Wachter and Megbolugbe[64] concluded that differences in household characteristics explained only four-fifths of the difference in home ownership rates between blacks and whites. Thus, racial discrimination remains a factor that cannot be ignored.[65]

Even with similar household characteristics and after controlling for virtually all risk factors, blacks are more likely than whites to be denied mortgage loans.[66] Indeed, several black applicants never reach the final stage in the lending process. They are discouraged or receive unfavorable treatment compared to whites at the preapplication stage.[67]

Such discriminatory activities, which still deny equal treatment to the black population, are legacies of a deeply entrenched history of discrimination that existed not only in the private housing market but in the federal government as well.[68] Although changes in federal housing policy are evident, they have not been sufficient to counter the long-term racial disparity in home ownership rates and the present covert practices of discrimination.

The Housing Discrimination Study 2000 measured the extent of housing discrimination against blacks and other racial minorities in 2000/2001.[69] It assessed whether discrimination had changed since 1989. The study was based on 4,600 paired tests in twenty-three metropolitan areas. The paired test, or the audit method, is the most effective method to measure housing-related discrimination.[70] The results showed large decreases in the level of discrimination experienced by blacks seeking to purchase a home. There were also modest decreases in discrimination against blacks seeking to rent a unit. However, the authors concluded that decreases notwithstanding, housing discrimination against blacks still exists at unacceptable levels. Moreover, geographic steering on the basis of neighborhood racial composition appears to have increased significantly between 1989 and 2000.[71]

Also, blacks continue to pay a "color tax" when it comes to home ownership. For example, blacks, on average, are almost two times as likely as whites to use subprime lenders for a home purchase.[72] Although subprime loans are important in expanding credit to blacks, they have higher interest rates, fees, and default rates than prime loans.[73] Home ownership in the United States is heavily subsidized by the federal government. Therefore the government has an obligation to eliminate the racial gaps.

SUMMARY AND CONCLUSIONS

This chapter has examined the status of blacks compared to whites at the turn of the twenty-first century. Based on the most recent demographic studies and U.S. Census data, black-white inequality was assessed using three indicators: residential segregation, suburbanization, and home ownership.

These three indicators were examined to assess the extent of black spatial assimilation and place stratification. A key analytical tool employed was the index of dissimilarity. The results revealed residential apartheid in that blacks remain the most racially segregated group in the United States. Indeed, blacks are the only group whose average levels of residential segregation from whites exceed 50 percent in metropolitan areas. When the neighborhood diversity experience of blacks is compared to that of other minority groups, blacks are more likely to reside in a neighborhood that is majority black.

The levels of black residential segregation vary, however, by the size of the metropolitan area. The largest metropolitan areas have the highest residential segregation. Segregation also varies by region. Blacks residing in the Midwest are the most segregated, followed by blacks in the Northeast. The South and West have the lowest levels of black segregation. Residential segregation varies by percent black. The higher the percent black, the higher is the level of residential segregation. Residential segregation also varies by the racial gap in median household income. The gap was highest in the Midwest and Northeast and lowest in the South and West. Blacks continue to live in different neighborhoods from whites regardless of their having similar income, education, and occupations. This suggests that race and not class is the most important factor explaining the residential segregation of blacks in 2000.

Because of the high level of black residential segregation, blacks remain at a significant disadvantage in their proximity to job opportunities. No racial group is more physically isolated from jobs than blacks. Since blacks are overrepresented in central cities, and jobs are more plentiful in the suburbs, this spatial mismatch is related to the lack of black suburbanization compared to other groups. Blacks residing in metropolitan areas of the Northeast and Midwest were the most physically isolated from employment opportunities. These two regions also had the highest black-white household income gap and the highest levels of black-white residential segregation.

Although black residential segregation at the turn of the century remained high, the level of segregation reflected a declining trend over the previous decade in most metropolitan areas. Segregation declined most sharply in metropolitan areas where the percentage of black population was changing and/or where the black population was small and/or located outside of the Northeast and Midwest.

This decline in residential segregation has resulted in a decline in the black spatial mismatch over the decade. The decline in black spatial mismatch has been related, in part, to the increase in black suburbanization. However, at the turn of the century, blacks remain the least suburbanized of any racial group. Moreover, unlike the case with other racial minority groups, black residence in the suburbs is no assurance of black residential integration. Blacks in the suburbs are residentially segregated like blacks in central cities. The census data revealed the emergence of more predominantly black suburbs. Black suburban segregation varied by region. It was greater in the Northeast and Midwest and least in the South and West. Nationally, a small decline in black suburban residential segregation occurred during the decade, with the largest decline occurring in suburbs with a small percentage of blacks.

This decline in suburban segregation was accompanied by an increase in black home ownership that occurred most often in the suburbs. Despite the increases in black home ownership, the racial gap in home ownership rates increased over the decade.

Finally, given the high level of black residential segregation, low level of black suburbanization, and persistent racial gap in home ownership, it appears that ecological theory and the concept of spatial assimilation are insufficient to explain the situation of blacks in metropolitan areas. Both the class-based ecological theory and spatial assimilation concept are distorted by the factor of racial discrimination in housing that restricts blacks of all incomes and educational and occupational levels from residing in certain white-dominated neighborhoods.

Thus, at the beginning of the twenty-first century, place stratification is evident in that blacks are still not able to convert socioeconomic gains into residentially integrated neighborhoods in the suburbs, where employment, housing, and other opportunities are greatest. This is residential apartheid American style.

NOTES

1. Douglas Massey, "Ethnic Residential Segregation: A Theoretical Synthesis and Empirical Review," *Sociology and Social Research* 69 (1985): 315–50; Richard Alba

and John Logan, "Minority Proximity to Whites in Suburbs: An Individual Level Analysis of Segregation," *American Journal of Sociology* 98, no. 6 (1993): 1388–1427.

2. Massey, "Ethnic Residential Segregation."

3. Douglas Massey and Nancy Denton, "Spatial Assimilation as a Socioeconomic Outcome," *American Sociological Review* 50 (1985): 94–106.

4. Joe T. Darden, "Differential Access to Housing in the Suburbs," *Journal of Black Studies* 21, no. 1 (September 1990): 15.

5. Eric Fong and Kumiko Shibuya, "Suburbanization and Homeownership: A Recapture of Assimilation Process in Contemporary American Society," *Sociological Perspectives* 43, no. 1 (2000): 139.

6. Richard Alba and John Logan, "Variations on Two Themes: Racial and Ethnic Patterns in the Attainment of Suburban Residence," *Demography* 28 (1991): 431–53.

7. Fong and Shibuya, "Suburbanization and Homeownership," 141.

8. Alba and Logan, "Minority Proximity to Whites in Suburbs."

9. Margery Turner et al., *What We Know About Mortgage Lending Discrimination in America* (Washington, DC: The Urban Institute, 1999).

10. Joe T. Darden and Sameh Kamel, "Black Residential Segregation in Suburban Detroit: Empirical Testing of the Ecological Theory," *Review of Black Political Economy* 27, no. 3 (2000): 103–23; Joe T. Darden and Sameh Kamel, "Black Residential Segregation in the City and Suburbs of Detroit: Does Socioeconomic Status Matter?" *Journal of Urban Affairs* 22, no. 1 (2000): 1–13.

11. John Iceland, Daniel Weinberg, and Erika Steinmetz, *Racial and Ethnic Residential Segregation in the United States: 1980–2000* (Washington, DC: U.S. Bureau of the Census, 2002), 59.

12. John Logan and Alenn Deane, *Black Diversity in Metropolitan America*, The Mumford Center, 2003, http://mumford1.dyndns.org/cen2000/blackwhite/blackwhite.htm (accessed August 15, 2004).

13. Joe T. Darden and Arthur Tabachneck, "Graphic and Mathematical Descriptions of Inequality, Dissimilarity, Segregation, or Concentration," *Environment and Planning A* 12 (1980): 227–34.

14. Logan and Deane, *Black Diversity in Metropolitan America*.

15. Ibid., 7.

16. John Logan, *Ethnic Diversity Grows, Neighborhood Integration Lags Behind*, The Mumford Center, 2001, http://mumford1.dyndns.org/cen2000 (accessed August 15, 2004); Joe T. Darden, "Residential Segregation: The Causes and Social and Economic Consequences," in *Racial Liberalism and the Politics of Urban America*, ed. Curtis Stokes and Theresa Melendez (East Lansing: Michigan State University Press, 2003), 321–44.

17. Iceland, Weinberg, and Steinmetz, *Racial and Ethnic Residential Segregation in the United States: 1980–2000*.

18. Ibid., 71.

19. Ibid., 71.

20. Joe T. Darden, "Choosing Neighbors and Neighborhoods: The Role of Race in Housing Preference," in *Divided Neighborhoods: Changing Patterns of Racial Segregation in the 1980s*, ed. Gary Tobin (Newbury Park, CA: Sage Publications, 1987), chapter 1; Nancy Denton and Douglas Massey, "Residential Segregation of Blacks, Hispanics, and Asians by Socioeconomic Status and Generation," *Social Science Quarterly* 69

(1988): 797–817; Douglas Massey and Mary Fischer, "Does Rising Income Bring Integration? New Results for Blacks, Hispanics, and Asians in 1990," *Social Science Research* 28, no. 3 (1999): 316–26; Mario Sims, "High Status Residential Segregation Among Racial and Ethnic Groups in Five Metro Areas, 1980–1990," *Social Science Quarterly* 80, no. 3 (1999): 556–73.

21. Scott South and Kyle Crowder, "Leaving the Hood: Residential Mobility Between Black, White, and Integrated Neighborhoods," *American Sociological Review* 63 (1998): 17–26; Darden and Kamel, "Black Residential Segregation in the City and Suburbs of Detroit."

22. John Iceland, Cicely Sharpe, and Erika Steinmetz, "Class Differences in African American Residential Patterns in U.S. Metropolitan Areas: 1990–2000," paper presented at the Annual Meeting of the Population Association of America, Minneapolis, MN, May 2003, 1–3.

23. U.S. Bureau of the Census, *Housing Vacancies and Homeownership: Annual Statistics, 2001*, 2002, http://www.census.gov/bhes/www/housing/hvs/annual01/ann01the 7.html (accessed January 25, 2004).

24. Iceland, Sharpe, and Steinmetz, "Class Differences in African American Residential Patterns in U.S. Metropolitan Areas: 1990–2000."

25. Darden, "Residential Segregation."

26. John Logan et al., *Separate and Unequal: The Neighborhood Gap for Blacks and Hispanics in Metropolitan America*, The Mumford Center, 2002, http://mumford1 .dyndns.org/cen2000/sepuneq/publicseparateunequal.htm (accessed October 15, 2004).

27. Joe T. Darden, *The Significance of White Supremacy in the Canadian Metropolis of Toronto* (Lewiston, NY: The Edwin Mellen Press, 2004).

28. Steven Raphael and Michael Stoll, *Moderate Progress in Narrowing Spatial Mismatch Between Blacks and Jobs in the 1990s* (Washington, DC: The Brookings Institution Center on Urban and Metropolitan Policy, 2002), 1.

29. John Kain, "Housing Segregation, Negro Employment and Metropolitan Decentralization," *Quality Journal of Economics* 82 (1968): 175–97.

30. Raphael and Stoll, *Moderate Progress in Narrowing Spatial Mismatch Between Blacks and Jobs in the 1990s.*

31. Ibid., 6.

32. Iceland, Weinberg, and Steinmetz, *Racial and Ethnic Residential Segregation in the United States: 1980–2000*, 59.

33. Raphael and Stoll, *Moderate Progress in Narrowing Spatial Mismatch Between Blacks and Jobs in the 1990s*, 3.

34. Iceland, Weinberg, and Steinmetz, *Racial and Ethnic Residential Segregation in the United States: 1980–2000.*

35. Logan, *Ethnic Diversity Grows, Neighborhood Integration Lags Behind*, 6.

36. David Cutler, Edward Glaeser, and Jacob Vigdor, "The Rise and Decline of the American Ghetto," *Journal of Political Economy* 107, no. 37 (1999): 455–506.

37. Ibid., 455.

38. Edward Glaeser and Jacob Vigdor, *Recent Segregation in the 2000 Census: Promising News* (Washington, DC: The Brookings Institution, 2001), 1.

39. Logan, *Ethnic Diversity Grows, Neighborhood Integration Lags Behind.*

40. Glaeser and Vigdor, *Recent Segregation in the 2000 Census*, 5.

41. Raphael and Stoll, *Moderate Progress in Narrowing Spatial Mismatch Between Blacks and Jobs in the 1990s.*

42. Ibid., 1.

43. Logan et al., "Separate and Unequal," 2.

44. Ibid., 6.

45. Logan, *Ethnic Diversity Grows, Neighborhood Integration Lags Behind.*

46. Logan et al., "Separate and Unequal," 6.

47. John Logan, *The Ethnic Enclaves in America's Suburbs*, The Mumford Center, 2001, http://mumford1.dyndus.org/cen2000 (accessed July 9, 2004).

48. Patrick Simmons, *Changes in Minority Homeownership During the 1990s* (Washington, DC: The Fannie Mae Foundation, 2001).

49. George Masnick, "Home Ownership Trends with Racial Inequality in the United States in the 20th Century," Joint Center for Housing Studies, Harvard University, Working Paper W01-4, 2001; Melvin Oliver and Thomas Shapiro, *Black Wealth/White Wealth: A New Perspective on Racial Inequality* (New York: Routledge, 1997).

50. Joint Center for Housing Studies, *State of the Nation's Housing* (Cambridge, MA: Harvard University, 2000).

51. George McCarthy, Shannon Van Zandt, and William Rohe, "The Economic Benefits and Costs of Homeownership," Research Institute for Housing America, Working Paper No. 01-02, 2001.

52. Masnick, "Home Ownership Trends with Racial Inequality in the United States in the 20th Century."

53. Donald Haurin, Robert Dietz, and Bruce Weinberg, "The Impact of Neighborhood Homeownership Rates: A Review of the Theoretical and Empirical Literature," *Journal of Housing Research* 13, no. 2 (2003): 119.

54. Ibid., 137.

55. Edward Glaeser and Bruce Sacerdote, "Why Is There More Crime in Cities?" *Journal of Political Economy* 107, no. 6 (1999): 225–58.

56. Mary Jackman and Robert Jackman, "Racial Inequalities in Homeownership," *Social Forces* 58, no. 4 (1980): 1221–34.

57. U.S. Bureau of the Census, *2000 Census Summary File 3* (SF3) (Washington, DC: 2002).

58. Simmons, *Changes in Minority Homeownership During the 1990s*, 1.

59. Ibid., 1.

60. Susan Wachter and Isaac Megbolugbe, "Racial and Ethnic Disparities in Homeownership," *Housing Policy Debate* 3, no. 2 (1993): 333–70; Joseph Gyourko and Peter Linneman, "The Changing Influences of Education, Income, Family Structure, and Race on Homeownership by Age Over Time," *Journal of Housing Research* 8, no. 1 (1997): 1–25; Simmons, *Changes in Minority Homeownership During the 1990s.*

61. Simmons, *Changes in Minority Homeownership During the 1990s.*

62. Joint Center for Housing Studies, *State of the Nation's Housing*, 12.

63. McCarthy, Van Zandt, and Rohe, "The Social Benefits and Costs of Homeownership," 5.

64. Wachter and Megbolugbe, "Racial and Ethnic Disparities in Homeownership."

65. Emily Rosenbaum, "Racial/Ethnic Differences in Home Ownership and Housing Quality," *Social Problems* 43, no. 4 (1996): 401–26.

66. Alicia Munnell, Lynn E. Browne, James McEneaney, and Geoffrey Tootell, "Mortgage Lending in Boston: Interpreting HMDA Data," *American Economic Review* 86, no. 1 (1996): 25–54.

67. James Carr and Isaac Megbolugbe, "The Federal Reserve Bank of Boston Study of Mortgage Lending Revisited," *Journal of Housing Research* 4, no. 2 (1993): 277–313; Turner, *What We Know About Mortgage Lending Discrimination in America.*

68. Darden, "Choosing Neighbors and Neighborhoods."

69. Margery Turner, Stephen Ross, George Galster, and John Yinger, "Discrimination in Metropolitan Housing Markets: National Results from Phase 1 HDS 2000" (Washington, DC: The Urban Institute, 2002), http://www.huduser.org/publications/asgfin/hds.html (accessed November 1, 2004).

70. Darden, *The Significance of White Supremacy in the Canadian Metropolis of Toronto,* 417.

71. Turner, Ross, Galster, and Yinger, "Discrimination in Metropolitan Housing Markets," 3–12.

72. Simmons, *Changes in Minority Homeownership During the 1990s,* 1.

73. Ibid.

4

Dilemma of Place and Suburbanization of the Black Middle Class[1]

Sheryll Cashin

An outspoken residential hubris and confident separatism is not uncommon among African Americans who are attracted to the black middle-class suburban enclaves that have begun to emerge outside of U.S. cities with sizable black populations.[2] They believe in the viability of black communities and black institutions. They believe it is possible to have the good life and the suburban dream in an overwhelmingly black setting. Marita Golden, a writer living in Mitchellville, Maryland, one of the highest-income, majority-black suburbs in America, put it this way in an essay for *Washingtonian* magazine, "Many families see themselves creating their own kind of promised land, bringing the good life with them and expecting even more. This is the classic American suburban dream, this time filtered through the lens of a history forged by inequality and the struggle to overcome." She says of her own choice to move from the District of Columbia to Mitchellville: "We were sold on the area because of a great deal on a house larger than anything we could afford in DC and because we liked the idea of living in this kind of black community."[3]

Prince George's County, Maryland, where Mitchellville is located, has received a great deal of public attention for its transformation from majority white to majority black[4] in the space of three decades while at the same time experiencing a substantial increase in average incomes and education levels.[5] In the 1960s, the county's resistance to open-housing laws and court-ordered busing earned it a reputation among black people as a rural backwater of rednecks, where the few pockets of blacks were subjected to a brand of justice with "good old boy" rules. Its evolution to a majority-black, buppie haven started in the 1970s when new black residents began moving in to take advantage of the large number of newly constructed garden apartments and condominiums in inner-Beltway communities like Capitol Heights and Forestville. White leaders in the county inadvertently promoted a large wave of black migration in the 1980s by building upscale homes intended to entice white-collar professionals in residential developments beyond the Beltway. The county's economic developers underestimated the sizable black middle class living in Washington, D.C., with money to spend and dreams of suburban living.

As blacks reached a critical mass in new single-family subdivisions originally intended for whites, whites began to shun the area. A notable amount of white flight took place in these years of black in-migration, and this exodus was probably exacerbated by a school desegregation order forcing court-ordered busing. By 2000, the county boasted a black population of over 500,000, 63 percent of the population, up from a mere 10 percent in the 1960s and exceeding the number of black residents of the District of Columbia, the so-called "Chocolate City," by more than 150,000.[6] Like many counties with clusters of suburban blacks, Prince George's developed a high degree of segregation at the neighborhood level. Over half of its neighborhoods are at least 70 percent black or 70 percent white.

Prince George's County is part of a larger trend of black suburbanization that began in earnest in the 1970s, after the passage of civil rights and fair housing laws.[7] Between 1970 and 1995 seven million black people moved to the suburbs, a number considerably greater than the four and a half million blacks who comprised the great migration from south to north between 1940 and 1970.[8] While most of these black suburban movers located in predominantly white settings, a new contemporary phenomenon of predominantly black, middle-class enclaves also developed.[9] More than forty U.S. metropolitan areas now boast at least 50,000 black suburbanites.[10] In many of the largest of these regions relatively affluent "buppie bubbles" have emerged; in Brook Glen, Panola Mill, and Wyndham Park in DeKalb County, southeast of Atlanta, Georgia; in Rolling Oaks in Dade County, Florida; in Black Jack, Jennings, Normandy, and University City in St. Louis County, and in suburbs to the south of Chicago.[11] In the Atlanta region, there are at least six suburban neighborhoods where blacks are both a majority and their income and education levels exceed the median for the entire metro region. These communities result from a variety of factors[12]— confident separatism, the pressures of a housing[13] market that presents stark choices, racial steering, relative affordability[14] compared to predominantly white affluent bastions, or some complex combination of all of these factors.

A black family of a certain means faces a dilemma when entering the housing market. They, like all Americans, desire superior environments[15] in which to live, work, play, and raise their children.[16] Their dream is the American dream. They want equal access to all of the resources society has to offer but they are frequently forced to choose between a black enclave that comes with some costs but provides a spirit-reviving balm against the stress of living as a black person in America, or a community[17] that offers a wealth of opportunities and benefits but where they would be vastly outnumbered by whites, a kind of integration[18] they may not want.

Painfully, I have come to the conclusion that external prejudice against black neighborhoods[19] makes it virtually impossible for the black middle class to form havens of their own that approximate the economic[20] or opportunity benefits of a white enclave. Black communities, even affluent ones, bear burdens and costs that predominantly white ones do not. Most of these costs can be tied either to race-laden decisions on the part of whites and predominantly white institutions to avoid black communities or to the propensity (in part fueled by discriminatory attitudes) of black communities to attract low-income people. Waves of black suburbanization have been fueled by the desire to escape the social distress of "the 'hood," including its crime and weak schools. But within the space of a decade, most black suburban movers will find that the social distress they sought to escape has migrated to them.

Therefore, integration or living in an integrated community is practically the only route black people have to escaping concentrated black poverty.[21] Try as they might, the black middle class cannot completely escape their lower-income brethren unless they move into predominantly white communities. It is a cruel truth. The black middle class carries much of society's load regarding concentrated black poverty.[22] They usually provide the buffer from ghettos[23] for the rest of society. The (racist) rules of the housing market are set against them.

In a nutshell, the rules operate as follows: Blacks form enclaves by preference and because they are steered to the least controversial areas—those deemed undesirable by whites—by a discriminatory real estate industry. These enclave areas usually form in the opposite direction from the centers of highest economic growth. In the booming 1990s, Prince George's County was situated (and still is) directly opposite the "white hot" technical juggernaut of Northern Virginia. In the Atlanta region, blacks suburbanized mostly south and eastward, while the fastest job growth has been in the suburbs due north, especially near the Perimeter Center.[24] This pattern is repeated virtually everywhere black people are suburbanizing in large numbers. When migrating blacks reach a critical mass, whites flee and demand in the local housing market falls, causing poorer blacks to move in behind middle-class blacks. Within a period as short as a decade, the black middle class finds itself once again in close proximity to social distress and often moves again, even farther away from the centers of economic growth.[25] Meanwhile commercial and retail investors shun these emerging black enclaves as the social distress they attract increases crime, often lowers property values, raises taxes,[26] and reduces school quality as the student population rapidly becomes impoverished.[27]

Black separatism, even of the affluent black kind, then, comes with palpable costs. When a white person chooses to move to a middle-class suburban enclave of "her kind of people," she makes this choice, perhaps unconsciously, with certain expectations and assumptions that society tends to live up to—assumptions that a black middle-class suburbanite, living in a similar haven of "one's own," cannot make, at least not confidently. Among those assumptions:

1. I can escape neighborhoods of poverty, particularly black ones.
2. My children will be able to attend good public schools. They will be prepared, maybe even well prepared, for college.
3. I will be free from crime.
4. My property taxes will be manageable and I will receive better government services at lower cost than I would in the city.
5. I will be able to shop and buy all the things I want and need, at stores located near where I live. I will have a nice range of options for eating out near where I live.

I'm sure I could extend this list of implicit assumptions about the benefits of suburban life; these are just the main ones. As I show below, these assumptions do not appear to be true for the middle-class and even affluent black people of Prince George's County. If this county, with its relatively affluent middle-class population base, cannot transcend the racial biases set against it, and if it cannot approximate the American suburban dream for its residents, then I do not see how any other black jurisdiction could.

THE COSTS OF BLACK SEPARATISM

In clarifying the costs of the separation for middle-class black suburbanites, I do not mean to denigrate majority-black communities. For some residents the soul-regenerating benefits of a black enclave will be worth the costs. My point is simply that there *are* pronounced costs associated with this choice and that, unfortunately for African Americans, it appears that the suburban ideal will elude them if they wish to pursue a separatist vision. I make my case below primarily by debunking the common assumptions about suburban middle class life, showing that they do not maintain in Prince George's County.

1. I can escape neighborhoods of poverty, particularly black ones. While the levels of income and education have risen as Prince George's has become blacker, the county is not immune to the brutally unfair rules of the real estate market—rules that favor majority-white communities and disfavor majority-black ones. Much to the chagrin of Prince George's County leaders, waves of low-income black people have been migrating to the county from the District of Columbia. This kind of poverty influx did not happen in the majority-white suburban counties surrounding the District.

Twenty-nine of the thirty-three suburban communities in the D.C. metro area that have been categorized as "at-risk" because of "present and growing social needs" are in Prince George's County.[28] Prince George's and the District itself carry a higher poverty burden than its predominantly white neighbors. In the 1990s, 15 percent of the metro region's welfare recipients lived in Prince George's, while other surrounding suburbs were home to less than 5 percent of this population. Not surprisingly, the whiter and more affluent communities have the least poverty burden. While I am not advocating class exclusion in this chapter, my point is that, to the extent that escaping poverty and attendant social distress is an aspiration of suburban movers, this aspiration is eluding the black middle class.

Most of the low-income folks who have migrated to Prince George's have settled inside the Beltway, in the western part of the county. Despite the divided nature of the county, the affluent black residents of Prince George's are not entirely insulated. With proximity comes conflict. Evidence of classism abounds, perhaps precisely because the poor folks from the 'hood are a reminder of what the upwardly mobile and upper-income black residents of Prince George's thought they had escaped. There is a quiet understanding among America's relatively small population of upper-income black people. It spills out in private conversations but is not widely or publicly admitted. In truth, most middle- and upper-income black people are just as uncomfortable living in close proximity to their lower-income brethren as are white folks and indeed, everyone else in America.

An infamous example of this black classism occurred in the summer of 1996 in the Prince George's community of Perrywood. When black kids from the streets of D.C. began traveling out to Perrywood to play basketball with their middle-income "brothers," the black bourgeoisie took notice. Upset with the nightly noise, recent break-ins and vandalism, and probably the mere presence of a 'hood element, they hired a private security company to screen nonresidents from the neighborhood. The irony of black people hiring private police to stop and check the identity of all black male youth in the neighborhood was not lost on many residents. Some expressed misgivings and anger, but not surprisingly, a consensus prevailed among the Perrywood residents around the need to protect their homes and property. A similar class dispute erupted in Prince George's in 2000 when the affluent residents of Lake Arbor objected to allowing lower-income students from neighboring Landover to attend a newly constructed high school. Prince George's also displayed its classist tendencies when it built a multimillion-dollar sports and recreational facility while consciously limiting the number of basketball courts.

This classist bent has also shaped politics in the county. Wayne Curry—Prince George's first black county executive and, reportedly at the time of his first election in 1994 the *only* elected black county executive in the nation—campaigned on the charge that housing was becoming too accessible to low-income D.C. families who would bring crime and other social problems with them. After his victory, he pressured developers to build larger and more expensive houses that inner-city working families could not afford. He also successfully sought a release from a court-ordered school busing program that brought poor students from the eastern fringes of the District into Prince George's schools. His stances were hugely popular with black and white middle-class residents.

To be fair, such efforts to exclude low-income residents from the county are economically rational and consistent with the zoning and economic development policies of many other majority-white suburban jurisdictions in the nation. Given the rules of the market, Prince George's county leaders probably have to fight a little harder than most suburban locales to meet the desires of its upwardly mobile residents, that is, escaping the ills of the central city with its perceived crime and high redistributive taxes. But Prince George's is not winning this battle, certainly not to the degree that majority-white communities are.

A personal friend of mine and resident of Prince George's has worried aloud to me about the urban influx. Ron tells me that he has been thinking about moving back into the District because "an element" has begun to creep into his neighborhood. It's not that these "lower-middle-class black folks" were causing an increase in crime. Instead Ron observes that they just have different habits. They don't maintain their houses as nicely. They sit outside at night, playing their radios loudly. Ron's property values were beginning to decline, and he thought maybe he should move back into a "Gold Coast" neighborhood in the District rather than into southern, more affluent parts of Prince George's, which would require him to endure longer commutes to his office in D.C. His family, like most black families with choices about where to live, is caught in the dilemma of the black middle class.

2. My children will be able to attend good public schools. They will be prepared, maybe even well prepared, for college. Schools are among the prime reasons people decide to live where they do; at least that is what realtors claim. The cruelest reality about Prince George's County is that its school district consistently ranks second-worst in the state of Maryland on test scores after Baltimore, a predominantly black and heavily poor city. In the D.C. metropolitan area, the Prince George's County school system ranked last on the 2002 *Washington Post* Challenge Index, which measures public high schools' efforts to challenge its students based on the percentage of students who take advanced placement and International Baccalaureate courses. Falls Church, an overwhelmingly white, affluent community in Northern Virginia at the opposite pole of the D.C. metropolitan universe, ranked first. Montgomery County, the highest ranked Maryland jurisdiction, came in at fifth place. The District ranked twentieth, two places ahead of Prince George's County, and one of its academic magnet schools ranked tenth among all schools. Of the 155 high schools evaluated for this ranking, the first Prince George's school to appear on the list was Eleanor Roosevelt, a magnet high school, ranked sixtieth. In that year, only 67 percent of the seniors at Roosevelt attended a four-year college, according to the latest available reported data. Of the first ten Prince George's high schools to appear on the Challenge Index ranking, only one other, Central High, had more than half of its seniors go on to a four-year college. At the other schools, college attendance ranged from 34 percent to 46 percent for graduating seniors. Ignominiously, Prince George's and District schools heavily occupy the bottom of the Challenge Index.[29]

In the late 1990s, only about a third of all of Prince George's third-, sixth-, and eighth-grade public school students scored at a satisfactory level or better on Maryland standardized tests—a level well above Baltimore's 16 percent proficiency but well below top-ranked Howard County's 60 percent. Test scores have improved of late, but apparently other school districts have improved as well. In the latest available school testing results, Prince George's third, fifth, and eighth graders still ranked second from last in the state, behind Baltimore. If one were shopping for a place to live in the D.C. metropolitan area based upon school quality, one would not put Prince George's on the list.

The causes of this poor performance are not entirely clear, but residents of the county have their theories. A West Indian immigrant couple who bought their home in Fort Washington in the early 1990s—I will call them Miles and Edith—tell me that their neighborhood has changed. Initially the neighborhood was very well integrated, but whenever a house was sold, a black family moved in. Hence, while still integrated, their neighborhood has become blacker over time. In their view, the schools are horrible. They initially put their kids in Prince George's public schools but withdrew them as the lower-income kids from families migrating from the District began to take over. The schools are bad, they say, because the middle-class parents have taken their children out, leaving them with much less parental involvement. Miles wonders aloud about why Prince George's cannot have good schools. "I am paying the same, maybe even higher property taxes than people who live in Montgomery County or Bethesda, but what do I have to show for it?" he says. He can cite examples of excellent schools in those jurisdictions but can't think of an excellent counterpart in Prince George's.

Ruth, a black woman in an interracial marriage raising three daughters, has similar misgivings about Prince George's schools. She offers the example of Friendly High School, which she describes as "predominantly black, middle class, and low achieving." She was appalled when her daughter was excitedly praised by school counselors for receiving a 950 on the SAT. "My daughter was sick the day she took the test. I would expect her to perform much better than that. In my mind, a 950 was nothing to be excited about." She says that her kids are receiving much worse schooling than they did in Montana, where she and her family lived before moving to Prince George's County to accommodate a career move by her husband. At a PTSA meeting at her daughter's high school, Ruth claims that as few as six parents might attend, for a school that has more than six hundred students.

If recently reported school data are to be believed, Friendly is not an impoverished school. Only 18 percent of its students receive free or reduced-price lunch. Ruth has similar frustrations at her younger daughter's elementary school, Henry G. Ferguson, a predominantly black magnet school. "The active parents of the PTSA are virtually all white," she says, suggesting that the black parents who do have their kids in public school are either overwhelmed, uninterested, or perhaps too accepting of what the school system offers their children. Alternatively, they may feel that the PTA has become the vehicle of white parents and is not focused on issues relevant to their own children. Or maybe African Americans are simply not used to being insistent consumers of public education. A history of being locked out may have translated over time into a feeling of disempowerment and a reluctance to demand or expect changes from public institutions, even ones that blacks now ostensibly control. Or, it could be that, now that African American administrators are largely in charge, black parents defer to their judgment and are content to drop their children off at the schoolhouse door.

Other relatively affluent Prince George's residents also share stories of woe about the schools. An African-American lawyer, working hard along with his wife to raise four sons, removed his oldest from a public middle school in Prince George's and elected to pay about $17,000 a year to send him to an elite private school in Washington, D.C., instead. He felt the teachers at the public school simply had low expectations for his son and were not striving to teach him. I think to myself about how he will be able to afford four such tuition bills as all of his sons come of school age.

When the lawyer moves his family temporarily to Atlanta for a work assignment, they live in the Dunwoody area of town. "I'm ambivalent about it," he says. "This is my first time living in a white neighborhood." But in Dunwoody, he has all his kids in public schools and remarks, "Here the schools return my phone calls."

John, an affluent Mitchellville doctor and resident of the premier Woodmore development, has taken his oldest daughter out of a Prince George's public school and placed her in a parochial school. His daughter tells me that in her public school some classes had as many as forty students. "The teachers could not control the students," she says. "They were often disrespectful toward teachers." John claims that at Ernest Everett Just Middle School, which one of his daughters attended, fewer than half of the students passed an initial round of state proficiency tests in reading and math.

Stacie Banks, a Fort Washington resident, tells the *Washington Post* she faced a similar situation. She took her daughter out of Indian Queen Elementary, a local public school, and enrolled her in the private Potomac School in McLean, Virginia, which she must drive to daily in addition to her commute to work in the District. Her main concern was overcrowding; with a boundary change, Queen was slated to receive 180 more students and only 3 more schoolteachers.[30]

Overcrowding is not the only problem. The Prince George's public schools also appear to be underresourced. Bridgette Tabor-Cooper, a Mitchellville resident who placed her daughter in a private Montessori school, says to the *Post*, "I would love the idea of being able to send my daughters to public school, but not the way most of them are now. . . . If you don't get into a good magnet program, you're sending your children to a school with uncertified teachers, not enough books, large numbers of children who don't behave."[31]

In conversation after conversation, middle- and upper-income black parents in Prince George's indicate that they do not have faith in the public school system. There are at least two factors contributing to the problems with Prince George's schools. First, the county is hampered by a property tax cap, approved by citizen referendum, that limits school spending—an additional fiscal constraint that other suburban school districts do not have to contend with. In 2000, for example, per-pupil spending in Prince George's was only $6,410, compared to Montgomery County's $7,584 and Fairfax County's $8,553. When County Executive Wayne Curry vigorously campaigned for the repeal of the tax cap in the fall of 1996, voters rebuffed him. Why, you might ask, would a majority-black county reject a repeal of a tax cap that would benefit majority-black schools? One possible explanation is that the people most likely to go to the polls, whites and affluent blacks in the county, were least likely to have their kids in public school.

Another potential explanation for the difference in school performance between Prince George's schools and its suburban counterparts is that there is a substantial difference in the numbers of poor children in these schools. School performance is closely tied to the family income of the student population. Indeed, the socioeconomic background of the students attending a school is probably the best predictor of the school's success. By the late 1990s, more than half of Prince George's public school system's students qualified for free or reduced-price lunches, indicating that many prosperous families in the county no longer sent their kids to the public schools. By comparison, only about 10 percent of the students in the Northern Virginia school districts of Falls Church and Loudon County—both on the opposite pole of the metropolitan region—qualified for free or reduced lunch.

The rules of the market work against middle-class black schools. Predominantly middle-class African American schools in the United States tend to impoverish rapidly because majority-black communities tend to attract lower-income populations over time, which, in turn, discourages middle-class parents from choosing such schools. Still, Prince George's boasts a number of predominantly black, predominantly middle-class schools, like Laurel, Surrattsville, Suitland, and Friendly high schools, that are decidedly underachieving; fewer than half of the seniors at these schools attended four-year colleges in recent years.[32] Another possible explanation for this difference between black middle-class achievement and that of white suburban counterparts is wealth differences. One researcher has found that high school graduation and college attendance rates are equal for blacks and whites when you control for wealth, rather than income.[33] Whether underachievement stems from an influx of poor children, a failure of the black middle class to cultivate a culture of achievement, or some other source, the end result is that many middle-class black parents who have opted to live in a "black sanctuary" are paying a premium for their separatism in the form of private school tuition. Meanwhile, their white counterparts in affluent white suburbs have the option of relying on high-quality, well-funded public schools that typically have few poor children and a host of engaged parents.

3. *I will be free from crime.* One of the primary reasons suburbanites leave or avoid central cities is crime. The bucolic suburbs offer the promise of freedom from fear. As with other common assumptions about suburban life, however, Prince George's is not doing as well as its predominantly white counterparts; its crime rate is higher and its citizens are more imperiled. Even the District saw improvements in crime during the 1990s that Prince George's did not enjoy, perhaps because the District was exporting poor people to the county. Crime within the District of Columbia dropped significantly in the 1990s, while it rose slightly in Prince George's. Although the total increase in crime in the county was marginal, the inner-Beltway communities experienced a crime explosion that was quite disproportionate to their population growth. Places like Berwyn Heights, a majority-white community of under 3,000 residents, grew by only 8 percent in population but saw crime rise 82 percent between 1990 and 1998. During the same period, the District of Columbia neighborhoods bordering inner-Beltway Prince George's communities experienced a rapid decrease in both crime and population. In fact, most of the communities with the highest crime rates in the entire D.C. metro region were all located inside the Beltway, in Prince George's County.

Once again, the laws of the market are undermining the suburban dream for Prince George's. The social distress formerly tied to the District's poorer neighborhoods is migrating to the county. Such distress contributes to rates of violent crime that are dramatically higher in Prince George's County than in neighboring counties. In 2000, for example, there were six times as many murders and five times as many aggravated assaults in Prince George's County as in neighboring Montgomery County, which has about 70,000 more people.[34]

Violent crime is not limited to the lower-income communities of the county. A creep of sorts has begun. Miles and Edith tell a tale of two classes in Fort Washington. According to them, Fort Washington Drive is a socio-economic dividing line and everyone knows it. "The lower-income families have different values," Edith frankly observes. "They get involved with crime and drugs." Edith mentions a murder a few years ago of a well-to-do couple at the hands of two young teenagers who came from the District. In the battle to escape the 'hood, Fort Washington residents are not entirely successful. In fact, some affluent blacks have begun to move even farther south into predominantly white and rural Charles County in part because it has "low crime."[35]

4. *My property taxes will be manageable and I will receive better government services at lower cost than I would in the city.* Academic studies show that the two primary motives for the formation of new suburban communities in the 1950s and 1960s were the desire to escape redistributive taxes of the central cities and to escape black people.[36] For affluent and middle-class blacks with choices, as I have argued above, escaping lower-income black folks, or the crime and distress that often plague their neighborhoods, seems to have been part of the rationale for moving to the suburbs. But black movers, like white movers, also want better services for less money. Unfortunately, this has not typically been the case for those who move to majority-black suburbs. Again, black communities tend to carry higher social service burdens than predominantly white ones because of their tendency to attract lower-income people. Majority-black jurisdictions like Prince George's also tend to be discriminated against in the market for commercial investment and economic growth. As a result, black communities tend to have higher taxes *and* services that are less responsive to the demands and aspirations of the black elite. Isolation from high-growth economic corridors also means that residents of majority-black communities face longer commutes.

Prince George's County is no exception to these trends. First, as I have mentioned, the county is part of a nationwide phenomenon of steering black people to areas deemed undesirable by whites and then steering economic growth in the *opposite* direction. The affluent bastions of Prince George's are outside the Beltway to the south and east of the District of Columbia. They could not be farther away from most of the areas of highest economic growth in the metro region: Tysons Corner, the I-66 Corridor, and the Dulles and Herndon areas in Northern Virginia, and Bethesda, Maryland, all of which are north and west of the District. As a result, residents of job-dense Fairfax County have shorter commute times than do Prince Georgians. Over half of Fairfax residents who work do so in their home county, while only 39 percent Prince Georgians have the luxury of working where they live.

This phenomenon of the black middle class suburbanizing in one direction and jobs and economic growth suburbanizing in another is true in Washington, D.C.; Atlanta; Chicago; and virtually any other metropolitan region that is home to a sizable black middle class. Affluent, largely white suburban communities tend to attract most of a metropolitan region's economic growth. Suburban communities with large black populations, on the other hand—communities that attract *less* economic growth and *more* social service burdens—tend to have higher tax rates, higher public debt, and substantially different patterns of expenditures than do other suburbs. Residents of black/multiethnic suburbs pay tax rates that are, on average, about 65 percent higher than those of white suburbs, *even after* differences in affluence are taken into account. And black/multiethnic suburbs spend more on redistributive services than any other type of suburb, independent of levels of wealth. Prince Georgians' property tax rates ($.962 per $100 of assessed value) are considerably higher than neighboring Montgomery County ($.754 per $100 of value), yet Montgomery spends more per pupil on public education than does Prince George's. Montgomery County, having higher-valued—read: whiter—residential properties and a stronger commercial base can generate more revenues for the services its citizens demand.

Overall, black suburbanites tend to reside in suburban communities characterized by lower property wealth, worse public finances, and poorer prospects for economic growth than suburbs with smaller black populations. As a result, blacks living in majority-black towns tend to receive worse government services than blacks who live elsewhere.[37] The lack of quality government services is a familiar refrain among some Prince George's residents. Bridgette Tabor-Cooper, who has lived in Prince George's her entire life, says she contemplated leaving after becoming a parent: "It's not black people that I want to escape. It's what this county does badly that other places do well. It's quality-of-life issues that I'm concerned about. There's more to life than nice neighborhoods, nice houses and great neighbors."[38]

The discriminatory rules of the market also mean that property values are more at risk in majority-black communities. Again, Prince George's is no exception. The northern parts of the county that have attracted many low- and moderate-income people from the District experienced a substantial decline in property values in the 1990s. Communities like Mt. Ranier, Berwyn Heights, and Hyattsville saw property values decline by between 15 and 18 percent in the mid- to late nineties. Indeed, most of the lowest-valued property in the D.C. metro area is in inner Prince George's County. This decline in property values was accompanied by a simultaneous increase in social distress, including a spike in child poverty and crime in these communities. On the other hand, the more affluent parts of the county have seen their property values increase. But the harsh reality is that Prince George's and other majority-black communities have been faring poorly in the competition for commercial tax base, with attendant negative consequences for their residents.

5. *I will be able to shop and buy all the things I want and need, at stores located near where I live. I will have a nice range of options for eating out near where I live.* Nothing seems to draw the ire of Prince George's black elite more than the fact that the county is shunned by higher-end retailers. The same attitude that leads a salesperson to ignore a black customer fuels a propensity of many retailers, restaurateurs, and commercial entities to ignore considerable black buying power. One affluent Prince George's resident describes this as her "civil rights" issue. Prince George's County has a higher median income than neighboring Baltimore County, yet that county has a Nordstrom at its Towson Town Center, while Prince George's doesn't have a Nordstrom, Lord & Taylor, or Neiman-Marcus. The Bowie Town Center, a 100-store, open-air mall designed to provide a "Main Street" environment, which opened in late 2001 to much celebration, is anchored by middle-market retailers like Hecht's (which became Macy's in 2006), Best Buy, and Sears. John, the doctor from Mitchellville, describes these stores as "crap." But even these so-called "crap" stores are located in the whitest community in the county. Bowie is 65 percent white, but its median income is $7,000 less than that of Mitchellville; it once considered trying to secede from predominantly black Prince George's to become a part of neighboring Montgomery County. The Boulevard at Capital Centre, another Main Street–style retail development that opened in the fall of 2003 closer to the center of black affluence, is about half the size of the Bowie Town Center, with fewer name-brand national stores.

Affluent black Prince Georgians bemoan having to drive to Tysons Corner, located just off the Beltway in Northern Virginia—"where the stores are," as this mall's marketing jingle ironically declares. Tysons boasts more than 250 stores to meet every taste and budget, especially at the high end. Marita Golden notes that the "retail equity activists" of Prince George's have "written letters to the editor, held demonstrations and news conferences, and complained to whoever would listen about the lack of respect for black buying power."[39] They want quality retail amenities that fit their tastes and budget in their own backyard.

If a Prince George's resident wants to experience fine dining, she also has to drive some distance outside the county to get it. Unlike in Bethesda,

Reston, Tysons, or the District, there is no Palm, no Four Seasons, not even a Houston's in Prince George's County. The dearth of eateries, especially at the high end, is such that when the Outback Steakhouse announced plans to open two new restaurants in the county and Starbucks announced plans to open a coffee shop, this was cause for celebration. The county's official website offers a listing of 66 restaurants located in Prince George's. A similar listing for Fairfax County offered over 340 eateries. In sum, white suburbanites living in havens of their own can take for granted the simple pleasure of eating out with their family in the vicinity at a nice place that offers some atmosphere and quality cuisine. Prince Georgians cannot.

One of the reasons for the dearth of restaurants may be that national chains rely heavily on the market profiles of companies like Claritas, Inc., of San Diego, or the crime profiles of CAP Index Inc., of Exton, Pennsylvania— profiles that do not convey the real positives in Prince George's—when they decide to open a new restaurant. The Inglewood Restaurant Park, in Largo, just off Route 202, near the Boulevard at Capital Centre, has had difficulty attracting a critical mass of tenants. Although crime is very low at this location and 35 percent of the households within a one-mile radius earn over $100,000, this location does not rate well under the Claritas and CAP profiles because it is within a six-mile radius of lower-income neighborhoods inside the Beltway and in the District.

The executives at a national headquarters of a restaurant chain located thousands of miles away can't seem to see past these rigid profiles.[40] Lacking any real experience with or understanding of black markets, it is easier to rely on stereotypes. As Marita Golden put it, "This is all part of the racial stigmatizing that education, affluence and expensive homes can't erase."[41]

This underinvestment in Prince George's highlights a central weakness of racially segregated communities: a concentration of racial minorities— particularly of black people—can and often does lead to a decline in access to and influence of dominant institutional actors that shape markets. This is not an apology for racist or ignorant market actors. It is a statement of fact. I have had colleagues in the academic community react angrily or skeptically when I present facts like these. They would like to explain away these unfair tendencies of markets based upon anything other than race. But I am not alone in pointing out these tendencies. Empirical studies show that commercial disinvestment in majority-black communities, even affluent ones, is commonplace.[42] I am reminded of a study commissioned by the FCC, which showed that even when minority-owned, minority-formatted radio stations were number one in terms of ratings, mainstream advertisers would send their advertising dollars elsewhere. The practice of making racist or ignorant assumptions about the buying habits of people of color in order to justify not spending advertising dollars with stations that were reaching more people than any other in their markets was widespread.[43] In short, black communities and the assets they bring are frequently devalued by nonblack institutions and people.

Prince George's County is not unique. The five common assumptions about suburban life do not seem to maintain for most other middle-class black communities. In DeKalb County, east of Atlanta, affluent blacks witnessed many stores, including Kmart and Cracker Barrel, pull up stakes and leave their community even as the influx of middle- and upper-income black movers was *raising* the income and education level of the county. A successful black lawyer who built her "dream home" in suburban DeKalb tells me she left it a few years later when she realized there were no viable public schools in DeKalb *or* public transportation routes for her son to get to a private school in Atlanta.[44]

Affluent blacks in the Atlanta suburbs face another dilemma. There are only a handful of predominantly black schools in which middle-class students are a majority. And because the residential areas where these schools are located are in constant flux, the schools do not remain middle-class very long. As a result, parents in the middle-class black suburban enclaves surrounding Atlanta are increasingly bypassing the public schools in favor of private schools.[45]

This pattern is replicated on the West Coast as well. An African American partner at a prominent Los Angeles law firm tells me that most of the black professionals in the City of Angels will live in one of three neighborhoods—Ladeira Heights, Baldwin Hills, or View Park—unless they have opted to move to "the Valley" because it offers larger, more affordable, and newer homes. All three of these neighborhoods are overwhelmingly black and in very close proximity to low-income, "inner-city" areas. Kim is a proud first-time owner of an older home in "lower Ladeira," which she says is only blocks away from a low-income neighborhood. Such proximity is okay with her. She mixes easily with all kinds of people. But it does tend to force black families with choices to opt out of the public schools. "All of the black professionals I know are either home schooling their children or they have them in private schools. I can't think of a single exception," Kim says.

I have searched the nation for a counterexample—a thriving black community with excellent public schools; an attractive and growing tax base; low crime rates; a host of stores, restaurants, and recreational amenities, in short, something approximating the advantages of majority-white communities, or of the vibrancy of black communities in the era of Jim Crow. In all honesty I have not found such a place. Obviously, black communities have their strengths, as waves of nonblack gentrifiers who have rediscovered the city and moved into black neighborhoods seem to recognize. Harlem is but one African American stronghold that is experiencing a second renaissance. Companies from Magic Johnson Theaters, to Starbucks, to IKEA are beginning to recognize the potency of minority buying power. Kim says of the

Crenshaw neighborhood in South-Central L.A. where Magic Johnson has cultivated an entertainment district of movie theaters and restaurants, "I just love going there and being around other black people of all different ranges of income. At the Starbucks, the Fridays, the Fat Burger, they are hanging out, talking, and playing chess. It is very vibrant and it makes you feel so good. There are lots of self-made people there. It's ours." Kim works in a predominantly white law firm but, she says, "I feel more comfortable, more secure, and better about myself" living and socializing in a black environment.

Despite their psychic benefits, there are some difficult issues that need to be addressed in order to make majority-black communities eminently viable, issues that we don't like to discuss openly. When it comes to where we live, integration may have eluded, failed, or simply been unappealing to many black people. But separation doesn't seem to be working entirely either. Because the black elite have choices about where to live, work, learn, and spend their money, blacks are no longer *forced* to depend upon one another—a key linchpin to the viability of black communities in the era of Jim Crow. Among the hardest of issues is how or whether we can cultivate high-performing public schools for our children.

Some Prince Georgians are beginning to look in the mirror. "In the black community we have to acknowledge the politically incorrect truth that too many of our students don't take school seriously and too many parents are conspirators," says Golden. Some are more pointed, laying the blame for the county's shortcomings squarely on the black middle class. Ernest Quarles, a Mitchellville lawyer who is married to a physician, cites "a lack of direction and self-esteem among some of the county's young blacks resulting from a lack of parental involvement in schools and recreational activities." He argues in the *Post* that "African Americans have failed to form a strong community bond and to mobilize politically to force change in schools, government, and services."[46]

To cultivate family-oriented communities that raise children well and offer "the good life" requires an insistent, organized citizenry that makes educating black children a priority and holds public institutions accountable. It also requires involved parents who join the PTA or find some other way to be involved in schools, and who turn off the television and are intimately involved with their children's development. We have to acknowledge that there is a black achievement gap and bring our resources and talents to bear to cultivate institutions and a culture where learning is taken seriously, teachers and elders are respected, and parents and the entire community are oriented toward educational achievement. I don't think this can happen in Prince George's or elsewhere without a full, rather than a partial, embrace on the part of the black middle class of their communities, including the low-income folks in their midst.

Black professionals who have chosen to live in separated neighborhoods but opt out of the schools, or who harbor a classism toward other black people pay for it in the long run. Their web of interconnection with the lower classes is indelible, whether they like it or not. They can roll up their sleeves and recruit others in their ranks to enter and stay committed to public schools or they can pay a price in the poor reputation of county schools and the spiraling costs of private school tuition. If they are not prepared to send their own kids to public school, they could at least lend time, resources, or votes that reinforce and nurture those schools and the children who attend them.

THE POSITIVE BENEFITS AND COUNTERARGUMENTS

I expect my conclusions about the costs of black separatism to be met with howls of dissent from some quarters. Let me be clear: I am not trying to be provocative to gain attention or career advancement. I am a progressive who cares passionately about the state of inequality in this nation. The facts I have presented are inconvenient, painful, even disturbing. I struggle with them because I am a "race" woman in many senses. I enjoy and thrive in the company of black people.

Such community feeling is what attracts many blacks to Prince George's County. The delight and pride they take in living in spirit-renewing black neighborhoods outweighs any costs associated with racial segregation. Many a Prince Georgian would also counter my "parade of horribles" by pointing to the county's strengths. After all, the county has a richer, better-educated population and tax base and a lower total poverty rate *because* of the influx of a sizable black middle-class population. Black professionals have saved the county from its former reputation, at least among black people, as a white, racist, rural backwater.

Prince Georgians also proudly argue that they prefer living in a county where African Americans now wield political power, providing the means to shape their own destiny. Since 1990, the school board chairman, county executive, and state and national legislative representatives are all black. And these black officials have been particularly effective in procuring state aid for the county, particularly for transportation, although it remains to be seen how the county will fair under a newly elected Republican governor. Prince Georgians also argue that their county offers attractive, even palatial, homes at relatively affordable prices.

CONCLUSION

Given the costs associated with separatism, where should African Americans who have choices elect to live? There is no universal answer to this conundrum because black people vary in their attitudes about racial solidarity, and their residential choices reflect this variety of opinion. Unfortunately, painfully, I have come to conclude that the only way for a person of color to approximate the suburban ideal is to live in a community that is both overwhelmingly white and relatively affluent. As I explain elsewhere, the same could also be said for blue-collar and middle-income whites and residents of a variety of other types of communities that, in our current separatist system, also cannot achieve the mythic ideal.[47] But even I, a prointegrationist, am not recommending this choice. I would not choose to live in an overwhelmingly white community. I am merely underscoring the fact of our very different, separated realities.

Between the extremes of overwhelmingly black and overwhelmingly white neighborhoods there are some, admittedly rarer, integrated or multiethnic alternatives. Elsewhere I have advocated for public policies that will encourage the creation of more stable, racially and economically integrated communities as a means of closing gaps of inequality.[48] With some ambivalence, I have reached the conclusion that the best—and likely the only—route to full equality for African Americans is a socioeconomically integrated one. While I support the integrationist ideal, I also understand the intrinsic value of black environments and institutions. Far from suggesting that blackness is inherently inferior, I am underscoring the discriminatory attitudes on the part of nonblacks and the impact this has on us.

As I have explained, one critical effect of racial steering and racial avoidance is the tendency for black communities to attract social distress. I am not suggesting that success in escaping from low-income people should be the standard by which a community is judged, although this seems to be precisely what buyers who have choices value. I am arguing, however, that in a system of racial and economic separation that is premised on the idea that the most valued communities should be farthest or most insulated from the minority poor, *some community* is going to have to bear the burden of proximity to social distress, and in American society, consciously or unconsciously, middle-class black communities have been assigned that role.

The close proximity of the black middle class to poor neighborhoods makes a black middle-class existence much more precarious than a white one. Children that grow up in middle-class, predominantly white communities that typically are well insulated from poverty, crime, and weak schools do not encounter the same risks that children living in black middle-class neighborhoods encounter on their passage to adulthood. In a different, socioeconomically integrated system, where low-income people of all races lived among middle- and upper-income people, we would not have the societal burden that comes with concentrated poverty and social distress. Nor would we have a situation where one group of people—African Americans—bear the disproportionate burden of concentrated poverty because they live either in or near a high-poverty neighborhood. On the other hand, the black middle class pays a price for its own classism. They pay for it with private school tuition or the steep price tag attached to "better" neighborhoods. And they pay a price for their neglect of or hostility to their lower-income brethren.

If middle-class black people kept their children in the Prince George's schools and stayed involved in those schools, they would be helping to create viable socioeconomically integrated institutions that support all black children regardless of economic background. But this is a heavy burden to lay on the black middle class. It is an unfair burden. In a more integrated society, black people would not have to do so much heavy lifting. There is a different way of thinking about this, however. Some have heatedly argued with me that *only* middle- and upper-class black people are capable of providing a viable solution to the problems challenging black communities, including black underachievement and weak schools, not to mention the erosion of marriage and family formation.

Only the black middle and upper classes have the possibility of having real empathy with the black poor, they argue, and therefore they should endeavor to make a difference—by fervently recommitting themselves to black institutions or by re-creating socioeconomically integrated black institutions reminiscent of the pre–civil rights era. Given the classist impulse in all of us, however, I am not optimistic about this possibility. In separated America, many folks are just struggling to get or stay ahead in the best community, the best school, or social track they can afford. We are all struggling not to fall through the cracks of a system that does not really attempt to bring everyone along. The black middle class experiences this dilemma more pointedly than other demographic groups because they, more than most, sit on the precipice between potential upward mobility and potential failure.

For the black middle class, then, the challenges abound. By living in a white neighborhood or sending their child to a heavily white, affluent private school they risk acculturating their children in ways that may be discomfiting. Black baby boomers who thrived on Howard, Fisk, or Meharry educations and the black network they afforded risk having children with very few black friends. Such dilemmas give rise to organizations like Jack and Jill, that exclusive social institution for the children of the black bourgeoisie. The challenge of raising well-rounded black children who can relate to all types, including their own, while also insulating them from the specter of death, low expectations, an oversexed popular culture, or anything else that might knock a young black child off course, especially a male, is mighty. The most pointed irony is that some of the most integration-weary black parents are paying thousands to send their kids to elite private institutions where their children are the integrators. Yet, a more integrated society that did not fear black people so much might manage to deliver a quality education in an integrated setting to black professional families for free.

The dilemma of the black middle class underscores larger issues of equity. Racial and economic segregation, whether caused by discrimination or voluntary separation leads to grave inequality. The social and economic trade-offs confronting the black middle class underscore the structural inequalities that permeate virtually every American metropolis. Blacks are hit harder because racial discrimination appears to be applied to them with unique intensity. But a similar, perhaps less stark, story of inequality also could be told for the vast majority of the metropolitan population that do not live in affluent, high-growth communities and suburbs.

Inequality is endemic to the fragmented American metropolis. The opportunity structure does not operate in the manner most Americans purport to believe in. Opportunities are much more unequal than we realize or will acknowledge, despite an overwhelming consensus that equality of opportunity should be the norm. And middle-income whites may be the group that is most blind to this reality.

NOTES

1. This chapter borrows heavily from a chapter in my book, *The Failures of Integration: How Race and Class Are Undermining the American Dream* (New York: Public Affairs, 2004). Used with permission.

2. Robert Halpern, *Rebuilding the Inner City: A History of Neighborhood Initiatives to Address Poverty in the United States* (New York: Columbia University Press, 1995).

3. Marita Golden, "Prince George's Convert," *Washingtonian* (July 2003): 35, 36.

4. Thomas R. Hendershot, "Prince George's County," http://www.washington-post.com/wp-srv/liveonline/01/metro/metro_hendershot062101.htm (accessed December 6, 2003).

5. David Dishneau, "Blacks' Income Gap Among Lowest in U.S.," *Washington Times*, November 25, 2003, http://www.washtimes.com/metro/20031124-094023-6661r.htm (accessed December 6, 2003); see also, Krissah Williams, "Investing Big Money, Lending Their Fame: Celebrities Bolster Business in Prince George's," *Washington Post*, October 4, 2004, http://www.washingtonpost.com/wp-dyn/articles/A4501-2004Oct3.html?sub=AR (accessed December 1, 2004).

6. Carol Ascher and Edwina Branch, "Precarious Space: Majority Black Suburbs and Their Public Schools," http://www.nyu.edu/iesp/publications/precariousspace.pdf (accessed December 1, 2004).

7. Dennis E. Gale, *Washington, D.C.: Inner-City Revitalization and Minority Suburbanization* (Philadelphia, PA: Temple University Press, 1990); Valerie C. Johnson, *Black Power in the Suburbs: The Myth or Reality of African American Suburban Political Incorporation* (Albany: State University of New York Press, 2002); *Insiders' Guide to Washington, D.C.*, 4th ed., "Metro Washington Overview, Suburban Maryland," http://www.insiders.com/washington-dc/main-overviews4.htm (accessed December 1, 2004).

8. Ascher and Branch, "Precarious Space."

9. Most of the empirical claims made in this chapter are supported in an extensive research article I recently published: Sheryll D. Cashin, "Middle Class Black Suburbs and the State of Integration," *Cornell Law Review* 86 (2001): 729.

10. See Steven Raphael and Michael A. Stoll, *Modest Progress: The Narrowing Spatial Mismatch Between Blacks and Jobs in the 1990s*, (Washington, DC: The Brookings Institution Center on Urban and Metropolitan Policy, 2002), 3–9.

11. john a. powell, "Race and Space: What Really Drives Metropolitan Growth," *Brookings Review* 16, no. 4 (1998): 20–22.

12. Peter Gordon and Harry W. Richardson, "Prove It: The Costs and Benefits of Sprawl," *Brookings Review* (September 1998): 8–11.

13. Kris Siglin, "Affordable Housing Is Smart for Regions," in *Smart Growth, Better Neighborhoods: Communities Leading the Way*, edited by National Neighborhood Coalition (Washington, DC: National Neighborhood Coalition, 2001), 75–76.

14. Robert D. Bullard, Glenn S. Johnson, and Angel O. Torres, *Sprawl City: Race, Politics, and Planning in Atlanta* (Washington, DC: Island Press, 2000), 122–125, 144, 146.

15. Steve Winkelman, Greg Dierkers, Erin Silsbe, Mac Wubben, Shayna Stott, and Funders' Network for Smart Growth and Livable Communities, *Air Quality and Smart Growth: Planning for Cleaner Air* (Coral Gables, FL: Funders' Network for Smart Growth and Livable Communities, 2005).

16. Carolyn M. Brown and David A. Padgett, "Top Cities for African Americans: The Results Are In: Here Are Readers' and Editors' Picks for the Best Places to Work, Live, and Play," *Black Enterprise* 34, no. 12 (July 2004): 78–103; see also, Monique R. Brown and David A. Padgett, "Readers' Choice: Best Cities for African Americans," *Black Enterprise* (July 2001), http://www.blackenterprise.com/ArchiveOpen.asp ?Source=ArchiveTab/2001/07/0701-45.htm (accessed December 28, 2006).

17. Kathleen Blaha, Peter Harnik, and Funders' Network for Smart Growth and Livable Communities, *Opportunities for Smarter Growth: Parks, Greenspace and Land Conservation*, Transition Paper Number Three (Miami: Funders' Network for Smart Growth and Livable Communities, 2000).

18. See Gregory R. Weiher, *The Fractured Metropolis: Political Fragmentation and Metropolitan Segregation* (Albany: State University of New York Press, 1991).

19. Naomi Friedman and Funders' Network for Smart Growth and Livable Communities, *Energy and Smart Growth: It's About How and Where We Build* (Miami: Funders' Network for Smart Growth and Livable Communities, 2004).

20. Greg LeRoy, Sara Hinkley, and Katie Tallman, *Another Way Sprawl Happens: Economic Development Subsidies in a Twin Cities Suburb* (Washington, DC: Good Jobs First, A Project of the Institute on Taxation and Economic Policy, 2000).

21. Paul A. Jargowsky, *Poverty and Place: Ghettos, Barrios, and the American City* (New York: Russel Sage Foundation, 1997); see also, Scott A. Bollens, "Concentrated Poverty and Metropolitan Equity Strategies," *Stanford Law and Policy Review* 8, no. 2 (1997): 11–23; and Karen Lucas, *Running on Empty: Transport, Social Exclusion and Environmental Justice* (Bristol, UK: Policy Press, 2004).

22. See john a. powell, "Race, Poverty, and Urban Sprawl: Access to Opportunities Through Regional Strategies," Institute on Race and Poverty, http://www1.umn .edu/irp/publications/racepovertyandurbansprawl.html (accessed December 1,

2004); George C. Galster and Edward W. Hill, *The Metropolis in Black and White: Place, Power, and Polarization* (New Brunswick, NJ: Center for Urban Policy Research, 1992).

23. John O. Calmore, "Racialized Space and the Culture of Segregation: Hewing a Stone of Hope from a Mountain of Despair," *University of Pennsylvania Law Review* 143 (1995): 1233.

24. Robert D. Bullard, Glenn S. Johnson, and Angel O. Torres, "Atlanta Megasprawl," *Forum for Applied Research and Public Policy* 14, no. 3 (Fall 1999): 17–23; Greg LeRoy, Sara Hinkley, and Funders' Network for Smart Growth and Livable Communities, *Opportunties for Linking Movements: Workforce Development and Smart Growth*, Transition Paper Number Two (Miami: Funders' Network for Smart Growth and Livable Communities, 2000); Angela Glover Blackwell, Heather McCulloch, and Funders' Network for Smart Growth and Livable Communities, *Opportunities for Smarter Growth: Social Equity and the Smart Growth Movement*, Transition Paper Number One (Miami: Funders' Network for Smart Growth and Livable Communities, 1999).

25. See Daniel J. Hutch, "The Rationale for Including Disadvantaged Communities in the Smart Growth Metropolitan Development Framework," *Yale Law and Policy Review* 20, no. 2 (2002): 353–68.

26. john a. powell, "How Government Tax and Housing Policies Have Racially Segregated America," in *Taxing America*, ed. Karen B. Brown and Mary Louise Fellows (New York: New York University Press, 1997).

27. Myron Orfield, Director, Metropolitan Area Research Corporation, to Leonard Downie Jr., Executive Editor, *Washington Post* (September 24, 1999) (on file with author); Gary Orfield and Carol Ashkinaze, *The Closing Door: Conservative Policy and Black Opportunity* (Chicago: University of Chicago Press, 1991), 81 (noting that "[h]ousing and neighborhood choice was seriously . . . limited for higher-income blacks" in the Atlanta area in the 1980s and that "rental and homeowner-ship markets, particularly in the more desirable suburbs, remained largely closed even to blacks with sufficient incomes"); Mary Pattillo-McCoy, *Black Picket Fences: Privilege and Peril Among the Black Middle Class* (Chicago: University of Chicago Press, 1999), 27 (noting that the black middle class has always been in a constant process of out-migration as it attempts to leave poor neighborhoods "but has never been able to get very far," and while black middle-class enclaves have developed in close proximity to poor neighborhoods, as the number of black middle-class persons has increased, the size of black middle-class enclaves has expanded and created greater physical separation in an otherwise contiguous "Black Belt").

28. Myron Orfield, *American Metropolitics: The New Suburban Reality* (Washington, DC: Brookings Institution Press, 2002), 2. For the listing of "at-risk" suburbs in the D.C. metro area, see Metropolitan Area Research Corporation, "Washington D.C.-Baltimore Region: Community Classification," Metropolitan Area Research Corporation, http://www.metroresearch.org/maps/national_report/DC_clus.pdf (accessed August 24, 2003).

29. "The 2002 Challenge Index," *Washington Post*, December 5, 2002; Jay Mathews, "High Schools Aim for More College-Level Classes," District Extra, *Washington Post*, December 5, 2002; *Washington Post*, "School Guide: Washington Area Education," *Washington Post*, http//www.washingtonpost.com/wp-dyn/education/schoolguide/ (accessed January 26, 2004).

30. Avis Thomas-Lester, "Fleeing Residents Cite County's Shortcomings, Schools, Lack of Amenities Criticized," *Washington Post*, June 21, 2001.

31. Ibid.

32. For information about individual schools see *Washington Post*, "School Guide."

33. Dalton Conley, *Being Black, Living in the Red: Race Wealth and Social Policy in America* (Berkeley: University of California Press, 1999), 68–79.

34. Fedstats, "Crimes Reported in Prince George's County, Maryland, Crime 2000," http://www.fedstats.gov/mapstats/crime/county/24033.html (accessed February 15, 2004) (showing 72 murders and 4,174 aggravated assaults); Fedstats, "Crimes Reported in Montgomery County, Maryland, Crime 2000," http://www.fedstats.gov/mapstats/crime/county/24031.html (accessed February 15, 2004) (showing 12 murders and 973 aggravated assaults).

35. Todd Shields, "For Some Black Pr. Georgians, Charles Is a Better Place to Be," *Washington Post*, June 22, 1997 (noting the increased migration of upwardly mobile African Americans from Prince George's County to Charles County).

36. Nancy Burns, *The Formation of American Local Governments: Private Values in Public Institutions* (Oxford: Oxford University Press, 1997).

37. Cashin, *Middle Class Black Suburbs*, 758. In addition to the empirical studies cited in Cashin, see Andrew A. Beveridge and Jeannie D'Amico, *Black and White Property Tax Rates and Other Homeownership Costs in 30 Metropolitan Areas: A Preliminary Report* (New York: Queens College of the City University of New York, Department of Sociology, Program for Applied Social Research, 1994); also see Diana Jean Schemo, "Suburban Taxes Higher for Blacks, Analysis Shows," *New York Times*, August 17, 1994.

38. Thomas-Lester, "Fleeing Residents."

39. Golden, "Prince George's Convert," 36.

40. Sara Kehaulani Goo, "County Residents Hunger for More Dining Options," *Washington Post*, June 21, 2001. The Borders bookstore chain is a notable exception. It goes beyond market profiles and attempts to make its stores fit to the markets it finds. Using that method, Borders "dug deep" into Prince George's County to find a location that would enable it to reach affluent black customers, opening a store at the Boulevard at Capital Centre. Krissah Williams, "For Sales, Focus on Local Interests, Borders Tries New Marketing Approach in Prince George's," *Washington Post*, November 24, 2003.

41. Golden, "Prince George's Convert," 37.

42. For an extensive analysis of the phenomenon of commercial disinvestment in contemporary black suburbs and the likely reasons for such disinvestment, including the risk that racial information leads investors to undervalue the assets of blacks, see Mary Jo Wiggins, *Race, Class, and Suburbia: The Modern Black Suburb as a "Race-Making Situation," University of Michiagn Journal of Law Reform* 35 (2002): 749. One recent study of the ten-county Atlanta region found that residents of affluent black neighborhoods were more likely to have to leave their neighborhood and drive some distance in order to dine at a non-fast-food restaurant, to grocery shop, or to see movies as compared to residents of white neighborhoods that had *less* aggregate buying power. Ruling out income or buying power differences as an explanation, the researchers concluded that the disparity was likely due to "inaccurate or

stereotyped marketing profiles of black neighborhoods or racial bias in business decision making." Amy Helling and David S. Sawicki, "Race and Residential Accessibility to Shopping and Services," *Housing Policy Debate* 14, nos. 1–2 (2003): 69, 96–97.

43. Civil Rights Forum on Communications Policy, "When Being Number One Is Not Enough: The Impact of Advertising Practices on Minority-Owned and Minority-Formatted Broadcasting Stations" (online report, January 1999), http://www.fcc.gov/Bureau/Mass_Media/Informal/ad-study/adsynposis.html (accessed January 26, 2004). In one case, a firm was quoted as encouraging advertisers to avoid urban stations and "instead buy time on those that would offer 'prospects, not suspects.'" Paul Farhi, "Advertisers Avoiding Minority Radio: FCC Study Cites Washington Market for Black and Hispanic 'Dictates,'" *Washington Post*, January 13, 1999.

44. Robert D. Bullard, Glenn S. Johnson, and Angel O. Torres, "The Routes of American Apartheid," *Forum for Applied Research and Public Policy* 15, no. 3 (2000): 66–74.

45. Orfield and Ashkinaze, *The Closing Door*, 115–16, 127.

46. Thomas-Lester, "Fleeing Residents."

47. Sheryll Cashin, *The Failures of Integration: How Race and Class Are Undermining the American Dream* (New York: Public Affairs, 2004), 168–201.

48. Ibid., 289–332.

5

Walling In or Walling Out: Gated Communities

Edward J. Blakely and Thomas W. Sanchez

It has been four decades since the United States legally outlawed all forms of public discrimination—in housing, education, transportation, and accommodations. Yet today, we are seeing a new form of discrimination—the gated, walled, private community. Americans are electing to live behind walls with active security mechanisms to prevent intrusion into their private domains by people of different races and cultures. For the first time, through data in the American Housing Survey (AHS), we are able to examine the choices of an increasingly frightened middle class as it moves to escape school and neighborhood integration and to gain or secure the economic advantages of home appreciation.[1]

Gated communities are an increasingly popular form of residential space that restricts access so that normally public spaces are privatized. They are intentionally designed security communities with designated perimeters, usually walls or fences, and entrances controlled by gates and/or guards. They include both new suburban housing developments and older, inner-city areas retrofitted with barricades and fences.[2] These communities represent a different phenomenon than apartment or condominium buildings with security systems or a doorman. There, a doorman precludes public access only to a lobby or hallway—private space within a building. Gated communities preclude public access to roads, sidewalks, parks, open space, playgrounds—resources that usually would be open and accessible to all citizens in a locality.

Gates range from elaborate two-story guardhouses that are manned twenty-four hours a day to rollback, wrought-iron gates, to simple electronic arms. Entrances are usually built with one lane for guests and visitors and a second lane for residents, who open the gates with an electronic card, a punched-in code, or a remote control. Some gates with round-the-clock security require all cars to pass the guard, issuing identification stickers for residents' cars. Unmanned entrances have intercom systems, some with video monitors, for visitors asking for clearance.

Security mechanisms are intended to do more than just deter crime. They are security from the shared life of the city and from such annoyances as solicitors and canvassers, mischievous teenagers, and strangers of any kind, malicious or not. The gates provide sheltered common space, open space not penetrable by outsiders, for the residents of upper-end gated communities, who already can afford to live in low-crime environments, with greater protection from crime as well as increased social status.[3] American middle-class families are electing the security screen of gates. They are "forting up" in an attempt to escape the changing social and economic face of America.

SEPARATE SPACES

Americans are suburbanizing. Over half of non-Hispanic whites and 36 percent of blacks live in the suburbs.[4] African American (black) suburbanization is income stratified in much the same way as white.[5] As blacks suburbanize, like all races, some are electing to live in gated and walled security compounds, but not as much as other minorities. More Asians and a slightly larger share of Hispanics find gates and walls to be one of their best choices at many income levels, based on housing size, costs, and other factors.

The gating phenomenon among suburban blacks takes on several different characteristics with regard to status, income, and personal security. While some middle- and upper-income blacks may be seeking different economic destinies, they have not as yet elected separate social and locational outcomes for their families. This is an important distinction: since black social and family ties cross income levels by necessity, the selection of a gated community seldom has the same social-disconnecting feature that it does for whites and even some Hispanics and Asians. In this chapter we explore some of these differences.

WHO'S IN?

The latest drive to redefine territory and protect neighborhood boundaries is being felt in communities of all income levels throughout the metropolitan world. In the last twenty years, gated communities, one of the more dramatic forms of residential boundaries, have been springing up across the United States and the developed world. According to our analysis in *Fortress America* and confirmed in the 2001 AHS, gated and controlled-access communities contain almost 7 million Americans. In the United States, walling is not random. It is a highly geographic phenomenon. Most of the walled areas are in parts of the nation facing the highest influx of new immigrants: the West (11.1 percent), the South (6.8 percent), the Northeast (3.1 percent) and the Midwest (2.1 percent). In this era of dramatic demographic, economic, and social changes, there is a growing crisis of future expectation in American civic life.[6]

The AHS covered 119,116,517 housing units, 106,406,951 occupied year round, with 7,058,427 units or 5.9 percent indicating that they were surrounded by walls or fences and 4,013,665 units (3.4 percent) with controlled or guarded access. The largest, most racially volatile areas have the highest concentrations of walled communities. These metropolitan areas are usually entry points for new immigrants and places of high mobility for blacks and other minorities.

METRO-POTTING OR METRO-POLLUTING

In social justice terms, metro-potting means growing different people in different environments and metro-polluting refers to the sprawl and congestion caused by racial flight that is strangling us with polluted air and unlivable conditions. Gated communities are a response to the rising tide of fear. They can be classified in three main categories. First are the lifestyle communities, where the gates provide security and separation for the leisure activities and amenities within. These communities include retirement communities such as golf country clubs and resort developments. For prestige communities, the gates symbolize distinction; they attempt to create and protect a secure place on the social ladder. These communities include enclaves for the rich and famous, developments for the "top fifth," and executive subdivisions. Finally, there are security zones where community safety is the primary goal. They may be central city or suburban, rich or poor. In the first two community categories, the developer builds gates as an amenity along with an image that helps sell houses. In the latter category, residents build the gates, retrofitting their low-income neighborhoods to shield them from the outside world.

Rising Status Walls

Prestige communities are the fastest growing development forms around the world. These developments feed on the aspiration of exclusion and the desire to differentiate. The services of gate guards and security patrols add to the prestige of exclusivity; residents value the simple presence of a security force more than the service they actually provide. Except for the oldest developments, prestige communities tend toward ostentatious entrances and showy facades. They differ from lifestyle communities in that they do not boast extensive recreational amenities, although they do have carefully controlled aesthetics and often enviable landscapes and locations. Here gating is motivated by a desire to project an image, protect current investments, and control housing values.

Prestige communities include the enclaves where actors and sports stars tend to locate. Rock stars, tennis pros, and other celebrities live in secluded, gated communities to ward off unwanted admirers and to lead some semblance of a regular life without dealing with unwanted photographers and other people who attempt to penetrate their privacy.

New Towns

One type of lifestyle development is the New Town. The suburban, gated New Towns are large-scale developments, with as many as several thousand housing units, that attempt to incorporate residential, commercial/industrial, and retail activities within or adjacent to the development. New Towns are not new, but the gating of their residential areas is. Living in these large, planned communities has always reflected a certain lifestyle choice; now more of them are offering the option of totally gated subdivisions or cities, particularly on the East Coast in places like Celebration, the Disney community near Orlando.

The New Town has a hard time attracting middle-class blacks because to them the New Town seems like a place of racial and income isolation. For example, Celebration had to advertise for minorities, and even after extensive campaigns in the nearby communities, failed to attract many residents from the large pool of Hispanics and blacks in the immediate area.[7] Canyon Lake, California, one of the half dozen fully gated cities, has a demographic profile very different from its surrounding areas. African Americans account for less than 1 percent, Hispanics 8 percent of the nearly 10,000 residents, where the adjacent city of Lake Elsinore, California, has a population of 5.6 percent black and over 30 percent Hispanic, and the county of Riverside is 7 percent black and over 35 percent Hispanic.

Security Zones

Security zones are places where the fear of crime and outsiders is the foremost motivation for defensive fortifications, areas where most black and Hispanic inner-city families are forced to live. Here the residents add barriers to their neighborhoods with gates or barricades, erecting fortifications to regain control or to fend off some outside threat. By marking their boundaries and restricting access, they are often trying to build and strengthen the feeling and function of community in their neighborhood. Gating and street closures occur at all income levels and in all areas. Keeping people out or keeping them in is the major issue in inner-city gating.

In many major cities security fences have been placed around public housing units to the outrage of the inhabitants. Blacks in these public housing units see the fences as containment and prison environments rather than protection. In 2003, the Virginia Supreme Court upheld the right of public housing authorities to use fences, gates, and guards to restrict access to high-crime public housing facilities—a decision that has spawned lively debate. Some residents and their allies claim that these housing units will "have similar status at the affluent gated communities."[8] This is clearly hyperbole, but there is merit to making places safer for the residents. However, unwanted security has many detractors: Virginia public housing residents argue that the gates and guards will seem more like penitentiary guards than the community greeters in affluent neighborhoods.

METRO GATE PATTERNING

Gating is not a universal metropolitan phenomenon; it is very geographic. Even across the regional geographic landscape, gating is distinctly metropolitan. Gated communities are very common in metropolitan New York, Chicago, Phoenix, and in Miami and other southern seaboard cities. They remain rarities in the Midwest except around large cities like Chicago, St. Louis, and Detroit because these cities have large pools of minorities and rising tides of immigrants.

The AHS data suggest that gated communities are most often found in areas with certain characteristics: metropolitan regions; areas with high levels of demographic change, especially foreign immigration; areas with high median income levels; regions with extreme residential segregation patterns or without a clearly dominant white majority; areas with high crime rates and high levels of fear; and areas to which whites are moving, either for retirement or because of "white flight," for example, Californian migrants to Arizona, Nevada, and Oregon.

Gated Community Builders

For developers gated communities can be a marketing angle, another way to target specific submarkets, or a necessity to meet demand. Builders in Southern California report faster sales in gated communities, with quick turnover ensuring thousands in additional profits. The developers of gated communities also see themselves as providing security, especially to certain large, racially diverse metropolitan areas. Gated communities have targeted the elderly since the 1970s, and gated second-home complexes are also well established, but those in need of walls now include empty-nesters, who are likely to take frequent, long vacations, and young double-income families in which no one is home during the day. Security systems such as gates are viewed by seniors as freedom not only from crime but from such annoyances as noisy children and teenagers.

Most developers, with the exception of some apartment complexes, don't prominently advertise, nor do they promise absolute security in their promotional brochures. Even the most advanced security system cannot guarantee a crime-free community, and developers fear liability if they make such claims.[9]

There is little doubt that metropolitan urban problems are the stimuli for this wave of gating. In many of the metropolitan areas with large numbers of gated communities, the drive for separation, distinction, exclusion, and protection is fueled in part by dramatic demographic change. A high level of foreign immigration, a growing underclass, and a restructured economy are changing the face of metropolitan areas like Los Angeles, Miami, Chicago, and New York at a rapid pace. Southern California's San Fernando Valley, for example, was 95 percent white in 1950, but today it is barely half white.[10] Many of the states with large numbers of gated communities, such as Oregon, Arizona, Montana, and Nevada, are destination states for increasing numbers of white Californians fleeing the state.

The need for gates and walls is created and encouraged by widespread changes in the social and physical structure of the suburbs. U.S. suburbs are becoming urbanized, such that many might now be called, in Mike Davis's term, "outer cities," places with many of the problems and pathologies traditionally thought to be restricted to big cities.[11] Gates reflect increasing separation by income, race, and economic opportunity. For example, the largest metropolitan areas were in general only slightly less segregated in 2000 than in 1990.[12]

Suburbanization has not meant a lessening of segregation, but only a redistribution of the urban patterns of discrimination. Minority suburbanization is concentrated in the inner-ring and old manufacturing suburbs.[13] In Chicago, as in many metropolitan areas, the inner-ring suburbs are attracting increasing numbers of minorities and immigrants. During the 1980s, nearly as many whites moved out of suburban Cook County as moved out of the city of Chicago, with African Americans and Hispanics moving in.[14] Major cities like Chicago are the new archetype of metropolitan spatial segregation, in which poverty is no longer concentrated in the central city but is suburbanizing, racing farther and farther out in the metropolitan fringe. The extension of gating and walling becomes a new way of maintaining race and class across our largest metropolitan areas. Segregation by income and race has led groups within the hypersegregated environment to wall and se-

Table 5.1.   Top Ten Metropolitan Areas

Metropolitan Area	% Walled	% Controlled Access
Atlanta	7.4%	5.5%
Boston	3.5%	0.6%
Chicago	5.3%	1.3%
Dallas	17.8%	13.4%
Detroit	2.3%	1.2%
Houston	26.7%	21.9%
Los Angeles	18.2%	11.7%
New York	5.2%	1.7%
Philadelphia	2.0%	0.8%
Washington, D.C.	4.3%	2.6%

Source: American Housing Survey, 2001. Data compiled by Tom Sanchez, "Security vs. Status: The Two Worlds of Gated Communities," Metropolitan Institute, Virginia Tech, 2003.

cure their space against the poor—to protect wealth, as in Pacific Palisades on the California coast, or to protect property values in inner-city Los Angeles or the South Side of Chicago. Those who try to escape poverty by moving away use walls to prevent it from reaching their newfound oases. Walls and gates add to the hardening of racial and spatial distancing, as in the ten largest racially mixed metropolitan areas shown in table 5.1.

Structural segregation, when seen in the metropolitan context, leads to distinct gating phenomena. Those feeling threatened by *poverty race creep* have two options: to "fort up" in place, or to move to a perceived safe zone farther from perceived danger. The typical fort-in-place suburb is white; wealthy; and with homes in desirable locations close to water, woods, or hillside views. The working and middle classes without the resources to move fort up in their inner- and midring suburbs. Low-income groups are forced to live in public housing projects or opt to live in contained, walled security zones to ward off surrounding crime. Finally, there are the far exurbs where walls and gates are becoming increasingly common for standalone housing developments.

Fear is one of the prime motivators, along with newer homes and better prices, for most suburbanites. A survey exploring the motivations of people moving out of Chicago to the suburbs found that the push of crime was far more important than the commonly assumed pull of a better place to raise children. Interviews from the *Chicago Tribune* series on the survey are illustrative:

- "I wanted a large, fabulous house with a yard—and no poor people."
- "We became worn out by the traffic, parking hassles, noise, crime, lack of being able to *feel* safe, dirty streets, etc. We did not feel the city of Chicago was a good place to start a family."

• "The turning point was being caught in a crossfire between police and others while I was with my child . . . also, within the last year, I was mugged and my car was stolen."[15]

Although crime is actually declining, crime perception and fear remain high. Domestic terrorism threats and news accounts add to the perception when prognosticators theorize that core city areas are under the greatest threat. As a result, the combination of race, class, crime, and terrorism creates an irrational push to protect home and family. Gates are one response to these fears.

WHO'S OUT?

Gated communities in the United States go directly back to the era of robber barons, when the very richest built private streets to seal themselves off from the hoi polloi. During the twentieth century more gated, fenced compounds emerged to serve the needs of the East Coast, automobile, and Hollywood movie aristocracies. These early gated areas were different from the gated subdivisions of today; they were uncommon places for uncommon people. Now, the merely affluent and the middle class can erect barriers between themselves and undesirables.

As Gerald Frug of Harvard Law School points out, "[T]he spread of walled areas . . . raises a legal policy issue: what is the proper nature and extent of one's property rights? . . . I think these walled enclaves should be treated more like public space."[16] Moreover, there is an ominous tone of race and class associated with gating. When more young black men are in prison than in college, walls and gates mean something different to black Americans.[17] White, black, and Hispanic gate-controlled and walled communities differ by owner, renter, and income. But blacks are low in all categories.

From their earliest examples, the suburbs aimed to create a new version of the country estate of the landed gentry: a healthy, beautiful, protected preserve, far from the noise and bustle of the crowded city. But demographic, social, and cultural changes permeate society, changing and diversifying the suburbs. "Suburban" no longer connotes safe, beautiful, or ideal. As suburbs age and as they become more diverse, they are encountering problems once thought of as uniquely urban: crime, vandalism, disinvestment, and blight. Gated communities seek to counter these trends by maintaining the ambiance of exclusivity and safety the suburbs once promised. They exist not just to wall out crime or traffic or strangers, but to lock in economic position. Gated communities hope that greater control over the neighborhood will mean greater stability in property values. The majority of gated, controlled-access (usually with guards) community home owners are white with a median income of more than $100,000. Blacks and Hispanics have different reactions to community elitism. Blacks with high incomes seldom elect to remove themselves from the surrounding community, even when they achieve the income and other status indicators of their white counterparts.

One gated, high-end community resident explained the symbolism of the gate: "The gate is something of a fallacy," he said. "Every time you go through with your clicker or your card, the computer has your code, and they know when you're coming and when you're going. Personally, I have nothing to hide, but I don't think it's anyone's goddamn business when I'm coming or when I'm going, and I wouldn't like my neighbors having that information, or the association. I personally would find that offensive."[18] A sentiment expressed by many African Americans too.

High-income black and Hispanic home owners find the gate offensive for other reasons as well. They view their roles as citizen models. If they remove themselves from their heritage communities and move in with "whitey" (gringos), they lose this vital connection with their birth community. Many blacks and Hispanics who "make it," we found in researching *Fortress America*, remain pillars of their communities because they are connected through their professions: doctors, lawyers, educators, ministers, local business owners, high-level public servants, and others who serve their ethnic communities. As one African American in South Florida described the separate enclaves, "They are not comfortable with us and I am not comfortable with them."[19]

Gating, and to some extent suburbanizing, represents a distancing from the community that is the foundation of the success of higher-income blacks and Hispanics. This is not to say that they feel compelled to live with the lowest-income groups. They can continue as role models living in racially diverse or even high-income racially separate suburbs. But closing themselves off could backfire and make them less popular in the very communities they represent to the broader population. Finally, the gates and guards are too symbolic of racial and economic divides that include slavery, racial stereotyping, and antidemocratic values. And for some Hispanic leaders, walls and gates recall the deeply polarized societies of Central and South America, which they left to seek a better, freer, less class-conscious way of life.

WHO HAS WHAT, WHERE?

Hispanics are more likely than blacks to live in gated compounds. We speculated that Hispanics, as recent arrivals, may be more likely to be confined to the inner-city, low-income, multifamily rental market where perimeter fences and locked gates to ward off crime are common. Thus we should see some differences in the gated form of housing by city and suburb for Hispanics. That is, Hispanic renters might live in gated, central-city compounds and be a smaller proportion of the residents in gated or walled suburban areas.

To test this hypothesis, we looked at the suburban/city gated percentages for the ten cities shown in table 5.1. We were unable to look at the suburbs of each city since the number of cases in the survey for the non-central-city areas is small. Table 5.2 shows that location is important for whites and Hispanics but not for blacks. Our general hypothesis is correct. However, Hispanic renters tend to make up a larger portion than blacks in gated central-city areas in all income categories.

Black attitudes toward the appearance and symbolism of the prisonlike gates seem to trump all other features of living in this form of community.[20] As one commentator put it regarding this issue, "[W]hen we feel we need to put barriers between ourselves and our neighbors, something is wrong with the American Dream."[21] The basic reason for these differences in housing preferences is that only black athletes, entertainers, and high-visibility personalities feel they can justify to themselves and to their heritage members the need to retreat from the public.

Blacks who are less visible, we speculate, tend to see the gates as barriers to civic engagement and as symbols of the plantation, racial separation, and segregation. Further, the gate-guarded areas present a dilemma for blacks who view being stopped by guards as opportunities for "racial profiling." As Frug argues, "the walls that surround privatized areas do more than relocate those identified as potential criminals . . . they have an important psychological impact on insiders as well. . . . They enable the property owners to assert more extensive property rights against outsiders than those that the legal system actually authorizes."[22]

WALLS AGAINST CRIME

Realistically, crime is a far greater problem for lower-income people than for higher-income groups. Data from the 1999 Bureau of Justice Statistics National Crime Victimization Survey indicate that crime is also a greater problem in cities than in suburbs or rural areas.[23] The rates for both violent crime and household crime (e.g., burglary) are about 35 percent lower in suburbs than in cities. City residents are one and a half times more likely than suburbanites to be a victim of a violent crime or a household burglary. Yet gates are primarily a suburban phenomenon. The real danger of crime bears no relationship to the fear of crime, a fear that can spur the gating of neighborhoods that were once open to their surroundings.

Table 5.2. **Suburban/City Gated/Walled Percentages for Top Ten Cities**

Top 10 Metros: Black Households—Owners

Weighted N = 1,484,228	Central City		Suburb	
	% Gated	% Walled	% Gated	% Walled
Income Quartile				
First	1.0%	2.9%	0.0%	0.0%
Second	0.0%	1.0%	0.0%	5.0%
Third	3.6%	8.8%	0.0%	1.5%
Fourth	1.1%	5.2%	0.0%	4.1%
All	1.4%	4.5%	0.0%	3.0%

Top 10 Metros: Nonblack Households—Owners

Weighted N = 7,592,840	Central City		Suburb	
	% Gated	% Walled	% Gated	% Walled
Income Quartile				
First	3.9%	8.0%	1.5%	3.8%
Second	4.2%	9.6%	1.8%	3.0%
Third	3.8%	6.6%	1.0%	4.8%
Fourth	3.3%	5.2%	0.8%	2.4%
All	3.7%	6.9%	1.1%	3.3%

Top 10 Metros: Hispanic Households—Owners

Weighted N = 949,579	Central City		Suburb	
	% Gated	% Walled	% Gated	% Walled
Income Quartile				
First	0.0%	14.9%	1.5%	4.8%
Second	0.0%	14.2%	1.8%	5.7%
Third	3.1%	3.2%	1.0%	10.6%
Fourth	2.3%	4.1%	0.8%	4.9%
All	1.5%	8.6%	1.1%	7.2%

Source: American Housing Survey, 2001.
Note: The top ten metros are: Atlanta, Boston, Chicago, Dallas, Detroit, Houston, Los Angeles, New York, Philadelphia, and Washington, D.C.

The results of our survey in *Fortress America* of home owner association boards in gated communities show that security is a primary concern for those who buy property in gated communities. Nearly 70 percent of respondents indicated that security was a very important issue in the ultimate decision of residents to live in gated communities. Only 1 percent thought security was not an important motivation.

But security does mean something to all gated-community residents, and it is spelled out in their perceptions of criminality. Recent data support the contentions of gated home owners in some high-crime areas that gates do count. Data from the high-crime South Florida area indicate that gates do protect but not perfectly. All communities experienced some crime. For the victim, one crime is too many, so it is hard to say whether residents can gain much comfort from the data. Few crimes occur at home and people have to leave their compounds and go into the wider community where they are just as likely to be a victim as anyone else. So, the data are somewhat misleading because we would have to find comparable communities for a true test.

In *Fortress America*[24] we found that community location, not gates, made the difference in crime rates. Within a half-mile to one-mile radius of gated communities, crime rates are generally the same with or without a gate. Further, it is noteworthy that the largest gated communities in this small sample have relatively high crime rates. Thus, it can be reasonably argued that crime is a function of size. However, most Americans react to the *image* of crime and criminality. Image means color and class in this country.

We found an excellent example of the criminal imaging of walled-in residents in our research for *Fortress America* in an older, downtown section of Palm Springs, California. One resident in this mixed-race, gated neighborhood described the gate effect as "a boon if you're a widow or a widower. I am not as apprehensive here coming into my house, it's a lot more safe feeling." One of the men seconded her relief. "Before it was gated, I had to keep everything locked. There were transients coming through, walking up and down the street. You can't question them, 'what are you doing here?' because these are public streets, or they were . . . now it's a good secure feeling."

Everyone in the sample group had experienced break-ins or robberies in the past, and they spent several minutes telling stories of past crimes. They believe that there is a real increase in security with gates, not just a psychological effect. Most significantly, they said traffic dropped by 75 percent, and that alone meant fewer strangers. Nonetheless, fences can be jumped, as one woman pointed out. "*Two Mexicans* have been coming to the park around eleven o'clock at night to drink beer by the pool." The property manager hadn't heard of this, although it had been going on for nearly a week, and she promised to watch for them that night and call the police (the development had no roving patrol or guards). She noted that no development can promise "security," to which one man responded that there are "federal prisons they call 'maximum security' and they break out of there!"[25] These comments are dripping with racial overtones.

Basically, crime is moved but not controlled by gates and guards. To some extent this is precisely what activists opposed to gating in the black and Hispanic communities contend. Sanchez and Lang's review of the AHS data of thirty-four variables of home owner or renter characteristics reinforces the above observations. They found that gated communities differed from ungated ones in people's acceptance of restrictions imposed through home owner rules in order to live in communities that had fewer signs of physical deterioration and in their perception that their communities possessed better neighborhood police protection.[26] But renters in gated and controlled-access communities perceived a high level of crime in the communities where they resided.[27] This is very likely a result of the locations of rental properties in high-crime areas, whereas gated home owner areas are in the suburbs away from crime.

WALLS AND GATES POLICY IN BLACK AND WHITE

Since the September 11, 2001, terrorist attack, more people feel vulnerable in the face of rapid change and the real or imagined threats of urban terrorism. Gated and barricaded communities are themselves a microcosm of a larger spatial pattern of segmentation and separation. The growing divisions between city and suburb, rich and poor are creating new patterns that reinforce the cost that isolation and exclusion impose on some while benefiting others. The actual crime statistics contradict the gated-community assertions of a need for further protection. Crime in every form is down across the nation. In fact, crime is very unlikely in the suburban areas where most gated communities are located. But crime in this case is definitely racially associated.

Residents of gated communities in our research pointed to the gates as protection against "those people," a not-so-subtle code for minorities who might come into their inner sanctum and commit acts of violence. As one young black expressed his visit to a gated compound in Seattle, "The guard was now visibly upset by my question, thinking perhaps that I was up to something, the vapor of some menacing crime loomed all around me. Why is a young black man [here]. Am I being fooled into letting down my guard and exposing my privileged patrons to the dangers of the streets?"[28]

These "turf wars," while most dramatically manifested by the gated community, are a troubling trend for the reemergence of racially inspired land use planning. As citizens separate themselves into homogeneous, independent cells, their ties to the greater polity and society become attenuated, increasing their resistance to efforts to resolve municipal, let alone regional, problems. Today, both new and old problems of race and class are joined with terrorism and immigration to make a more complex network of attitudes that drive the gating phenomenon.

In the suburbs, gates are the logical extension of the original suburban drive. In the city, gates and barricades are sometimes called "cul-de-sac-ization," a term that clearly reflects the design goal of creating a suburblike street pattern out of the existing urban grid. Gates and walls are an attempt to suburbanize our cities. Neighborhoods have always been able to exclude potential residents through housing costs. Now, gates and walls exclude not only undesirable new residents, but even casual passers-by and people from the neighborhood next door.

The exclusivity of gated communities goes beyond the question of public access to streets. Gated communities are yet another manifestation of the trend toward privatization of public services—the private provision of recreational facilities, open space and common space, security, infrastructure, even social services and schools. Gated communities substitute for or augment public services with services provided by the home owner association. The same is true of all the private-street subdivisions that are now the dominant form of new residential development. But in gated communities, this privatization is enhanced by physical control of access to the development.

The trend toward privatized government and community is part of the more general trend of fragmentation; the resulting loss of connection and social contact is weakening the bonds of mutual responsibility and the social contract. The weakening social contract is illustrated by the self-interested nature of gated-community residents, who increasingly act as a group to vote against public expenditures for the total community.

The basic problem is that in gated communities and other privatized enclaves, the local community that many residents identify with is the one within the gates. Their home owner association dues are like taxes; their responsibility to their community, such as it is, ends at the gate. One city official in Plano, Texas, summed up the attitude of the gated-community residents in his town: "I took care of my responsibility, I'm safe in here, I've got my guard gate; I've paid my (home owner association) dues, and I'm responsible for my streets. Therefore, I have no responsibility for the commonweal, because you take care of your own."[29]

Residents of gated communities, like other people in cities and suburbs across the country, vary in the degree to which they feel the connections and duties of community within and outside of their developments. The primary difference is that in gated communities, with their privatized streets, recreation, local governance, and security, residents have less need of the public realm outside the gates than residents of traditional open neighborhoods. If they choose to withdraw, there are fewer ties to break, less daily dependence on the greater community.

As one resident of Blackhawk, a gated country club development in Northern California with a white, high-income majority told us, "People are tired of the way the government has managed issues . . . because you don't really have control over how the money is spent. . . . I feel disenfranchised . . . if the courts are going to release criminals, and we're going to continue not to prosecute people and continue to spend money the way we've been spending it, and I can't impact it, [at least here] in Blackhawk . . . I have a little control over how I live my life."[30]

This Blackhawk resident speaks for millions of white Americans who are using public policy to "fort up." This phenomenon has enormous policy consequences: In allowing some citizens to secede from public contact by internalizing and excluding others from sharing in their economic and social privilege, it aims directly at the conceptual base of community and citizenship in America. The old notions of community mobility and mutual responsibility are loosened by these new community patterns. What is the measure of nationhood when the divisions between neighborhoods require armed patrols and electric fencing to keep out other citizens? When public services and local government are privatized, when the community of responsibility stops at subdivision gates, what happens to the function and the idea of a social and political democracy? Can this nation so divided by gates and walls offer the dream of equality to all? If we lose this dream, what is the case and cause for this nation where all men are supposedly equal?

NOTES

1. HUD User Policy Development Research Information Service, *American Housing Survey* (Washington, DC: U.S. Department of Housing and Urban Development, 2002).

2. Edward J. Blakely and Mary Gale Snyder, Interviews in gated communities in 1995 for *Fortress America* (Washington, DC: Brookings Institution, 1997).

3. Edward J. Blakely and Mary Gale Snyder, *Fortress America* (Washington, DC: Brookings Institution, 1997).

4. U.S. Census Bureau, *Annual Demographic Supplement to the March 2002 Current Population Survey*, figure 2 in the Black Population in the United States (Washington, DC: U.S. Census Bureau, April 2003), 2.

5. Ibid., 2.

6. HUD User Policy Development Research Information Service, *American Housing Survey*.

7. "Integrated Community Is Part of Trend Toward Suburban Segregation," *New York Times*, September, 23, 2001, C12.

8. George van Delaras, "Gated Communities for the Poor, a New Phenomena in Public Housing," E. Web Conversation Root Article, 2003 http://www.e-thepeople.org/article/2034/view?viewtype (accessed March 15, 2004).

9. Blakely and Snyder, Interviews in gated communities in 1995 for *Fortress America*.

10. Jocelyn Stewart, "Valley Being Balkanized by Name Changes," *Los Angeles Times*, September 11, 1991, B1.

11. Mike Davis, *City of Quartz: Excavating the Future in Los Angeles* (New York: Verso, 1990).

12. U.S. Census Bureau, *Annual Demographic Supplement*, 2.

13. Douglas S. Massey and Nancy A. Denton, *American Apartheid: Segregation and the Making of the Underclass* (Cambridge, MA: Harvard University Press, 1993).

14. Greg Hinz, "Moving Violation," *Chicago Tribune*, March 1994, 21.

15. Patrick T. Reardon, "Fear, Anger, Regret: Ex-Chicagoans Speak Out," *Chicago Tribune*, November 29, 1993.

16. Gerald Frug, "Citizens and Property Rights: Beyond Walled Enclaves," *Re-Vista: Harvard Review of Latin America* (Winter 2003): 1–2.

17. Van Delaras, "Gated Communities for the Poor, a New Phenomena in Public Housing."

18. Blakely and Snyder, Interviews in gated communities in 1995 for *Fortress America*.

19. "Integrated Community Is Part of Trend Toward Suburban Segregation," C12.

20. Van Delaras, "Gated Communities for the Poor, a New Phenomena in Public Housing."

21. Jonathan Chisdes, "Gated Communities Promote False Security, Segregation," *Content of Character*, September 20, 2000, http://ww.chisdes.com/gated.html (accessed May 27, 2004).

22. Frug, "Citizens and Property Rights: Beyond Walled Enclaves," 2.

23. Bureau of Justice Statistics, *National Crime Victimization Survey* (Washington, DC: U.S. Department of Justice, 1999).

24. Blakely and Snyder, Interviews in gated communities in 1995 for *Fortress America*.

25. Blakely and Snyder, Interviews in gated communities in Palm Springs, June 8, 1995, for *Fortress America*.

26. Thomas W. Sanchez and Robert E. Lang, "Security versus Status: The Two Worlds of Gated Communities," Census Note Metropolitan Institute, Virginia Tech, 2003, 12.

27. Ibid., 12.

28. Charles Maude, "A Tale of Two Gated Communities: An African Memoir," *Radical Urban History: An e Journal* 6, at http//ww.rut.com (accessed May 16, 2004).

29. Blakely and Snyder, Interviews in gated communities in Plano, Texas, September 5, 1995, for *Fortress America*.

30. Blakely and Snyder, Interviews in gated communities in Blackhawk, April 11, 1995, for *Fortress America*.

6

Spatial Mismatch and Job Sprawl

Michael A. Stoll

Over the past few decades, a central feature of metropolitan life for African Americans is the extent to which they face employment challenges. For example, over the past twenty years, the black employment rate (or the fraction of the population that is employed) for adult men and women has been consistently about twenty and eight percentage points, respectively, lower than that for comparable whites.[1] During the latter half of the twentieth century, changes in the spatial location of employment opportunities within metropolitan areas have served to increase the physical distance between predominantly black residential areas and the locations of important employment centers. Despite moderately increasing rates of residential mobility to the suburbs over the past few decades, black residential locations have remained fairly centralized and concentrated in older urban neighborhoods of the nation's metropolitan areas, but employment has continuously decentralized toward metropolitan-area suburbs and exurbs.

Many argue and document that this "spatial mismatch" between the location of blacks and jobs is in part responsible for the stubbornly inferior labor market outcomes experienced by African Americans. Given the difficulties of reserve commuting to suburbs in many metropolitan areas, coupled with the fact that high proportions of blacks do not own cars, such spatial mismatch disconnects blacks from many jobs for which they may be suited, thereby increasing their employment difficulties.[2]

This chapter provides an exploratory analysis of whether sprawl is associated with the spatial isolation of blacks from jobs. There has been growing attention to the varied impacts of sprawl, understood here as low-density, geographically spreading patterns of development. Some have engaged in debate about how to measure sprawl[3] and whether it is increasing,[4] while others have examined its causes, such as the role of government policy, and preferences and discrimination.[5] Some have attempted to identify the impacts of sprawl, for example on increasing health problems, pollution, concentrated poverty, and other concerns,[6] but few have done so systematically, and few have focused on race, with some exceptions.[7]

This chapter seeks to add to this literature by systemically exploring whether metropolitan areas that are characterized by more sprawl are also those areas where blacks are more spatially isolated from jobs. A priori, one might expect this to be the case. After all, the spatial mismatch hypothesis is predicated on the notion that metropolitan areas are growing and that new employment opportunities disproportionately locate on the suburban fringe. To the extent that sprawl characterizes suburban development, such employment opportunities will locate in areas far from areas where blacks are concentrated, thereby increasing their physical isolation from jobs. This is likely to be especially true if racial discrimination in suburban (and particularly exurban) housing markets persists, thereby limiting blacks' ability to move near these growing areas of opportunity.

On the other hand, it is plausible that sprawl could reduce blacks' physical isolation from jobs. As Kahn[8] argues, sprawl is likely to increase housing affordability by producing housing rapidly relative to demand. He demonstrates that blacks' housing consumption, especially their home ownership rates, is greater in metropolitan areas with higher rather than lower levels of sprawl. To the extent that the homes that blacks locate to in sprawling metropolitan areas are disproportionately located in suburban areas, their physical proximity to growing suburban employment centers is likely to be reduced, thereby reducing mismatch for blacks. Hence, it is an empirical question as to whether sprawl further spatially isolates blacks from jobs.

The remainder of the chapter proceeds as follows. First, the measures of sprawl and mismatch used in the analysis are discussed and defined; then, the average levels of sprawl and mismatch are estimated and compared across metropolitan areas defined by size and region. Next, the chapter systematically examines the relationship between sprawl and mismatch conditions for blacks and compares these to those for Latinos and whites. Finally, the paper explores heterogeneity in the relationship between sprawl and the blacks/jobs mismatch across different characteristics of metropolitan areas and examines one mechanism, racial segregation, that could influence the relationship between sprawl and the mismatch. The conclusion then follows.

MEASURING SPRAWL AND SPATIAL MISMATCH

While there is currently an ongoing debate about the definition of sprawl, in this chapter, sprawl is defined as a dimension of concentration and centralization of employment activity within and across metropolitan areas. More precisely, sprawl is measured as the percent of jobs that are located outside of a five-mile radius centered on the metropolitan area's central business district (CBD).[9] This measure of sprawl has been used elsewhere,[10] and it is highly correlated with other concepts of sprawl, such as the concentration/centralization of people (since the spatial distribution of all people and all jobs are highly correlated), and with measures typically used by economists to measure employment density, such as spatially based employment density gradients.[11]

Thus, this measure has a straightforward interpretation: lower percentages of a metropolitan area's employment located outside the five-mile ring around the CBD implies lower sprawl, while higher sprawl is associated with higher percentages of a metropolitan area's employment located outside the five-mile ring. For example, table 6.1 shows a sprawl measure of 57.8 in the Northeast, indicating that about 57.8 percent of jobs in metropolitan areas in the Northeast are located outside of the five-mile ring centered on CBDs

Table 6.1. Average Levels of Sprawl and Mismatch by Metropolitan Statistical Area Size and Region, 2000

		Total Jobs Mismatch for:		
	Sprawl	*Blacks*	*Whites*	*Latinos*
All MSAs	63.2	53.5	33.8	44.1
Larger MSAs (500,000 People or More)	69.5	56.5	35.6	45.8
Region:				
Northeast	57.8	64.2	32.7	54.6
Midwest	64.1	61.4	31.6	48.8
South	64.4	45.9	35.8	38.7
West	64.3	52.1	34.7	44.0
Black Population Size:				
Less than 10,000	33.9	30.3	25.8	28.9
10,000 to 100,000	49.6	42.2	30.6	38.1
Greater than 100,000	71.3	55.9	36.3	47.3
Percent MSA Black:				
Less than 5 percent	46.5	38.0	29.2	36.3
5 to 10 percent	63.7	51.7	32.9	44.8
Greater than 10 percent	67.4	54.5	35.8	46.9

Notes: Sprawl is defined as the fraction of jobs in metropolitan areas that is located outside of a five-mile radius centered on the central business district.

The sprawl measure is weighted by metropolitan area total population size.

The people/jobs mismatch for each racial/ethnic group is weighted by each respective racial/ethnic group's metropolitan area population size.

$N = 267$ metropolitan areas.

of metropolitan areas in this region. Table 6.1 also shows a sprawl index of 64.4 in the South, indicating that levels of sprawl are higher in the South than in the Northeast.

The data used to construct this measure of sprawl come from the U.S. Department of Commerce's 1996 ZIP Code Business Patterns and provide information on total employment counts by zip code. Zip code business pattern data are extracted from the Standard Statistical Establishments List, a file maintained and updated by the Census Bureau of all known single and multiestablishment companies. The data to calculate each zip code's distance from the CBD come from Chu.[12] With these data, the percent of jobs within metropolitan areas that are located outside the five-mile radius of the CBD can be calculated.[13]

Of course, this measure of sprawl has some potential problems. Most importantly, this measure could depend on and be correlated with the metropolitan area's population size. In a larger metropolitan area, or as the metropolitan area grows, one might expect that the employment share within the five-mile radius will be lower. This is because the five-mile radius around the CBD is fixed, while suburban boundaries may grow. This is of concern because the development patterns informing the growth of larger metropolitan areas need not be characterized by sprawl. This concern is addressed in this chapter by including controls for population size and land area (in square miles) in the analysis. But because metropolitan areas that are large, growing rapidly, or spread out over large expanses of land could also have gotten that way through sprawl development patterns, the estimates of the relationship between sprawl and mismatch shown here are likely to be conservative, once population and area size are taken into account.

The measure of mismatch between blacks and jobs is based on the index of dissimilarity, which is most well known in the social science literature as a measure of residential segregation between groups. The mismatch index of dissimilarity measures the degree of segregation between blacks and jobs and has been used elsewhere to measure spatial mismatch.[14] This index is calculated using data on jobs from the 1999 Zip Code Business Patterns files and data on people from the 2000 U.S. Census for the 267 metropolitan statistical areas in the United States included in this analysis. A technical discussion of the dissimilarity index along with a detailed discussion of the data sources used is presented in the technical appendix.

The dissimilarity index ranges from 0 to 100, with higher values indicating greater segregation between people and jobs. Hence, the index value between blacks and jobs for all metropolitan areas in the United States describes the extent to which the areas (measured as zip codes) where blacks tend to reside are different from the areas in which jobs are located.[15] In the analysis, mismatch indexes are presented for total jobs and retail jobs. Indexes based on total employment provide an overall measure of the imbalance between people and jobs. Indexes based on retail employment provide estimates of the geographic imbalance between people and relatively low-skilled jobs, since a large fraction of retail jobs are low skilled. Retail jobs account for about 18 percent of jobs in the United States.[16]

The actual numerical value of the dissimilarity index has a convenient interpretation. Specifically, the index can be interpreted as the percent of either the black population or of jobs that would have to relocate to different areas to completely eliminate any geographic imbalance. For example, as table 6.1 indicates, the 2000 index value describing the imbalance between the residential distribution of blacks and jobs is 53.5. This indicates that in 2000, about 54 percent of blacks would have had to relocate within the metropolitan area to be spatially distributed in perfect proportion with the geographic distribution of jobs.

In the remainder of this chapter, the average values of sprawl and mismatch in the United States will be examined. Then, metropolitan areas with high and low levels of sprawl and mismatch, and their overlap, will be identified. Next, the analysis will explore the systematic relationship between mismatch and sprawl and how this relationship may vary with characteristics of metropolitan areas such as their region, size, and the fraction of their population that is black. Finally, the chapter investigates the potential mechanisms by which sprawl might affect blacks' spatial isolation from jobs, focusing on the role of racial residential segregation.

CHARACTERIZING SPRAWL AND MISMATCH

Table 6.1 presents the average levels of sprawl and mismatch (for blacks, whites, and Latinos) in the United States. These average values are weighted by the metropolitan area's population size. For all metropolitan areas combined, the average sprawl level is 63.2, indicating that on average about 63 percent of metropolitan area jobs lie outside the five-mile radius of the CBD. As suggested earlier, larger metropolitan areas, here shown as those with a population of 500,000 or more, have higher levels of sprawl. In larger metropolitan areas, about 70 percent of metropolitan area jobs lie outside the five-mile radius of the CBD.

Table 6.1 shows that sprawl varies across regions in the United States. In particular, the Northeast is characterized by less sprawl, while the South (and West and Midwest) show higher levels of sprawl. While one might speculate that the differences in sprawl across regions are accounted for by the age of metropolitan areas, this is not the case, as the age of the metropolitan area's major city is largely uncorrelated with sprawl.[17]

Sprawl is also higher in metropolitan areas that have larger African American populations and where the percentage of the population that is black is larger. To be sure, this could be an artifact of the fact that metropolitan areas with larger black populations are also larger metropolitan areas more generally, and that these areas, as noted previously, are likely to be characterized by sprawl. Another story is that sprawl might be greater in such areas because whites might be prompted to move farther from the urban core as a consequence of their racial residential preferences. That is, as blacks reach a certain percentage in the metropolitan areas, whites, especially those who harbor preferences not to live near African Americans, may choose to live in suburban and exurban areas far from these groups, thereby providing the demand for developers and local government to build in sprawl-like manner.

Table 6.1 also presents average values of mismatch between people and total jobs for blacks, whites, and Latinos. These averages are weighted by the metropolitan area population counts for the racial/ethnic group being described by the index.[18] Perhaps the most striking pattern observed in table 6.1 is the clear racial/ethnic differences in the degree of mismatch between people and jobs, with blacks the most spatially isolated from jobs. This pattern is also true in each region. In 2000, the overall mismatch index for blacks indicates that more than 50 percent of blacks would have had to relocate to even out the distribution of blacks relative to jobs. The comparable figure for whites is twenty percentage points lower at 33.8. The degree of geographic mismatch from employment opportunities experienced by Latinos lies between the values for whites and blacks. The value for Latinos is 44.1.

Despite these patterns, recent research has indicated that over the 1990s, modest improvements occurred in blacks' proximity to employment. This occurred as a result of blacks' increased residential mobility within metropolitan areas over the 1990s, and not because jobs began to relocate to black neighborhoods during this period of robust economic growth. That is, the residential mobility of blacks from mostly central cities to suburban areas over the 1990s, and not job generation in black communities, helped lower mismatch levels over the 1990s, though only minimally. Still, as the bottom panel of table 6.1 shows and as Raphael and Stoll[19] confirm, the mismatch between blacks and jobs is most severe in areas where a relatively large percentage of the population is black and where the absolute value of the black population is large.

Table 6.1 shows that mismatch levels for blacks vary by region. Mismatch levels are higher in the Northeast and Midwest than in the West and South, where they are the lowest. Interestingly, despite blacks' high rate of net inmigration to the South over the 1990s, where mismatch levels for blacks are much lower, this migration accounted for very little of the decline in mismatch observed for blacks over this period.[20] Racial residential segregation patterns across regions are one potential factor that might help account for the observed variation in mismatch by region for blacks. As noted earlier, racial segregation in housing markets strongly contributes to the mismatch between blacks and jobs, and this segregation is higher in the Northeast and Midwest than the West and especially the South.[21]

The variation in mismatch levels across regions is much greater for blacks than whites, and slightly more so than for Latinos. Indeed, whites' mismatch levels are low to begin with and do not vary much across regions. On the other hand, the patterns in the variation of mismatch for Latinos are very similar to those of blacks, just at slightly lower levels.

Finally, a comparison of the patterns of sprawl and mismatch for blacks across regions provides some interesting insight into the potential direction of this relationship. While sprawl is lower in the Northeast than in the South, the mismatch index for blacks shows the opposite pattern. One might be tempted to conclude that the expected direction of sprawl and mismatch is negative given these patterns, suggesting that sprawl improves blacks' spatial proximity to jobs. This conclusion would be premature since within a region, patterns of sprawl and mismatch across metropolitan areas could be very different, but this view provides the biggest contribution to this relationship. In the following section, this relationship between sprawl and mismatch is explored more directly and in more detail.

Before this examination, however, we look at the fifteen metropolitan areas with the highest and lowest levels of sprawl and mismatch between blacks and jobs. This analysis includes only larger metropolitan areas, or those with 500,000 or more people. Table 6.2 lists these areas and shows some interesting patterns. First, the variation in sprawl and mismatch levels is much greater for those metropolitan areas with high rather than low levels of these indexes. That is, low-sprawl areas range from 8.6 percent to 50 percent, a gap of about forty-one percentage points, while the equivalent gap for high-sprawl areas is nearly twenty points. Still, at the extremes, Ann Arbor is nearly an all-sprawl metropolitan area, while Jersey City is characterized by almost no sprawl. Alternatively, in Milwaukee, blacks are nearly perfectly segregated from jobs, while in Greenville, blacks are much more proportional to the spatial distribution of jobs.

There are a number of metropolitan areas that overlap across high and low distinctions of sprawl and mismatch. Table 6.2 shows where areas are characterized either by both high sprawl and mismatch or by both low sprawl and mismatch. Detroit, St. Louis, and Philadelphia are characterized by high sprawl and also have high levels of blacks/jobs mismatch. On the other hand, Bakersfield, Albuquerque, McAllen, and Fresno are low-sprawl areas that have low levels of mismatch.

Quite interestingly, there are metropolitan areas where the opposite patterns occur. Greensboro and Riverside are characterized by high-sprawl patterns but have low levels of mismatch between blacks and jobs. On the

Table 6.2. Metropolitan Areas with the Fifteen Highest and Lowest Levels of Sprawl and Mismatch, 2000 (Metropolitan Areas with Population Size of 500,000 or More)

A. Sprawl

High		Low	
1. Ann Arbor, MI	98.1	1. Jersey City, NJ	8.6
2. *Detroit, MI*	90.7	2. Honolulu, HI**	25.1
3. Greensboro, NC*	90.6	3. Fort Wayne, IN**	34.6
4. Riverside, CA*	87.6	4. *Bakersfield, CA*	34.7
5. Hartford, CT	86.6	5. Colorado Springs, CO	36.4
6. Los Angeles, CA	86.4	6. *Albuquerque, NM*	37.8
7. West Palm Beach, FL	86.2	7. Las Vegas, NV	38.7
8. Tampa, FL	86.2	8. *McAllen, TX*	39.4
9. Atlanta, GA	85.1	9. New York, NY**	41.4
10. *St. Louis, MO-IL*	82.8	10. Syracuse, NY	41.7
11. New Haven, CT	82.7	11. Wichita, KS	44.1
12. Allentown, PA	81.0	12. Sarasota, FL	48.2
13. Oakland, CA	80.9	13. Tacoma, WA	48.8
14. Dallas, TX	80.2	14. Columbia, SC	49.9
15. *Philadelphia, PA*	79.4	15. *Fresno, CA*	50.0

B. Blacks/Jobs Mismatch

High		Low	
1. Milwaukee, WI	72.4	1. Greenville, SC	27.0
2. *Detroit, MI*	71.4	2. Tucson, AZ	28.3
3. Fort Wayne, IN**	70.9	3. Charleston, SC	30.4
4. New York, NY**	70.3	4. *Albuquerque, NM*	34.2
5. Chicago, IL	69.5	5. Charlotte, NC	34.5
6. Buffalo, NY	68.3	6. Columbia, SC	34.9
7. Newark, NJ	65.2	7. Raleigh-Durham, NC	35.3
8. Miami, FL	64.7	8. Norfolk, VA	36.2
9. Omaha, NE	64.7	9. Wilmington, DE	36.6
10. Kansas City, KS	64.4	10. *McAllen, TX*	37.5
11. *Philadelphia, PA*	64.2	11. Greensboro, NC*	38.3
12. Honolulu, HI**	63.2	12. *Bakersfield, CA*	38.4
13. Denver, CO	62.6	13. *Fresno, CA*	40.5
14. *St. Louis, MO-IL*	62.6	14. Phoenix, AZ	41.6
15. Dayton, OH	62.4	15. Riverside, CA*	41.7

Notes: Metropolitan areas in italics indicate both high sprawl and high mismatch, or both low sprawl and low mismatch.
* Indicates metropolitan areas with both high sprawl and low mismatch.
** Indicates metropolitan areas with both low sprawl and high mismatch.

other hand, Fort Wayne, New York, and Honolulu indicate high levels of black/jobs mismatch but are characterized by low-sprawl patterns.

One factor that could account for these patterns is racial residential segregation. For example, though not shown here, the index of dissimilarity between blacks and whites in 2000 in Greensboro and Riverside is 59.0 and 46.2, respectively, somewhat lower than the black/white segregation index for U.S. metropolitan areas as a whole (60.4). On the other hand, the index of dissimilarity between blacks and whites in Fort Wayne (70.9), New York (81.8), and Honolulu (the exception at 35.8) is in general higher than that for U.S. metropolitan areas as a whole.[22] Thus, these patterns raise the interesting question of to what extent sprawl is related to racial segregation and whether this relationship is weaker or stronger than that between residential segregation and blacks/jobs mismatch. These questions will be explored later in the analysis.

IS SPRAWL RELATED TO THE BLACKS/JOBS MISMATCH?

To assess whether sprawl is in any way related to the mismatch between blacks and jobs, figure 6.1 presents a scatter plot of the sprawl index values for the 267 metropolitan areas in the sample against the mismatch index values for blacks for these areas. The scatter plot also includes a trend line that is fitted to the data using a simple linear regression, whose equation is presented in the lower right panel of the graph.

As can be seen, sprawl is positively and significantly correlated with mismatch conditions for blacks. This indicates that metropolitan areas that are characterized by more sprawl are also characterized by greater levels of mismatch between blacks and jobs. Conversely, metropolitan areas that are characterized by less sprawl are also characterized by lower levels of mismatch between blacks and jobs. The coefficient estimate on sprawl from a regression equation predicting mismatch for blacks is shown in the graph and is statistically highly significant. It indicates that an increase in the sprawl index by 10 percentage points (or about the difference in sprawl conditions between Philadelphia and Detroit—see table 6.2) is associated with a 3.1 percentage point increase in mismatch conditions for blacks. Moreover, as indicated by the R^2, sprawl by itself accounts for about 27 percent of the variation in the mismatch index for blacks.

Though not shown here, even when population size of metropolitan areas is controlled for, there remains a statistically significant relationship between mismatch and sprawl, with a coefficient estimate on sprawl of 0.22. This indicates that once population size is taken into account, an increase in the sprawl index by 10 percentage points is associated with a 2.2 percentage point increase in mismatch conditions for blacks. So although population size of

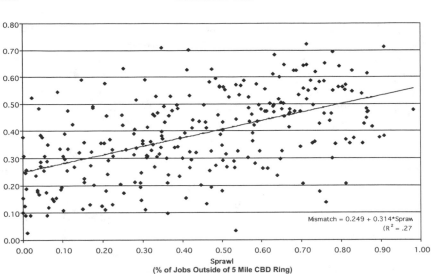

Figure 6.1.   Blacks/Jobs Mismatch Versus Urban Sprawl in U.S. Metropolitan Areas, 2000
Note: Correlation is statistically significant at below the 0.001 percent level.

metropolitan areas does account for some of the observed relationship between sprawl and mismatch (about 29 percent), it does not explain all.

Sprawl may not be uniquely associated with mismatch conditions for
blacks. Conceivably, sprawl could harm other groups that might experience
some residential concentration in the urban core, such as Latinos, and
could even harm whites if development patterns at the metropolitan fringe
occur rapidly and with very low density. Thus, figures 6.2 and 6.3 are also
presented to show the association between sprawl and mismatch conditions for whites and Latinos, respectively. Figure 6.2 presents this association for whites and shows that sprawl is slightly positively correlated with
their mismatch conditions. However, this association is not statistically significant, as shown in the regression equation. Moreover, sprawl accounts
for only about 6 percent of the variation in the mismatch index for whites,
as indicated by the R^2.

The pattern for Latinos is more similar to that of blacks than whites. Figure 6.3 presents the association between sprawl and mismatch conditions
for Latinos. Like blacks, sprawl is positively and significantly correlated with
mismatch conditions for Latinos, but the strength of the relationship is
weaker than that for blacks. The regression equation indicates that an increase in the sprawl index by 10 percentage points is associated with a 1.8
percentage point increase in mismatch conditions for Latinos (3.1 for
blacks). Moreover, sprawl accounts for about 15 percent of the variation in
the mismatch index for Latinos, much less than the 27 percent for blacks.
Like blacks, however, this relationship remains statistically significant even

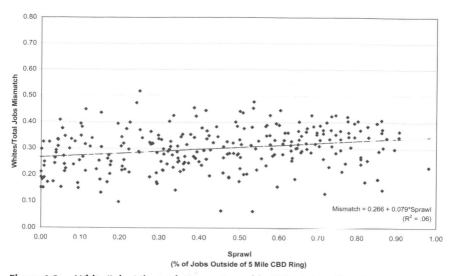

Figure 6.2.   White/Jobs Mismatch Versus Sprawl in U.S. Metropolitan Areas, 2000
Note: Correlation is not statistically significant.

when one controls for the population size of metropolitan areas. Though not shown, when this is done, the coefficient estimate on sprawl is 0.10, indicating that population size of metropolitan areas accounts for about 44 percent of the association between sprawl and mismatch for Latinos, a much larger percentage than that for blacks.

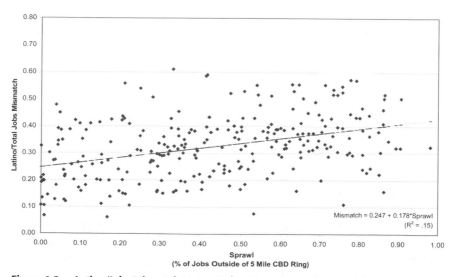

Figure 6.3.   Latino/Jobs Mismatch Versus Urban Sprawl in U.S. Metropolitan Areas, 2000
Note: Correlation is statistically significant at below the 0.001 percent level.

To summarize, a simple and direct examination of the relationship between sprawl and mismatch conditions reveals that sprawl is positively and significantly related to mismatch for blacks, and to a lesser extent Latinos, but not whites. This relationship holds for blacks and Latinos even when the population size of metropolitan areas is taken into account. Though not definitive, these patterns suggest that as metropolitan areas become more sprawled, blacks', and to a lesser extent Latinos', spatial isolation from employment does not improve, it worsens. Given these patterns, a number of descriptive questions emerge, such as whether or how these patterns, especially for blacks, vary with the characteristics of metropolitan areas. The next section of the chapter explores these questions by examining potential variations in the relationship between sprawl and mismatch conditions for blacks by the regional and population characteristics of metropolitan areas.

SPRAWL, MISMATCH, AND REGIONS

As shown earlier in table 6.1, the average values of the sprawl and the blacks/jobs mismatch indexes across regions suggested that sprawl improves blacks' spatial proximity to jobs. While the previous analysis documents that this is not the case for metropolitan areas as a whole, in this section the relationship between sprawl and mismatch is examined more rigorously across regions. In this section and for much of the remainder of this chapter, results from regression equations predicting the blacks/jobs mismatch index are presented because of its presentation and interpretation ease.

Figure 6.4 presents the coefficient estimates on sprawl that are based on regression equations predicting mismatch for blacks for each major region in the United States. Estimates are shown for the mismatch index for blacks for total jobs and for retail jobs. These estimates (especially those for total jobs mismatch index) are directly comparable to those presented in the lower right panel of figure 6.1. However, in these regression equations, controls are included for metropolitan-area population and land-area size, and thus the figures shown here are conservative estimates of the relationship between sprawl and mismatch as discussed earlier.

The coefficient estimates for sprawl shown in figure 6.4 indicate that there is variation in the relationship between sprawl and mismatch across regions. For both the total jobs and retail jobs mismatch index for blacks, the association between sprawl and mismatch is much stronger in the Northeast and the Midwest than in the West and South. Still, sprawl is strongly related to mismatch in the West, particularly for total jobs. This relationship is the weakest in the South. Indeed, the coefficient estimate on sprawl in the South for the blacks/retail trade mismatch index is not statistically significant (i.e., indicating no relationship between these two factors).

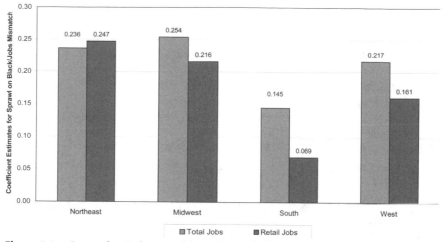

Figure 6.4. Regression Estimates of Sprawl (% of Jobs 5 Miles outside of CBD Ring) on Blacks/Jobs Mismatch by Region
Notes: All estimates include controls for metropolitan area population and land area size. All coefficient estimates are statistically significant at least at the 10 percent level.

Thus, although sprawl levels are lowest and mismatch levels (for blacks) highest in the Northeast, the relationship between these two factors is strongest in this region. One potential explanation for this apparent incongruence is racial segregation patterns. Racial segregation levels between blacks and whites are higher in the Northeast and Midwest than elsewhere such that it may be more difficult and challenging for blacks to move to outer-suburban areas in these regions (for a variety of reasons not discussed here) even when metropolitan areas in the Northeast are characterized by lower levels of sprawl.[23]

SPRAWL, MISMATCH, AND POPULATION SIZE CHARACTERISTICS OF METROPOLITAN AREAS

The relationship between sprawl and mismatch conditions for blacks could vary across the size of metropolitan areas. This could be true despite evidence provided above that the relationship between these two factors remains statistically significant even after controlling for the population size of metropolitan areas. This is because sprawl and the population size of metropolitan areas are highly correlated, as indicated above. Indeed, the correlation coefficient between the sprawl index used in this analysis and the population size of metropolitan areas is .50 and statistically significant. Given these factors, we might expect that sprawl is most strongly related to mismatch for blacks in larger metropolitan areas, especially since racial residential segregation is higher in larger metropolitan areas.

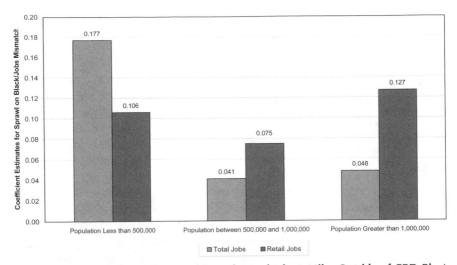

Figure 6.5. Regression Estimates of Sprawl (% of Jobs 5 Miles Outside of CBD Ring) on Blacks/Jobs Mismatch by Metropolitan Size
Notes: All estimates include controls for metropolitan land area size and region. All coefficient estimates are statistically significant at least at the 10 percent level.

Figure 6.5 presents the results of regression equations that summarize the relationship between sprawl and mismatch for blacks by the size of metropolitan areas. Small metropolitan areas are classified as those with less than 500,000 people, while medium and large metropolitan areas are classified as those with populations between 500,000 and 1 million, and over 1 million, respectively. The regression equations that generate the coefficients on sprawl control for metropolitan-area land-area size and region, but not population size, for obvious reasons.

First, the results indicate differing patterns of the relationship between sprawl and mismatch across these areas for mismatch indexes using total and retail trade jobs. Sprawl is most strongly and positively related to blacks' mismatch from retail trade jobs in larger metropolitan areas (as expected), and to a lesser extent in small metropolitan areas. On the other hand, sprawl is most strongly related to blacks' mismatch from total jobs in smaller metropolitan areas. The reasons for the latter observation are not clear from these data, however.

Instead, sprawl may be more strongly related to mismatch conditions for blacks in metropolitan areas that have larger black populations or that are blacker as a percentage. This is because in such metropolitan areas existing color barriers may be more extreme, thus making it more difficult for blacks to move to (suburban or exurban) areas with growing employment opportunities. Figures 6.6 and 6.7 present the coefficient estimates on sprawl from regression equations that summarize the relationship between sprawl

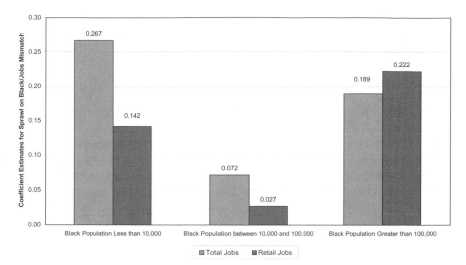

Figure 6.6. Regression Estimates of Sprawl (% of Jobs 5 Miles Outside of CBD Ring) on Blacks/Jobs Mismatch by Metropolitan Black Population Size
Notes: All estimates include controls for metropolitan population and land area size and region. All coeffi cient estimates are statistically significant at least at the 10 percent level

and mismatch for blacks by the size of the black population and the per-centage of the metropolitan area that is black, respectively.

The results in figures 6.6 and 6.7 show mixed support for this idea. Sprawl is most strongly related to mismatch conditions for blacks in metropolitan areas with large black populations (greater than 100,000) for retail jobs, but not for total jobs (though sprawl is still strongly related to mismatch in these areas). But sprawl is not the most strongly related to mismatch conditions in metropolitan areas with a large percentage of blacks (over 10 percent). Al-ternatively, sprawl is strongly related to mismatch conditions for blacks (for both total and retail trade jobs) in metropolitan areas with smaller (less than 10,000) black populations and where blacks represent a modest fraction of the metropolitan area's population (between 5 and 10 percent) for reasons that are not altogether clear.

THE INFLUENCE OF RACIAL SEGREGATION

Racial segregation is one mechanism that could influence the relationship between mismatch and sprawl. In large part, and as the spatial mismatch hypothesis suggests, the degree of mismatch experienced by blacks across metropolitan areas is strongly related to the extent of racial segregation. In areas where blacks are more segregated from whites, blacks are also more centralized in metropolitan areas and largely physically more isolated from

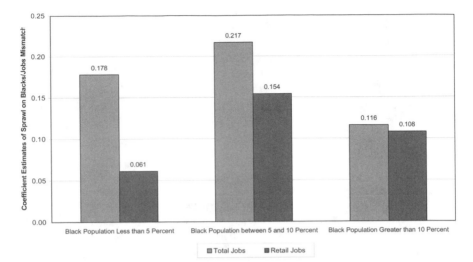

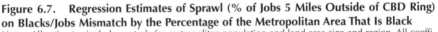

Figure 6.7. **Regression Estimates of Sprawl (% of Jobs 5 Miles Outside of CBD Ring) on Blacks/Jobs Mismatch by the Percentage of the Metropolitan Area That Is Black**
Notes: All estimates include controls for metropolitan population and land area size and region. All coefficient estimates are statistically significant at least at the 10 percent level.

job-generating suburban areas that are typically located on the suburban fringe (and where a disproportionate share of whites live). Thus, metropolitan areas that are characterized by more sprawl could be areas where blacks are located farther from employment centers partly because such metropolitan areas may also be more racially segregated.

Figure 6.8 presents results of a variety of coefficient estimates from a variety of regression equations aimed at addressing these questions. All regression equations control for metropolitan-area population and land-area size, and region. The first column on the left of the figure presents the coefficient estimate of the index of dissimilarity between blacks and whites (i.e., a measure of racial segregation) from a regression equation predicting the blacks/jobs mismatch index used throughout this analysis. Consistent with the spatial mismatch hypothesis, this estimate indicates that racial segregation is strongly related to blacks' mismatch from total jobs. This estimate indicates that a 10 percentage point increase in the index of dissimilarity between whites and blacks is associated with an 8.2 percentage point increase in the index of dissimilarity between blacks and jobs, all else being equal. Thus, racial segregation is strongly related to mismatch conditions for blacks.

The remaining columns in the figure show the coefficient estimates of sprawl from separate regression equations predicting segregation measures (i.e., indices of dissimilarities) among different racial/ethnic groups. The coefficient estimate on sprawl indicates that sprawl is significantly and pos-

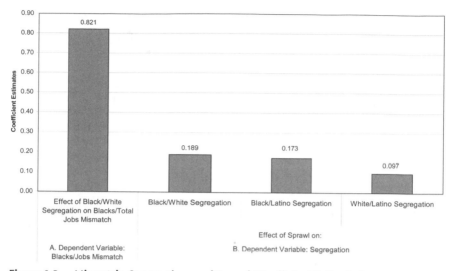

Figure 6.8.   Mismatch, Segregation, and Sprawl (Coefficient Estimates)
Notes: All estimates include controls for metropolitan area population size and land area, and region. The segregation measures are indexes of dissimilarity. All coefficient estimates are statistically significant at least at the 10 percent level except the estimate of sprawl on white/Latino segregation.

itively related to racial segregation between blacks and whites. This estimate indicates that a 10 percentage point increase in sprawl conditions across metropolitan areas is associated with a 1.9 percentage point increase in the index of dissimilarity between blacks and whites, all else being equal.

This result qualifies recent research on the effect of sprawl on increasing black housing consumption.[24] It suggests that while sprawl may indeed positively influence blacks' housing consumption as a result of its influence in lowering housing prices, such consumption is taking place in or near existing black residential communities and not in suburban areas that are disproportionately white (for a variety of reasons not discussed here). This may result in increased racial segregation between blacks and whites.

But the causal arrow of the relationship between sprawl and residential segregation is not clear. On the other hand, it could also be the case that racial segregation patterns influence sprawl. Whites, especially those with strong preferences to live far from blacks, may attempt to further isolate themselves from blacks by increasingly moving to the suburban fringe or by supporting policies that promote growth and/or limit blacks' access to the suburbs, such as restrictions on low-income housing developments.

Sprawl is also positively related to segregation between blacks and Latinos, but not between whites and Latinos. Indeed, the figure indicates that a 10 percentage point increase in sprawl conditions across metropolitan areas is associated with a 1.7 percentage point increase in the index of dissimilarity between blacks and Latinos, all else being equal. These results suggest that sprawl may also be positively influencing Latinos' housing consumption as a result of lower housing prices, but that unlike blacks, Latinos are more likely than blacks to consume housing in suburban areas that are disproportionately white. It is an open question as to whether the difference between where blacks and Latinos are locating across areas characterized by sprawl is a function of racial housing discrimination against blacks in suburban areas or to differences in the preferences between blacks and Latinos for neighborhoods that are predominantly white.

CONCLUSIONS

This chapter has provided an exploratory analysis of the relationship between urban sprawl and the spatial mismatch between blacks and jobs. Much attention has been paid recently to the question of sprawl, especially whether it is increasing and what its impacts are on social and economic life. This chapter has looked at the connection between sprawl and race to evaluate the welfare impacts of sprawl on blacks in the employment sphere. The direction of the influence of sprawl on such mismatch was less than clear. On the one hand, sprawl could further isolate blacks from jobs if racial segregation is a persistent, structural feature of metropolitan life. On the other hand, sprawl could lessen blacks' isolation from jobs if sprawl improves housing affordability and (as a result) blacks move disproportionately to suburban areas where employment is disproportionately located.

The results of the chapter show a few clear patterns. The results reveal that urban sprawl is positively and significantly related to mismatch conditions for blacks, and to a lesser extent Latinos, but not whites. But sprawl is highly correlated with the size of metropolitan areas in the United States, leading one to speculate that higher mismatch conditions for blacks in more sprawled areas was driven by the size of metropolitan areas. This was not the case. In fact, the relationship between sprawl and mismatch held for blacks and Latinos even after the population size of metropolitan areas was taken into account, though the relationship became somewhat weaker as a result. Thus, these findings strongly suggest that as metropolitan areas become more sprawled, blacks', and to a lesser extent Latinos', spatial isolation from employment worsens.

The results also revealed variations in the strength of this relationship across characteristics of metropolitan areas. The relationship between sprawl and mismatch conditions for blacks was found to be stronger in the Northeast than in other regions. This was true despite the fact that average levels of sprawl are lower there than the other regions. Sprawl is also a much more strongly related mismatch condition for blacks in metropolitan areas that have larger black populations. Both of these patterns are likely to be strongly influenced by racial residential segregation. Such segregation is higher in these metropolitan areas than elsewhere and as such may serve to limit blacks' residential mobility to suburban areas despite the possibility that housing, especially suburban housing, may be more affordable in metropolitan areas characterized by higher rather than lower sprawl.

Thus, the results of this chapter strongly suggest that urban sprawl negatively affects blacks' physical isolation from jobs and therefore may be a chief contributor to the continuing employment difficulties of African Americans. But the important question that emerges from this view is how sprawl might matter. The results suggest that in areas with greater sprawl racial segregation between blacks and whites is also higher. Since black/white segregation is strongly related to mismatch conditions for blacks, sprawl appears to limit blacks' physical access to jobs by increasing segregation.

How does sprawl increase segregation? The answer to this question is not clear from the data, but one possibility is that whites' preferences to live far from blacks are driving sprawl. Alternatively, it could be that sprawling areas develop disproportionately single-family housing that may limit blacks' access to suburbs as a result of affordability issues, though the support of developing this kind of housing could be related to whites' racial preferences as well. Still, what is clear is that more research needs to be conducted to examine how, why, and in what other domains sprawl might affect African Americans.

TECHNICAL APPENDIX

Description of the Dissimilarity Index between People and Jobs

Data on population and job totals for subgeographic units of the metropolitan area are used to calculate the dissimilarity index described in the main text. In this chapter, the data are measured at the zip code level for the 267 metropolitan areas included in the analysis. The equation for the dissimilarity index is quite straightforward. Define *Black$_i$* as the black population residing in zip code *i* (where *i* = (1, . . . ,*n*) and indexes the zip codes in a given metropolitan area), *Employment$_i$* as the number of jobs in zip code *i*, *Black* as the total black population in the metropolitan area, and *Employment* as the total number of jobs in the metropolitan area. The dissimilarity score between blacks and jobs is given by

$$(1) \quad D = \frac{1}{2} \sum_i \left| \frac{Black_i}{Black} - \frac{Employment_i}{Employment} \right|.$$

As written, the dissimilarity index ranges between 0 (perfect balance) and 1 (perfect imbalance). In the text and figures presented above, this figure is multiplied by 100. This transformation allows one to interpret the index values as the percent (rather than the proportion) of either of the populations that would have to move to yield perfect balance.

Population data tabulated at the zip code level from the 2000 U.S. Census of Population and Housing is used; in particular, the 2000 population data come from the 2000 Summary Tape Files 1. The jobs-people mismatch indexes are calculated for whites and blacks. For the 2000 census, racial background is defined as those that marked one race alone. Those who marked more than one race are not used in these calculations.

The employment data comes from the 1999 ZIP Code Business Patterns files. The ZIP Code Business Patterns files provide an actual enumeration of the number of jobs located in each zip code in the country. Hence, data from the 1999 ZIP Code Business Patterns files are used to measures total employment. For the total employment/population mismatch indexes, the 1999 employment data are matched to the 2000 population data. In the main text, the mismatch indexes are referred to by whether the employment data used are total employment or retail employment.

Description of the Dissimilarity Index among People

Similarly, to measure racial segregation, the dissimilarity score is also used but between racial groups. To measure the dissimilarity score between blacks and whites (or Hispanics or Asians) the following equation is used:

$$(2) \qquad D = \frac{1}{2} \sum_i \left| \frac{Black_i}{Black} - \frac{White_i}{White} \right|.$$

As written, the dissimilarity index ranges between 0 (perfect balance) and 1 (perfect segregation). Again, in the text and figures presented above, this figure is multiplied by 100. This transformation allows one to interpret the index values as the percent (rather than the proportion) of either of the populations that would have to move to yield perfect balance.

NOTES

1. Michael A. Stoll, *African Americans and the Color Line* (New York: Russell Sage Foundation and Population Reference Bureau, 2004).

2. There is a large and established literature on why and how space matters in employment. It establishes that time and money costs of travel and information limit the distances workers are willing or able to commute to get to work, especially for those workers that are low-skill or young. Public transit increases the time cost

of travel, as does how far workers must commute to employment opportunities. Purchasing and maintaining a car, as well as paying for gas and insurance, increases the money cost of travel. Furthermore, distance from employment opportunities raises the costs of getting information about these jobs. As any of these costs rise, workers will be less willing to travel an additional mile.

3. Russ Lopez and H. Patricia Hynes, "Sprawl in the 1990s: Measurement, Distribution, and Trends," *Urban Affairs Review* 38, no. 3 (2003): 325–55; Hal Wolman, George Galster, Royce Hanson, Michael Ratcliffe, and Kimberly Furdell, "Measuring Sprawl: Problems and Solutions," paper presented at the Association of Collegiate Schools of Planning, Baltimore, MD, November 2002.

4. Edward Glaeser and Matthew E. Kahn, "Decentralized Employment and the Transformation of the American City," *Brookings-Wharton Papers on Urban Affairs* 2 (2001): 1–64.

5. Gregory D. Squires, "Urban Sprawl and the Uneven Development of Metropolitan America," in *Urban Sprawl: Causes, Consequences, and Policy Responses*, ed. Gregory D. Squires (Washington, DC: Urban Institute, 2002), 1–22; David Rusk, *Inside Game Outside Game: Winning Strategies for Saving Urban America* (Washington, DC: Brookings Institution, 1999); Kenneth Jackson, *Crabgrass Frontier: The Suburbanization of the United States* (New York: Oxford University Press, 1985).

6. Robert D. Bullard, Glenn Johnson, and Angel Torres, *Sprawl City: Race, Politics and Planning in Atlanta* (Washington, DC: Island Press, 2000); R. Heinlich and W. Andersen, *Development at the Urban Fringe and Beyond: Impacts on Agriculture and Rural Land*, ERS Agriculture Economics Report no. 803 (Washington, DC: U.S. Department of Agriculture, 2001); David J. Cieslewicz, "The Environmental Impacts of Sprawl," in *Urban Sprawl: Causes, Consequences, and Policy Responses*, ed. Gregory D. Squires (Washington, DC: Urban Institute, 2002), 23–38; Paul A. Jargowsky, "Sprawl, Concentration of Poverty, and Urban Inequality," in *Urban Sprawl: Causes, Consequences, and Policy Responses*, ed. Gregory D. Squires (Washington, DC: Urban Institute, 2002), 39–72.

7. john a. powell, "Sprawl, Fragmentation, and the Persistence of Racial Inequality: Limiting Civil Rights by Fragmenting Space," in *Urban Sprawl: Causes, Consequences, and Policy Responses*, ed. Gregory D. Squires (Washington, DC: Urban Institute, 2002), 73–118.

8. Matthew E. Kahn, "Does Sprawl Reduce the Black/White Housing Consumption Gap?" *Housing Policy Debate* 12, no. 1 (2001): 77–86.

9. The CBD is a specific geographic area whose spatial boundaries are defined by the U.S. Census Bureau and is that area within the central city of a metropolitan area commonly referred to as downtown. The locations of the CBDs in this analysis are drawn from the 1982 Economic Census, *Geographic Reference Manual* (Washington, DC: U.S. Bureau of the Census, 1993).

10. Kahn, "Does Sprawl Reduce the Black/White Housing Consumption Gap?"; Glaeser and Kahn, "Decentralized Employment and the Transformation of the American City."

11. See Glaeser and Kahn, "Decentralized Employment and the Transformation of the American City."

12. Chenghuan Chu, *Employment Decentralization* (undergraduate thesis, Harvard University, Department of Economics, 2000).

13. Chu provided these data to Matthew E. Kahn to calculate these measures.

14. Steve Raphael and Michael A. Stoll, *Modest Progress: The Narrowing Spatial Mismatch between Blacks and Jobs in the 1990s* (Washington, DC: The Brookings Institution Center on Urban and Metropolitan Policy, 2002).

15. To be sure, a mismatch index based on the dissimilarity measure does not actually measure the physical distance between the average member of a given population and jobs. The index measures the imbalance across geographic subunits of the metropolitan area (for example, zip codes or census tracts) between members of the population and jobs. To take an extreme example, suppose that all black residents resided in one zip code of a city while all jobs were located in a different zip code. Whether these two zip codes are one mile apart from one another or twenty miles apart will not influence the dissimilarity measure. In both instances, the dissimilarity index will be equal to 100. Nonetheless, as a summary measure, the dissimilarity measure does allow comparisons across geographic areas.

16. Bureau of Labor Statistics, *Employment and Earnings* (Washington, DC: U.S. Department of Commerce, 2001).

17. Glaeser and Kahn, "Decentralized Employment and the Transformation of the American City."

18. Weighting the calculation of the average will place more weight on metropolitan areas with large populations. For example, New York, Chicago, and Atlanta will all receive relatively large weights in the calculation of the black mismatch measures, given the relatively large black populations of these cities. The weighting permits us to interpret the patterns in table 6.1 as the average degree of mismatch experienced by the typical member of each group.

19. Raphael and Stoll, *Modest Progress*.

20. Stoll, *African Americans and the Color Line*; Raphael and Stoll, *Modest Progress*.

21. See Joe T. Darden, "Residential Apartheid American Style," chapter 3 of this volume, 2007.

22. Data on black/white index of dissimilarity for 2000 for each metropolitan area mentioned here come from the Lewis Mumford Center for Comparative Urban and Regional Research website. These data are available at http://mumford1 .dyndns.org/cen2000/data.html (accessed March 29, 2004).

23. See Darden, "Residential Apartheid American Style"; Edward Glaeser and Jacob Vigdor, *Racial Segregation in the 2000 Census: Promising News* (Washington, DC: The Brookings Institution Center on Urban and Metropolitan Policy, 2001).

24. Kahn, "Does Sprawl Reduce the Black/White Housing Consumption Gap?"

7

Atlanta: A Black Mecca?

Robert D. Bullard, Glenn S. Johnson, and Angel O. Torres

Metropolitan Atlanta has experienced constant growth since the 1900s. The region has grown in population at an annual rate of 2.9 percent since 1950. The 1960s were considered the boom years, in which Atlanta established its regional dominance. The 1970s and 1980s were characterized as a time when the city became increasingly black. During this same period, the city experienced a steady decrease in its share of the metropolitan population since 1960. Metropolitan Atlanta continued to experience breakneck growth from the 1990s through 2004.[1]

An average of 87,000 people moved into the metropolitan area each year during the 1990s, compared to 61,788 in the 1980s.[2] The region has gained more than 77,000 new residents each year since 2000. The ten-county metropolitan area (Cherokee, Cobb, Douglas, Clayton, Fayette, Fulton, Henry, Gwinnett, DeKalb, and Rockdale) had a population of over 3.7 million people in 2004.[3] The twenty-eight-county metropolitan statistical area (MSA) of Atlanta grew from 4.2 million in 2000 to 4.7 million in 2004—making it the eleventh largest MSA in the United States.[4] Planning officials' estimates indicate that the area will receive another 2.3 million people by 2030.[5]

During 2000–2004, African Americans, Hispanics, and other racial minorities accounted for more than 80 percent of population growth in the twenty-eight-county Atlanta MSA. In 2000, whites represented 71 percent of the area's population. Today they make up 57 percent of the 4.7 million people in metropolitan Atlanta.[6] Each year, the region adds about 100,000 people, the vast majority moving into the suburban and exurban counties surrounding the city. Four of every five of the newcomers are racial and ethnic minorities.[7]

Atlanta proper is only the forty-first-largest city in the nation, largely due to its suburban sprawl development patterns and the city's inability to annex surrounding unincorporated areas as in the case of Houston, Phoenix, and San Diego. According to the Atlanta Regional Commission's (ARC) 2006 population estimates, the city's population of 451,600 is higher than it has been in at least twenty-five years. During 2000–2004, the Atlanta metropolitan area added over 183,000 African Americans. The number of new African Americans to the region was nearly twice the number of African Americans who moved into the next fastest-growing metro area for African Americans in the United States, Miami–Fort Lauderdale. Atlanta moved from having the seventh-largest population in 1990 to having the third-largest in 2004.[8]

Today, white school-age children in the region are in the minority—making up just 49.8 percent of that age group. If current trends continue, Atlanta will soon overtake Chicago in total black population. The Miami metropolitan area was second, adding nearly 97,000 blacks during the five-year period. Miami rose from having the eighth-largest black population in 2000 to sixth in 2004. The city of Atlanta added nearly 10,000 people in 2005. Atlanta's population stood at 416,474 in 2000, 415,200 in 1990, 424,922 in 1980, and 495,039 in 1970.[9]

The in-migration of mostly well-heeled middle-income and upper-income newcomers is bringing new sources of revenue for the city to support roads, sewers, parks, schools, and other city services. The city's budget has risen 31 percent since 2000—from $448 million to $589 million in 2006. Not everyone sees these changes as a good thing—especially if that person is losing a home and the entire neighborhood can't pay their property taxes because of gentrification.

Property taxes have skyrocketed—making Atlanta unaffordable for many long-time African American residents.[10] Older neighborhoods are being taken over by mostly white childless couples, singles, and middle-age "empty nesters" who have grown weary of the gear-grinding commutes—the longest in the country. Conflicts abound between older residents who are struggling to stay in their in-town neighborhoods and newcomers who are intent on pushing them out to make way for their upscale "McMansions," large new houses that are far beyond the size of their older neighbors.

The face of Atlanta is rapidly changing. For the first time since the 1920s, the African American share of the city's population is declining and the white percentage is rising.[11] In 2004, African Americans were 54 percent of the city's population—down from 61 percent in 2000, and 67 percent in 1990. Changing demographics have created uncertainty in local Atlanta politics, where African Americans have dominated since 1973. Some African American community leaders warn of the dilution and possible demise of black power. They even suggest that Mayor Shirley Franklin, who is in her second term and cannot run again because of term limits, may be the last African American mayor for some time.

Even the Old Fourth Ward, the neighborhood where Dr. Martin Luther King Jr. was born, is less than 75 percent African American, down from 94 percent African American in 1990. The neighborhood has seen housing prices and property taxes skyrocket while low-rent apartments are demolished and replaced with new developments and new residents. *Black Commentator* writer Bruce Dixon describes the last thirty years of the "Black Mecca" as a "failure of the Black leadership class" to deliver significant benefits to the poor and working-class African Americans who have assisted and supported them in governing Atlanta.[12] Dickson writes:

> Maynard Jackson's former chief of staff Shirley Franklin today presides over 475,000 Atlantans in the hollowed out core of a metro area ten times that size. For a generation, Georgia's white business and political elite have relentlessly punished Atlanta for the sin of being ruled by black faces, confining most public and private investment to the sprawling suburban donut that surrounds the city. Hence metro Atlanta is the least densely populated of the nation's large cities. The airport, freeways and a small number of subway lines are already built.
>
> The only remaining goodies left to hand out in Shirley Franklin's Atlanta are the few remaining public services that can be privatized, the future tax revenue which can be diverted to favored bankers and middlemen via bond issues, and the land under the city itself, which can be eased into the hands of well-connected developers by a number of means.[13]

The legacy of past residential segregation as well as the more recent phenomenon of urban sprawl both work against inner-city blacks. This is the "Atlanta Paradox."[14] The "Black Mecca" leads the nation in numbers of African American millionaires; at the same time, it leads the nation in the percentage of its children in poverty. Mayor Maynard Jackson is heralded with making from thirty-three to thirty-five black millionaires during his administration. Andrew Young and Shirley Franklin kept the momentum going. On the other hand, in 2004, nearly half (48.1 percent) of Atlanta's black children lived in poverty.[15]

UNEVEN GROWTH AND UNEQUAL HOUSING

In the past, suburbanization largely meant out-migration of whites. However, the 1990s saw a sizable number of middle-income and poor black Atlantans also make the move to the suburbs. Middle-income blacks have found expanded home ownership opportunities in some Atlanta suburbs, while low-income blacks have found suburban rental units in the post–1996 Olympics apartment glut period. Nevertheless, suburban residence has translated into few economic gains for poor blacks who are "stuck in the burbs" long distances from jobs, public transit, and their informal community network.

Atlanta is encircled by the "Perimeter" Highway, Interstate 285, which delineates the majority-black interior of the city from the mostly white—though rapidly diversifying—suburbs. Many locals use the terms ITP (inside the Perimeter) and OTP (outside the Perimeter) to describe neighborhoods, residents, and businesses. Thus, the Perimeter often serves as a geographical, social, and racial "code" similar to that of the Capital Beltway around Washington, D.C.

New housing subdivisions mushroomed in Atlanta's suburbs, forests, and rural farmland. Eight of every ten new units built during the 1990–2000 period were single family.[16] The ten-county Atlanta metropolitan region added 180,425 housing units during the 2000–2004 period, a 13.6 percent increase. The bulk of the housing was concentrated in the northern Atlanta suburbs, north of I-285. One of every four housing units built in the region during the period was in Gwinnett County. Together, Gwinnett, Fulton, and Cobb counties accounted for nearly two-thirds of the region's net increase in housing during the period.[17] The housing inventory in north Fulton County more than doubled between 1990 and 2004.

Much of the housing boom passed over the city of Atlanta. The city added only 14,732 new housing units in the 2000–2004 period, or a 7.9 percent increase, compared to 41,983 units in Gwinnett (20.0 percent increase), 31,593 units in Fulton (9.1 percent increase), and 22,332 units in Cobb (9.4 percent increase).[18] These growth trends point to clear disparities between the mostly black city of Atlanta and its mostly white suburbs.

Black expansion into Atlanta's suburbs quite often reflected the segregated housing pattern typical of central-city neighborhoods. Segregated middle-income black suburban "enclaves" have become a common residential pattern. For example, south DeKalb rivals Prince George's County, Maryland, as one of the most affluent African American communities in the nation. Nevertheless, obstacles still keep many affluent and poor blacks out of the newer suburban developments, including low income, housing discrimination, restrictive zoning practices, inadequate public transportation, and fear.

Race matters in urban credit and insurance markets.[19] The insurance industry, like its housing industry counterpart, "has long used race as a factor in appraising and underwriting property."[20] Many inner-city neighborhoods are left with check-cashing stations, pawn shops, storefront grocery stores, liquor stores, and fast-food operations—all well buttoned up with wire mesh and bulletproof glass.[21] A 1996 *Atlanta Journal-Constitution* survey discovered stark disparities in property insurance rates between black and white Atlanta neighborhoods.[22] The redlining issue prompted newspaper reporter Shelly Emling to title her story: "Insurance: Is It Still a White Man's Game?"[23] Emling answered her question as follows: "Insurance companies create pricing zones that are mostly white or mostly black, and home owners in the black zones are paying top dollar."[24]

Insurance redlining is not isolated to an individual insurance agent. The practice is widespread among big and small companies. The largest insurance companies in Georgia (i.e., State Farm, Allstate, Cotton States, Cincinnati Insurance, and USAA) routinely charge consumers 40 to 90 percent more to insure homes in Atlanta's predominantly black neighborhoods than for similar or identical houses in mostly white suburbs.[25] The premium disparity holds true whether blacks live in the low-income Vine City neighborhood or the wealthy Cascade neighborhood that houses Atlanta's black elite. As the racial composition of a neighborhood becomes mostly black, the price of home owner insurance rises dramatically.[26]

Using the state rates for a hypothetical $125,000 brick house (with $250 deductible), the *Atlanta Journal-Constitution* study concluded that "State Farm and Allstate, Georgia's largest insurers, tend to charge their highest rates in zip codes that also contain the highest proportion of black residents."[27] The premium differentials become apparent when one compares the hypothetical $125,000 brick house in different locations in metropolitan Atlanta. Shelly Emling writes: "To insure that house with State Farm in black sections of the city of Atlanta would cost about $612 a year; in Buckhead, the rate falls to $459. In Cobb, Gwinnett and north Fulton, all more than 80 percent white, the price falls to $363 a year."[28]

The premium differentials between black and white neighborhoods cannot be explained solely by loss data, that is, theft, vandalism, fire, and larceny crimes. In reality, the highest loss ratios are not in black areas. A loss ratio is the sum an insurance company pays in claims versus the amount it collects in premiums. For example, a ratio of 68 percent means that a company paid out 68 cents for each $1 it collected. In general, a company that has a loss ratio of 65 percent turns a healthy profit.

The loss ratio in mostly black Allstate Zone 2 (Central Atlanta) is 79 percent, yet they pay a whopping $705 in annual premiums. On the other hand, the loss ratio in mostly white Atlanta Zone 18 (north Fulton, northwest DeKalb) is 92 percent, and the home owners pay $349—less than half what is paid by residents in Zone 2. There is little doubt that the mostly white suburban communities with the highest loss ratios are not paying their fair share. These premium disparities further illustrate the benefits suburban whites derive from discrimination.

Predatory lending also creates separate and unequal housing opportunities.[29] Predatory lending disproportionately hurts black Atlantans.[30] Predatory practices by some subprime lenders have resulted in extremely high foreclosures in once stable neighborhoods.[31] There were 1,313 foreclosures in the five largest counties in Georgia in August 2001, near the record of 1,578 in April 1991.[32] Fulton County had 568 foreclosures in March 2002 compared to 340 in March 2001,[33] while DeKalb had 619 foreclosures in March 2002.[34] Over 41 percent of advertised foreclosures in DeKalb County were actually on loans that were less than two years old.[35]

Using HUD's list of subprime lenders for the Atlanta MSA, the Home Mortgage Disclosure Act (HMDA) data show there has been dramatic growth in subprime lending in the Atlanta MSA, over 500 percent from 1993 to 1998 (from 1,864 to 11,408).[36] The volume of foreclosures grew 232 percent from 1996 to 1998, while the number of mortgages only grew 7 percent. Forty-four percent of subprime loans had high interest rates (defined as 4 percent above the Treasury bill rate). Subprime lending was three times more significant in low-income neighborhoods than in the overall market, and 74 of the 101 census tracts with high subprime activity (25 percent or more of mortgages) were predominantly black.

The overall share of foreclosures for subprime went from 5 percent to 16 percent for 1996 to 1998; median age of subprime foreclosures was two years compared with four years for prime loans. In the end, predatory lending has a devastating impact on black home owners in the Atlanta area by denying them a basic form of wealth. It also destabilizes entire neighborhoods.

REGIONAL MOBILITY

The boundaries of the Atlanta metropolitan area doubled in the 1990s. The region measured 65 miles from north to south in 1990. Today, Atlanta's economic dominance reaches well beyond 110 miles from north to south.[37] Much of the region's growth in the 1990s was characterized by suburban sprawl and economic disinvestment in Atlanta's central city.[38] The Sierra Club rated Atlanta as the "most sprawl-threatened" large city (over 1 million people) in the nation.[39]

Atlanta rose from having the seventh-largest black population in 1990 to having the third-largest in 2004—more than doubling its African American population during that time.[40] Among large metropolitan areas, Atlanta led all others in its black population gains during both the 1990s and in 2000–2004.[41] Atlanta's diversified and growing economy, large black middle class and several black businesses, and concentration of historically black colleges and universities (Atlanta University Center) all serve as a draw for African Americans from across the United States.

Atlanta is also a magnet for commuters. Daytime Atlanta is very different from resident nighttime Atlanta. In 2005, the U.S. Census Bureau released its first ever report highlighting the differences between the residential populations of various cities and the numbers of people present during the workday or "daytime population."[42] The daytime population refers to the number of people, including workers, who are present in an area during normal business hours, in contrast to the resident population present during the evening and nighttime hours.

For medium-size cities (250,000 to 500,000), Atlanta topped the list, with the daytime population rising 62.4 percent. Other cities with large daytime gains include: Tampa, 47.5 percent; Pittsburgh, 41.3 percent; St. Louis, 35.1 percent; Cincinnati, 31.0 percent; Minneapolis, 25.0 percent; Cleveland, 24.0 percent, and Buffalo, 16.3 percent. No city showed a larger daytime population shift than the nation's capital. The steady stream of government and other office workers that flows into Washington, D.C., swells the District's population by 71.8 percent. Other big cities (500,000 to 1 million) with large daytime population gains include: Boston, 41.1 percent; Memphis, 15.8 percent; Indianapolis, 15.6 percent; and Baltimore, 14.2 percent. Detroit saw its daytime population dip below its resident population by 0.1 percent.

Between 1990 and 2005, the Atlanta region added 1.25 million persons. Population growth was slow in the city of Atlanta, increasing by only 26,900, or less than 3 percent of the total population gain. On the other hand, the northern portion of the region gained 616,000 residents, or almost 50 percent of the region's population growth; the southern part of the region gained 289,900 persons, or 23.1 percent of the population gains during 1990–2005. Fulton County continues to be the region's largest county, with 874,100 residents in 2005. Gwinnett County led the region in net population increase, adding more than 21,000 persons each year since 2000.[43]

The Atlanta regional economy has boomed since 1990. The total workers in the region increased 33.6 percent during the 1990s, the sixth-largest percentage increase among all the metropolitan areas in the United States (the national average was 11.5 percent). The region had 2 million jobs in 2001, a 42 percent increase over 1990, or nearly 600,000 new jobs.[44]

Newcomers flocked to the region for obvious reasons—jobs. Unemployment remained low and job growth remained strong. Between 1990 and 2003, over 508,000 jobs were added to the region. Most new jobs and newcomers settled outside the city. The city of Atlanta lagged far behind the job-rich suburbs. The city captured about 40 percent of the region's jobs in 1980. By 1990, Atlanta's share had slipped to 28.3 percent, and 22.0 percent in 2000.[45]

Clearly, Atlanta's northern suburbs reaped the lion's share of new jobs. From 1990 to 2003, Atlanta's northern suburbs added 267,200 jobs. This accounted for 52.6 percent of all jobs added in the region. Another 96,800 jobs, or 19.1 percent, were added in the southern part of the region. Only 13,970 jobs were added in the region's central core of Atlanta, representing only 2.8 percent of all jobs created during the height of the region's booming economy.[46]

Fulton County, where Atlanta is located, continued to be the largest employment center in the region, with more than 738,200 jobs in 2001, accounting for 36.5 percent of the region's total employment. In all, Fulton, DeKalb, Cobb, and Gwinnett accounted for 76 percent of jobs, 67 percent of the workers, and 65 percent of the population in the region.[47]

Most poor black Atlantans are not near the jobs. This economic isolation of black Atlantans is complicated by inadequate public transit (limited, unaffordable, or inaccessible service and routes, and security and safety problems), lack of personal transportation (no privately owned car available to travel to work), spatial mismatch (location of suitable jobs in areas that are inaccessible by public transportation), and concentrated poverty.

The majority of entry-level jobs in metro Atlanta are not within a quarter mile of public transportation. Only 11.3 percent of metro Atlanta's jobs are located within a three-mile radius of the central business district (CBD); 38.1 percent are located within a ten-mile radius, and 61.9 percent are located outside the ten-mile ring.[48] Getting to job sites is next to impossible if you are carless in Atlanta since the Metropolitan Atlanta Regional Transit Authority, or MARTA, is limited to only two counties—Fulton and DeKalb.

MARTA—MOVING AFRICANS
RAPIDLY THROUGH ATLANTA

The ten-county Atlanta metropolitan area has a regional public transit system in name only. Race was a major driver in shaping public transit in the Atlanta region. The Metropolitan Atlanta Rapid Transit Authority (MARTA) serves just two counties, Fulton and DeKalb. For many white suburbanites, "MARTA" stood for "Moving Africans Rapidly Through Atlanta."[49] According to the MARTA board chairman Bill Moseley, "People in the suburbs think MARTA is a black, transit-dependent system." In 2001, the financially strapped MARTA system budgeted $700,000 to hire a marketing firm to "study and implement a program to polish its image."[50]

In the 1960s, MARTA was hailed as the solution to the region's growing traffic and pollution problems. The first referendum to create a five-county rapid rail system failed in 1968. However, in 1971, the City of Atlanta, Fulton County, and DeKalb County approved a referendum for a 1 percent sales tax to support a rapid rail and feeder bus system. Cobb County and Gwinnett County voters rejected the MARTA system. The vote ran strictly along racial lines. Yet, Clayton and Gwinnett were allowed to sit on the MARTA board and determine its fate—including raising fares and cutting service.

The unequal representation picture does not stop at the county level, since the MARTA board is also made up of state officials—even though the state does not fund MARTA. In the end, Gwinnett, Clayton, and state officials make decisions about MARTA but are not accountable to the political jurisdictions whose residents pay for the system—the city of Atlanta and Fulton and DeKalb counties. This form of "representation without taxation" lies at the heart of the growing transportation equity movement in metro Atlanta.

The percentage of Atlanta commuters using public transit to get to work, 4.7 percent, is lower than the national average. Overall, African American Atlantan commuters are more likely to use public transit than are whites. In Atlanta, 28.2 percent of black males and 35.0 percent of black females take public transit to work. On the other hand, 4.4 percent of white male and 6.7 percent of white female Atlantans ride public transit to work.[51]

MARTA has grown from thirteen rail stations in 1979 to its current thirty-eight rail stations. It is the ninth-largest transit system in the United States, operating 556 buses (441 compressed natural gas and 145 clean diesel) with 120 bus routes.[52] The agency also operates 110 lift-vans for paratransit services. MARTA operates 338 rail cars on 47.6 miles of rail. Some 31.6 miles of rail are located in Fulton County, 14.7 miles in DeKalb County, and 7 miles (to Hartsfield-Jackson Atlanta Airport) are located in Clayton County. The system handles more than 451,600 passengers on an average weekday. It operates 120 bus and van routes. MARTA's rail lines carry 259,000 passengers on an average weekday.

Where MARTA builds the next lines is hotly debated among diverse neighborhood constituents in Atlanta, Fulton County, and DeKalb County. Competition between MARTA's service area haves and have-nots will likely intensify in the future. Just how far MARTA lines extend has proved to be a thorny issue. In July 2002, the MARTA board of directors asked staff to initiate the Alternatives Analysis for the North Line Corridor from the North Springs Station to Windward Parkway Locally Preferred Alternative, which features a heavy rail extension to the interchange of Martin Luther King Jr. Drive and I-285 and a Bus Rapid Transit (BRT) segment along I-20 to Fulton Industrial Boulevard.

In October 2002, MARTA initiated the West Line Alternatives Analysis/Draft Environmental Impact Statement (AA/DEIS) for Fulton Industrial Boulevard. The DEIS was submitted to the Federal Transit Administration (FTA) for review in March 2005. And in the spring of 2003, MARTA initiated a study identifying strategies to implement BRT-type service in the Memorial Drive corridor from the former Avondale Mall location to the park and ride lot at Stone Mountain. The timeline for implementation of the Memorial Drive BRT is early 2008.[53]

Most Metro Atlanta counties decades ago opted not to join MARTA. This decision was tinged with racial overtones. Today, Fulton and DeKalb taxpayers are still questioning where MARTA lines go and where they do not go. There is no agreement where MARTA should go next, and politics will likely play a role in determining the answer.[54] Only Fulton and DeKalb County residents pay for the upkeep and expansion of the system with a one-cent MARTA sales tax. Revenues from bus fares generated $5 million more revenue than taken in by rail in 1997.[55]

MARTA offers over 28,000 parking spaces at its rail stations and parking is free unless overnight. A 1999 license tag survey, "Who Parks-and-Rides," covering the period 1988–1997, revealed that 44 percent of the cars parked at MARTA lots were from outside MARTA's Fulton/DeKalb County service area.[56] Thus, Fulton and DeKalb County tax payers are subsidizing people who live in outlying suburban counties who park their cars at the park-and-ride lots and ride on MARTA trains into the city and to the airport.

On November 28, 2000, the Metropolitan Atlanta Transportation Coalition (MATEC), a coalition of eleven black Atlanta organizations, filed an administrative complaint with the U.S. Department of Transportation on behalf of their minority and disabled members.[57] The MATEC organizations charged MARTA with racial discrimination under Title VI of the Civil Rights Act of 1964. The coalition pointed out overcrowded bus lines, lack of clean compressed natural gas (CNG) buses, lack of bus shelters, and fewer amenities provided in communities of people of color compared with white communities. The group also charged MARTA with failure to comply with the federally mandated Americans with Disability Act (ADA).[58]

Race has always played a pivotal role in MARTA's creation and governance. In nearly four decades, MARTA has had five general managers—all of whom have been white males. It was not until December 2000, after growing community pressure, that MARTA selected its first African American general manager.[59] However, having a black person at the helm of MARTA brings an added dimension of race to the table. As long as the transit agency is identified as being a black-run system, it will face an uphill battle of securing earmarked regional and state funding.

The Atlanta region needs a strong MARTA. Raising fares and providing substandard transit services to its riders do not equal smart growth. MARTA's transit-dependent riders are typically children and the elderly, lower-income, carless or own fewer automobiles, from larger households, living near transit stations, and generally nonwhite. African Americans make up 73 percent of its customers.[60] MARTA is a necessity for the individuals who do not own cars. Only 6.3 percent of whites compared to 26.5 percent of blacks who live in the MARTA service area are without cars. More than 34.6 percent of Atlantans are carless—compared with 44.4 percent in Baltimore, 42.1 percent in Washington, D.C., 36.2 percent in St. Louis, and 34.8 percent in pre-Katrina New Orleans—all majority-black cities.

In September 2002, the FTA advised the MATEC groups of its plan to me-
diate their complaint with MARTA representatives. Mediation was completed in mid-October 2002. Some changes at MARTA were cosmetic and
mere window dressing. Others were more substantive.[61] Today, MARTA provides sign language at all of its public meetings. It has taken steps to remedy the disparity in service toward Latino riders. Currently, MARTA provides
Spanish-English literature and flyers at train stations and public meetings.
A Spanish-English interpreter is now available at all board meetings and
public hearings. Also, MARTA's Customer Service Hot Line is now able to
provide assistance to Spanish-speaking customers. Beginning in 2003, all
emergency information has been published in Spanish.

In December 2002, MARTA received fifty new "clean diesel" buses to re-
place old (some more than twelve years old and with more than 600,000
miles) buses at the Hamilton Garage—which serves the mostly black south
Fulton County. While this concession does not get clean CNG buses in the
mostly black service area, this is the first time in over ten years that this facility received new buses, as the previous practice was to move the old buses
to this facility and place the new buses at the other two garages.

Several train stations in black areas have received upgrades and maintenance, such as Hamilton Holmes (new roof), West End (power scrubbings),
and Ashby Street (elevator and escalator repairs). MARTA has begun a program to install 600 shelters and 300 benches giving minority, low-income,
and transit-dependent areas priority placements. It established the SMART
Team program. This program uses a number of the agency's employees to
identify, assess, and recommend solutions to maintenance problems in and
around MARTA's train stations.

There is no regional transit system that can work in metropolitan Atlanta
without having the mature MARTA system at the core. MARTA is the most
comprehensive transit system in the region, operating both buses and rail.
This mature transit system has taken four decades to develop, with only two
of the counties in the region paying for the system. Race still matters in
planning transit in metropolitan Atlanta. Until racism is reined in, the Atlanta region will continue to have a patchwork of unlinked, uncoordinated,
and "separate but unequal" transit (bus) systems "feeding into" and "feeding off" MARTA.

The three governments supporting MARTA (Fulton and DeKalb counties
and the City of Atlanta) with a one cent sales tax since 1971 are balking at
extending local-option sales tax (MARTA tax) long term. The ARC's proposed $8.5 billion Transportation Improvement Plan (TIP) has a mere $24
million allocated to MARTA—mainly to pay a small fraction of the cost to
upgrade MARTA's fare-collection system, which will help suburban bus systems feed into MARTA.[62]

Cobb County created it own transit system in 1991. Cobb Community Transit (CCT) operates 41 buses that cover 345 miles. The suburban system carries an average of 9,300 passengers on weekdays. The one-way fare inside Cobb County is $1.25. The fare to a MARTA connection is $3 one-way and $4 round-trip (both include MARTA transfers). CCT has limited links to MARTA. However, CCT buses take riders directly into several MARTA stations and stop at the curb in front of major employers. It also operates express routes that run from park-and-ride lots. The two systems do not share funds when riders transfer.

The Georgia Regional Transit Authority (GRTA) has express buses from Clayton and Rockdale counties that drop passengers off in downtown Atlanta. Commuters can board one of the eight buses with plush seats, individual lighting, wheelchair lifts, and some laptop ports.[63] These are the first of twelve routes that GRTA is planning on operating from suburban sites to employment centers in the metropolitan area. These express buses are supposed to provide suburban drivers an option for dealing with traffic gridlock. Critics of the new "Xpress" buses argue that the convenient new buses are threatening to turn old Peachtree Street into a full-blown bus station.[64]

Funding problems are likely to hit the Gwinnett, Clayton, and other start-up circulator bus systems in Atlanta's suburbs since they, like MARTA, have not found long-term funding for transit. The U.S. Department of Transportation provided three-year operating assistance for transit start-up systems. The ARC is commissioning an in-depth study of transit funding and possible solutions. The consultants were expected to complete the study in 2006. MARTA and other transit systems in the region could be dismantled or gone by the time the "experts" sort through the facts and present their findings.

In April 2004, Governor Sonny Perdue introduced his $15.5 billion plan to address traffic congestion in the Atlanta metropolitan area. To pay for his plan, Perdue relied on $11 billion in existing funds and $4.5 billion in new loans, mostly advances on future federal transportation grants and state gas tax collections. They are only incremental financial boosts, not the ongoing new funding source needed in a state struggling to control traffic gridlock.

MARTA officials were surprised to see only $2 million of Perdue's plan given to the financially struggling transit system. MARTA's operating budget comes from sales tax (46 percent), fares (34 percent), and the FTA and other sources (20 percent). MARTA is the nation's largest transit agency that does not receive earmarked state or regional funds. By contrast, the Massachusetts Bay Transit Authority (Boston) gets 20 percent of the state's five cent sales tax, or about $680 million a year.[65]

In August 2006, MARTA officials reported that its 2005–2006 fiscal year indicated an estimate of $19 million in the black,[66] after starting the year projecting a $16 million deficit on an operating budget of $323.5 million. Between 1998 and 2005 MARTA lost $59 million on its operation side, which includes $21 million in 2003.[67] MARTA officials indicated that they will use the surplus to improve transportation services for Atlanta, Fulton, and Dekalb counties. Current MARTA investments are concentrated in non-black communities.

Many black Atlanta neighborhoods have waited decades for the economic benefits associated with MARTA stations. Of particular concern is the significant decline in employment in central-city neighborhoods. In recent years, MARTA has begun to take a more active role in encouraging transit-oriented development (TOD) around its rail stations. MARTA and the Atlanta Development Authority (ADA) have identified some nine sites for mixed-use developments.[68] TOD got a shot in the arm in 1999 when Bell-South (one of the area's largest employers) announced that it would move 13,000 of its employees to new offices to be built near the MARTA Lindbergh station.[69]

MARTA's TOD projects are in various stages at Lenox, North Avenue, Medical Center, Chamblee, Sandy Springs, Avondale, King Memorial, and Lakewood/Ft. McPherson stations. In fiscal year 2005, construction started on Uptown Square, a 362-family apartment development, as well as 208,893 feet of retail space at Lindbergh City Center. Combined, the two projects are projected to eventually generate over $200 million in lease revenue for MARTA. At Lakewood/Ft. McPherson station, nearly six acres of land was sold for $982,000 to the Urban Residential Finance Authority to build 192 apartments.[70]

Atlanta has undergone one of the largest expansions of any urban area in history. Its traffic congestion was having a severe impact on the region's economy, which is one reason why BellSouth decided to locate at the Lindbergh City Center. "Lindbergh City Center, a joint development effort of BellSouth and the Metropolitan Atlanta Rapid Transit Authority (MARTA) is [housing] 1 million square feet of offices right on top of the Lindbergh metro station, making it Atlanta's most recent and at forty-seven acres, most ambitious transit-oriented development project."[71]

In an effort to assist Atlanta in conforming to the Clean Air Act (CAA) standards, BellSouth thought it would be a great idea to build its new offices in the city instead of the suburbs (suburban corporate campus), which was their original plan. This was a way to make MARTA attractive to Atlanta residents and thus to address both the region's traffic gridlock problems and air quality issues. BellSouth is a company with 20,000 employees who are spread out over seventy-five suburban locations, and it was to its business advantage to build in the city because its employees were not willing to settle down in suburban communities. The location of this station was "cheaper, easier, and more productive" for the workers of BellSouth.

The second phase of the Lindbergh TOD would include 330,000 square feet of retail space along the center's main street, 259 condominiums, and 566 apartments. MARTA and the developer of the Lindbergh TOD went into conflict negotiation with five groups (Garden Hills, Peachtree Heights East, Peachtree Park, Peachtree Hills, and Lindbergh Gardens) in the area over parking and pedestrian and traffic improvements for the area. The groups were able to get fewer parking spaces for the area and improvements for pedestrians and bicyclists, wider sidewalks on Piedmont, traffic calming medians, textured crosswalks, and bike lanes.

However, the Atlanta Neighborhood Development Partnership (ANDP) argued that Lindbergh did not plan any affordable housing.

In the final analysis, many of the new immigrants and low-income residents would be displaced. Moreover, the Lindbergh TOD has exacerbated the traffic problem in the area instead of providing a solution.

The lessons learned from the Lindbergh TOD are as follows: (1) Community involvement is essential to creating good projects; (2) Research shows that too much parking has a deleterious effect on transit ridership, aggravates traffic congestion, and drives up the cost of projects; (3) TOD projects should be integrated into their surroundings. Investments in pedestrian infrastructure and streetscape improvements are key; (4) Affordable housing needs to be a component of TOD; and (5) TOD cannot solve congestion and emissions problems without supportive policies and investments at the regional and state level.

Housing and commerce have been rising along MARTA's rail lines, and the system's bus routes have been rethought for the first time in two decades. For example, the Metro Atlanta Chamber of Commerce spent months pushing the "flex-trolleys" for the busiest metro corridors. Other transit talks in the city have focused on the proposed Beltline—a twenty-two-mile transit loop. The proposed Beltline would connect forty-nine Atlanta neighborhoods with a new transit line and linear park; bicycle and pedestrian pathways will follow along the loop. It will connect with existing MARTA stations at five locations and it will utilize the Old "Belt Line" Railroads developed after the Civil War.

The Beltline would provide transportation choices by linking existing transportation hubs with new regional transit projects, create a greenspace network, spur mixed-use redevelopment along 2,500-plus acres of underutilized land that lie within a quarter mile of the corridor, and reduce congestion. The Beltline has a high population density within a half mile of the corridor. MARTA is coordinating a $2.5 million feasibility study of the Beltline and the proposed C-Loop. It applied for inclusion in the 2005–2010 TIP and ranked fourth in GRTA's Draft Regional Transit Action Plan. The project is also included in Atlanta's Comprehensive Development Plan and the ARC's *Mobility 2030* Regional Transportation Plan. The nonprofit

Friends of the Beltline group has begun discussions with CSX, Norfolk Southern, and the Georgia Department of Transportation.[72]

In August 2006, transit advocates met to discuss a transportation study of the Beltline that gave Bus Rapid Transit (BRT) an edge over two rail-based alternatives, light rail and the modern street car.[73] BRT is a relative new technology and the transit advocates viewed it as the cheapest of all the transportation options. There are mixed feelings about choosing BRT among the transit advocates; however, they want a mode of transportation that is cost-effective, covers a good amount of land use, and moves people along the corridor.[74]

HIGHWAY SPRAWL

Building highways to the suburbs and subsidizing the construction of suburban homes were considered two of our government's primary responsibilities.[75] However, many transportation activities had unintended negative consequences of dividing, isolating, disrupting, and imposing different economic, environmental, and health burdens on some communities. Writing in the Foreword to *Just Transportation*, longtime civil rights activist and Georgia congressman John Lewis states:

> Even in a city like Atlanta, Georgia—a vibrant city with a modern rail and public transit system—thousands of people have been left out and left behind because of discrimination. Like most other major American cities, Atlanta's urban center is worlds apart from its suburbs. The gulf between rich and poor, minorities and whites, the "haves" and "have-nots" continues to widen.[76]

Metropolitan Atlanta has been shortchanged in the state allocation of transportation funding for years. Much of this disparate treatment emanates from the state's rules on how motor fuel taxes can be spent. The gas tax can only be used for roads and bridges—and not a dime can go toward transit. Still, metro Atlantans do not get a fair return on the money they pay in gas taxes. For example, between 1992 and 1997, the ten-county region received back only fifty-five cents on every dollar paid out in gas taxes—resulting in a $518 million shortfall.[77] Metro Atlanta has 42 percent of the state's population, but only 17 percent of the states gas tax revenue actually comes back to the region—a classic case of transportation injustice.

Metro Atlanta is expected to add another 2 million people by 2030. To address this growth, ARC's *Mobility 2030* plan calls for spending $50 billion over the next twenty-five years on transportation. Yet this massive expenditure is expected to do little in terms of relieving congestion, mainly because it again shortchanges transit—and practically leaves MARTA off the funding table. Public transit in metro Atlanta is in a "catch-22" predicament—by state law it is easier to spend money for roads and not transit, so the region gets more roads and gridlock.[78] The decision by the thirty-nine-member ARC board to spend $50 billion mostly on roads makes more political sense than economic sense.

Atlanta's regional transportation policies are implicated in land-use patterns, unhealthy air, and sprawl. Traffic and air pollution have made Atlanta the sprawl poster child. Sprawl has caused the region's ranking as a favored corporate location to be downgraded. The region's economy depends heavily on keeping traffic moving along the three interstate highways (I-20, I-75, and I-85). Atlanta sits at the hub of this sprawling auto-dependent region. The Tom Moreland Interchange, or "Spaghetti Junction" (the interchange where I-85 and I-285 come together), typifies the traffic and pollution that poor planning has brought to greater Atlanta. Sprawl represented progress. And the automobile is the undisputed king of the road.

Atlanta's political class considered sprawl an inevitable fact of life until confronted with the realities of the federal Clean Air Act.[79] The Atlanta metropolitan area has been in violation of the Clean Air Act for some time now. The region is a nonattainment area for ground-level ozone, with cars, trucks, and buses as the largest source of this pollution. Ozone is formed by the reaction of oxygen radicals with precursors such as volatile organic compounds and nitrogen oxides, common components of car exhaust.[80]

Transportation and land-use plans have also contributed to and exacerbated social and economic inequities. Freeway congestion tells the story. Building roads to everywhere is the problem—not the solution. Despite decades of transportation investments, residents of the region face severe congestion, drive farther, breathe unhealthier air, and are more automobile dependent than ever before. For many Atlantans, the car has become their home away from home.

Sprawl is the reason why Atlanta residents drive long distances to work, shop, play, and get to school. For the period 1990–2020, Atlantans are expected to travel an average of 15,000 miles per year. On average, people in the region drive 34 miles per day—more than anyone else on the face of the planet (50 percent farther than Los Angeles–area residents). Atlantans lead the nation in miles driven per day (over 100 million miles per day).

Traffic gridlock and polluted air help make Atlanta one of the most sprawl-threatened large cities in the United States.[81] The Atlanta region had more than 2.9 million registered vehicles in 2003, up from 1.5 million registered vehicles in 1980. Most Atlantans drive to work. The region's economic activity centers and emerging activity centers are concentrated in the northern suburbs. Fifteen of the eighteen activity centers are located north of I-20, a freeway that historically divided the region racially and geographically. Only one of the five emerging activity centers is located south of I-20.

The region's transportation dilemma is complicated by the amount of the state's motor fuel tax and how it gets used. Georgia's motor fuel tax is one of the lowest in the nation, thus hardly discouraging driving. Conversely, the state taxing structure has no built-in incentives to support mass transportation. Since the Georgia motor fuel tax currently can only be used for roads and bridges, the state transportation agency only pays lip service to mass transit. The real money goes to sprawl-driven roads and more roads.

Atlantans are growing weary of traffic gridlock, long commutes, and polluted air. The smog is also hurting Atlanta's image as an attractive business climate. Amid signs that federal highway dollars would be frozen, Georgia's Environmental Protection Division (EPD) helped to create the Partnership for a Smog-Free Georgia (PSG). The PSG operates from the workplace and is the beginning point for changing Atlantans' commuting habits. Since its birth in 1998, PSG has recruited over 160 "partners" into its program. The program also has a dozen public sector partners and links to eighty-five state agencies and universities and twenty-five federal agencies. Some of the large corporate partners include the Coca-Cola Company, Delta Airlines, Turner Broadcasting Systems, BellSouth, and IBM.[82]

After making some progress in reducing nitrogen-oxide emissions in the early 1990s, as a result of cleaner-running cars and tighter emission inspections, the region is now experiencing reversals in air quality. In the summer of 1999, the Atlanta region experienced thirty-seven consecutive ozone alert days. The region exceeds the National Ambient Air Quality Standards for ozone by 33 to 50 percent.

The Atlanta Regional Commission is the metropolitan planning organization (MPO) responsible for land use and transportation planning in the region. In order to receive federal transportation funds, ARC was required to develop a Transportation Improvement Plan (TIP) that would conform to federal standards. ARC developed an Interim Transportation Improvement Plan (ITIP).[83] Because of the severe ozone nonattainment, the federal government criticized the ARC's plan for concentrating too heavily on roads and its failure to show how it would improve the region's poor air quality. Federal officials have also identified public participation as a major problem in ARC's planning and decision making.[84]

In 1998, two separate coalitions of citizens' groups challenged ARC's leadership, planning, and decision making, which is tilted toward new roads. A group of environmental organizations and a coalition of mainly African American environmental justice, neighborhood, and civic groups filed a notice to sue under the Clean Air Act the ARC and the state and federal governments for approving sixty-one "grandfathered" new road projects funded under the Interim TIP they felt would add to and exacerbate the region's already severe air quality problem.[85]

In addition to challenging the illegal exemption of grandfathered road projects, the environmental justice coalition raised equity concerns with the grandfathered roads and the region's $700 million transportation spending plan.[86] The groups charged that highway-dominated plans would disproportionately and adversely affect the health and safety of African Americans and other people of color.

The environmental group followed through with a lawsuit that resulted in a settlement that eliminated forty-four of the sixty-one grandfathered road projects.[87] The seventeen other projects were allowed to proceed because the Georgia Department of Transportation (DOT) had already awarded contracts to construct the roads. The settlement freed up millions of dollars for transportation alternatives that will improve air quality and mobility in the region.[88] The settlement restricts projects from proceeding until the state includes them in a regional transportation plan that meets federal clean air standards. The settlement requires the ARC to make its computer traffic modeling public, requires Georgia DOT to conduct a major study of transportation and congestion in the northern suburbs, and requires the U.S. DOT to study the social equity impacts of transportation investments in the region.[89]

Shortly after the June 1999 settlement, the environmental justice coalition entered into informal negotiations with the U.S. Department of Transportation, state, and local agencies, including the ARC, that would begin addressing transportation equity, environmental justice, and Title VI concerns of the groups.[90] Equity concerns revolve around three broad areas: how environmental justice issues are addressed in the planning process, how the benefits are distributed across various populations, and how the burdens of transportation investments are distributed across various populations.

Preliminary negotiations called for a two-phase analysis of transportation equity in the Atlanta region. Phase one consisted primarily of addressing the "procedural aspect of the planning process, focusing on how public participation of low-income and minority communities can be enhanced and how the concerns of these communities can be better identified and addressed in the planning process."[91] Phase two focused on the "substantive outcomes of the planning process, examining the distribution of transportation burdens and benefits to low-income and minority communities and expanding effective participation by low-income and minority communities in the planning process."[92]

Getting metro Atlantans out of their cars and into some form of coordinated and linked public transit may well be the key to solving a major part of the region's traffic and air quality problems. Widespread support for an integrated transit system exists, from ordinary citizens to powerful civic leaders. A June 1998 *Atlanta Journal-Constitution* poll showed that seven of every ten suburban residents supported some form of unified rail and bus system.[93] Realizing the urgent need to address traffic gridlock and metro Atlanta's growth problems, gubernatorial candidate Roy Barnes promised to create a "superagency" to handle transportation.

One of the first acts the newly elected Democratic Governor Barnes pushed for was the creation of the Georgia Regional Transportation Agency or GRTA.[94] The GRTA received final approval from the Georgia General Assembly on March 1999.[95] A fifteen-member GRTA board was appointed by the governor in June 1999.[96] Governor Barnes cautioned Atlantans not to expect GRTA to be a "miracle cure" that brings immediate relief to gridlocked commutes and the thick smog that blankets the skyline. He stated: "This is not the end of problems. . . . It's not even the beginning of the end. But its does give us the tools to begin with."[97]

On January 14, 2004, the GRTA board revised its mission statement and set out some guiding principles and roles for the authority with specific focus on transportation investments and land use. Its new mission statement is "to improve Georgia's mobility, air quality, and land use practices."[98] Republican Governor Sonny Perdue applauded GRTA for revising its mission and concluded that "combined with the roles and principles the board defined at their retreat last month, they have set GRTA on a clear track toward reducing traffic congestion and improving air quality in our region and state."[99] GRTA is still an unproven quantity. When most residents in metro Atlanta think of transportation, cars and highways come to mind—not public transit. One need only follow the dollars to determine the region's transportation priorities. Highways still grab the lion's share of transportation funds.

The Atlanta metropolitan area grew at record speed. The region's housing starts, job growth, and low unemployment rate are envied across many regions. Although Atlanta's share of the metropolitan population has declined over the years, the health of the majority African American city is still important to the overall metropolitan region's vitality. Atlanta as the "hole in the doughnut" does not bode well for the region. New challenges are being raised to address imbalances resulting from sprawl. What happens outside the city affects all Atlantans. The future of the region is intricately bound to how government, business, and community leaders address Atlanta's quality of life and equity issues.

Will the Atlanta region take a bold stance and address central city reinvestment and redevelopment, fair housing, public schools, public transit, and public health needs? Or will it keep pandering to the forces of racial segregation, discrimination, and blocked economic opportunity? Clearly, the "Black Mecca" continues to attract large numbers of African Americans seeking opportunity and a better life. Atlanta is no "Mecca" for a large slice of the African American community—families stuck in concentrated poverty with little hope of escape. Lack of a comprehensive regional transit plan blocks thousands of black Atlantans from accessing job centers and "opportunity-rich" suburbs. Dismantling this "invisible" wall will benefit the entire region.

NOTES

1. William H. Frey, *Diversity Spreads Out: Metropolitan Shifts in Hispanic, Asian, and Black Population Since 2000* (Washington, DC: The Brookings Institution, March 2006).

2. The 1998 Atlanta Regional Commission estimates are based on 1990 U.S. census, building permits, and other growth formulas.

3. Atlanta Regional Commission, *Atlanta Region Transportation Planning: Fact Book 2003* (Atlanta: Atlanta Regional Commission, 2003), 9.

4. The counties are Barrow, Bartow, Butts, Carroll, Cherokee, Clayton, Cobb, Coweta, Dawson, DeKalb, Douglas, Fayette, Forsyth, Fulton, Gwinnett, Harrison, Heard, Henry, Jasper, Lamar, Meriwether, Newton, Paulding, Pickens, Pike, Rockdale, Spalding, and Walton. Mike King, "Racial Shifts Speak Volumes and Metro Atlanta Will Have to Listen," *The Atlanta Journal-Constitution*, March 9, 2006, A15.

5. Atlanta Regional Commission, *Envision 6: Envision Our Future* (Atlanta: Atlanta Regional Commission, 2006), 4.

6. King, "Racial Shifts Speak Volumes."

7. Ibid.

8. Frey, *Diversity Spreads Out.*

9. David Pendered, "Flourishing Intown Becomes the In Place to Live and Play," *The Atlanta Journal-Constitution*, August 20, 2006, D13.

10. Shaila Dewan, "Gentrification Changing Face of New Atlanta," *New York Times*, March 11, 2006, http://www.nytimes.com/2006/03/11/national/11atlanta .html?ei=5088&en=3f1cb81bbd4f4341&ex=1299733200&partner=rssnyt&emc=rss &pagewanted=all (accessed March 15, 2006).

11. Ibid.

12. Bruce Dixon, "Failure of the Black Misleadership Class," *Black Commentator*, February 9, 2006, 1, http://www.blackcommentator.com/170/170_cover_dixon_ misleadership_class.html (accessed February 12, 2006).

13. Ibid., 3.

14. David L. Sjoquist, *The Atlanta Paradox* (New York: The Russell Sage Foundation, 2000).

15. U.S. Census Bureau, "Percent of Children Under 18 Years Below Poverty Level in the Past 12 Months (For Whom Poverty Status Is Determined)," *American Community Survey* (Washington, DC: U.S. Census Bureau, 2004).

16. Atlanta Regional Commission, *Population and Housing 2005* (Atlanta: ARC, 2005), 21.

17. Ibid.

18. Ibid.

19. Gary Arthur Dymski, "The Theory of Bank Redlining and Discrimination: An Exploration," *Review of Black Political Economy* 23 (Winter 1995): 37–74; Gregory Squires, "Race and Risk: The Reality of Redlining," *National Underwriter (Property & Casualty/Risk & Benefits Management)* 100 (September 16, 1996): 63, 70.

20. Gregory Squires, "Policies of Prejudice: Risky Encounters with the Property Insurance Business," *Challenge* 39 (July 1996): 45–50.

21. Robert D. Bullard, J. Eugene Grigsby III, and Charles Lee, *Residential Apartheid: The American Legacy* (Los Angeles: UCLA Center for African Studies, 1994), 3.

22. Shelly Emling, "Black Areas in City Pay Steep Rates," *The Atlanta Journal-Constitution*, June 30, 1996, A16.

23. Shelly Emling, "Insurance: Is It Still a White Man's Game," *The Atlanta Journal-Constitution*, June 30, 1996, A17.

24. Emling, "Black Areas in City Pay Steep Rates."

25. Ibid.

26. Ibid.

27. Ibid.

28. Ibid.

29. ACORN, *Separate and Unequal: Predatory Lending in America* (Washington, DC: Association of Community Organizations for Reform Now, February 2004).

30. See CNN Money, "Subprime Lenders Target Minorities: Study Finds African-Americans, Hispanics Pay Higher Loan Rates Than Whites with Similar Incomes," May 1, 2002, http://money.cnn.com/2002/05/01/pf/banking/subprime (accessed May 6, 2005).

31. See Glenn Canner, "The Role of Specialized Lenders in Extending Mortgages to Low-Income and Minority Homebuyers," *Federal Reserve Bulletin* 85, no. 11 (November 1999): 709–23; U.S. Department of Housing and Urban Development and U.S. Department of Treasury Joint Task Force, *Curbing Predatory Home Mortgage Lending* (Washington, DC: U.S. Department of HUD and U.S. Department of Treasury, 2000); Robert D. Bullard, Glenn S. Johnson, and Angel O. Torres, "Race, Equity, and Smart Growth: Why People of Color Must Speak for Themselves," Environmental Justice Resource Center at Clark Atlanta University, December 1999, http://www.ejrc.cau.edu/raceequitysmartgrowth.htm (accessed January 13, 2004).

32. D. L. Bennett, "Losing a Home Is So Easy, It's Scary," *The Atlanta Journal-Constitution*, July 28, 2001, A1.

33. Bill Torpy, "Foreclosures Set One-Month Record for State," *The Atlanta Journal-Constitution*, March 28, 2002, J1.

34. John Adams, "Foreclosure Sales in Metro Atlanta Hit Record High," *The Georgia Real Estate Report* 3, no. 3 (March 2002): 19.

35. Bennett, "Losing a Home Is So Easy, It's Scary."

36. See Abt Associates, *Analyzing Trends in Subprime Originations and Foreclosures: A Case Study of the Atlanta Metro Area*, February 2000; J. Vincent Eagan, "Predatory Lending and Black Atlanta," in *The Status of Black Atlanta 2002* (Atlanta: The Southern Center for Studies in Public Policy, Clark Atlanta University, 2002).

37. Christopher Leinberger, "The Metropolis Observed," *Urban Land* 57 (October 1998): 28–33.

38. David Goldberg, "Regional Growing Pains," *The Atlanta Journal-Constitution*, March 10, 1997.

39. Sierra Club, *The Dark Side of the American Dream: The Cost and Consequences of Suburban Sprawl* (College Park, MD: Sierra Club, August 1998), 3.

40. Frey, *Diversity Spreads Out.*

41. Ibid.

42. U.S. Census Bureau, *Estimated Daytime Population*, Population Division, Journey to Work and Migration Statistics Branch, December 6, 2005, http://www.census.gov/population/www/socdemo/daytime/daytimepop.html (accessed April 17, 2006).

43. Atlanta Regional Commission, *Envision 6: Envision Our Future* (Atlanta: Atlanta Regional Commission, 2006), 3.

44. U.S. Census Bureau, *Estimated Daytime Population*, 10.

45. Atlanta Regional Commission, *Atlanta Region Outlook*, Atlanta: Atlanta Regional Commission, December 1998); Atlanta Regional Commission, *Envision 6: Envision Our Future*, 10.

46. Ibid.

47. Center for Neighborhood Technology, *Making the Case for Mixed-Income and Mixed-Use Communities* (Chicago: Center for Neighborhood Technology, June 2004), 32.

48. Edward L. Glaeser, Matthew Kahn, and Chenghuan Chu, *Job Sprawl: Employment Location in U.S. Metropolitan Areas* (Washington, DC: The Brookings Institution, Center on Urban and Metropolitan Policy, May 2001), 5.

49. Robert D. Bullard, Glenn S. Johnson, and Angel O. Torres, eds., *Sprawl City: Race, Politics, and Planning in Atlanta* (Washington, DC: Island Press, 2000), 39–68.

50. John McCosh, "MARTA Calls on Marketers for Image Air: Can Soft Drinks Fill Empty Seats?" *The Atlanta Journal-Constitution*, February 11, 2001, A1; John McCosh, "MARTA: Its Image Is So Bad, New Name Might be Smarta," *The Atlanta Journal-Constitution*, February 11, 2001, A1.

51. Sidney Davis, "Transportation and Black Atlanta," in *Status of Black Atlanta 1994*, ed. Bob Holmes (Atlanta: The Southern Center for Studies in Public Policy, 1994), 79.

52. Metropolitan Atlanta Rapid Transit Authority, *Fiscal Year Annual Report* (Atlanta: MARTA, 2005), 5.

53. Ibid., 11.

54. Susan Laccetti Meyer, "Where Should MARTA Go Next," *The Atlanta Journal-Constitution*, December 5, 1998, A18.

55. Metropolitan Atlanta Rapid Transit Authority, Division of Planning and Policy Development, Transit Research and Analysis, Chronology, June, 1996, 17.

56. See Metropolitan Atlanta Rapid Transit Authority, Division of Planning and Policy Development, Department of Research Analysis, "A Tag Survey 1988–1997," 1999; Goro O. Mitchell, "Transportation, Air Pollution, and Social Equity in Atlanta," in *The Status of Black Atlanta*, ed. Bob Holmes (Atlanta: Southern center for Studies in Public Policy, Clark Atlanta University, 1999), 120.

57. Complaint letter from Metropolitan Atlanta Transportation Equity Coalition (MATEC) to Ron Stroman, U.S. DOT, Office of Civil Rights, and Nuria Fernandez, Administrator of the Federal Transit Administration, November 28, 2000.

58. Ernie Suggs, "Complaint: MARTA Hike Based on Bias," *The Atlanta Journal-Constitution*, December 7, 2000, D5. The complainants included a broad array of groups, including some well known civil rights organizations (SCLC, NAACP, and Rainbow/PUSH Coalition), neighborhood organizations (Rebel Forest Neighborhood Task Force, Campbellton Road Coalition, Second Chance Community Services, Inc.), a disabled persons advocacy group (Santa Fe Villa Tenant's Association), an environmental organization (Center for Environmental Public Awareness), a

youth group (Youth Task Force), and a labor union that represents MARTA drivers (Amalgamated Transit Union Local 732).

59. Stacy Shelton, "MARTA Appoints New Chief," *The Atlanta Journal-Constitution*, December 1, 2000, D16.

60. MARTA, "5th Annual Quality of Service Survey," September 1999.

61. Robert D. Bullard, Glenn S. Johnson, and Angel O. Torres, *Highway Robbery: Transportation Racism and New Routes to Equity* (Cambridge, MA: South End Press, 2004).

62. Maria Saporta, "Transit 'Catch-22' Is Bad for Atlanta," *The Atlanta Journal-Constitution*, August 16, 2004, E3.

63. Julie B. Hairston, "Express Buses Revved Up for Rollout," *The Atlanta Journal-Constitution*, June 7, 2004, http://www.cobbrides.com/Express%20buses%20 revved%20up%20f.htm (accessed July 1, 2005).

64. Colin Campbell, "Xpress Buses Overcrowd Already Busy Peachtree," *The Atlanta Journal-Constitution*, June 8, 2004, http://www.cobbrides.com/Xpress%20buses%20 overcrowd%20al.htm (accessed July 8, 2005).

65. Maria Saporta, "Transit Funding in Mass. Opens Eyes of Atlantans," *The Atlanta Journal-Constitution*, May 17, 2004, E6.

66. See Paul Donsky, "MARTA Reports Surplus," *The Atlanta Journal-Constitution*, August 1, 2006, B1.

67. Ibid.

68. David Pendered, "MARTA Aims to Help Shape Development," *The Atlanta Journal-Constitution*, October 19, 1998; David Pendered, "MARTA Makes Its Move," *The Atlanta Journal-Constitution*, March 29, 1999.

69. Joey Ledford, "Beating Traffic Woes by Moving to Town," *The Atlanta Journal-Constitution*, February 5, 1999.

70. MARTA, *Fiscal Year 2005 Annual Report*, 13.

71. Sharon Reigon, David Hoyt, and Gloria Ohland, "The Atlanta Case Study: Lindbergh City Center," in *Transit Town: Best Practices in Transit-Oriented Development*, ed. Hank Dittmar and Gloria Ohland (Washington, DC: Island Press, 2004), chap. 9.

72. "Metropolitan Atlanta Rapid Transit Authority (MARTA)," http://www .georgiaencyclopedia.org/nge/Article.jsp?path=/Transportation/LandTransportation/ UrbanMassTransit&id=h-1023 (accessed May 15, 2005).

73. Paul Donsky, "Bus Transit Looks Like the Ticket for Beltline," *The Atlanta Journal-Constitution*, August 9, 2006, D1.

74. Ibid.

75. Conservation Law Foundation, *City Routes, City Rights: Building Livable Neighborhoods and Environmental Justice by Fixing Transportation* (Boston: Conservation Law Foundation, 1998), 18.

76. John Lewis, "Foreword," in Robert D. Bullard and Glenn S. Johnson, *Just Transportation* (Gabriola Island, BC: New Society Publishers, 1997), xi–xii.

77. Maria Saporta, "Transportation Funds Must Be Shared Fairly," *The Atlanta Journal-Constitution*, February 24, 2003, E3.

78. Maria Saporta, "Transit 'Catch-22' Is Bad News for Atlanta."

79. David Goldberg, "Atlanta Suburbanites Thinking Regionally," *The Neighborhood Works*, November/December 1997, 13.

80. Charles W. Schmidt, "The Specter of Sprawl," *Environmental Health Perspectives* 106 (June 1998): 276.

81. Sierra Club, *The Dark Side of the American Dream*, 5.

82. Gita M. Smith, "Atlanta's Working Solution to Smog," *The Atlanta Journal-Constitution*, August 30, 1999, E1, E5.

83. Atlanta Regional Commission, *Proposed 1998 Amendments to the Interim Atlanta Region Transportation Improvement Program, FY 1999–FY 2001* (Atlanta: ARC, October 1998).

84. U.S. Department of Transportation, *Federal Highway Administration, Certification Report for the Atlanta Transportation Management Area* (Washington, DC: FHA, September 1998).

85. On November 10, 1998, three environmental groups, Georgians for Transportation Alternative, Georgia Conservancy, and Sierra Club, filed a sixty-day notice to sue local, state, and federal transportation agencies under the Clean Air Act.

86. On December 16, 1998, a coalition of social justice and environmental groups filed a "Notice of Intent to Sue to Remedy Violations of the Clean Air Act" with local, state, and federal transportation agencies. The groups that signed the letter included the Environmental Defense Fund, Southern Organizing Committee for Economic and Social Justice, Rainbow/PUSH Southern Region, Save Atlanta's Fragile Environment, North Georgia African American Environmental Justice Network, Southwest Atlanta Community Roundtable, Center for Democratic Renewal, Rebel Forest Neighborhood Task Force, and Georgia Coalition for People's Agenda.

87. David Goldberg, "Deal Kills Money for 44 Roads But 17 Others Get Go-ahead as Environmentalists Drop Suit," *The Atlanta Journal-Constitution*, June 21, 1999.

88. Southern Environmental Law Center, "SELC Scores Major Victory in Atlanta Lawsuit," *Southern Resources* (Summer 1999): 1, 5.

89. Ibid.

90. U.S. Department of Transportation, Federal Highway Administration, "Assessment of Environmental Justice Issues in Atlanta Proposed Work Plan," for discussion meeting held on June 28, 1999.

91. Ibid., 1.

92. Ibid., 2.

93. David Goldberg, "Polls Say Suburbanites Aren't Hostile to MARTA," *The Atlanta Journal-Constitution*, June 28, 1998.

94. David Goldberg, "A Guiding Hand: Does Metro Atlanta Need a New Agency to Handle Growth Problems? Many Residents Say Yes, But Making It Happen Could Be Tough," *The Atlanta Journal-Constitution* July 20, 1998.

95. Kathey Pruitt, "GRTA Clears Final Legislature Hurdles," *The Atlanta Journal-Constitution*, March 24, 1999.

96. David Goldberg and Kathey Pruitt, "GRTA Occupies Hot Seat," *The Atlanta Journal-Constitution*, June 4, 1999, A1.

97. Governor Roy Barnes as quoted in Kathey Pruitt, "Barnes: GRTA No Miracle Cure," *The Atlanta Journal-Constitution*, April 7, 1999, B1.

98. See GRTA News, http://www.grta.org/news_section/current_articles/revised_mission_011404.htm (accessed January 20, 2004) and http://www.grta.org/news_section/current_articles/attachedment_011404.htm, p. 19 (accessed January 20, 2004).

99. Ibid.

8

Black New Orleans: Before and After Hurricane Katrina

Beverly H. Wright and Robert D. Bullard

The history of New Orleans is intrinsically tied to the Vieux Carre. In fact, early New Orleans history is the history of the Vieux Carre. In 1718, Bienville, a French Canadian, along with a small group of men, left Mobile to establish a city on the banks of the Mississippi.[1] Located ninety miles from the Gulf of Mexico, this new city was to be named in honor of the Duke of Orleans. La Nouvelle Orleans was initially established to be a military outpost, a trading post, and an administrative center for French holdings in Louisiana.

The new French settlement was located "on one of the most beautiful crescents of the river" and in time New Orleans became known as the Crescent City.[2] Adrien de Pauger, a French military engineer, was instructed to execute a plan for the city. De Pauger laid out the streets in a "simple gridiron plan" with the public square (Place d'Armes, later renamed Jackson Square) in the center and four square blocks extending in each direction above and below and six blocks back from the river.[3]

The Vieux Carre has retained its original charm by maintaining its original street system (eleven blocks along the Mississippi River and six blocks deep) and also much of its colonial and antebellum character and charm. It also has a diversity of architectural styles, reflecting its multinational cultural and historic evolution. Although the Vieux Carre is called the French Quarter, little remains from the French colonial period, due to a disastrous fire in 1788 that destroyed eight hundred and fifty buildings. This included all the business houses and residences of the most aristocratic families. Although the rebuilding of the Vieux Carre was done under the Spanish Colonial period, most of the work was done by French architects, influenced by earlier French building styles and techniques. Before the city had fully recovered from this fire, in 1794 a second fire devastated the city. Although New Orleans was a Spanish colonial city for thirty-seven years, it remained essentially French. After the Louisiana Purchase, there was an influx of Americans, but because a majority of the new settlers lived outside the colonial city, the dominant character of the Vieux Carre remained French.

EARLY BLACK NEW ORLEANS HISTORY

As a result of the official launching of the American slave trade, blacks began to appear in large numbers in New Orleans. The 1726 census recorded only 300 slaves living in the city, but by 1732 there were nearly 1,000 slaves living in New Orleans.[4] New Orleans was not only unique because of its European inhabitants, uncommon in most southern cities, but it also had a significant number of "free colored people." The first free blacks were recorded in New Orleans in the 1720s; by 1803, there were 1,335 free blacks living in the city.

After the Civil War, New Orleans's black population experienced a dramatic increase. This resulted in the inability of many ex-slaves to find work or housing. Consequently, the poorest blacks lived where they could. They lived along the battures, or backswamps. Because the city of New Orleans was built facing the Mississippi River, her course followed the great crescent bend of the river. Hence, the batture was "the area on the riverside of the artificial levee without flood protection and without private ownership." The poorest blacks built shacks in the batture away from the dock area. These houses were, however, temporary because the river would periodically overflow and wash away the shacks.

Keeping in mind that New Orleans is a seaport town that is located at the mouth of the Mississippi and is situated below sea level, with flooding her main problem, it is not surprising that whites occupied the highest and best land, protected by natural levees. Poor blacks lived in the backswamps on the inland margin of the natural levee, where drainage was bad, foundation material precarious, streets atrociously unmaintained, mosquitoes endemic, and flooding a recurrent hazard. It is along this margin that a continuous belt of black population developed. Free blacks in New Orleans, many of whom were economically well off, originally lived and owned property in the French Quarter. After the Civil War and the onset of Jim Crow laws, however, they were pushed out of that section.

Many of the blacks moved their families to the Treme, or Sixth Ward, an area adjacent to the French Quarter. As the Sixth Ward became crowded, many moved to the old Seventh Ward, an area that was contiguous to the Sixth Ward and represented a natural extension of the black community. These early black residential patterns developed over the years into long-standing, traditionally black neighborhoods, although early New Orleans's residential patterns were peculiarly integrated.

Several inventions influenced the racial geography of New Orleans in the twentieth century. These included the development of the Wood pump and the expansion of the city's public transportation system through use of the streetcar. The onset of World War I brought with it a virtual halt in the construction of housing. Black residents of New Orleans at this time lived in housing comparable to their white working-class counterparts. Blacks, however, were relegated to the less desirable homes in the backswamp area. There was also a large in-migration of rural blacks and whites, attracted by defense jobs in the city.

It became clear in the early 1920s that additional housing units were needed in the city. There were, however, many early barriers to their construction. There was an apparent drive to improve housing conditions when the 1920 census showed that New Orleans had dropped from twelfth to sixteenth place in population. The loss of population was blamed on the local authorities' inability to solve the housing problems of the city, resulting in many of the townspeople moving out beyond the city's boundaries.

The expansion of the city's streetcar system also affected its racial geography. As public transportation expanded, old black neighborhoods established in the nineteenth-century backswamp areas expanded into the newly drained margins of that area. The expanded transportation system made it possible for blacks to live in areas away from their jobs. The Wood pump, therefore, made it possible for whites to move to the suburbs and for blacks, with the aid of the expanded streetcar system, to move closer into the city. The black and white populations, it seems, were moving in opposite directions.

For a quarter century, beginning in 1978, with the election of Ernest "Dutch" Morial, New Orleans has had an uninterrupted succession of black mayors. In 2002, Orleans Parish (county) had the highest percentage of black residents of any older county in the United States. Roughly 68 percent of New Orleans area residents were black. The so-called "white flight" from New Orleans to the suburbs and continuing racial segregation, poverty, unemployment, crime, and low levels of educational achievement stand as marked contrasts to the city's growing black middle class, which has elected to settle in all-black affluent areas of New Orleans East.[5]

New Orleans, like most major urban centers, was a city in peril long before Hurricane Katrina's floodwaters devastated the city in August 2005.[6] New Orleans (Orleans Parish) had a population of 484,674 in 2000. Of this total, 325,947 (68 percent) were African American, 135,956 (28 percent) were non-Hispanic whites, and 22,871 (4 percent) were of other ethnic groups. Like many great cities, New Orleans also had its share of problems. The economic structure of the city made it difficult to provide jobs with wages high enough to support a family. New Orleans's economy was built around low-wage service jobs to service tourism.

Eastern New Orleans in the 1970s was the fastest growing section of the city. Riding high on the prosperity of the oil industry, building construction in the east was at an all-time high. Newly constructed moderate to expensive homes with comparable luxury apartments dotted the landscape of New Orleans's newest residential area. Unexpectedly, the "oil boom" turned to bust, and the city likewise fell into decline. Banks that held the mortgages on large luxury apartment complexes built by contractors who overestimated the housing needs of the city and the ability of the population to pay, were losing money. At the same time, the city was facing a housing shortage. The inner-city housing stock was dilapidated and becoming more so each year. Public housing was in ruin and in short supply. The city was in deep trouble and the city council was desperate for answers.

Population patterns in the 1980s changed the race and class composition of eastern New Orleans. White residents very quickly began to migrate to St. Tammany Parish, a bedroom community across Lake Pontchartrain. Middle-class African Americans began buying more homes in the eastern suburbs, and more and more luxury apartments were becoming filled with poorer African American New Orleanians on rent subsidies.

Interstate 10 not only made it possible for middle-class black New Orleanians to move to the eastern suburbs, it also made it easier for white New Orleanians to move to St. Tammany Parish and drive into the central business district every day for work, taking the city's tax dollars with them. The result of this new migration pattern devastated the city's economy. Suburban New Orleans East, just like its inner city, became increasingly black, with "pockets of poverty."

New Orleans blacks were more geographically isolated from jobs than whites. The spatial mismatch index measures the degree of segregation between blacks and jobs. The index ranges from 0 to 100, with higher values indicating greater segregation between people and jobs. This index indicates that a little over half of blacks would have had to relocate within metropolitan areas to be geographically distributed in the same way as jobs. The spatial mismatch index for New Orleans's blacks was 65.1 in 2000.[7] Lack of transportation kept thousands of black New Orleanians located outside of the central city.

TRANSPORTATION APARTHEID AND AN UNNATURAL DISASTER

On August 28, 2005, Mayor Ray Nagin ordered New Orleans's first ever mandatory evacuation since the city was founded in 1718.[8] Buses evacuated thousands of residents to the Superdome and other shelters within the city. It has been the policy of the Red Cross for years not to open shelters in New Orleans during hurricanes greater than Category 2. Red Cross storm shelters were moved to higher ground north of Interstate 10 several years ago.[9]

New Orleans's emergency plan called for thousands of the city's most vulnerable population to be left behind in their homes, shelters, and hospitals.[10] A *Times-Picayune* reporter, Bruce Nolan, summed up the emergency transportation plan: "City, state and federal emergency officials are preparing to give the poorest of New Orleans' poor a historically blunt message: In the event of a major hurricane, you're on your own."[11] The New Orleans Rapid Transit Authority (RTA) emergency plan designated sixty-four buses and ten lift vans to transport residents to shelters. This plan was woefully inadequate since the larger buses only hold about sixty people each.

On August 29, 2005, Hurricane Katrina made landfall near New Orleans, leaving death and destruction across the Louisiana, Mississippi, and Alabama Gulf Coast.[12] Katrina is likely the most destructive hurricane in U.S. history. Katrina was also one of the deadliest storms in decades, with a death toll of 1,325. Bodies were still being discovered under rubble in New Orleans's mostly black Ninth Ward nearly a year after the storm. Disaster planners failed the "most vulnerable" in New Orleans—individuals without cars, nondrivers, disabled, homeless, sick persons, the elderly, and children. As a result, many vulnerable people were left behind and may have died as a result of lack of transportation. Nearly two-thirds of the Katrina victims in Louisiana were older than sixty. These data confirm what many believe, that Katrina killed the weakest residents.[13]

Hurricane Katrina exposed a major weakness in urban mass evacuation plans. It also shone a spotlight on the heightened vulnerability of people without cars—a population that faces transportation challenges in everyday life.[14] Katrina's evacuation plan worked relatively well for motorists but failed to serve people who depend on public transit.[15] More than one-third of New Orleans's African American residents did not own a car. Over 15 percent of the city's residents relied on public transportation as their primary mode of travel. Local, state, and federal emergency planners have known for years the risks facing transit-dependent residents.[16]

At least 100,000 New Orleans residents did not have cars to evacuate in case of a major storm.[17] A 2002 article titled "Planning for the Evacuation of New Orleans" detailed the risks faced by hundreds of thousands of carless and nondrivers in the New Orleans area. Of the 1.4 million inhabitants in the high-threat areas, government officials assumed that only approximately 60 percent of the population, or about 850,000 people, would be able to leave the city.[18]

Although the various agencies had knowledge of this large vulnerable population, there simply was no effective plan to evacuate these New Orleanians away from rising water. This problem received national attention in 1998 during Hurricane Georges, when emergency evacuation plans left behind mostly residents who did not own cars.[19] The city's emergency plan was modified to include the use of public buses to evacuate those without transportation. When Hurricane Ivan struck New Orleans in 2004, many carless New Orleanians were left to fend for themselves, while others were evacuated to the Superdome and other "shelters of last resort."[20]

Transporting an estimated 100,000 to 134,000 people out of harm's way was no small undertaking.[21] Most of the city's 500 transit and school buses were without drivers. About 190 RTA buses were lost to flooding. Most of the New Orleans Rapid Transit Authority (NORTA) employees were dispersed across the country and many were made homeless.[22] Before the onslaught of Katrina, NORTA employed more than 1,300 people. A year after the storm, NORTA's board of directors laid off 150 of its 730 employees. These figures include about 125 of NORTA's 400 operators and 21 of its 162 maintenance employees.

A year after the storm, less than half of all bus and streetcar routes were back up and running and only 17 percent of the buses were in use.[23] NORTA once operated twenty-eight bus routes, two streetcar lines, and paratransit for persons with disabilities. Today, its core black ridership scattered, NORTA is struggling financially.

LOSS OF COMMUNITY INSTITUTIONS

Katrina was complete in its devastation of homes, neighborhoods, institutions, and communities. Katrina floodwaters laid waste to dozens of African American churches—the most stable institution in black New Orleans. African American churches were the first responders to the Katrina disaster. Once these institutions were flattened, many black residents were stripped of the "safety net" they fall back on in times of trouble.

Katrina closed the entire New Orleans school system. Blacks made up 93 percent of New Orleans's students before the storm. Evacuated children were enrolled in school districts from Arizona to Pennsylvania, including more than 25,000 attending schools in Houston.[24] In January 2006, state and local officials approved new charter schools in some of the same buildings that once housed New Orleans's traditional public schools before Katrina.[25] In June 2006, ten months after the storm, only 25 of New Orleans's 117 schools were open—and half were charter schools.[26]

Public schools in New Orleans are rapidly being privatized under the "charter" school banner. In June 2006, the elected New Orleans school board controlled just four schools. The city is now the nation's laboratory for charter schools—publicly funded schools run by private bodies. Schools in the New Orleans metro area will get $213 million less in 2006 than in 2005 in state money because tens of thousands of public school students were displaced by Katrina. At the same time, the special allocation of $23.9 million can only be used for charter schools in Louisiana. The teachers' union, the largest in the state, has been told there will be no collective bargaining.[27]

Katrina also closed a number of colleges and universities in New Orleans—displacing over 75,000 college students. The storm severely damaged three historically black colleges and universities (HBCUs) in New Orleans (Dillard University, Southern University in New Orleans, and Xavier University). These three universities were home to over 10,500 African American college students. New Orleans holds the distinction as the only U.S. city, besides Atlanta and Nashville, that is home to three or more HBCUs. Atlanta has five and Nashville has three HBCUs. New Orleans's HBCUs struggled before Katrina. The disaster exacerbated the financial problems of these underfunded institutions.

Katrina evacuees who have made it back to their home region have much lower levels of joblessness. This is especially important for African Americans, whose joblessness rate fell over thirty percentage points for returnees. The unemployment rate for white Katrina evacuees was 24 percent, compared with just under 50 percent for blacks and 42 percent for Hispanics.[28] The November 2005 jobless rate for Katrina returnees was 12.5 percent, while 27.8 percent of evacuees living elsewhere were unemployed. However, the black jobless rate was 47 percent in November compared with 13 percent for whites who have not gone back.[29]

The problem is that most Katrina evacuees have not returned to their home region. Black Katrina evacuees are less likely than whites to have returned to their home region. Four months after the storm, only 21 percent of black evacuees had returned, compared with 48 percent of whites. The U.S. Census Bureau estimates that between July 2005 and January 2006, New Orleans's population had fallen by 64 percent, to 158,353, with a 22 percent black population, down from 67 percent.[30] New Orleans's prestorm population was about 455,000. After the hurricane, the city shrank to 93,000. By January 2006, it had recovered to 174,000. By July 2006, New Orleans still had only 214,000 residents, less than half of its pre-Katrina population.

INSTITUTIONALIZED DISCRIMINATION

Hurricanes have historically increased competition for housing in unaffected areas. Before Katrina, African Americans in New Orleans were more than three times as likely as white borrowers to get high-interest loans.[31]

African American conventional loan applicants were also two and one-third times more likely to be turned down for a mortgage than white applicants. One of every three African American applicants, 29.83 percent, were denied conventional home purchase loans in 2002, down from 39.73 percent in 2001 and down from 56.6 percent in 1997.[32] In 2004, African Americans in New Orleans were twice as likely as their white counterparts to have their loans rejected—20.41 percent and 10.5 percent, respectively.[33]

In December 2005, the National Fair Housing Alliance (NFHA) released a report, *No Home for the Holidays: Report on Housing Discrimination Against Hurricane Katrina Survivors*, documenting high rates of housing discrimination against African Americans displaced by Hurricane Katrina.[34] The NFHA conducted tests over the telephone to determine what both African American and white home seekers were told about unit availability, rent, discounts, and other terms and conditions of apartment leasing. In 66 percent of these tests—forty-three of sixty-five instances—white callers were favored over African American callers.

The NFHA also conducted five matched-pair tests in which persons visited apartment complexes. In those five tests, whites were favored over African Americans three times. NFHA conducted an investigation of rental housing practices in five states to determine whether victims of Katrina would be treated unfairly based on their race.[35] Based on the evidence uncovered by testing conducted in seventeen cities, the NFHA filed five race-based housing discrimination complaints against rental housing complexes located in Dallas, Texas; Birmingham, Alabama; and Gainesville, Florida.[36]

Katrina ravaged an eight-parish labor market that supported 617,300 jobs.[37] In September, nearly 100,000 Katrina evacuees were still housed in 1,042 barracks-style shelters scattered across twenty-six states and the District of Columbia.[38] By mid-October, most shelters were emptied of Katrina evacuees. The Federal Emergency Management Agency (FEMA) has contracted for 120,000 mobile homes for Louisiana, Mississippi, and Alabama storm victims until they find more permanent housing in homes and apartments. However, the pace of getting evacuees out of shelters has been slowed because few sites have been found with the necessary infrastructure—water, sewer, and electricity—to accommodate trailers. Six weeks after the storm hit, FEMA had placed 4,662 Louisiana families in trailers, hotel rooms, or cruise ships docked in New Orleans.[39]

Some Louisiana parishes near New Orleans adopted "emergency ordinances" limiting density of mobile-home parks.[40] Some small white rural towns have adopted "NIMBY-ism" (Not in My Back Yard) to keep out "temporary housing."[41] No one, including FEMA (which provided the trailers and mobile homes), home owners (who were trying to protect their property values), and Katrina victims (who must live in the tight quarters) are served well if temporary "Katrina ghettos" are created. FEMA and the Red

Cross did little to address institutional barriers that block housing and other aid from flowing to African American storm victims who have historically been underserved by local and state government.

Katrina may have wiped out up to half of New Orleans's 115,000 small businesses.[42] A 2002 U.S. Census Bureau report indicates that New Orleans had 9,747 black-owned firms, 4,202 Hispanic-owned firms, and 3,210 Asian-owned firms. Katrina hurt over 60,000 black-owned businesses in the Gulf Coast region, which generate $3.3 billion a year.[43] This is not a small point, since most black-owned firms employ blacks.

Black-owned firms have met endless roadblocks and have been virtually frozen out of the cleanup and rebuilding of the Gulf Coast region. Billions of dollars were spent cleaning up the mess left by Katrina. However, only 1.5 percent of the $1.6 billion awarded by FEMA went to minority businesses, less than a third of the 5 percent normally required by law.[44] The Army Corps of Engineers awarded about 16 percent of the $637 million in Katrina contracts to minority-owned firms.

Katrina allowed government to suspend the Davis-Bacon Act, passed in 1931 during the Great Depression, which sets a minimum pay scale for workers on federal contracts by requiring contractors to pay the prevailing or average pay in the region.[45] Some leaders saw the suspension of the prevailing wage combined with the relaxation of federal rules requiring employees to hire only people with proper documents as spurring an influx of low-wage illegal immigrant workers.[46] This heightened tension between African Americans and Latino immigrant workers. A month later, after mounting pressure from Democrats, moderate Republicans, organized labor, and workers in the Gulf Coast region, the Bush administration reinstated the prevailing-wage rule.[47] The relaxation of document rules was designed to assist Gulf coast hurricane victims who lost their IDs, not a suspension of immigration laws.

Some Katrina victims claim they were unfairly denied emergency aid.[48] They accuse FEMA of leaving them behind a second time. In general, black business entrepreneurs are still significantly more likely to be denied bank credit, and when successful, receive smaller loans relative to comparable nonminority businesses.[49] A *New York Times* study discovered that the Small Business Administration (SBA) has processed only a third of the 276,000 home loan applications it has received.[50]

The SBA rejected 82 percent of the applications it received, a higher percentage than in most previous disasters. Well-off neighborhoods like Lakeview received 47 percent of the loan approvals, while poverty-stricken neighborhoods received only 7 percent. The loan denial problem is not limited to poor black areas. Middle-class black neighborhoods in New Orleans East also have lower loan rates. This trend could spell doom for rebuilding black New Orleans neighborhoods.

Historically, black-owned banks and savings and loans have provided loans and other services to black communities that were redlined by white banks and mortgage companies. Dryades Savings and Loan and Liberty Bank are two well-established black-owned lending institutions in New Orleans. *Black Enterprise Magazine* listed Liberty Bank as the third-largest African American bank in the United States. Liberty Bank and Dryades Bank had assets of $348.2 million and $102.9 million, respectively.[51] Before Katrina, Liberty Bank operated nine branches in New Orleans, three in Baton Rouge, and one in Jackson, Mississippi. Katrina cost Liberty Bank an estimated $40 million and 80 of its 160 employees are out of work.[52]

Katrina set the stage for a monumental tug of war between insurers and the storm victims. The total economic losses from the storm are expected to exceed $125 billion.[53] Katrina is expected to generate $40 to $60 billion in insurance losses, all of the claims of which will take at least two years to process.[54] In August 2006, insurance companies had already paid $41 billion.[55] How much financial responsibility the insurance companies end up bearing will depend on how insurers handle the claims—determination of "wind" or "flood" damage. Damage from rising water is covered only by government-backed flood insurance.

FEMA estimates that the majority of households and businesses in the twelve Hurricane Katrina–affected counties in Alabama, Mississippi, and Louisiana do not have flood coverage. FEMA also estimates that 12.7 percent of the households in Alabama, 15 percent in Mississippi, and 46 percent in Louisiana have flood insurance. Similarly, only 8 percent of the businesses in hurricane-affected counties in Alabama, 15 percent in Mississippi, and 30 percent in Louisiana have flood coverage.[56]

Thousands of African American consumers in the Louisiana, Mississippi, and Alabama Gulf Coast region are concentrated in the secondary insurance market—smaller and less well-known insurance firms. This could prove problematic, especially for black home owners. Nearly a dozen small insurance companies collapsed after Hurricane Andrew—the most expensive single hurricane until Katrina—which cost the industry about $23 billion in today's dollars.[57]

In an attempt to head off a flood of insurance disputes, Mississippi Attorney General Jim Hood filed suit to block insurance companies from denying flood claims when those floods are caused by wind. He claims the insurance exclusion of water damage violates Mississippi's Consumer Protection Act and "deprives consumers of any real coverage choices."[58] The lawsuit also accuses some insurance companies of forcing storm victims into signing documents that stipulate their losses are flood related, not wind related, before they can receive payment or emergency expenses; the lawsuit would ban such practices.[59]

In August 2006, U.S. District Judge L. T. Senter Jr. ruled on the claims brought forward by a Mississippi couple that their insurance company, Nationwide, was liable for damage caused by the storm surge brought ashore by Katrina.[60] In *Leonard v. Nationwide Mutual Insurance Co.*, Judge Senter ruled that the Leonards are entitled to $1,228.16 over the $1,661 already offered by the insurance company to cover damages to their property.[61] The Leonards' estimates found combined wind and flood damages in excess of $130,000.

The judge ruled that the majority of the damages to the property in questions were mostly caused by water intrusion, which is not covered under basic home owners insurance.[62] Senter's ruling could set a precedent for hundreds of other court challenges against the insurance industry for denying billions of dollars in claims from Katrina victims, since the same judge will preside over all of the Katrina insurance disputes in Mississippi.[63]

WILL THE "MOTHER OF ALL TOXIC CLEANUPS" BE FAIR?

Before rebuilding and reconstruction can begin in some neighborhoods, mountains of storm debris and waste need to be cleared and cleaned up. Flooding in New Orleans largely resulted from breached levees and flood walls, flaws in design, construction, and maintenance—a man-made disaster.[64] Too many unnecessary shortcuts were made over the past forty years. These shortcuts cost people's lives.

Katrina was one of the worst environmental disasters in U.S history.[65] A September 2005 *Business Week* commentary described the handling of the untold tons of "lethal goop" as the "mother of all toxic cleanups."[66] However, the billion-dollar question facing New Orleans was which neighborhoods will get cleaned up, which ones will be left contaminated, and which ones will be targeted as new sites to dump storm debris and waste from flooded homes.

Hurricane Katrina left debris and waste across a 90,000-square-mile disaster area in Alabama, Mississippi, and Louisiana, compared to a 16-acre tract in New York on September 11, 2001.[67] Debris from Katrina could well top 100 million cubic yards compared to the 8.8 million cubic yards of disaster debris generated after the 9/11 terrorist attacks on New York City.

In addition to wood debris, Environmental Protection Agency (EPA) and Louisiana Department of Environmental Quality (LDEQ) officials estimate that 140,000 to 160,000 homes in Louisiana may need to be demolished and disposed.[68] More than 100,000 of New Orleans's 180,000 houses were flooded, and half sat for days or weeks in more than six feet of water.[69] Government officials estimate that as many as 30,000 to 50,000 homes citywide may have to be demolished.

One year later, FEMA had spent $3.7 billion to remove 99 million cubic yards of debris from Katrina.[70] This is enough trash to pile two miles high across five football fields. Still, an estimated 20 million cubic yards littered New Orleans and Mississippi waterways—with about 96 percent or 17.8 million cubic yards of remaining wreckage in Orleans, St. Bernard, St. Tammany, Washington, and Plaquemines parishes. Louisiana parishes had already hauled away twenty-five times more debris than was collected after the 9/11 terrorist attack in 2001.[71]

Despite barriers and red tape, a few Katrina evacuees are slowly moving back into New Orleans's damaged homes or setting up travel trailers in their yards. They want to know if it's safe. Home owners are gutting their houses, treating the mold, fixing roofs and siding, and slowly getting their lives back in order. It will be years before the repopulation of New Orleans is completed. For example, a March 2006 RAND Corporation study projected the population of New Orleans to reach about 272,000 in September 2008—amounting to 56 percent of the population of 485,000 before Hurricane Katrina struck.[72]

Returning residents are getting mixed signals from government agencies when it comes to contamination and potential public health threats. In December, LDEQ announced that "there is no unacceptable long-term health risk directly attributable to environmental contamination resulting from the storm." Two months later, in February, the Natural Resources Defense Council (NRDC) came out with different conclusions.[73] NRDC's analyses of soil and air quality after Hurricane Katrina revealed dangerously high levels of contaminants in some New Orleans neighborhoods.

Government and independent scientists remain worlds apart and offer divergent interpretations of what contamination is in the ground, how harmful it is to returning residents, and the appropriate remediation plan. Although government scientists insist the soil is safe, an April 2005 multi-agency task force press release raises some questions. Still, the government cautions residents to "keep children from playing in bare dirt. Cover bare dirt with grass, bushes, or 4–6 inches of lead-free wood chips, mulch, soil, or sand."[74]

The EPA and LDEQ recommend that "residents in the vicinity protect themselves and their children from potential exposure to lead in the home and in the surrounding soil of their neighborhoods."[75] New Orleans pre-Katrina lead statistics speak for themselves. It is no secret that before Katrina, over 50 percent (some studies place this figure at around 70 percent) of children living in the inner-city neighborhoods of New Orleans had blood-lead levels above the current guideline of ten micrograms per deciliter.[76] Childhood lead poisoning in some New Orleans black neighborhoods was as high as 67 percent. Some of the lead problem comes from old lead paint in homes and some from lead in the soil.[77]

Post-Katrina government samples turned up levels of benzo(a)pyrene, a carcinogenic petroleum constituent, exceeding EPA's residential guidelines in the mostly black Agriculture Street community. This is not the first time contamination was uncovered in this neighborhood. In the early 1980s, the Agriculture Street community (Gordon Plaza Subdivision, Housing Authority of New Orleans [HANO] housing, Gordon Plaza Apartments, the Moton Elementary School, the Press Park residential area and community center) was constructed over the Agriculture Street Landfill site.[78]

The ninety-five-acre site was used as a municipal landfill receiving municipal waste and construction debris for more than fifty years prior to being developed for residential and light commercial use—including debris from Hurricane Betsy in 1965. It closed in 1966. Metals, pesticides, and polycyclic aromatic hydrocarbons (PAHs) were found in surface and subsurface soils during environmental studies. The EPA refused to declare the site eligible as a Superfund program in 1986, but, using different standards that gave more weight to soil contamination, added the landfill to the National Priorities List as a Superfund site in 1994.[79] Residents pushed for a buyout of their property and to be relocated. The federal EPA disagreed and ordered a cleanup at a cost of $20 million. The actual cleanup began in 1998 and was completed in 2001.

Government officials assured the Agriculture Street community residents that their neighborhood was safe after the 1998 "cleanup." The Concerned Citizens of Agriculture Street Landfill disagreed and filed a class-action lawsuit against the city of New Orleans for damages and cost of relocation. Katrina accomplished the relocation—albeit forced relocation. After thirteen years of litigation, Seventh District Court Judge Nadine Ramsey ruled in favor of the residents. Her ruling, coming five months after Katrina, could end up costing the city, the Housing Authority of New Orleans, and the Orleans Parish School Board tens of millions of dollars.[80]

Judge Ramsey described the plaintiffs as overwhelmingly poor minority citizens who "were promised the American dream of first-time home ownership. The dream turned out to be a nightmare."[81] The case is on appeal. A dozen or so FEMA trailers now house residents on the contaminated site.

Federal officials debate the appropriate course of action to take in the Agriculture Street community and a dozen or so New Orleans neighborhoods where contamination by toxic metal predates Katrina.[82] The EPA and LDEQ debate what remediation action is needed for the fourteen neighborhood environmental "hot spots" scattered across older New Orleans neighborhoods: three sites in Gentilly, two in Treme, two in Central City, and one each in Bywater, Lower Ninth Ward, Carrollton, Uptown, Mid City, St. Roch, and Seventh Ward.[83] The fourteen neighborhoods were narrowed down from a list of forty-six sites examined by state and federal officials last fall that showed high levels of lead, arsenic, or benzo(a)pyrene.

Not waiting for government to clean up the toxic sediments left behind by Katrina floodwaters, in March 2006 organizers of "A Safe Way Back Home," the Deep South Center for Environmental Justice at Dillard University (DSCEJ), and the United Steelworkers (USW) undertook a proactive pilot neighborhood cleanup project—the first of its kind in New Orleans.[84] The coalition assembled partners from historically black colleges and universities, organized labor, community-based organizations, environmental groups, faith-based groups, and more than 125 college-student volunteers from across the country.

The DSCEJ/USW coalition received dozens of requests and inquiries from New Orleans East home owner associations to help clean up their neighborhoods block by block.

State and federal officials labeled the voluntary cleanup efforts as "scaremongering."[85] The EPA and LDEQ tested 800 sample locations in New Orleans and found cause for concern in only 46 samples. Generally, government officials contend the soil in New Orleans is consistent with what was found before Katrina. LDEQ called the "Safe Way Back Home" program "completely unnecessary."[86] A week after the voluntary cleanup project began, an LDEQ staffer ate a spoonful of dirt scraped from the Aberdeen Road pilot project. The dirt-eating stunt was clearly an attempt to disparage the voluntary neighborhood cleanup initiative. LDEQ officials later apologized.

In August 2006, the EPA gave New Orleans and surrounding communities a clean bill of health, while pledging to monitor a handful of toxic hot spots.[87] EPA and LDEQ officials concluded that Katrina did not cause any appreciable contamination that was not already there. Although EPA tests confirmed widespread lead in the soil, a prestorm problem in 40 percent of New Orleans, the EPA dismissed residents' calls to address this problem as outside of its mission.

THE POLITICS OF "CHOCOLATE CITY"

Almost 300,000 registered voters left New Orleans after Katrina.[88] The storm damaged or destroyed 300 of 442 polling places. Holding a city election poses major challenges regarding registration, absentee ballots, city workers, polling places, and identification for displaced New Orleanians. Nevertheless, the city held its elections in April 2005, even though the vast majority of its citizens were living outside of the city. During a highly contested primary, two mayoral candidates, incumbent Ray Nagin and challenger Lieutenant Governor Mitch Landrieu, were chosen to face off later in May.

Landrieu is the son of Moon Landrieu—the last white mayor of New Orleans. Dissatisfaction with Nagin's performance during and after Hurricane

Katrina was running so high that twenty-two mayoral candidates were on the primary ballot.[89] The incumbent Mayor Nagin, who was trailing in the polls a week before the May primaries, won by more than 5,000 votes.[90]

In 2001, Nagin won the mayoral elections with overwhelming white support and less than 40 percent of the black votes.[91] The majority of African American voters supported his opponent, former New Orleans police chief Richard Pennington—who now heads up the Atlanta Police Department. Nagin's lowest levels of support were in black neighborhoods such as the Ninth Ward, one of the areas hardest hit by Katrina floodwaters.

However, white voters turned out to the polls in record numbers, helping ultimately to tip the scales in Nagin's favor.[92] In the end, Nagin rewarded his white supporters, assembling an administration that drew heavily on Republican and white appointees. Nagin even endorsed Republican Bobby Jindal over Democrat Kathleen Blanco for governor of Louisiana. Blanco's narrow victory led to the strained relationship that many insiders put as a prime cause of the poor communication that paralyzed Southern Louisiana days after Hurricane Katrina.[93]

Campaigning was a difficult task. With most registered voters out of the area, campaigns moved to Baton Rouge, Birmingham, Atlanta, Houston, Memphis, Dallas, and Jackson (Mississippi). Some voters in these cities organized buses to travel to New Orleans to vote.[94] The candidates had to travel to these host cities and campaign there. Some candidates opened campaign offices out of state. Mail campaigns proved ineffective, since FEMA refused to release mailing lists of relocated voters. Even after many obstacles, the out-of-state campaign paid off, since about 113,000 registered voters were able to cast ballots, even though some estimates put the New Orleans population at the time of the election at less than 100,000.

Civil rights groups sued unsuccessfully to gain access for Katrina evacuees to out-of-state polling places.[95] They argued that if Iraqi nationals could be provided polling stations in the United States, surely American citizens could be provided out-of-state polling stations. The Louisiana legislature and the federal courts disagreed and approved a plan to allow ten state satellite polls for displaced voters.[96] New Orleans voters trying to cast absentee ballots found it to be difficult; they either needed Internet access to download forms or to follow a two-step process that required them to write to request a ballot and later return it with supporting documentation.[97] The peculiar twist of New Orleans elections is yet another attempt to dilute and suppress the potent African American vote in the state.

Rebuilding New Orleans will be one of the largest urban reconstruction programs in the country. In a meeting held in Baton Rouge a few weeks after the storm, a cross-section of black New Orleans elected officials, business and civic leaders, and educators expressed concern about "bringing people home."[98] The repopulation of New Orleans is a major challenge.

Who the city is repopulated with has important social, economic, cultural, civil rights, and political implications.

Katrina emptied out black New Orleans in a way successive waves of "urban renewal" programs could not. The Housing Authority of New Orleans, or HANO, as it is popularly called, had been dismantling traditional public housing for nearly a decade before Hurricane Katrina through the U.S. Department of Housing and Urban Development's (HUD) "Home Ownership and Opportunity for People Everywhere" or HOPE VI. The program demolished traditional public housing and "vouchered out" most residents in order to make way for mixed-use, market-rate developments.[99] The St. Thomas redevelopment in New Orleans in the late 1990s became the prototype for dismantling strategically sited public-housing developments—housing that provided a safety net for thousands of poor people. New Orleans's St. Thomas homes were demolished to make way for neotraditionalist townhouses and a Wal-Mart store.

The rebuilding of New Orleans and the Gulf Coast region after Hurricane Katrina has caused some black community leaders to cry foul. They see a rebuilding plan moving forward that excludes them or limits their presence in the "new" New Orleans. A dispatch from the Associated Press agreed. "Hurricane Katrina [may] prove to be the biggest, most brutal urban-renewal project Black America has ever seen."[100] Displacement is often viewed as an inevitable by-product of HOPE VI–inspired urban revitalization efforts.[101] Some of these efforts mirror the old urban renewal programs—creating "rehab refugees" that are traded in for a "better class of poor people."[102]

In September 2005, a month after Katrina, HUD Secretary Alphonso Jackson, who is African American, predicted it will be years before New Orleans regains the half-million population it had before the storm, and the population might never again be predominantly black. The comments were made by the HUD chief during a visit to Houston. "Whether we like it or not, New Orleans is not going to be 500,000 people for a long time. New Orleans is not going to be as black as it was for a long time, if ever again."[103] Secretary Jackson's comment about a "whiter" New Orleans was not met with the same public uproar as Mayor Ray Nagin's "Chocolate City" remarks. Nagin apologized for a Martin Luther King Day speech in which he predicted that New Orleans would be a "chocolate" city once more and asserted that "God was mad at America."[104]

Secretary Jackson said publicly what some business and political leaders in New Orleans have been discussing privately. Congressman Richard H. Baker, a ten-term Republican from Baton Rouge, was overheard telling lobbyists: "We finally cleaned up public housing in New Orleans. We couldn't do it, but God did."[105] Government failure to devise a repopulation plan a full year after the storm ushered in a form of "ethnic cleansing" of public housing and many hard-hit low-income and middle-income black neighborhoods.[106]

In May 2006, HUD announced it would invest $154 million in rebuilding public housing in New Orleans and assist the city to bring displaced residents home.[107] But critics fear that government officials and business leaders are quietly planning to demolish the old projects and privatize public housing. Before the storm, New Orleans had close to 8,000 public housing units. A year after Katrina, at least 80 percent of public housing in New Orleans remained closed. Six of ten of the largest public housing developments in the city were boarded up, with the other four in various states of repair.

Over 49,000 people lived in public housing before Katrina, 20,000 in older, large-scale developments such as St. Bernard, and 29,000 in Section 8 rental housing, which was also devastated by the storm. Although the city faces a severe housing crunch, in June 2006, federal housing officials announced that more than 5,000 public housing apartments for the poor would be razed and replaced by developments for residents from a wider range of incomes.[108] This move heightened the anxiety of many low-income black Katrina survivors who fear they will not be allowed to return in favor of higher-income families.

The demolition of four sprawling public housing projects—the St. Bernard, C. J. Peete, B. W. Cooper, and Lafitte housing developments, represents more than half of all of the conventional public housing in the city, where only 1,097 units were occupied ten months after the storm. HUD raised by 35 percent the value of disaster vouchers for displaced residents because the city's housing shortage has caused rents to skyrocket.

Louisiana governor Kathleen Babineaux Blanco announced in February 2006 the establishment of a new housing initiative called The Road Home program.[109] The program was designed by the Louisiana Recovery Authority (LRA) in conjunction with the Office of Community Development and national housing experts. The plan is intended to provide up to $150,000, minus insurance payments and FEMA assistance, for home owners to repair, rebuild, take a buyout or relocate, or sell their homes.

The program is so complicated that it is sometimes difficult for the staff to explain. The Road Home Program is intended to provide information to help home owners and owners of small-scale rental property understand their options and make informed decisions regarding their properties. The proposal also includes a plan for repairing and rebuilding affordable housing through incentives for rental property owners and developers.[110]

There is renewed hope that the housing situation will improve. In June 2006, the AFL-CIO announced plans to invest $1 billion to develop 10,000 affordable homes and a new downtown hotel.[111] The investment plan includes $250 million in financing for housing construction over the next seven years, with more than 5,000 rental units expected to be built. Another $100 million will be equity investments for commercial real estate and re-vitalization projects.[112]

Hundreds of groups around the country have taken the position that no Katrina victims, including former residents of New Orleans public housing, should be left behind in the rebuilding of lives and communities in the Gulf Coast region. Katrina is forcing organizations to regroup and rethink how the nation responds to natural and man-made emergencies. In a joint statement, *Principles and Priorities for Rebuilding New Orleans*, more than a half dozen black groups stressed the importance of "using the expertise and knowledge of local and grassroots resources with the large-scale means of the federal government to directly benefit the residents and businesses in the areas affected by the disaster."[113]

National Urban League president Marc Morial, a former mayor of New Orleans, called for a "Katrina Victims Bill of Rights."[114] Morial urged Congress to move forward on initiatives that address personal injury, economic dislocation, and voting rights—a Victims Compensation Fund for the hundreds of thousands of citizens injured, killed, and displaced by Katrina.

Finally, there appears to be a general consensus that Katrina survivors have a right to self-determination and all displaced persons should be allowed to return to their home and neighborhood and allowed to exercise their democratic rights guaranteed under the U.S. Constitution. Making this happen will not be easy.

NOTES

1. Regional Planning Commission of Orleans, Jefferson, and St. Bernard Parishes, "History of Regional Growth of Jefferson, Orleans, and St. Bernard Parishes," November 1969, 13; Richard Baumbach and William E. Borah, *The Second Battle of New Orleans: A History of the Vieux Carre? Riverfront Expressway Controversy* (Tuscaloosa: University of Alabama Press, 1981), 5.

2. Ibid.

3. Bureau of Governmental Research, *"The Vieux Carre" New Orleans: Its Plan, Its Growth, Its Architecture*, report published December 1968, 10–11.

4. See B. H. Wright, "Black in New Orleans: The City That Care Forgot," in *In Search of the New South: The Black Urban Experience in the 1970s and 1980s*, ed. Robert D. Bullard (Tuscaloosa: University of Alabama Press, 1989), 45–74.

5. Beverly Wright, "New Orleans Neighborhoods under Siege," in *Just Transportation: Dismantling Race and Class Barriers to Mobility*, ed. Robert D. Bullard and Glenn S. Johnson (Gabriola Island, BC: New Society Publishers, 1997), 121–44.

6. Manuel Pastor, Robert D. Bullard, James K. Boyce, Alice Fothergill, Rachel Morello-Frosch, and Beverly Wright, *In the Wake of the Storm: Environment, Disaster*

and Race After Katrina (New York: Russell Sage Foundation, May 2006); Michael Eric Dyson, *Come Hell or High Water: Hurricane Katrina and the Color of Disaster* (New York: Basic Books, 2006).

7. Michael Stoll, *Job Sprawl and the Spatial Mismatch between Blacks and Jobs* (Washington, DC: Brookings Institution, February 2005).

8. Associated Press, "Mandatory Evacuation Ordered for New Orleans," August 28, 2005.

9. American Red Cross, "Hurricane Katrina: Why Is the Red Cross Not in New Orleans," available at http://www.redcross.org/faq/0,1096,0_682_4524,00.html (accessed October 1, 2005).

10. Mark Schleifstein, "Preparing for the Worst," *Times-Picayune*, May 31, 2005.

11. Bruce Nolan, "In Storm, N.O. Wants No One Left Behind," *Times-Picayune*, July 24, 2005.

12. Douglas Brinkley, *The Great Deluge: Hurricane Katrina, New Orleans, and the Mississippi Gulf Coast* (New York: William Morrow, 2006); Ivor Van Heerden, *The Storm: What Went Wrong and Why During Hurricane Katrina* (New York: Viking, 2006).

13. Nicholas Riccardi, "Many of Louisiana Dead Over 60," *The Atlanta Journal-Constitution*, November 6, 2005, A6.

14. Dyson, *Come Hell or High Water*.

15. Todd Litman, *Lesson from Katrina and Rita: What Major Disasters Can Teach Transportation Planners* (Victoria, BC: Victoria Transport Policy Institute, September 30, 2005).

16. See State of Louisiana, *Southeast Louisiana Hurricane Evacuation and Sheltering Plan*, State of Louisiana, 2000, available at www.ohsep.louisiana.gov/plans/EOPSupplementala.pdf (accessed November 2, 2005); Mark Fischett, "Drowning New Orleans," *Scientific American*, October 2001, available at www.sciam.com (accessed November 5, 2005); Joel K. Bourne Jr., "Gone with the Water," *National Geographic*, October 2004, available at http://magma.nationalgeographic.com/ngm/0410/feature5/ (accessed November 5, 2005); City of New Orleans, *City of New Orleans Comprehensive Emergency Management Plan*, City of New Orleans, 2005, available at www.cityofno.com (accessed December 6, 2005).

17. City of New Orleans, *City of New Orleans Comprehensive Emergency Management Plan*.

18. Brian Wolshon, "Planning for the Evacuation of New Orleans," *Institute of Transportation Engineers Journal* (February 2002): 45, available at http://www.ite.org/ (accessed December 6, 2005).

19. Michael Perlstein and Brian Thevenot, "Evacuation Isn't an Option for Many N.O. Area Residents," *Times-Picayune*, September 15, 2004, A1.

20. Shirley Laska, "What If Hurricane Ivan Had Not Missed New Orleans?" *National Hazards Observer* (November 2004): 5–6.

21. Littman, *Lessons from Katrina*.

22. Bruce Eggler, "RTA Back on Track Slowly, Surely," *Times-Picayune*, October 14, 2005, B1.

23. Amy Liu, Matt Fellowes, and Mia Mabanta, *Special Edition of the Katrina Index: A One-Year Review of Key Indicators of Recovery in Post-Storm New Orleans* (Washington, DC: Brookings Institution, August 2006), 6.

24. Clay Robison and Samantha Levine, "Perry, White Thrash FEMA," *Houston Chronicle*, November 1, 2005, available at http://www.chron.com/cs/CDA/rssstory .mpl/special/05/katrina/3432394 (accessed November 25, 2005).

25. Susan Saulny, "Students Return to Big Changes in New Orleans," http://www .nytimes.com/2006/01/04/national/nationalspecial/04schools.html?ex=12940308 00&en=00ef41bc6a36bc6a&ei=5088&partner=rssnyt&emc=rss (accessed November 16, 2005).

26. Amy Liu, Matt Fellowes, and Mia Mabanta, *Katrina Index: Tracking Variables of Post-Katrina Reconstruction* (Washington, DC: Brookings Institution, June 2006), http://www.brookings.edu/metro/pubs/200512_katrinaindex.htm (accessed June 10, 2006).

27. Bill Quigley, "Ten Months After Katrina: Gutting New Orleans," *Common Dreams News Center*, June 29, 2006, found at http://www.commondreams.org/ views06/0629-20.htm (accessed July 5, 2006).

28. Environmental Policy Institute, "Katrina Evacuees Face Extreme Levels of Joblessness," November 9, 2005, available at http://www.epinet.org/content.cfm/ webfeatures_snapshots_20051109 (accessed December 7, 2005).

29. Louis Uchitelle, "Jobs Surged Last Month in Rebound from Storm," *New York Times*, December 3, 2005.

30. INFOPLEASE, "Profile of the 50 Largest Cities of the United States," available at http://www.infoplease.com/ipa/A0108567.html (accessed September 29, 2006).

31. ACORN, *The Great Divide: Home Purchase Mortgage Lending Nationally and in 115 Metropolitan Areas* (Washington, DC: Association of Community Organizations for Reform Now, October 2003), 3.

32. Ibid., 5.

33. See Federal Financial Institutions Examination Council (FFIEC), *Home Mortgage Disclosure Act, Aggregate Report Search by State*, found at http://www.ffiec.gov/ hmdaadwebreport/aggwelcome.aspx (accessed December 8, 2005).

34. National Fair Housing Alliance, *No Home for the Holidays: Report on Housing Discrimination Against Hurricane Katrina Survivors*, Executive Summary (Washington, DC: NFHA, December 20, 2005), available at http://www.nationalfairhousing.org/ html/Press%20Releases/Katrina/Hurricane%20Katrina%20Survivors%20-%20 Report.pdf (accessed December 28, 2005).

35. From mid-September through mid-December 2005, the NFHA conducted telephone tests of rental housing providers in seventeen cities in five states: Alabama (Birmingham, Mobile, Huntsville, and Montgomery); Florida (Gainesville, Tallahassee, and Pensacola); Georgia (Atlanta, Columbus, Macon, and Savannah); Tennessee (Nashville, Chattanooga, and Memphis); and Texas (Houston, Dallas, and Waco).

36. National Fair Housing Alliance, *No Home for the Holidays*, 2.

37. Ned Randolph, "State Will Suffer Sans N.O.," *Advocate* (Baton Rouge), September 11, 2005, 1A.

38. Thomas Frank, "Blanco Pushes FEMA for Hotel Rooms," *USA Today*, September 21, 2005, A3.

39. Laura Maggi, "Shelter Shutting: Next Steps," *Times-Picayune*, October 14, 2005, A1.

40. Ibid.

41. Jeff Chang, Thenmozhi Soundararajan, and Anita Johnson, "Getting Home Before It's Gone," Alternet.org, September 26, 2005, found at http://www.alternet.org/katrina/2593 (accessed October 12, 2005).

42. Jacqui Goddard, "No People, No Power, No Money: A City Struggling to Live Again," *Times* (London), November 12, 2005, available at http://www.timesonline.co.uk/article/0,,23889-1868323,00.html (accessed November 21, 2005).

43. Alan Hughes, "Blown Away by Katrina," *Black Enterprise Magazine*, November 2005, 150.

44. Hope Yen, "Minority Firms Getting Few Katrina Pacts," *Business Week*, October 4, 2005, available at http://www.businessweek.com/ap/financialnews/D8D1CE901.htm?campaign_id=apn_home_down&chan=db (accessed October 14, 2005).

45. Thomas B. Edsall, "Bush Suspends Pay Act in Areas Hit by Storm," *Washington Post*, September 9, 2005, D3.

46. Mary Lou Pickel, "Immigrant Workers Rile New Orleans," *The Atlanta Journal-Constitution*, October 19, 2005, A1.

47. Griff Witte, "Prevailing Wages to Be Paid Again on Gulf Coast," *Washington Post*, October 27, 2005, A01, available at http://www.washingtonpost.com/wp-dyn/cont ent/article/2005/10/26/AR2005102601706.html (accessed October 30, 2005).

48. Bob Sullivan, "FEMA Grants Leave Some Behind," MSNBC, October 19, 2005, available at http://www.msnbc.msn.com/id/9655113 (accessed October 24, 2005).

49. For an in-depth discussion of urban poverty and minority economic development see Thomas D. Boston and Catherine L. Ross, eds., *The Inner City: Urban Poverty and Economic Development in the Next Century* (New Brunswick, NJ: Transaction, 1997).

50. Leslie Eaton and Ron Nixon, "Loans to Homeowners Along Gulf Coast Lag," *New York Times*, December 15, 2005.

51. Hughes, "Blown Away by Katrina," 152.

52. Ibid., 149.

53. Kathy Chu, "Wind or Flood: Fights with Insurers Loom," *USA Today*, September 20, 2005, A2.

54. Ibid.

55. Joseph B. Treaster, "Storm Passes, but Insurance Worries Stay," *New York Times*, August 31, 2006.

56. Kathy Chu, "Flooding Victims to Get Funds Quicker," *USA Today*, September 21, 2005, A1.

57. Joseph B. Treaster, "Gulf Coast Insurance Expected to Soar," *New York Times*, September 24, 2005; Walter Gillis Peacock and Chris Girard, "Ethnic and Racial Inequalities in Hurricane Damage and Insurance Settlements," in *Hurricane Andrew: Ethnicity, Gender, and the Sociology of Disasters*, ed. Walter Gillis Peacock, Betty Hearn Morrow, and Hugh Gladwin (London: Routledge, 2007), 180–81.

58. Anita Lee, "Wind or Water: The Debate Rages, But Who Will Pay?" *Sun Herald* (South Mississippi), December 21, 2005, available at http://www.sunherald.com/mld/sunherald/news/special_packages/hurricane_katrina/13454363.htm?source=rss&channel=sunherald_hurricane_katrina (accessed December 22, 2005).

59. Péralte C. Paul, "You've Got to Make Them Feel Good about Something," *Pulse Journal*, September 19, 2005, found at http://www.pulsejournal.com/hp/content/shared/news/nation/stories/09/0918_COXKATRINA_INSURE.html (accessed December 1, 2005).

60. Andrew Ward, "Insurer Wins Test Case Over Katrina Liability," MSNBC, August 16, 2006, available at http://www.msnbc.msn.com/id/14364907/ (accessed August 20, 2006).

61. Please see for the complete ruling: http://www.mssd.uscourts.gov/news/Leonard%20v.%20Nationwide%20final%20opinion.pdf#search=%22leonard%20v.%20Nationwide%20Mutual%20Insurance%20%22 (accessed September 30, 2006).

62. Associated Press, "Judge: Insurance Policy Excluded Flood Damage: Ruling Could Set a Precedent for Hundreds of Other Court Challenges," MSNBC, August 15, 2006, available at http://www.msnbc.msn.com/id/14362386/ (accessed August 22, 2006).

63. "Judge Who Decided First Katrina Case Now Faces Hundreds," *Insurance Journal*, August 18, 2006, available at: http://www.insurancejournal.com/news/national/2006/08/18/71525.htm (accessed September 1, 2006).

64. Thomas Gabe, Gene Falk, Maggie McCarthy, and Virginia W. Mason, *Hurricane Katrina: Social-Demographic Characteristics of Impacted Areas*, Washington, DC: Congressional Research Service Report RL33141, November, 2005; John Schwartz, "New Study of Levees Faults Design and Construction," *New York Times*, May 22, 2006.

65. See Stephen Jackson, "Un/natural Disasters, Here and There," *Understanding Katrina: Perspectives from the Social Sciences*, Social Science Research Council, 2005, 1; Chester Hartman and Gregory Squires, *There Is No Such Thing as a Natural Disaster* (New York: Routledge, 2006); Susan Cutter, *Hazards, Vulnerability and Environmental Justice* (New York: Earthscan, 2006); See Robert D. Bullard, "Katrina and the Second Disaster: A Twenty-Point Plan to Destroy Black New Orleans," Environmental Justice Resource Center at Clark Atlanta University, December 23, 2005, found at http://www.ejrc.cau.edu/Bullard20PointPlan.html (accessed December 25, 2005).

66. Catherine Arnst and Janet Ginsburg, "The Mother of All Toxic Cleanups," *Business Week*, September 26, 2005. Available at http://www.businessweek.com/magazine/content/05_39/b3952055.htm (accessed September 22, 2006).

67. Linda Luther, *Disaster Debris Removal After Hurricane Katrina: Status and Associated Issues* (Washington, DC: Congressional Research Service Report to Congress, June 16, 2006), 1.

68. U.S. EPA and Louisiana Department of Environmental Quality, "News Release: Top State and Federal Environmental Officials Discuss Progress and Tasks Ahead After Katrina," September 30, 2005, available at http://www.deq.state.la.us/news/pdf/administratorjohnson.pdf#search='katrina%20debris%20350%2C000%20automobiles (accessed October 1, 2005).

69. Adam Nossiter, "Thousands of Demolitions Are Likely in New Orleans," *New York Times*, October 23, 2005, available at http://www.nytimes.com/2005/10/23/national/nationalspecial/23demolish.html?ex=1287720000&en=feb9b1cfc0b344ba&ei=5090&partner=rssuserland&emc=rss (accessed September 26, 2006).

70. Federal Emergency Management Agency, "By the Numbers: One Year Later," FEMA Recovery Update for Hurricane Katrina Press Release, August 22, 2006, http://www.fema.gov/news/newsrelease.fema?id=29108 (accessed August 23, 2006).

71. Gerard Shields, "Five Parishes to Receive Help with Debris Cleanup," *Advocate* (Baton Rouge), June 30, 2006.

72. Kevin F. McCarthy, D. J. Peterson, Narayan Sastry, and Michael Pollard, *The Repopulation of New Orleans After Hurricane Katrina* (Santa Monica, CA: The RAND Corporation, March 24, 2006).

73. Gina M. Solomon and Miriam Rotkin-Ellman, *Contaminants in New Orleans Sediments: An Analysis of EPA Data* (New York: NRDC, February 2006), available at http://www.nrdc.org/health/effects/katrinadata/sedimentepa.pdf (accessed February 19, 2006).

74. U.S. EPA, "Release of Multi-Agency Report Shows Elevated Lead Levels in New Orleans Soil, Consistent with Historic Levels of Urban Lead," EPA Newsroom, March 4, 2006, available at http://yosemite.epa.gov/opa/admpress.nsf/0/BA5F2460D6C777F58525714600693B5B (accessed March 8, 2006).

75. Ibid.

76. Howard Mielke, "Lead in the Inner Cities: Policies to Reduce Children's Exposure to Lead May Be Overlooking a Major Source of Lead in the Environment," *American Scientist* 87, no. 1 (January/February 1999): 62–73.

77. Felicia A Rabito, LuAnn E. White, and Charles Shorter, "From Research to Policy: Targeting the Primary Prevention of Childhood Lead Poisoning," *Public Health Reports* 119 (May/June 2004): 271–78.

78. Agency for Toxic Substances and Disease Registry, "Public Health Assessment: Agriculture Street Landfill New Orleans, Orleans Parish, Louisiana," available at http://www.atsdr.cdc.gov/HAC/PHA/agriculturestreet/asl_p3.html (accessed September 15, 2005).

79. See Agency for Toxic Substances and Disease Registry, "Public Health Assessment", Alicia Lyttle, *Agriculture Street Landfill Environmental Justice Case Study* (Ann Arbor: University of Michigan School of Natural Resources, January 2003).

80. Susan Finch, "Ag Street Landfill Case Gets Ruling: City Ordered to Pay Residents of Toxic Site," *Times-Picayune*, January 27, 2006.

81. Ibid.

82. Matthew Brown, "Lead Found in Soil of Many Areas of N.O.: Contamination by Toxic Metal Predates Katrina, Scientists Say," *Times-Picayune*, April 6, 2006.

83. Amy Wold, "EPA Looks at N.O.'s Soil's Lead Content: Pre-Katrina Problem May Need Remediation," *Advocate* (Baton Rouge), April 6, 2006, http://www.2theadvocate.com/news/suburban/2586821.html (accessed April 9, 2006).

84. "Residents to FEMA: This Is How to Clean Up Tainted Properties in New Orleans," press release, United Steelworkers and Deep South Center for Environmental Justice at Dillard University, March 23, 2006, available at http://biz.yahoo.com/bw/060323/20060323005549.html?.v=1 (accessed March 27, 2006).

85. Ann M. Simmons, "New Orleans Activists Starting from the Ground Up," *Los Angeles Times*, March 24, 2006, available at http://newreconstruction.civilrights.org/details.cfm?id=41606 (accessed March 27, 2006).

86. Leslie Williams, "Groups Warn About Arsenic in Soil," *Times-Picayune*, March 24, 2006.

87. Matthew Brown, "Final EPA Report Deems N.O. Safe," *Times-Picayune*, August 19, 2006.

88. Ed Anderson, "City May Hire Extra Workers for Absentee Ballots," *Times-Picayune*, October 14, 2005, A3.

89. Kim Cobb and Kristen Mack, "Nagin Revels in His Unconventional Win," *Houston Chronicle*, May 22, 2006, available at: http://www.chron.com/disp/story .mpl/front/3878784.html (accessed September 12, 2006).

90. Louisiana Secretary of State, "Official Parish Election Results for Election Date: 5/20/06, Parish of Orleans," available at: http://www.sos.louisiana.gov:8090/ cgibin/?rqstyp=elcpr&rqsdta=05200636 (accessed September 13, 2006).

91. Christopher Tidmore, "New Orleans Mayor Nagin and City Election Analysis," May 26, 2006, available at: http://www.bayoubuzz.com/articles.aspx?aid=7176 (accessed September 13, 2006).

92. Institute for Southern Studies, "One Year After Katrina: The State of New Orleans and the Gulf Coast," available at: http://www.reconstructionwatch.org/images/ One_Year_After.pdf (accessed September 13, 2006).

93. Tidmore, "New Orleans Mayor Nagin and City Election Analysis."

94. Peter Whoriskey, "A Mayoral Free-for-All in Changed New Orleans," *Washington Post*, March 6, 2006, A03, available at http://www.washingtonpost.com/ wp-dyn/content/article/2006/03/05/AR2006030500884_pf.html (accessed September 13, 2006).

95. Ibid.

96. Mark Schleifstein, "Absentee Voting by the Numbers," *Times-Picayune*, May 20, 2006, available at http://www.nola.com/newslogs/tpupdates/index.ssf?/mtlogs/ nola_tpupdates/archives/2006_05_20.html (accessed September 13, 2006).

97. Whoriskey, "A Mayoral Free-for-All in Changed New Orleans."

98. Meeting of black New Orleans community leaders held at the Louisiana state capitol building, Baton Rouge (September 12, 2005).

99. National Housing Law Project, Poverty & Race Action Council, Sherwood Research Associates, Center for Community Change, ENPHRONT, *False Hope* (Washington, DC: NHLP, 2002).

100. Mike Davis, "Gentrifying Disaster," *Mother Jones*, October 25, 2005, 1.

101. Larry Keating, "Redeveloping Public Housing: Relearning Urban Renewal's Immutable Lessons," *Journal of the American Planning Association* 66, no. 4 (2000): 384–96.

102. Christopher Swope, "Rehab Refugees," *Governing Magazine* (May 2001): 1.

103. Lori Rodriguez and Zeke Minaya, "New Orleans' Racial Makeup Up in Air: Some Black Areas May Not Be Rebuilt, HUD Chief Says," *Houston Chronicle*, September 29, 2006.

104. Associated Press, "New Orleans Mayor Apologizes for Remarks," *USA Today*, January 17, 2006.

105. Charles Babington, "Some GOP Legislators Hit Jarring Notes in Addressing Katrina," *Washington Post*, September 10, 2005, A4.

106. Davis, "Gentrifying Disaster."

107. Gwen Filosa, "Public Housing Residents Plan to 'Take Over' Shuttered Complex," *Times-Picayune*, May 31, 2006.

108. Susan Saulny, "5,000 Public Housing Units in New Orleans Are to Be Razed," *New York Times*, June 15, 2006.

109. Louisiana Recovery Authority, "Public Invited to Comment on The Road Home Housing Plan," press release, no date, available at http://www.lra.louisiana .gov/pr4_5_pr.html (accessed August 16, 2006).

110. State of Louisiana, Office of the Governor, "Displaced Louisiana Residents Are Encouraged to Call 24-hour, 7-day Housing Registry and Start on the Road Home," March 8, 2006, available at http://www.gov.state.la.us/index.cfm?md =newsroom&tmp=detail&articleID=1711 (accessed March 9, 2006).

111. Michelle Roberts, "AFL-CIO Plans Investment in La. Projects: AFL-CIO Plans to Invest $700 Million in Housing, Other Projects to Help Rebuild New Orleans," Associated Press, June 13, 2006, available at http://www.cbsnews.com/stories/ 2006/06/13/ap/national/mainD8I7HQQ00.shtml (accessed September 14, 2006).

112. AFL-CIO Now, "Latest AFL-CIO Initiative in Rebuilding New Orleans Through Investment Trust Corp," August 14, 2006, available at http://blog.aflcio.org/ 2006/08/14/latest-afl-cio-initiative-in-rebuilding-new-orleans-through-investment-trust-corp/ (accessed September 16, 2006).

113. Joint Statement by Black Social Scientists, *Principles and Priorities for Rebuilding New Orleans* (October 26, 2005), 1, available at http://www.epi.org/content .cfm/webfeatures_viewpoints_rebuilding_new_orleans (accessed October 29, 2005).

114. U.S. Newswire, "National Urban League Calls for a Katrina Victims Bill of Rights," September 8, 2005, available at http://releases.usnewswire.com/GetRelease .asp?id=52942 (accessed September 25, 2005).

9

Health Disparities in Black Los Angeles

J. Eugene Grigsby III

The 1965 Watts riots focused the nation's attention on the plight of black Angelenos as no other event ever had. In part, this was because 34 people were killed, nearly 1,000 injured, and almost 4,000 more arrested in addition to property damage estimated at $40 million. For nonblacks, this may have been the first indication that the gulf between black and white was more serious than heretofore believed. For black Angelenos, the riot emphasized their continued frustration with police brutality, segregated housing, and lack of access to needed services.

One issue became clear from the numerous postriot studies: residents did not have access to comprehensive health care services and, in particular, to emergency care.[1] This lack contributed significantly to major disparities in mortality and morbidity. A proposed solution was the construction of a new state-of-the-art county hospital capable of providing health services to the area's predominantly African American population. In addition, a new medical school with the ability to train health professionals as well as physicians was also proposed.[2] The Charles R. Drew Medical School opened in August 1966. The Martin Luther King Jr. General Hospital opened on March 27, 1972. Through a contract with the county of Los Angeles, the Drew school provides medical staffing for the hospital. In 1982, by unanimous vote of the County Board of Supervisors, the name was changed to the King/Drew Medical Center.

Today, nearly forty years after the riots, the much-vaunted medical center has been forced to curtail services and close many of its residency training programs.[3] In considering the current situation, two questions must be answered. What has happened to the health status of African Americans in Los Angeles since the uprising of 1965? What will the future hold if this critical facility for addressing health access for African Americans in Los Angeles ceases to exist?

The California Endowment's recent report *Unequal Treatment, Unequal Health* finds that the infant mortality rate for African Americans in California is more than twice as high as that of whites and that African Americans living in Los Angeles County have a 78 percent higher death rate from heart disease than the overall population.[4] Furthermore, the Office of State Health Planning and Development in its *Fact Book on Racial and Ethnic Disparities in Health Care in California* reports that health status, health service utilization, and health outcomes are where disparities occur.[5] These findings indicate that in spite of efforts to provide needed health care services, health disparities between African Americans and other ethnic/racial groups remain.

The remainder of this chapter is divided into three sections. In the first, census data are used to document both the growth and geographic dispersion (suburbanization) of the Los Angeles region's African American population between 1960 and 2000. Section two explores the question of how well the health needs of the African American population have been served over the past four decades, particularly since during this time many African Americans have moved to the "suburbs." Data from the Los Angeles County and California Departments of Health Services are used to assess whether health disparities persist and whether they are less severe for African Americans living in the suburbs than for those living in central Los Angeles. Finally, some proposed contemporary solutions for addressing these disparities are reviewed to better understand what steps might be taken to improve the health status of Los Angeles's African Americans in this decade.

SUBURBANIZATION OF LOS ANGELES'S AFRICAN AMERICAN POPULATION

Many readers unfamiliar with the Los Angeles metropolitan area may mistakenly believe that African Americans reside primarily in the central city of Los Angeles.[6] While this was the case in the 1960s when 73 percent of the African Americans in the county lived within Los Angeles city limits, it is not presently true. Today a majority of African Americans (55 percent) live in other cities throughout the county.

Suburbanization of African Americans has been occurring for over forty years. The African American population in the cities of Carson, Inglewood, Pasadena, and Pomona, for example, grew to 11 percent or greater between 1960 and 1970. Ten years later (1980) the proportion of African Americans in two of these four cities had more than doubled (Carson, 12 percent to 29 percent, Inglewood, 11 percent to 57 percent). This suburbanization

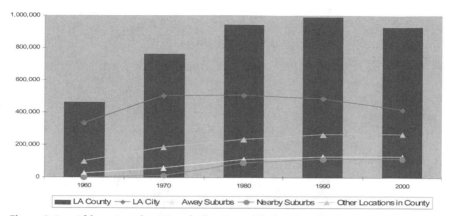

Figure 9.1.   African American Population Growth in Los Angeles County, 1960 to 2000
Source: 1960–2000 Census Data compiled by the National Health Foundation.

trend began a decade earlier for the city of Compton. In 1950 African Americans comprised 4 percent of Compton's population. By 1960 this had increased to 39 percent and by 1980 to 75 percent.

On the other hand, African American population growth in suburban Long Beach lagged by ten years. In 1980 African Americans constituted 14 percent of Long Beach's population. By 2000 their number had reached 45 percent. During this same period the size of the African American population also began to increase in other neighboring cities, including Gardena (26 percent) and Hawthorne (33 percent).

Since 1980, however, Los Angeles and Compton have experienced declines in their African American population proportions by 6 percent and 35 percent, respectively. This decline is attributed to both immigration of other ethnic groups (particularly Latino) and increased out-migration of African Americans to other cities in the county (see figure 9.1).

For over five decades there has been a continued growth in the region's total African American population, but it was not limited to the city of Los Angeles. Where once Los Angeles was the central place of residence for African Americans, today there are twelve other cities that host 27 percent of the county's African American residents. Furthermore, 29 percent of the county's African Americans are dispersed throughout the remaining seventy-three cities and the unincorporated territory in the county (see figure 9.2).

So, when one thinks in terms of such key issues for African Americans as health status, it is important to frame these issues from the perspective of the residential community in which people live. This is particularly important if information about health disparities is to be used to motivate local decision makers to address the problem more effectively. Health planners, more often than not, aggregate data to the county or state level, making it

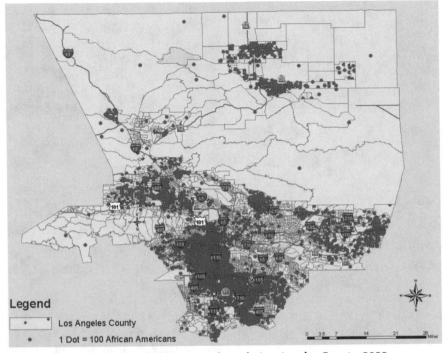

Figure 9.2.   Distribution of African Americans in Los Angeles County, 2000
Source: 2000 Census Data mapped by the National Health Foundation.

difficult to address questions of how suburbanization might impact health disparities.

To analyze whether or not suburbanization reduces health disparities for African Americans, cities with large African American populations were grouped into three types: first, nearby suburban cities (those that share borders with Los Angeles, including Carson, Culver City, Gardena, Lynwood, Long Beach, Inglewood, and Hawthorne); second, away suburbs (those cities that do not share borders with Los Angeles, including Pasadena, Paramount and Pomona, Monrovia, and Signal Hill); and third, the seventy-three cities and unincorporated areas that do not individually have large African American populations but who collectively house 29 percent of the county's African population.

Figure 9.3 shows the spatial distribution of African Americans in the thirteen cities with the largest African American populations. Figure 9.4 provides a more detailed view of the nearby suburbs, which account for 23 percent of the county's African American population. The maps graphically portray the spatial dispersion of the region's African American population. The next section of this chapter assesses the health status of African Americans in the Los Angeles metropolitan area.

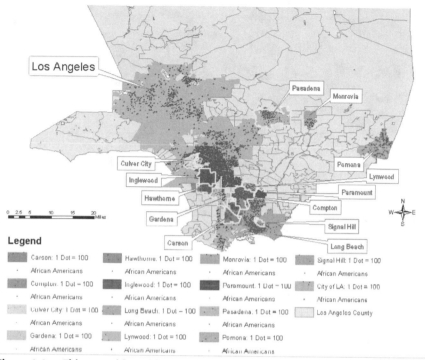

Figure 9.3. Thirteen Cities with the Largest African American Populations in Los Angeles County in 2000
Source: The National Health Foundation.

HEALTH DISPARITIES AMONG
AFRICAN AMERICANS IN LOS ANGELES

The National Institutes of Health (NIH) define health disparities as "differences in the incidence, prevalence, mortality, and burden of disease and other adverse health conditions that exist among specific population groups in the United States."[7] By far the greatest disparities—in terms of number of people affected and width of the gaps—are experienced by people of color.[8]

Primary care is the underpinning of the health care system, and research studies have shown that having a regular source of care increases the chances that people receive adequate preventive care and other important health services. Data from the Agency for Health Care Research and Quality (AHRQ) reveal that about 30 percent of Hispanics and 20 percent of African Americans lack a regular source of health care compared with less than 16 percent of whites. Hispanic children are nearly three times as likely as non-Hispanic white children to have no usual source of health care. African American and Hispanic Americans are far more likely to rely on

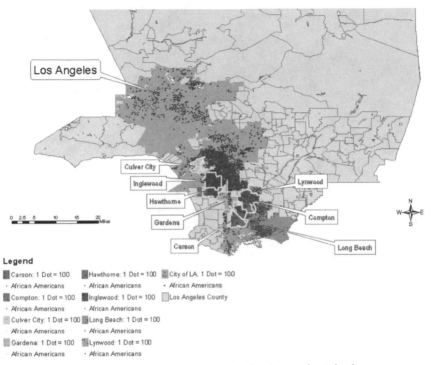

Figure 9.4.   Density of African American Population in Nearby Suburbs, 2000
Source: The National Health Foundation.

hospital emergency rooms or clinics for their usual source of care than are white Americans (16 and 13 percent, respectively, versus 8 percent).[9]

African Americans are 13 percent less likely to undergo coronary angioplasty and one-third less likely to undergo bypass surgery than are whites. Among preschool children hospitalized for asthma, only 7 percent of African American and 2 percent of Hispanic children, compared with 21 percent of white children, are prescribed routine medications to prevent future asthma-related hospitalizations.[10] African Americans with human immune deficiency virus (HIV) infection are less likely to be on antiretroviral therapy, less likely to receive prophylaxis for pneumocystis pneumonia, and less likely to be receiving protease inhibitors than other persons with HIV.[11]

Several studies conducted by the UCLA Center for Health Policy identify diabetes, access to primary care, heart disease, asthma, and HIV infection as major health care issues facing African Americans in Los Angeles County. Over 25 percent of African American adults sixty-five and over have been diagnosed with type 2 diabetes. More than six in ten African American adults (62.7 percent) and three in ten not diagnosed with diabetes (33.5 percent) have weight above healthy levels.[12]

Table 9.1.   Age-Adjusted Rates (per 1,000) of YLLs, YLDs, and DALYs by Ethnicity

	RATE		
Race/Ethnicity	*YLLs*	*YLDs*	*DALYs*
Black	106.4	83.9	190.3
White	55.8	56.7	112.5
Latino	43.4	50.7	94
Asian/PI	28.5	48.5	76.9
AI/AN	67.4	81.7	149.2

Source: Los Angeles County Department of Health, UCLA Health Policy Center.

The Los Angeles County Health Department and the UCLA Health Policy Center employed a new measure called the Global Burden of Disease to assess the total burden of disease and injury among Los Angeles County residents. This approach combines measures of premature mortality (Years of Life Lost, YLLs) and morbidity (Years Lived with Disability, YLDs), into a single measure of burden known as Disability Adjusted Life Years (DALYs). This approach found Los Angeles's African Americans had the highest age-adjusted rate per 1,000 population (190.3), followed by American Indians/Alaska Natives (149.2), whites (112.5), Latinos (94.0), and Asians/Pacific Islanders (76.9) (see table 9.1).[13]

African Americans and American Indians also have higher rates of disability as measured by Years Lived with Disability (YLDs) per 1,000 population. These findings underscore the importance of addressing the markedly increased rate of premature mortality among African Americans in the county.[14] Homicide/violence was also identified as the leading cause of DALYs in African Americans and the second leading cause in Latinos, but does not appear among the leading ten causes in whites and Asian/Pacific Islanders (see table 9.2).[15]

Given the disparities that have been identified for African Americans in Los Angeles County, it should come as no surprise that this population perceives that its quality of life is adversely impacted by its health status. As can be seen in table 9.3, African Americans reported in a survey conducted by the Los Angeles County Health Department that they had a higher number of unhealthy days (8.3 percent) than whites (7.1 percent), Latinos (6.3 percent), and Asian/Pacific Islanders (4.7 percent). African Americans also reported having the highest number of activity limitations related to poor health. When it came to rating their overall health, only Latinos (35.6 percent) reported that their health was worse than African Americans' (21.2 percent). Whites, on the other hand, were half as likely to rate their health as being poor to fair (13.1 percent).

Table 9.2. Leading Causes of DALYs by Race/Ethnicity in Los Angeles County, 1997

	DALYs Years	Rate	Rank
AFRICAN AMERICAN			
Homicide/Violence	14,264	15.79	1
Coronary Heart Disease	11,380	12.6	2
Diabetes Mellitus	9,737	10.78	3
Alcohol Dependence	6,966	7.71	4
Stroke	6,950	7.69	5
Trachea/Bronchus/Lung Cancer	5,526	6.12	6
HIV/AIDS	5,514	6.1	7
Asthma	4,712	5.22	8
Emphysema	4,388	4.86	9
Depression	4,151	4.59	10
WHITE			
Coronary Heart Disease	44,010	13.63	1
Emphysema	20,411	6.32	2
Alcohol Dependence	19,933	6.28	3
Trachea/Bronchus/Lung Cancer	19,073	5.91	4
Alzheimer's/Other Dementia	18,533	5.74	5
Diabetes Mellitus	15,287	4.74	6
Osteoarthritis	15,174	4.7	7
Stroke	14,931	4.63	8
Depression	14,268	4.45	9
Drug Overdose/Other Intoxication	14,268	4.42	10

	Years	Rate	Rank
LATINO			
Alcohol Dependence	28,305	6.7	1
Homicide/Violence	23,927	5.67	2
Depression	18,530	4.39	3
Diabetes Mellitus	15,116	3.58	4
Osteoarthritis	14,864	3.52	5
Motor Vehicle Crashes	14,222	3.37	6
Coronary Heart Disease	12,207	2.89	7
Drug Overdose/Other Intoxication	9,542	2.26	8
Stroke	8,873	2.1	9
Cirrhosis	7,994	1.89	10
ASIAN/PI			
Alcohol Dependence	8,345	6.78	1
Depression	6,151	5	2
Osteoarthritis	5,758	4.68	3
Coronary Heart Disease	5,219	4.24	4
Stroke	4,290	3.49	5
Diabetes Mellitus	4,118	3.35	6
Alzheimer's/Other Dementia	3,864	3.14	7
Emphysema	3,015	2.45	8
Motor Vehicle Crashes	2,745	2.23	9
Unintended Firearm Injury	2,487	2.02	10

Source: Los Angeles Department of Health Services, UCLA Health Policy Center.

Table 9.3. Percentage of Poor to Fair Self-Rated Health and Mean Number of Unhealthy Days and Activity Limitation Days among Adults in Los Angeles County

Race/Ethnicity	Poor to Fair Health Percent	Unhealthy Days Mean	Activity Limitation Days Mean
African American	21.2% (n=835)	8.3	3.5
White	13.1% (n=3376)	7.1	2.7
Latino	35.6% (n=3267)	6.3	2.4
Asian/Pacific Islander	15.3% (n=716)	4.7	1.7

Source: 1999 Los Angeles County Health Survey.

How can such disparities in health status and perceptions of limitations be evaluated in light of the extent of African American suburbanization that has occurred since the Watts riots of 1965? To attempt to answer this question, data from the California State Department of Health Services were utilized to locate hospitals, emergency rooms, and clinics in nearby and away suburbs as well as in the city and county of Los Angeles. These facilities were overlaid on density maps showing the location of African Americans (see figures 9.5 and 9.6). With this information, and by focusing on ambulatory care sensitive diagnoses, it is possible to assess the ability of African Americans to access health care as measured by clinics, hospitals, and emergency room locations. These data also make it possible to determine the extent of certain health disparities based upon residential location.

The results of this mapping analysis revealed that access to health care resources varies widely by city. African Americans living in Compton (a nearby suburb with a 40 percent African American population) have no hospitals or emergency rooms and only four clinics available to meet their health needs. In Inglewood (nearby suburb), where African Americans comprise 47 percent of the population, there are two hospitals, both with emergency rooms, and eleven clinics, Hawthorn (nearby suburb), with a 33 percent African American population, has one hospital with an emergency room and one clinic, and Long Beach (nearby suburb), with a 45 percent African American population, has six hospitals (four with emergency departments) and eighteen clinics. Clearly there is a great deal of variation in the availability of hospitals, emergency rooms, and clinics depending on the city where African Americans live. Residents of Compton, for example, have the fewest number of health care facilities available to them. African American residents in Long Beach, on the other hand, have more hospitals, emergency rooms, and clinics available to them than do African Americans in any other city except Los Angeles.

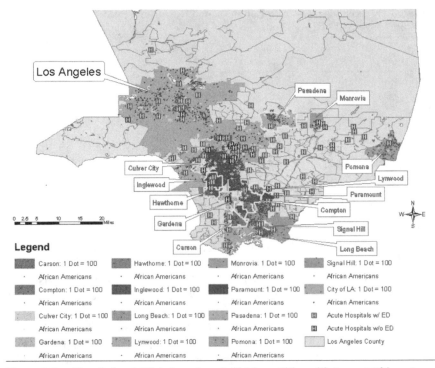

Figure 9.5.   Hospital and Clinic Locations in Thirteen Cities with Largest African American Population in Los Angeles County, 2000
Source: The National Health Foundation.

Los Angeles, with 11 percent African American population (representing 45 percent of the county's total African American population), presents a different picture. While there are 38 hospitals (29 with emergency departments) and 123 clinics, none of the hospitals is located in close proximity to the city's African American community. The Drew/King Medical Center and five other hospitals are located at the extreme edges of the communities where most African Americans live. In 1972, however, when Drew/King opened, two-thirds of the county's African American population lived in the city of Los Angeles, with the majority being concentrated relatively close to the new hospital. As a result of suburbanization, the King/Drew Medical Center has become less and less relevant as a local facility capable of serving the health care needs of the county's African American population.

The suburban city types identified earlier were used to organize ambulatory sensitive discharge data in order to determine if suburbanization reduced health care disparities. Two cities, Pasadena and Long Beach, have their own

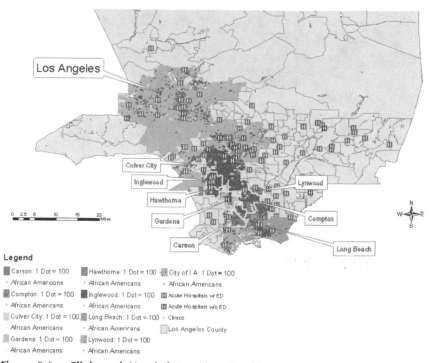

Figure 9.6. Clinic and Hospital Locations in Thirteen nearby Suburbs with Large African American Populations
Source: The National Health Foundation.

independent health departments and are not part of the Los Angeles County Health Department.[16] A separate analysis was conducted using this grouping in order to determine if health disparities might vary depending on whether African Americans were served by different public health systems.

Hospital discharge data for select ambulatory care–sensitive conditions were compiled for hospitals in each suburb type.[17] A disparity was identified if the discharge percent exceeded the percent of the total population for a specific ethnic group in a given geographic area. Figure 9.7 shows health disparities for African Americans persist irrespective of residential location. However, the results show that analyzing disparity data by different geographic locations shows that African Americans' disparity differences decline with suburbanization.

Countywide, African Americans comprise 10 percent of the population but represent 15 percent of the hospital discharges for all ambulatory care–sensitive conditions. Whites on the other hand have a lower percentage of discharges for these conditions compared to their population base (42 percent versus 47 percent). The remainder of the county's residents show little

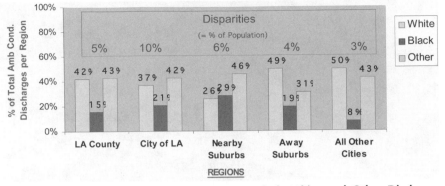

Figure 9.7. Comparison of Disparities Among Black, White, and Other Discharges Across LAC Regions (All Ambulatory Care Conditions)
Source: OSHPD Data Compiled by the National Health Foundation.

variance between their proportion of the population (42 percent) and their percentage of ambulatory discharges (43 percent).

Within the city of Los Angeles, African Americans represent 11 percent of the population and account for 21 percent of the ambulatory care–sensitive discharges. Whites on the other hand constitute 47 percent of the city's residents but only 37 percent of the ambulatory care discharges. There is no difference between the remainder of the population in terms of their proportion of the population versus their discharge rate (42 percent in both cases).

In the nearby suburbs the ambulatory care–sensitive discharge difference for African Americans is higher than their percentage of the population (29 percent versus 23 percent). As was the case countywide, the white discharge difference is lower than their population base (26 percent versus 35 percent). The discharge difference for the remainder of the population in this area is also higher (46 percent) than would be expected given the population rate (42 percent).

This pattern of higher African American discharges compared to their population base (19 percent versus 15 percent) is found in the away suburbs also. However, this is the only area where discharges for whites are greater than expected (49 percent versus 45 percent). The remainder of the population in the away suburbs also has lower discharge differences than the proportion of their population (31 percent versus 39 percent).

In the third group of other suburban cities, African Americans also have ambulatory care–sensitive discharge differences higher than their population base (8 percent versus 5 percent). Whites have lower than expected ambulatory care–sensitive discharge differences (50 percent versus 53 percent), but the discharge difference for others is higher (43 percent versus 41 percent).

Ambulatory care–sensitive discharge differences in the independent areas (Pasadena and Long Beach) show that disparities for African Americans are much larger than for any other areas (33 percent versus 14 percent), while for whites and the others they are lower (34 percent versus 47 percent for whites) and (33 percent versus 39 percent for others).

The disparities difference for African Americans living in Los Angeles City is 10 percent, in the nearby suburbs 6 percent, in the away suburbs 4 percent, and in the other suburbs 3 percent. For the two cities with independent public health systems, the disparity rate for African Americans is 19 percent. These findings suggest that greater African American suburbanization may result in decreasing the health disparities gap (at least as measured by these cumulative ambulatory care–sensitive conditions).

There are several possible explanations for these findings. First, the concentration of poor African Americans declines the further one moves from central Los Angeles and the median income of African Americans increases inversely to proximity to Los Angeles City. Therefore controlling location to a certain extent also accounts for socioeconomic status. A second reason for these findings may be that a number of African Americans in the nearby suburbs actually are hospitalized in the city of Los Angeles due to its greater number of facilities. A third reason could be that the ambulatory care discharge data in this report do not capture the most severe illnesses suffered by African Americans documented by other studies.

IMPLICATIONS FOR THE FUTURE

Many studies show African Americans have higher incidences of specific diseases, do not always obtain the services they need, and may receive different interventions than whites. The resulting health disparities cannot be denied. To reduce these disparities, most previous research has recommended one or more of the following: (1) improve access; (2) reduce structural barriers by providing more culturally relevant education and increasing funding, particularly to community-based organizations; (3) enable community-based organizations to have more of a leadership role in directing research and educational programs. Implementing such recommendations should make a difference, but the previous forty-year history does not encourage the idea that these strategies actually reduce disparity rates.

The recent report by the Public Health Institute (PHI), *Building Public Health Systems to Improve Community Health in California*, states that to create good community health there "must be a capacity to work in collaboration with others to confront the changing social and environmental source of preventable illness and injury."[18] It emphasizes that this is especially true if efforts to eliminate disparities in health among different populations and communities are to be successful.

A key finding of the present study is that as African Americans disperse from a core central city to surrounding suburbs, disparities in health status may decline. If this is in fact the case, then using smaller geographic units, for example, cities, to monitor health disparities provides a vehicle for facilitating greater collaborations and fostering partnerships. By using cities rather than counties as an organizing framework, it is easier to engage local elected officials, the media, community- and faith-based organizations, foundations, and the business community in discussions regarding the problem and possible solutions. Presenting the problem at the county level, particularly in a county of 9 million people like Los Angeles, makes it extremely difficult for diverse stakeholders to form meaningful partnerships for problem solving.

According to PHI, "healthy people in healthy communities" refers not only to common interests, but also to a common location—where people live. The notion of place must be fundamental because that is where the constellation of forces influencing health comes together and creates the conditions in which people are—or are not—healthy, and where disparities in health are most dramatically revealed.

With more systematic and focused disparity information, it also becomes possible to lobby regulatory bodies, such as the Joint Commission on Accreditation of Healthcare Organizations (JCAHO), to develop criteria for what hospitals should do to identify, reduce, and ultimately eliminate these disparities. Requiring hospitals to monitor disparities and, where necessary, develop remedy action plans could become part of the accreditation process. The importance of both monitoring disparities and making this mandatory has been shown in various arenas.

As a recent study by the National Health Foundation on the collection and reporting of quality data among California hospitals found, frequency of data collection and reporting are highest when required by outside authorities. Also, the Kaiser Permanente group has found that by monitoring disparities as a part of their quality assurance activities, they have been able to demonstrate significant progress in reducing disparities across racial/ethnic groups. Other major hospital systems should be encouraged to do the same.

By monitoring disparities at focused geographic units such as cities, it becomes possible to produce reports indicating where and if progress is being accomplished. Development of disparity "report cards" would be used effectively to stimulate media coverage, which in turn can be used by advocacy groups to focus attention on workable solutions.

APPENDIX

African American Population Growth in Los Angeles County, 1960 to 2000

	1960	1970	1980	1990	2000	% of County Total
LA County	**461,546**	**762,850**	**942,328**	**992,974**	**930,957**	**100%**
City of Los Angeles	334,917	503,931	505,301	487,674	415,195	45%
	73%	66%	54%	49%		
Nearby Suburbs						
Culver City	13	166	3,149	4,026	4,644	
Inglewood	29	10,051	54,029	56,861	53,060	
Hawthorne	3	1,746	7,532	20,212	27,775	
Gardena	8	1,743	10,212	11,713	15,010	
Lynwood	9	315	16,892	14,652	9,451	
Paramount	2	29	1,190	5,098	7,508	
Subtotal	64	14,050	93,004	112,562	117,448	13%
	0%	2%	10%	11%		

(continued)

	1960	1970	1980	1990	2000
Away Suburbs					
Long Beach	9,531	19,294	40,463	58,761	68,618
Carson	50	8,405	23,879	21,953	22,808
Pasadena	14,587	18,255	24,554	24,952	19,319
Monrovia	2,551	2,679	2,926	3,626	3,202
Pomona	880	10,022	17,627	19,013	14,398
Signal Hill	1	401	699	884	1,212
Subtotal	27,600	59,056	110,148	129,189	129,557
% of County Total	6%	8%	12%	13%	14%
Other Locations in County	98,965	185,813	233,875	263,549	268,757
% of County Total	21%	24%	25%	27%	29%
Independent Health Departments					
Long Beach	9,531	19,294	4,063	58,761	68,618
Pasadena	14,587	18,255	24,554	24,952	19,319
Subtotal	24,118	37,549	28,617	83,713	87,937
% of County Total	5%	5%	3%	8%	9%

Source: The National Health Foundation

Number of Hospitals and Clinics in Each City

Clinics	#	% of Total	African American Population	Per 1,000/Population
Los Angeles	123	0.64	415,195	0.30
Inglewood	11	0.06	53,060	0.21
Hawthorne	1	0.01	27,775	0.04
Compton	4	0.02	37,690	0.11
Long Beach	18	0.09	68,618	0.26
Carson	2	0.01	22,804	0.09
Commerce*	1	0.01		
Culver City	2	0.01	4,644	0.43
Gardena	3	0.02	15,010	0.20
Lynwood	3	0.02	9,451	0.32
Hollywood*	1	0.01		
Monrovia	2	0.01	3,202	0.62
Paramount	1	0.01	7,508	0.13
Pasadena	11	0.06	19,319	0.57
Pomona	8	0.04	14,398	0.56
Signal Hill	0	0.00	1,212	0.00
Total	193			

Hospitals	#	% of Total	African American	Per 1,000/Population
Culver City	1	0.02	4,644	0.22
Gardena	2	0.04	15,010	0.13
Lynwood	1	0.02	9,451	0.11
Monrovia	1	0.02	3,202	0.31
Paramount	1	0.02	7,508	0.13
Pasadena	1	0.02	19,319	0.05
Pomona	1	0.02	14,398	0.07
Signal Hill	0	0.00	1,212	0.00
Los Angeles	31	0.65	415,195	0.07
Inglewood	2	0.04	53,060	0.04
Hawthorne	1	0.02	27,775	0.04
Compton	0	0.00	37,690	0.00
Long Beach	6	0.13	68,618	0.09
Total	48			

* data not available
Source: National Health Foundation

King/Drew Crisis Chronology

12/10/02—Accreditation Council for Graduate Medical Education withdraws accreditation of a diagnostic radiology program. The council found "significant deficiencies," such as inadequate supervision of residents in the emergency room. The council also found that between 1997 and 2001, only 15.4% of residents who took oral board certification examinations passed the first time. To take effect June 2004 (Ornstein/Riccardi, *LA Times*).

12/12/02—Los Angeles County Board of Supervisors orders county Department of Health Services to prepare a "corrective action plan" by January 7, 2003, to "ensure the maintenance" of graduate education and residency programs at Martin Luther King/Drew Medical Center (*LA Times*, 12/11).

6/5/03—Los Angeles County to eliminate jobs at Martin Luther King Jr./Drew Medical Center, including 79 physicians, 152 nurses, and 210 administrative positions by June 30 (*LA Times*, 6/05).

6/26/03—Judge bars cuts in patient services at Martin Luther King Jr./Drew Medical Center but allows the county to eliminate about 400 jobs at the hospital by July 1 (Fox, *LA Times*, 6/26).

7/16/03—Judge extends ban on cuts in patient services at King-Drew Medical Center (Ornstein, *LA Times*, 7/16).

9/03/03—Martin Luther King Jr./Drew Medical Center loses accreditation to teach general surgeons. The Accreditation Council for Graduate Medical Education revoked the accreditation of King/Drew because it had two more residents than the 38 permitted; the program was placed on probation last year because its residents were not provided with an adequate amount of surgical experience, faculty research was inadequate, and its curriculum did not follow recommended guidelines. The decision takes effect immediately (Ornstein/Weber, *LA Times*, 8/26).

9/17/03—Los Angeles County Supervisors establish task force to review problems with King/Drew residency program (Ornstein/Weber, *LA Times*, 9/17).

10/31/03—King/Drew Medical Center does not face immediate sanctions, contrary to earlier report. Accreditation Council for Graduate Medical Education said King/Drew would have at least two years to correct deficiencies in its physician training programs before actions are taken to close them (Ornstein/Weber, *LA Times*, 10/31).

12/04/03—Accreditation Council for Graduate Medical Education has recommended closing Martin Luther King Jr./Drew Medical Center's neonatal residency program (Weber/Ornstein, *LA Times*, 12/04).

12/09/03—Nurses at Martin Luther King Jr./Drew Medical Center "shirk patient care." Physicians "allow known problems to fester" and county officials offer "poor oversight," according to a memo sent by Los Angeles County. Department of Health Services Director Dr. Thomas Garthwaite to the county Board of Supervisors (Ornstein/Weber, *LA Times*, 12/09).

12/10/03—Los Angeles County health officials said that they are planning "sweeping management changes" at the Martin Luther King Jr./Drew Medical Center, but members of the county Board of Supervisors advocated a "more complete overhaul" of the hospital (Briscoe et al., *LA Times*, 12/10).

12/16/03—Los Angeles County Department of Health Services suspends nursing director at King/Drew Medical Center (Ornstein, *LA Times*, 12/16).

1/9/04—President of Drew School placed on paid administrative leave (*LA Times*, 1/10).

1/12/04—Assembly hearing addresses problems at King/Drew (Briscoe, *LA Times*, 1/10).

1/13/04—Los Angeles County Department of Health Services recommends downgrading King/Drew neonatal unit from a regional unit to an intermediate care unit, which would restrict the facility's services for newborns in intensive care and infants who need ventilators to breathe for more than four hours. The proposed downgrade is set for July 04 (*LA Times*).

1/14/04—The Los Angeles County Board of Supervisors approved recommendations by Dr. Thomas Garthwaite, director of the county Department of Health Services, to consolidate or restructure clinical services at Martin Luther King Jr./Drew Medical Center and give the medical center more flexibility to pay nurses at competitive rates (Landsberg/Briscoe, *LA Times*, 1/14).

1/14/04—"Colorblind" approach urged for King/Drew. Los Angeles County Supervisor Yvonne Braithwaite Burke said administrators need to be hired on the basis of their qualifications, not their race (Landsberg/Briscoe, *LA Times*, 1/14).

2/02/04—Lawyers for the Los Angeles County–owned Martin Luther King Jr./Drew Medical Center released a "lengthy" response to a "blistering" CMS report on problems at the hospital, insisting the facility had taken "swift and decisive action" to correct the problems (Landsberg, *LA Times*, 2/2).

2/09/24—Los Angeles County Department of Health Services reduces trauma patient volume at King/Drew Medical Center. The annual patient load in Martin Luther King Jr./Drew Medical Center's trauma unit will be reduced by 18%, or by about 500 patients, beginning February 16. The change, which involves redrawing the geographic limits of King/Drew's service area, is intended to allow the hospital a chance to address other patient care issues. King/Drew's trauma unit, which is the second busiest in the county, currently treats more than 2,700 patients annually and handles the highest number of gunshot victims in the county (*LA Times*, 2/09).

2/27/04—Los Angeles Sheriff's Deputies Call on State to Take Over Martin Luther King Jr./Drew Medical Center alleging that patients are "perishing needlessly because of the deteriorating health services provided by the hospital" (Molly, AP, *Contra Costa Times*, 2/27).

3/01/04—Board of Pharmacy Cites Martin Luther King Jr./Drew Medical Center for Medication Error. The Board of Pharmacy has cited Los Angeles County–owned Martin Luther King Jr./Drew Medical Center over an incident in which the hospital mistakenly administered a cancer medication to a patient without cancer over a period of four days last month (*LA Times*, 2/28).

3/5/04—King/Drew Is Again Assailed Over Prescription Drug Flaws. State inspectors are second group in a week to chastise the hospital for giving the wrong medication to a patient with meningitis (Ornstein, *LA Times*, 3/5).

3/10/04—Los Angeles County Supervisors Request Plan to Operate King/Drew Medical Center Without Medical School. The Los Angeles County Board of Supervisors on Tuesday requested that the county Department of Health Services develop operating procedures to run county-owned Martin Luther King Jr./Drew Medical Center by May 1 without its affiliated medical school, Charles Drew University of Medicine and Science (AP, *Fresno Bee*, 3/10).

3/22/04—Changes at King/Drew Medical Center Sufficient to Maintain Medicare Funding, CMS Says. CMS said Friday that it would not revoke Martin Luther King Jr./Drew Medical Center's certification to participate in Medicare because it found that the hospital "submitted adequate plans for correcting widespread flaws in the way it administers drugs to patients" (Hyman, *LA Times*, 3/20).

NOTES

1. Governor's Commission on the Los Angeles Riots, *Violence in the City: An End or Beginning?* (1965).

2. Los Angeles County Department of Health Services Web site, http://www.ladhs .org/MLK/history.htm (accessed March, 2004).

3. Starting in December 2002, the *Los Angeles Times* began running a series of articles chronicling problems at the Drew/King Medical Center. See the appendix for this chronology.

4. The California Endowment, *Unequal Treatment, Unequal Health: What the Data Tell Us About Health Gaps in California* (2003).

5. Office of Statewide Health Planning and Development, *Racial and Ethnic Disparities in Healthcare in California* (November 2003).

6. In 2004 there were a total of eighty-eight municipalities in Los Angeles County. The county consists of 4,084 square miles, making it 800 square miles larger than Delaware and Rhode Island combined. Source: www.lacounty.info/overview.htm (accessed May 2004).

7. National Institutes of Health, http://healthdisparities.nih.gov/whatare.html (accessed April 30, 2004).

8. California Campaign, *Health for All: California's Strategic Approach to Eliminating Racial and Ethnic Health Disparities* (2003), 1.

9. Agency for Healthcare Research and Quality, *Addressing Racial and Ethnic Disparities in Healthcare Fact Sheet*, 2003, http://www.ahcpr.gov/research/disparit.htm (accessed May 1, 2004).

10. Ibid., 2.

11. Agency for Healthcare Research and Quality, Publication No. 00-p041, Current as of February 2000.

12. Antronette Yancy, Melissa Gachell, E. Richard Brown, and William McCarthy, "Diabetes Is Major Health Problem for African Americans," UCLA Center for Health Policy Research Fact Sheet, November 2003.

13. *The Burden of Disease*, produced by the Los Angeles County Department of Health and the UCLA Center for Health Policy Research, 12.

14. Ibid., 14.

15. Ibid., 12.

16. State law in California requires that counties provide public health services. The cities of Pasadena and Long Beach are exceptions. Each of these cities has maintained independent public health functions from those of the County of Los Angeles.

17. These ambulatory care conditions include Asthma with Status Asthmaticus, Chronic Obstructive Pulmonary Disease (COPD), Congestive Heart Failure (CHF), Diabetes with complication, Diabetes without complication, Hypertension, and HIV. Similar data for clinics are not available.

18. Public Health Institute, Partnership for the Public's Health, *Building Public Health Systems to Improve Community Health in California*, 15.

10

Black Political Power in the New Century

David A. Bositis

Since the time of the civil rights movement, black political power in the United States has generally increased at the federal, state, and local levels except when Republicans controlled both legislative and executive power. These gains were substantially due to increasing black voting power. Subsequent to the passage of the Voting Rights Act in 1965, the gap between black and white registration rates and turnout has consistently narrowed, albeit during a period of generally declining participation across both populations. Black voters are a key constituency in general elections in at least fifteen states and represent a key voting block in Democratic primaries in more than twenty states. Maintaining this voting power is especially important because the country is very evenly divided in partisan preferences, and the federal courts, which were at one time supportive of black political empowerment, have become at best neutral on black empowerment issues.

The number of black elected officials has increased steadily since the passage of the Voting Rights Act, with more than 9,100 black elected officials in January 2001. After the Voting Rights Act was amended in 1982 to deal with vote dilution practices, the creation of new black-majority legislative districts has led to a large and substantial increase in the number of black legislators at the local (city council), state, and federal levels.

Following the 1992 elections, black representation in the southern state legislatures increased dramatically, and in many of those states, legislative black caucuses and individual black lawmakers gained significant political power and influence. Since 1994, several of the southern state legislative bodies witnessed changes in partisan control, and in each of those instances black lawmakers saw their influence diminish. The Congressional Black Caucus experienced a similar period of influence during the 103rd Congress

(1993–1995), and a subsequent loss of power following the Republican takeover of the U.S. Congress in 1995.

Following the passage of the Voting Rights Act, many black leaders also emerged in urban politics, with most of the large cities in the United States electing black mayors for the first time. This includes many cities with white-majority populations. However, these mayors, mostly Democrats, confronted their leadership challenges during a period of diminished influence for cities. Influence was diminished due to state legislative action, loss of population, and the increasing portability of capital; since the early 1970s, companies have shifted operations to lower-cost locations in nonurban areas, rural areas, southern states, and then out of the country.

Since the mid-1960s, African Americans have expressed their political choices through the Democratic Party and have become an essential part of the party's base vote; they also occupy leadership positions in party organizations at all levels. When Democrats control legislative and/or executive power, this black support translates into considerable influence for black political elites. However, when Democrats are out of power, the absence of black influence within the Republican Party represents a significant challenge to black political empowerment.

Despite the gains in black political power that have occurred during this period, racially polarized voting, while diminishing, continues to be a problem for black voters and their candidates running for office at the state level. While the current number of black statewide elected officials is at a historic high nationally, the number remains small—forty—and there is only a single black governor and only one black U.S. Senator. There have been two black governors and three black senators in modern times, despite the fact there have been thirty-six black candidates for those offices. Three southern states, including two with black populations greater than 30 percent, have never elected a black candidate to statewide office: Mississippi, South Carolina, and Arkansas.

In the past decade, a new challenge has confronted black politics, with younger African Americans increasingly identifying themselves as politically independent. The problem with lack of identification with a political party is that independents are less likely to vote than strong partisans. This is especially important because the black population is very young compared to the white population. The median age (2003 estimate) for the non-Hispanic white population is forty years, while it is thirty-one years for the African American population. Hence, younger black voters assume greater importance to the overall black vote. Younger voters of all races vote with less frequency than older voters, but younger voters lacking partisan ties vote least of all.

The strongest partisans among younger black adults—and among all African Americans—are black women. And black women, including younger black women, vote with greater frequency than black men of similar age. Further, there is a partisan gender gap in the black electorate. One of the possible consequences of this trend is that black women are substantially increasing their representation among black elected officials; the relationship between the two trends remains conjectural, but is nonetheless persuasive.

Black elected officials have increased since 1970, which has led to black urban leadership, but black political power and influence remains limited. African Americans are important to the Democratic Party, but racially polarized voting impacts African Americans running in federal and statewide elections. Moreover, there is a generation gap between younger and older blacks where young black adults have different political views than their parents and grandparents, which dilutes the strength of the influence blacks can wield. The future of black empowerment may be with black women, because they vote with greater frequency and they are increasing their representation among black elected officials.

THE VOTE AND VOTING RIGHTS

In 1960, the year John F. Kennedy was elected president, 5.2 percent of the nonwhite voters of Mississippi were registered to vote, as were 13.7 percent of nonwhite voters in Alabama and South Carolina, and 23.1 percent in Virginia; by 1968, the first presidential election following the passage of the Voting Rights Act, a majority of African Americans were registered to vote in every southern state.[1] In the decade following, black registration and turnout rates tended to lag white rates by about ten percentage points.

Starting in 1982, the gap between black and white registration and turnout rates narrowed, especially in the southern states. This narrowing gap in the South attests to a strong political commitment by black voters since a large percentage of black voters are permanently disenfranchised from voting due to ex-felon status.[2] In Alabama and Florida, 31 percent of all black men are permanently disenfranchised, as are one-quarter of black men in Mississippi and Virginia.

The importance, and perseverance, of the black vote, as seen in exit polls conducted after major elections over the past decade, show the black share of the votes actually cast in elections is approximating, and even exceeding, the black voting-age population in many states. In the 2000 presidential election, the black share of the statewide vote in Alabama, Florida, Missouri, Tennessee, and Texas exceeded the black voting-age population in those states.

Of the eighteen states examined, the black share of the vote in 2000 exceeded the black voting-age population in seven, and was below the black voting-age population in nine; in two states the black share equaled the voting-age population. In these eighteen states in 2000, the black share of the actual vote averaged 0.8 of a percentage point below the black voting-age population. Among these eighteen states, the black share of the statewide vote was 20 percent or greater in five; in ten of these states the black share of the vote was between 10 and 19 percent.

The black vote has become an important factor in statewide elections in at least a dozen states, including several swing states that frequently decide presidential elections, including Florida, Missouri, and Ohio. African Americans have changed from an essentially marginal political status pre–Voting Rights Act, to having the capacity to determine the outcome of major elections, including presidential elections. With one caveat (to be discussed below), the voting trends suggest the black vote will continue to have a major influence on election outcomes, especially with a closely divided electorate—where voter suppression becomes a tactic to minimize the impact of black voters.

In some cases the only tool to combat black voter suppression is the Voting Rights Act of 1965 (VRA). This act is often regarded as one of the single most important pieces of civil rights legislation.[3] The main purpose of the VRA was to protect every American against racial discrimination in voting; it also protects the voting rights of many people who have limited English skills.[4] The act was adopted initially in 1965 and extended in 1970, 1975, and in 1982. The act guarantees that no person shall be denied the right to vote on account of race or color. In addition, the act contains several special provisions that impose even more stringent requirements in certain jurisdictions throughout the country.[5] Three key provisions of the act were scheduled to expire in 2007. Those sections were Section 5 (Preclearance), Section 203 (Language Minority Assistance), and Sections 6–9 (Federal Monitors and Observers). During the reauthorization process in Congress, Section 5 was the most hotly debated. This provision directly impacts nine states with a documented history of discriminatory voting practices and local jurisdictions in seven others by requiring them to submit planned changes in their election laws or procedures to the U.S. Department of Justice or the District Court in Washington, D.C. for preapproval.[6]

The states whose voting procedures still are overseen by the federal government are Alabama, Alaska, Arizona, Georgia, Louisiana, Mississippi, South Carolina, Texas, and Virginia. Legislators from the mostly southern states claimed that the act was no longer necessary and that it punished them for past racist deeds that no longer existed in their states.[7] Other conservatives fought provisions requiring jurisdictions with large populations of non-English-speaking citizens to print ballots in languages other than English.

In July 2006, amid fanfare and before a South Lawn audience that included members of Congress, civil rights leaders, and family members of civil rights leaders, President George W. Bush signed legislation extending for twenty-five years the Voting Rights Act. President Bush declared, "Congress has reaffirmed its belief that all men are created equal."[8]

BLACK ELECTED OFFICIALS

The increasing influence of black voters has been matched by the growth in the number of black elected officials. Since 1970, the number of black elected officials has increased more than fivefold, from 1,469 in 1970 to 9,101 in 2001, the most recent year for which national data are available. The increases have been most impressive since the Voting Rights Act was amended in 1982 to deal with the problem of vote dilution, that is, dispersing black voters across several districts to prevent them from influencing the outcomes of elections. The increases have been important in legislative offices, both state and federal. From 1982, when the Voting Rights Act was amended, to 1993, after most state legislative elections had been held in newly drawn districts (post-1990 census), the number of black state legislators increased from 336 to 533, or 58.6 percent.[9] The changes in the Voting Rights Act did not impact U.S. House elections until 1992, when the size of the Congressional Black Caucus increased by 50 percent.

For a brief period of time in the early 1990s, the increased number of black state and federal legislators experienced a significant growth in power, while serving in legislative bodies dominated by Democrats.[10] In 1992, the Democrats controlled both chambers in twenty-nine states, while the GOP did so in only six states, and the U.S. House of Representatives was firmly in Democratic hands. Also, at that time in the southern states, Democrats controlled all state legislative bodies, and all black state legislators in the South save one were Democrats and served in the majority.[11]

Starting in 1994, a major partisan shift occurred, where Republicans captured the U.S. House and over the remainder of the decade eroded the previous Democratic dominance in the state legislatures. In 2001, according to the National Conference of State Legislatures, the Democrats controlled both chambers in only seventeen states, while the Republicans dominated in twenty-one states; there was split control in the remaining states. In the southern states, the Republicans controlled ten of twenty-two state legislative bodies, and controlled both chambers in Florida, South Carolina, Texas, and Virginia.[12] There were only 111 black state legislators in the South serving in the minority, or 37.1 percent of all southern black state legislators.

This shift in partisan control in both the U.S. House and in several state legislatures diminished black power and influence there between 1995 and 2006. Rather than as committee and subcommittee chairmen, many black state legislators found themselves in the role of ranking member. Representatives Charles Rangel (D-NY) and John Conyers (D-MI) would be the chairmen of the U.S. House Ways and Means, and Judiciary, committees.

Black Democrats experienced a reversal of fortune following the 2006 midterm elections with the Democrats regaining partisan control. Black members in the 110th Congress will arguably be more influential than their numbers, or the black voting-age population, would suggest. First, Rep. Jim Clyburn (SC) will be Assistant Democratic Leader (Whip). Black members will chair the House Ways and Means Committee (Rangel), Judiciary Committee (Conyers), and Homeland Security Committee (Thompson); in addition, there will be about eighteen black subcommittee chairs in the U.S. House after the Democrats assume control.

Related to the trends and status of black legislators during this period are the trends and status of black mayors. Since 1970, there has been a more than tenfold increase in the number of black mayors, to 454 in 2001, including 49 black mayors of cities with populations larger than 50,000; of the 49 large cities with black mayors, 58.3 percent do not have a black majority population. Most of the largest cities in the U.S., including New York, Chicago, and Los Angeles, have had black mayors.

These black mayors have confronted some of the same problems as the black legislators. Black mayors are almost exclusively Democratic, and as the number of Republican state legislatures, and governors, has increased since the early 1990s, these mayors have often confronted diminished influence in the state capitals. City budgets depend on state assistance for schools,[13] public safety, roads and infrastructure, and other needs—and city leaders often require state approval to raise taxes or issue bonds. Needless to say, black Democratic mayors frequently get a poor reception from white suburban and rural Republican legislators when negotiating with the state.

Another factor that has diminished the influence of black mayors is that capital has become portable. In the past, steel (Pittsburgh), autos (Detroit), rubber (Akron), oil (Houston), and other valuable industries were fixed in particular locations, and mayors could rely on taxes from those companies to finance city government. Since the early 1970s, companies, large and small, have abandoned cities and relocated in suburban areas, rural areas, in southern states, and in more recent years, Mexico and the Far East. Mayors now have a limited ability to tax, and negotiations often involve lifting or limiting taxes in order to keep or attract new business.

Many cities have experienced population loss due to more middle-class residents, including African Americans, moving to the suburbs, or population loss due to loss of industries and jobs. Politically, fewer people translates to diminished influence.

These factors have affected all big cities to some degree, but black majority cities, such as Detroit, and their black mayors have been particularly affected. Thus, while there has been a significant increase in black urban leadership, the political power and influence of black mayors remains constrained.

AFRICAN AMERICANS AND THE TWO-PARTY SYSTEM

Since 1964, African Americans' political influence has been effectively confined to the Democratic Party, in large part because the Republican Party has become the party of the white South. When the Democrats exercise political control, this alliance has given black leaders more influence than there would be otherwise. While the black adult population is about 13 percent of the U.S. total, African Americans represent 20 percent, and often more, of the Democratic Party. Black voters represented 15.4 percent of Bill Clinton's vote in 1992,[14] 17.1 in 1996, and 18.9 percent of Al Gore's vote in 2000.[15] In contrast, only 1.9 percent of President Bush's voters in 2000 were African Americans.[16] Among the states that Clinton won in 1996, black voters represented 18 percent of his vote in Florida, 22 percent in Illinois, 52 percent in Louisiana, 33 percent in Maryland, 21 percent in Michigan, and 24 percent in Tennessee. Black voters represented an even higher proportion of Gore's voters, including 28 percent of his vote in Florida.

Since black voters are Democrats, their representation in Democratic Party primaries is usually much larger than their representation in the voting-age population. Because of this, their voice in selecting Democratic nominees is magnified. In recent contested Democratic presidential primaries, the black share of the vote has been quite substantial, and occasionally determinative.

In 1988, the last year that the Rev. Jesse Jackson ran for the Democratic nomination, the black share of the Democratic primary vote in Louisiana and Mississippi exceeded 40 percent, and was 35 percent in Alabama and Georgia; in eleven states black voters were at least 20 percent of the Democratic primary vote. In 1992, the black share of the primary vote was greater than 40 percent in Mississippi and South Carolina, 30 percent in North Carolina, and greater than 20 percent in eight states. In the early 2004 Democratic presidential primaries, the black share of the Democratic primary vote was 47 percent in South Carolina, 33 percent in Virginia, and 23 percent in Tennessee.

The black vote in federal elections has been solidly Democratic since 1964. Since Ronald Reagan ran for president in 1980, no Republican candidate has received more than 12 percent of the black vote. In 2000, President Bush received only 9 percent of the black vote. He received 11 percent of the black vote in 2004. Also, since that time, Republican congressional candidates have received no more than 13 percent of the black vote, except

in 1990, when an extremely low black voter turnout (black voters represented only 5 percent of all voters that year) magnified the influence of
black Republican voters that year. As a general rule, there is an inverse relationship between the Republican share of the black vote and black turnout;
greater black turnout correlates with a smaller Republican share of the black
vote.

Black elected officials are also predominantly Democrats. All 39 members of the Congressional Black Caucus are Democrats, and 608 of 613
black state legislators nationwide are Democrats. A comparison of Democratic and Republican party organizations also highlights the role of African
Americans in the Democratic Party. While only 4.1 percent of Republican
delegates at the 2000 Republican National Convention were black, 20.1
percent of all Democratic delegates were African Americans. There were
only 6 African Americans on the Republicans' three convention committees
(Rules, Platform, and Credentials), but there were 101 black members on
the Democrats' committees, including a co-chair of the Platform committee. Furthermore, at that time, the GOP had only 1 black national committee member (0.7 percent of the total), while there were 91 black members
on the Democratic National Committee, or 21.1 percent of the total.

RACIALLY POLARIZED VOTING

While there have been solid and tangible gains in black political power,
racially polarized voting continues to constrain the prospects for black voters and their candidates running for office—especially in federal and
statewide elections. There is only one black governor, Deval Patrick (MA),
and one black U.S. senator, Barack Obama (IL), at the present time. There
has been only one other black governor (Douglas Wilder, D-VA) and two
other black senators (Edward Brooke, R-MA, and Carol Moseley Braun, D-
IL) in modern times.[17] Senator Brooke is the only African American to be
reelected to the U.S. Senate in modern times. The United States has had
only five black U.S. senators in its history.[18]

Since 1966, there have been thirty-six black major-party nominees for
governor and U.S. senator, with black candidates winning six of those elections. There are forty black statewide elected officials at this time, twenty-
three of them justices on courts of last resort. Of the seventeen black elected
officials in administrative offices in the United States, the highest ranking
black elected officials are one governor, two lieutenant governors (MD and
NY), and an attorney general (GA); however, the two lieutenant governors,
both Democrats, were not elected on their own, but as part of a ticket with
a white gubernatorial candidate. In addition, there are three southern states,
including two with black populations greater than 30 percent, that have

never elected a black candidate to statewide office: Mississippi, South Carolina, and Arkansas.

Racially polarized voting also continues to endure at the U.S. Congressional level. Between 1990 and 2000, there were forty-eight U.S. House races in the South featuring black and white opponents. During this period, at least one such contest occurred in every southern state. Black candidates won forty of these contests; all black incumbents won, and the seven black non-incumbents were elected in open-seat contests in majority-minority districts. Of the eight black candidates who lost, seven ran in non-Hispanic white majority districts (the eighth ran in a majority Hispanic district), three were Republicans, and all but two-faced opponents who were incumbents.

A regression analysis for these races suggests that the vote for the black candidates was dependent on the black voting-age population (BVAP) of the district and incumbency status. The two-variable model had reasonably good explanatory power, with 75 percent of the variance in the vote for the black candidate explained by the two factors. The model equation is:

Black candidate vote = 31.7 ⏐ 0.50 ? *BVAP* + 10.7 ? *Incumbency status*

The implications of this model are these. A black incumbent would need a BVAP of at least 15.2 percent to win (i.e., 50+ percent) against a white opponent in the South. A black candidate in an open-seat contest would need a BVAP of at least 36.6 percent to win. A black candidate facing a white incumbent opponent would require a district with a BVAP of at least 58 percent.

The implications of the model bear further scrutiny. First, to become an incumbent, a black candidate would have to run in either a majority-minority district or in an open-seat election with a black voting-age population of at least 36.6 percent. Therefore, a black incumbent would never run in a district with a 15.2 percent BVAP. Further, at this time in the South, it is highly unlikely that a white incumbent would be elected from nor run for reelection in a district with a 58 percent BVAP (even assuming it was a newly redistricted district).

Therefore, the most interesting finding from the model is the 36.6 percent BVAP needed for a black candidate to win in an open-seat contest, which gives a fair sense of where the level of racially polarized voting stands at this time: a black candidate would have a 50 percent chance of winning an open-seat election (for any office) providing the constituency had at least 36.6 percent black voting-age population.

DIVERGING GENERATIONS?

Since 1996, yearly surveys at the Joint Center for Political and Economic Studies have found that many younger black adults, that is, those eighteen to thirty-five years old (roughly corresponding to Gen X and Gen Y), differ from their parents and grandparents in certain of their political views. Thematically, many younger African Americans tend toward individualistic views rather than the more collectivist views of their elders, at least in the realm of politics and policy. In partisan politics, this has correlated with a rise in the number of self-identified independents (see table 10.1). Since independents by definition lack strong partisan ties, and strength of partisanship is strongly and positively associated with voting, this means lower voter turnout among younger blacks.[19]

In a 2001 Joint Center for Political and Economic Studies national survey of young black adults, eighteen- to thirty-five-year-old African Americans, while predominantly Democratic in partisanship (62 percent), were substantially less Democratic than older blacks, who are more than 80 percent Democratic identified. These younger African Americans were not Republicans: less than 10 percent identified with the GOP. Rather, they are increasingly political independents, with 30 percent characterizing themselves that way.[20]

The partisanship (or rather the lack of partisanship compared with older blacks) of eighteen- to thirty-five-year-old African Americans has a direct bearing on their rates of political participation, and voting in particular.[21] This impacts participation rates because strong partisans are more likely to vote than weak partisans, independent leaners, and independents generally. In this survey of young black adults, 54 percent of Democratic and Republican partisans said they always vote, and only 28 percent of independents said they always vote.

Surveys have rather consistently shown that independents tend to be less well informed (and less interested), feel conflicted between the two parties and therefore not strongly motivated to support either one, believe they have less political influence, or are alienated from the political system. Only 36.1 percent of the eighteen- to thirty-five-year-old African Americans interviewed characterized themselves as strong partisans. Thus, it is no surprise that the more independent young African American adults vote at very low rates, since they do not identify, or at most weakly identify, with the two major parties.

In the 1998 midterm election, only 15.8 percent of eighteen- to twenty-four-year-old African Americans voted. Further, only 36.9 percent of twenty-five to forty-four-year-old African Americans voted. This contrasted with turnout rates greater than 50 percent for blacks over forty-five years old. In the 2000 presidential election, slightly more than one-third of eighteen- to twenty-four-year-old blacks voted (34.2 percent), as did a slight majority of those between twenty-five and forty-four. However, in that election well over 60 percent of older African Americans voted.

Younger African Americans hold many attitudes about voting that are alien to older blacks. In the Joint Center's Youth Survey noted above, young

Table 10.1. Black Partisan Identification by Age Cohort, 1999–2002

	Democratic %			Independent %			Republican %			(N)		
	1999	2000	2002	1999	2000	2002	1999	2000	2002	1999	2000	2002
Total	68	74	63	23	20	24	5	4	10	925	850	850
18–25	58	51	54	30	36	34	7	9	9	123	76	116
26–35	67	70	56	26	24	29	4	5	15	149	148	169
36–50	66	79	65	26	18	21	4	4	12	238	234	233
51–64	69	77	70	20	18	21	5	3	5	234	173	154
65+	80	82	75	13	13	16	4	1	7	140	150	123

Source: Joint Center for Political and Economic Studies National Opinion Polls.

black nonregular voters were asked why they did not always vote. A majority, 56.1 percent, of the eighteen- to thirty-five-year-old nonregular voters said they did not always vote because "politicians don't keep their campaign promises," while almost half, 47.5 percent, of them said they did not always vote because they "don't have enough information about the candidates." More than two in five (41.7 percent) suggested that "neither candidate was worth supporting," and about one-third of these nonregular voters said they did not vote because their "one vote won't make any difference to the outcome" (31.4 percent) or that "not voting is a way to show dissatisfaction with the system" (33.8 percent).

BLACK WOMEN'S ROLE IN FUTURE BLACK POLITICAL EMPOWERMENT

The strongest partisans among younger black adults—and among all African Americans—are black women. And black women, including younger black women, vote with greater frequency than black men of similar age. In the Joint Center's Youth Survey, eighteen- to thirty-five-year-old-black women are more Democratic (70 percent) than young black men (52 percent); eighteen- to thirty-five-year-old black men are almost twice as likely to characterize themselves as independent (39 percent) as younger black women (22 percent). Further, these attitudinal differences translate into a partisan gender gap in the black electorate. According to Voter News Service exit polls, black women voted eleven percentage points more Democratic than men in 1996, and nine percentage points more in 2000.

The lack of partisan attachment translates into lower levels of voting participation for younger black men. In the 1998 midterm election, only 13.2 percent of eighteen- to twenty-four-year-old African American males voted (according to the Census Bureau's Current Population Survey), while 18 percent of eighteen- to twenty-four-year-old black women voted. Further, only 33.7 percent of twenty-five- to forty-four-year-old African American males voted, and only 39.5 percent of twenty-five- to forty-four-year-old black women.

In the 2000 presidential election, only 31.8 percent of eighteen- to twenty-four-year-old African American males voted (according to the Census Bureau's Current Population Survey), while 36.3 percent of eighteen- to twenty-four-year-old black women voted. The gap increased for twenty-five- to forty-four-year-old blacks, with only 47.5 percent of men and 57.0 percent of women voting.

One of the possible consequences of this trend, that is, black women voting at higher rates and being more strongly attached to the Democratic Party, is that black women are substantially increasing their representation among black elected officials. Black women officeholders now represent 35.4 percent of all black elected officials. In recent years, there has been no net growth in the number of male black elected officials.[22] On the other hand, between 1995 and 2001, there have been 5.9 new black women elected to office for every newly elected black man.

Black women have experienced much greater success in elected office than other groups of women. According to the Center for American Women and Politics (CAWP) at Rutgers University, 14 percent of all U.S. House members are women. However, 38.5 percent of the members of the Congressional Black Caucus are women. Also, 20.5 percent of all state senators are women, but 35.2 percent of all black state senators are women. Further, 23 percent of all state representatives are women, while 32.6 percent of all black state representatives are women.

FELONY DISENFRANCHISEMENT AND THE PRISON INDUSTRIAL COMPLEX

There are 4.4 million Americans who are disenfranchised due to a past or current felony conviction.[23] No other nation in the world imprisons a larger share of its population or marks so large a share of its population with the lifelong mark of a serious (felony) criminal record. More than 13 million Americans—fully 7 percent of the adult population and an astonishing 12 percent of the adult male population—possess felony records.[24]

Clearly, state disenfranchisement laws hit African American and Latino males hardest. Nationwide, over 13 percent of African American adult males are denied the right to vote, and African American men make up 36 percent of the total disenfranchised population. Similarly, 16 percent of Latino men will enter prison in their lifetime, compared to only 4.4 percent of white men.

According to the Human Rights Watch and the Sentencing Project's *Losing the Vote* report, ten states disenfranchise all ex-offenders who have completed their criminal sentences; thirty-two states prohibit felons from voting while they are on parole, and twenty-nine of these exclude felony probationers from voting also.[25] In Alabama and Florida, 31 percent of all black men have lost their right to vote. In five other states (Iowa, Mississippi, New Mexico, Virginia, and Wyoming), one in four black men (24 to 28 percent) is permanently disenfranchised.

Over 1.4 million African American men, or 13 percent of African American men, are disenfranchised—a rate seven times the national average and representing 36 percent of the total disenfranchised population. At the current rate of incarceration, three in ten of the next generation of black men can expect to be disenfranchised at some point in their lifetime. Civil rights groups shone the national spotlight on Florida's disenfranchisement of innocent voters before the infamous 2000 presidential election—an election George W. Bush won in Florida by a scant 537 votes.

The NAACP and other groups described the state's action as a deliberate attempt to remove blacks from the rolls and deny them their constitutional right to vote.[26] Some of the state's actions were throwbacks to the Jim Crow era when white officials went to great length to prevent blacks from voting.

The 2000 presidential election in Florida was marred by thousands of eligible African American voters who were erroneously purged from the rolls and wrongly turned away from the polling places based on a faulty list compiled by a private contractor. African Americans accounted for 44 percent of those removed from the rolls, though they make up only 11 percent of the population. They also account for 13 percent of Florida's voting population but cast 15 percent of the state's 5.9 million votes for president. Democrats reap the lion's share of Florida's black votes. The suppression of the black voter turnout, whether legal or illegal, helps Republicans.

It took a federal lawsuit against the state of Florida for it to restore the rights to thousands of voters. The purging of felons from the voter rolls has continued to be a sore point since the 2000 presidential elections. Felons lists keep popping up, since the Republican-dominated state government is determined to "cleanse" the voting list of felons. In July 2004, nine days after making the names of more than 47,000 potential felon voters public, state officials scrapped the list, created by the Florida Department of Law Enforcement, saying it was too flawed to be trusted.[27]

The felons list included only sixty-one Hispanics, about 1 percent of the names on the list. The felons database had no Hispanic category, which excluded many people from the list.[28] Nearly one in five residents in Florida is Hispanic. Many Hispanics vote Republican. The *Miami Herald* reported that more than 2,100 Florida voters, many of them African American Democrats, were on the list even though their civil rights had been formally restored by the state.[29]

It is amazing that the U.S. Census Bureau counts people in prison where their bodies are confined, not the communities they come from and of which they are genuine members.[30] Imprisonment moves people in predictable patterns—typically out of large urban centers and into rural communities.[31] Research in the geographic disparities of incarceration is ongoing, but a clear pattern is emerging:

- Although 60 percent of Illinois's prisoners call Cook County (Chicago) home, 99 percent of the state's prison cells are outside the county.[32]
- Philadelphia is the legal residence for 40 percent of Pennsylvania's prisoners, but the county contains no state prisons.[33]

- Wayne County (Detroit) is home for 20 percent of Michigan's population. Almost 30 percent of the state's prisoners are from Wayne County, but only 11 percent of the state's cells are there.[34]

Interestingly, in the 1980s, 5 percent of all growth in the U.S. rural population was people in prison.[35] In the 1990s, an astonishing 30 percent of new residents of upstate New York were prisoners.[36] Guard towers are slowly replacing small towns and family farms as the struggling heartland turns to prisons as an industry of last resort.

All kinds of communities are affected. West Feliciana Parish, Louisiana, is classified by the Census Bureau as a 100 percent rural community, but 5,000 of its 15,000 residents live in custody—fully a third.[37] In comparison, Walker County, Texas, is more urban, with small cities totaling 60,000 people—but more than 13,000 of them cannot eat breakfast without permission of the warden. Altogether, nearly 200 counties in America have more than 5 percent of their population in prison.[38] Eighteen counties have more than 20 percent of their population in prison. This extraordinary transformation can be seen in the fine print of the 2000 census, but it is unnoticed unless looked for.[39] See table 10.2, which shows the top twenty prison counties in the United States.

BLACK POLITICAL POWER AND INFLUENCE

The 2000 census is indicating that as the African American population decreases relative to other racial/ethnic groups, so will their political power and influence. In the cities of Los Angeles, Washington, Houston, Miami, and Chicago, African Americans will reluctantly—and grudgingly—give up their current political leverage and positions as their numbers dwindle relative to other racial groups. Black political power and influence in U.S. cities must be reconceptualized with the idea of an America that is far more diverse than simply white and black people. What then does racial integration mean in the context of an American population in flux?[40]

The shifts in the racial mix of U.S. cities, with the percentage of African Americans falling, and growing black skepticism toward the value of integration undercut traditional notions of "integration" and "assimilation."[41] In the 1960s, "integration" meant inclusion in a United States largely defined by European Americans. Today, integration must mean inclusion, involvement, and participation in a nation that has evolved far beyond the black-white paradigm.[42]

African Americans will have to participate in reviving political coalitions—and, when necessary, help form new ones to ensure that their issues and interests remain on the nation's political agenda.[43] African American political

Table 10.2. Top Twenty Prison Counties in the United States

State	County	Population	%Rural	Prison Pop.	Prison %
1. Louisiana	W. Feliciana Parish	15,111	100.0%	4,995	33.1%
2. Texas	Concho	3,996	100.0%	1,299	32.8%
3. Florida	Union	13,442	52.2%	4,052	30.1%
4. Illinois	Brown	6,950	41.8%	1,912	27.5%
5. Tennessee	Lake	7,954	100.0%	2,090	26.3%
6. Virginia	Greensville	11,560	64.4%	3,027	26.2%
7. Texas	Mitchell	9,698	32.0%	2,523	26.0%
8. California	Lassen	33,828	58.7%	8,367	24.7%
9. Texas	Hartley	5,537	57.6%	1,343	24.3%
10. Missouri	DeKalb	11,597	67.1%	2,626	22.6%
11. Texas	Jones	20,785	60.9%	4,650	22.4%
12. Texas	Walker	61,758	36.3%	13,691	22.2%
13. Texas	Bee	32,359	30.6%	7,070	21.8%
14. Texas	Childress	7,688	34.0%	1,652	21.5%
15. Arkansas	Lincoln	14,492	100.0%	3,003	20.7%
16. Texas	Madison	12,940	69.9%	2,681	20.7%
17. Illinois	Johnson	12,878	79.1%	2,640	20.5%
18. Nevada	Pershing	6,693	100.0%	1,370	20.5%
19. Texas	Anderson	55,109	41.3%	10,750	19.5%
20. Virginia	Sussex	12,504	100.0%	2,379	19.0%

Source: Eric Lotke and Peter Wagner, "Prisoners of the Census: Electoral and Financial Consequences of Counting Prisoners Where They Go, Not Where They Come From," *Pace Law Review* 24 (2005): 587–607.

leaders will need to represent not just a black political agenda, but a fresh, progressive brand of politics that is all-encompassing and places "identity interests" within the context of the overall civic good.[44]

What is really needed is a multiracial vision, forged at the grassroots level, wedded to a political agenda of social change that makes all people feel as if they are stakeholders in their respective communities. Black elected officials must recognize that the people they represent are of many different ethnicities who want a better education for their children, safer streets, quality schools, and good jobs. These "survival issues" were important to African American voters in the 2000 and 2004 national elections.

The black vote is still important in national elections. African American voters still have to fight to get their vote counted. Significant problems were reported in several states in the 2004 national elections, most notably, Ohio. Ohio was a pivotal state in the 2004 national election. In its 2005 study, *Democracy at Risk: The 2004 Election in Ohio*, the Democratic National Committee (DNC) examined extensive litigation and questions relating to administration of the election, both before and after Election Day.[45] Their findings included:

- Twice as many African American voters as white voters reported experiencing problems at the polls (52 percent versus 25 percent). African American voters who had voted in the past election but had moved since the last time they voted were nearly twice as likely to be forced to vote provisionally than white voters who had voted in the past but had moved since they voted.
- Statewide, 16 percent of African Americans reported experiencing intimidation versus only 5 percent of white voters.
- Statewide, African American voters reported waiting an average of fifty-two minutes before voting, while white voters reported waiting an average of eighteen minutes.
- Younger voters and African Americans were more likely to vote provisionally than older voters and whites, even when you account for differences in registration and residential mobility. African American voters were 1.2 times more likely than white voters to be required to vote provisionally.
- African American voters statewide were 47 percent more likely to be required to show identification than white voters. And 61 percent of African American men reported being asked to provide identification at the polls.

Given these astounding findings, it is little wonder why blacks and whites see the world through different lenses. For example, 71 percent of white Ohio voters were very confident their vote was counted correctly versus 19 percent of African Americans.[46] The fact that African Americans were more likely to be challenged, and more likely to wait in line, than were white voters does nothing to close this confidence gap.

Voter suppression has been a technique used by both the Democrats and Republicans. But today, the Republican Party has more to gain by suppressing the black vote, especially in areas with large African American populations and some other heavily Democratic voting groups. Most African Americans vote Democratic. Generally when black votes are suppressed, Republicans benefit.[47]

There is rarely "smoking-gun" proof of black voter suppression schemes. However, this proof came in 2004, when then-seventy-three-year-old state representative John Pappageorge of Michigan, who was running for a state senate seat, was quoted by the *Detroit Free Press*: "If we do not suppress the Detroit [read: black] vote, we're going to have a tough time in this election cycle." African Americans comprise 83 percent of Detroit's population and overwhelmingly vote Democratic.

Florida in 2000 and Ohio in 2004 provide a fairly clear picture of the roadblocks some officials are willing to erect to stop African Americans from voting in future elections. In 2000, African American voters in Florida

were ten times more likely than nonblack voters to have their ballots rejected and were often prevented from voting because their names were erroneously purged from registration lists. Other recent direct assaults on
African American voters' rights include:

- In 2003, voters in African American areas of Philadelphia were systematically challenged by men carrying clipboards and driving sedans
  with magnetic signs designed to look like law enforcement insignia.
- Controversy erupted over the use in the Orlando area of armed, plain-
  clothes officers from the Florida Department of Law Enforcement
  (FDLE) to question elderly black voters in their homes as part of a state
  investigation of voting irregularities in the city's March 2003 mayoral
  election. Critics charged that the tactics used by the FDLE intimidated
  black voters, which could suppress their turnout in future elections. Six
  members of Congress called on Attorney General John Ashcroft to in-
  vestigate potential civil rights violations in the matter.
- In Kentucky in July 2004, black Republican officials joined to ask their
  state GOP party chairman to renounce plans to place "vote chal-
  lengers" in African American precincts during the upcoming elections.
- In historically black colleges and universities (HBCUs) across the
  South, students are too often told erroneously that they can't vote
  where they go to school. Registrars refuse to set up registration and voting booths on campus, hoping to discourage student turnout. In 2004
  in Waller County, Texas, a local district attorney told students at predominantly black Prairie View A&M University that they were not eligible to vote in the county where the school is located—the same
  county where, twenty-six years earlier, a federal court order was required to prevent discrimination against the students.[48]

Clearly, African American and other minority voters bear the brunt of every
form of illegal disenfranchisement scheme, including pernicious efforts to
keep them away from the polls. Julian Bond, NAACP board chairman,
summed up the challenges detailed in *The Long Shadow of Jim Crow*, "While
we are keeping an eye on state officials and new voting machines, we cannot
relax our vigilance against these kinds of direct assaults on voters' rights."[49]

CONCLUSION

In order for black political power to continue to grow in the new century,
there are three key issues that must be addressed. First, racially polarized
voting must continue to diminish and reach a low enough level that black
candidates can begin to more regularly win statewide elective office.

Second, younger black voters, who represent a very large part of the black population, and who vote at very low levels, must be mobilized at higher levels than has been the case in the past; the elimination of felony disenfranchisement laws would also contribute significantly to black voting power.

Third, black political power at this time is entirely invested in the Democratic Party, and Democratic control is essential for the full expression of that power. However, in the long term, in order to achieve a stable and substantial level of political power, African Americans need to make more inroads within the Republican Party.

Fourth, African Americans and other people of color must strengthen their alliances to combat voter intimidation and suppression schemes—no matter how benign they appear on the surface. They must demand that the Voting Rights Act and other civil rights laws are rigorously enforced across this nation—including tallying electronic voting. The struggle does not end with the right to vote; the real issues in upcoming elections revolve around the U.S. Department of Justice ensuring African Americans and other historically disenfranchised groups that all of their votes cast will be counted.

There are, of course, other important issues to future black political empowerment, including collaborations with other progressive groups. Black and Hispanic voters and leaders have been close allies in the past and will further enhance their powers with future collaborations, due to the substantial growth in both populations.

NOTES

1. See *Political Participation: A Report of the United States Commission on Civil Rights* (Washington, DC: U.S. Government Printing Office, 1968), 12–13.

2. See the Sentencing Project and Human Rights Watch, *Losing the Vote: The Impact of Felony Disenfranchisement Laws in the United States* (Washington, DC: The Sentencing Project, 1998), 8. Also found at http://www.mindfully.org/Reform/2003/Racist-Felony-Disenfranchisement11dec03.htm (October 2, 2006).

3. United States Commission on Civil Rights, "Reauthorization of the Temporary Provisions of the Voting Rights Act: A Briefing Before the United States Commission on Civil Rights," Washington, DC: USCCR, October 7, 2005, 1, available at http://www.usccr.gov/pubs/060706VRAbrief524.pdf (accessed October 2, 2006).

4. U.S. Department of Justice, Civil Rights Division, Voting Section, "Frequently Asked Questions," available at http://www.usdoj.gov/crt/voting/misc/faq.htm (accessed October 2, 2006).

5. United States Department of Justice, Civil Rights Division, Voting Section, *Introduction to Federal Voting Rights Laws*, http://www.usdoj.gov/crt/voting/intro/intro.htm (accessed October 2, 2006).

6. American Civil Liberties Union, *ACLU Voting Rights: About the VRA*, available at http://www.votingrights.org/more.php#sect5 (accessed October 2, 2006).

7. Artur Davis, "Voting Rights Act Is Still Needed to Build on Progress," *The Hill*, available at: http://www.hillnews.com/thehill/export/TheHill/Comment/OpEd/061406_oped3.html (accessed October 2, 2006).

8. "Bush Signs Voting Rights Act Extension amid Midterm Election Season," *USA Today*, July 27, 2006.

9. *Black State Legislators: A Survey and Analysis of Black Leadership in the State Capitals* (Washington, DC: Joint Center for Political and Economic Studies, 1992), 4.

10. *Black Elected Officials: A Statistical Summary, 2001* (Washington, DC: Joint Center for Political and Economic Studies, 2003), table 1.

11. *Black State Legislators*, 4.

12. See *Black Elected Officials: A Statistical Summary, 2001*, table 8.

13. See David A. Bositis, *National Opinion Poll: Education* (Washington, DC: Joint Center for Political and Economic Studies, 2002).

14. Joint Center for Political and Economic Studies, *Blacks and the 1996 Elections: A Preliminary Analysis* and *Blacks and the 2000 Elections: A Preliminary Analysis* (Washington, DC: Joint Center for Political and Economic Studies, 1996; 2000).

15. David A. Bositis, *The Black Vote in 2000: A Preliminary Analysis* (Washington, DC: Joint Center for Political and Economic Studies, 2000), 2; see National Conference of State Legislatures, table 4: "Partisan Change in Southern State Legislatures, 1990–1992 vs. 2003," in *Blacks and 2000 Elections* (Washington, DC: Joint Center for Political and Economic Studies, 2003).

16. See National Conference of State Legislatures, table 4: "Partisan Change in Southern State Legislatures, 1990–1992 vs. 2003."

17. Joint Center for Political and Economic Studies, Blacks and the 2004 Democratic National Convention, table 7, "Black Major Party Nominees for U.S. Senator and Governor, 1966–2002" (Washington, DC: Joint Center for Political and Economic Studies, 2004).

18. Christopher Wills, "Obama Headed to Senate After Easy Win," Associated Press, November 2, 2004, http://www.obamaforillinois.com/index.asp?Type=B_PR&SEC={3003DBAB-64B6-4DCE-901A-6E42E444239D}&DE={B7A944D4-61EA-45B3-8E4A-FE590460C030}&Design=PrintView (accessed December 6, 2004).

19. See David A. Bositis, *The Political Perspectives of Young African Americans: A National Opinion Poll Special Report* (Washington, DC: Joint Center for Political and Economic Studies, 2001), 1–2.

20. Ibid.

21. Ibid.

22. National Conference of State Legislatures, table 4: "Partisan Change in the Southern State Legislatures, 1990–1992 vs. 2003."

23. Paul Street, "The Political Consequences of Racist Felony Disenfranchisement," www.blackcommentor.com http://www.mindfully.org/Reform/2003/Racist-Felony-Disenfranchisement11dec03.htm (accessed December 6, 2004).

24. Ibid.

25. The Sentencing Project and Human Rights Watch, *Losing the Vote*.

26. Robert E. Pierre, "Botched Name Purge Denied Some the Right to Vote," *Washington Post*, May 31, 2001, A01.

27. Matthew Waite, "Florida Scraps Felon Vote List," *St. Petersburg Times*, July 11, 2004.

28. The Associated Press, "Florida Won't Use Flawed Felon List," *New York Times*, July 11, 2004.

29. Mary Ellen Klas, "State Kills Flawed Felon Purge List (Florida)," *Miami Herald*, July 10, 2004.

30. Peter Wagner, "Locked Up, Then Counted Out: Prisoners and the Census," *Fortune News* (Winter 2002–2003), published by the Fortune Society, http://www.prisonpolicy.org/articles/fn011703.shtml (accessed December 15, 2004).

31. Eric Lotke and Peter Wagner, "Prisoners of the Census: Electoral and Financial Consequences of Counting Prisoners Where They Go, Not Where They Come From," *Pace Law Review* 24 (2005): 587–607.

32. Rose Heyer and Peter Wagner, "Too Big to Ignore: How Counting People in Prisons Distorted Census 2000," Prisoners of the Census Executive Summary, http://www.prisonersofthecensus.org/toobig/exec_sum.shtml (accessed December 5, 2004).

33. Ibid.

34. Ibid.

35. Calvin L. Beale, "Prisons, Population, and Jobs in Nonmetro America," *Rural Development Perspectives* 8 (1993): 16, 17.

36. Rolf Pendall, *Upstate New York's Population Plateau: The Third-Slowest 'State'* (Washington, DC: The Brookings Institution, 2003), available at http://brookings.edu/dybdocroot/es/urban/publications/200308_Pendall.pdf (accessed December 15, 2004).

37. Compare U.S. Census Bureau, "Group Quarters Population by Group Quarters Type," at http://factfinder.census.gov/servlet/DTTable?_bm=Y&state=DT&context=DT& ds_nameDEC_2000_SF1_U&mt_name=DEC_2000 SF1_U_PCT016&-tree_id=4001&-all_geo-types=N&-geo_id=05000US22125&-search_results=01000 US&-format=&_lang=EN with U.S. Census Bureau, "State and County Quick Facts, West Feliciana Parish, Louisiana," at http://quickfacts.census.gov/qfd/states/22/22125.html (accessed December 15, 2004).

38. Out of 3,140 counties, 197, or 6.3 percent, have more than 5 percent of their population in prison. See U.S. Census Bureau, U.S. Dept of Commerce, *2000 Census*, at http://www.census.gov/ (accessed December 6, 2004).

39. See U.S. Census Bureau, U.S. Dept. of Commerce, 2000 Census of Population and Housing: Summary File 1 Technical Documentation 6-68 to 6-69 (2002) available at http://www.census.gov/prod/cen2000/doc/sf1.pdf (accessed December 15, 2004); Lotke and Wagner, "Prisoners of the Census."

40. Joe Hicks, "The Changing Face of America," California Association of Human Relations Organizations. Editor's note: This first appeared in the July 20, 1997, edition of the *Los Angeles Times*, http://www.cahro.org/html/augsept97-1.html (accessed December 15, 2005).

41. Ibid.

42. Ibid.

43. Ibid.

44. Ibid.

45. Democratic National Committee, *Democracy at Risk: The 2004 Election in Ohio* (Washington, DC: DNC, 2005).

46. Ibid., 4.

47. Bob Herbert, "Protect the Vote," *New York Times*, September 13, 2004.

48. People for the American Way and NAACP, *The Long Shadow of Jim Crow* (Washington, DC: PFAW and NAACP, 2004), 3–6.

49. Ibid., 1.

11

Achieving Equitable Development

Angela Glover Blackwell

The next generation of Americans will be "majority-minority," with the Latino population exceeding all other ethnic minority populations combined. The U.S. population hit 300 million in October 2006. The nation's population is expected to top 400 million in the 2040s, with white non-Hispanics making up a bare majority. Hispanics are projected to make up close to one-quarter of the population, and African Americans more than 14 percent. Asians will increase their share of the population to more than 7 percent.[1] And by 2050, people of color are expected become the majority.

This projection represents nothing short of a *demographic sea change*.[2] The first signs of this shift were in California, but it is now evidenced in nearly every region of this country. Does this demographic change suggest that the black-white framework that has dominated the discourse regarding full participation for people of color in the United States is no longer relevant? While it is not the only lens needed to understand the past and develop analysis and plans for the future, the black-white paradigm colors the experiences of *all* minorities. In this country it is defining, embedded, and persistent. Strategies that build from this racial analysis but respond to the current reality are needed to achieve full inclusion in today's context.

The black-white paradigm defines the conditions in urban America. For example, if a Southeast Asian family moves into a poor inner-city neighborhood in any large U.S. city, they will likely find: deteriorating housing stock, a community with a tense relationship with the police, no full-service grocery store with fresh produce and vegetables, and failing public schools. They will find this *not* because of their skin color or language or country of origin, but because the conditions in the neighborhood have been defined by the way the country has chosen to relate to people who are African American.

That neglect of these communities and the lack of investment stem from the embedded nature of racial discrimination. Racial inequality in America has become so deeply embedded—especially in housing patterns—that literally where you live could stand as a proxy for what your life opportunities will be. In communities of inner-city, concentrated poverty, children attend schools that lack the resources and political support to thrive. These schools fail to equip the children in the surrounding communities with the skills needed to become contributing members of society. Adults in these communities often lack the skills required for good jobs, and those that have the skills too often find that the jobs they could get are too distant from their homes—a situation exacerbated by the absence of mass transit.

But having posited that the black-white paradigm remains important in understanding the present condition in urban America, it is insufficient for fully grasping and addressing the challenge of full inclusion. Many of the neighborhoods of the black metropolis, while developed during some of the worst periods of black exclusion, are now populated by people who bring new sets of needs. Latinos, Asians, and Pacific Islanders have language needs that are different from those of African Americans. Latinos often suffer from what should be an oxymoron, "working poverty," in ways that are profound and complicated by issues of citizenship documentation. Housing overcrowding and stereotyping affect these groups in unique ways.

All low-income people of color, however, are being impacted by the way development patterns are shaping opportunity. How the nation continues to grow will impact the opportunity structure for all of those living in neighborhoods being left behind. What hope, what opportunities, then, for achieving and ensuring any kind of quality of life for future inhabitants of the black metropolis?

EQUITABLE DEVELOPMENT:
A VIABLE REGIONAL STRATEGY

A focus on race and housing in the context of regional development and growth is the only way to achieve regional equitable development. Within sprawling regions, housing opens or shuts the doors to other life opportunities. Land-use policies determine whether low- and moderate-income families—people of color in particular—will be concentrated in underserved communities or be able to choose neighborhoods with good schools and access to jobs. Regional development patterns play a significant role in housing gentrification and displacement. Yet as contributors to this volume attest, without political will and a strategic agenda, little progress will be made.

Many jurisdictions shun responsibility for producing affordable housing; external enforcement mechanisms are the exception. To make matters worse, public commitment to housing affordability problems in the United States has significantly diminished. Xavier de Souza Briggs has called housing affordability the "most invisible social policy issue in America"—placing greater dependence, but no pressure, on the private sector to address the challenge.[3]

Building a coherent housing strategy that responds to geographic concerns and promotes racial equity requires bundling a number of tactics, policies, and practices that have been around for years in various forms. A new movement is emerging around "equitable development."[4] This strategy is anchored by the fair distribution of affordable housing, rooted in community building, and guided by the pursuit of equity. It promotes strategies that move toward inclusion and that safeguard the interests of long-term residents in communities undergoing change. In asking "who benefits," this strategy provides win-win solutions that benefit all, including low-income communities of color.

Four principles inform equitable development:

- *Integrating people and place.* Regional development and revitalization policies and practices must integrate *people*-focused strategies—efforts that support low-income community residents and families—with *place*-focused strategies—those that stabilize and improve housing, commercial establishments, and other aspects of the physical environment.
- *Reducing local and regional disparities.* One's address should *not* be the determinant of his or her life chances. The services, amenities, and opportunities that are essential for healthy, livable communities should be accessible to *all* neighborhoods. Win-win solutions must be crafted that simultaneously improve conditions in low-income communities of color *and* build healthy metropolitan regions that—if they pay attention to both regional growth and central-city poverty—are more likely to thrive.
- *Promoting double bottom-line investments.* Public and private investments in low-income communities are key to revitalization, but to reduce poverty as well as to promote advancement, these investments must produce a double bottom line: (1) financial returns to investors, and (2) economic and social benefits for the residents (e.g., jobs; requisite services; entrepreneurial opportunities; and access to desirable, affordable housing, including ownership options).
- *Ensuring meaningful community voice, participation, and leadership.* Widespread participation by community residents and organizations in planning and development helps ensure that the results benefit the community, respond to the needs of low-income people of color, and reflect the principles articulated above. To achieve these results, community

residents and organizations must have access to the tools, knowledge, and resources that can guarantee their significant participation.

The principles of equitable development present the challenge to simultaneously address the needs of the people in a community while improving the quality of its housing stock and commercial and service environment. This means paying attention, from the beginning of the process, to finding ways to keep housing affordable over time. It also means that development outside of the black metropolis should seek ways to create affordable housing opportunities and that transportation and other regional public investments should enhance the value of housing throughout the region by making jobs and recreational activities broadly accessible.

The equitable development paradigm ensures that low-income people and communities of color benefit from local and regional economic activity by requiring that affordable housing development and distribution be seen as the *centerpiece* of geographic and racial fairness. It collectively targets transportation, asset and work-force development, as well as public and private investment policies and practices, to maximize community benefits and to mitigate unintended negative consequences of development—lack of access to opportunity, displacement of low-income people of color, or the creation of a jobs/housing mismatch. Advocates for racial, economic, and social equity are beginning to understand this new regional paradigm, to grapple with the opportunities and challenges that it presents, and to develop strategies to achieve equity in local and regional contexts.

In November 2002, PolicyLink, with the Funders' Network for Smart Growth and Livable Communities, hosted the Summit on Promoting Regional Equity. The original plans were to attract 250 participants; the overwhelming response, however, forced registration to close at 650. More than half of the participants were people of color; 35 states were represented. An array of policy issues was explored, with in-depth strategic discussions and experiences from specific places lifted up and dissected; their successes were celebrated and shared, their difficulties instructive to others seeking guidance. The need for affordable housing as a key part of local, regional, state, and federal agendas was reinforced, as was the need for comprehensive approaches.[5] Advancing Regional Equity, the next summit, held in May 2005, drew a racially and geographically diverse group of over 1,200 participants, illustrating the movement's growing momentum.

A FRAMEWORK FOR ACTION

Clearly the concept of equitable development has broad appeal, and it is a useful lens by which to view strategies to craft policy campaigns for social and economic justice.[6] But what does equitable development look like on the ground, in communities? What are the most promising points of intervention, given the fact that sprawling development patterns affect nearly every facet of opportunity, and that action on multiple fronts is needed?

Using these equitable development principles as a guiding light in crafting regional policies seeks to ensure that *all* members of the region both contribute to and benefit from local and regional development. This section examines how these principles are being advanced in four important arenas for regional equity action:

- living near regional opportunities;
- linking people to regional opportunities;
- promoting equitable public investment; and
- making all neighborhoods stable, healthy, and livable.

While there are many more promising efforts that could be discussed in this short chapter, the examples below are illustrative of the diverse actors and intervention points for achieving regional equity.

Living Near Regional Opportunities

Housing is more than shelter—it is a critical determinant of opportunity when located in a community with resources and amenities. Living in a decent house in a good neighborhood creates access to high-quality schools, strong social networks, opportunities for physical activity, and public services. Paying an affordable rent or mortgage makes resources available for other important needs such as health insurance, transportation, and investing in the education of one's children.

Owning a home is the primary vehicle for wealth building in this country, yet despite some closing of the gap, significant racial disparities exist in home ownership rates. As the Millennial Housing Commission explains, housing matters, not just to individual and family well-being, but also to neighborhood, community, and national social and economic well-being.[7]

Given this, a key arena for promoting regional equity is ensuring that quality housing is affordable and available throughout metropolitan areas. Low-income families who reside in affordable housing close to good schools, employment centers, transportation centers, parks, grocery stores, civic institutions, and services are better positioned to succeed economically and socially. While large-scale public housing projects are no longer built in the most undesirable places and there exists an explicit goal of deconcentrating poverty through housing policy (Housing Choice Vouchers, Hope VI, Low-Income Housing Tax Credits), the nation's housing markets remain starkly divided by race and income. This division is not simply an urban vs. suburban phenomenon.

Many older, inner-ring suburbs are increasingly the destination for working families of color looking for affordable and safe housing choices. These declining first-tier suburbs face many of the same challenges found in urban communities being left behind, creating the ironic situation of working families moving away from, not to, opportunity. Multiple forces conspire to prevent the production of affordable housing in opportunity-rich communities where quality transit, employment, schools, and civic institutions exist; a multifaceted approach is required to overcome the barriers these forces create.

Dismantling Exclusionary Land-Use Practices

Regional inequity is often the result of exclusionary land use and zoning practices. A survey of jurisdictions in the twenty-five largest metropolitan areas showed that low-density zoning consistently reduced rental housing in jurisdictions where it was enacted, and the resulting shortage limited the number of African Americans and Latinos in that community.[8] Local jurisdictions employ a variety of land use and zoning techniques, minimum-square-footage requirements or large-lot regulations—to exclude affordable housing choices and those who could benefit from them. Regulatory policies such as fair-share housing agreements, inclusionary zoning, and zoning overlays that raise density and allow multifamily housing development can shift these exclusionary land-use practices and open up opportunity-rich communities for affordable housing development.

Inclusionary zoning requires private developers to contribute to affordable housing in exchange for benefits that reduce construction costs such as zoning variances, density bonuses, development rights, or expedited permits. Since Montgomery County, Maryland, passed the first ongoing ordinance in 1974, numerous jurisdictions with housing needs as varied as Sacramento, Santa Fe, Denver, Boulder, Cambridge, East Palo Alto, and Fairfax County (Virginia) have found inclusionary zoning to be an important affordable housing tool.

In recent years inclusionary zoning has seen resurgence, with campaigns being led by diverse community coalitions from Los Angeles, California, to Madison, Wisconsin, and Washington, D.C. A New York City coalition is focused on ensuring that infill development planned on formerly industrial land will set aside 20 percent of its projected 75,000 new housing units as affordable.[9] Inclusionary zoning has been proven effective at both producing and equitably distributing affordable housing in line with smart-growth principles.

Inclusionary Zoning in the San Francisco Bay Area

An innovative approach to thinking regionally about inclusionary zoning can be found in the San Francisco Bay Area. The Bay Area Inclusionary Housing Initiative is a unique partnership of community organizations and foundations advancing a multiyear, regional campaign to help Bay Area cities and counties accelerate adoption of inclusionary housing policies. Led by the Nonprofit Housing Association of Northern California, the goal of this regional initiative is to double the rate of inclusionary housing production. Communities that already have inclusionary zoning in place have demonstrated that it is a critical tool for providing much needed low- and moderate-income housing for working families. The participating foundations are the S. H. Cowell Foundation, Fannie Mae Foundation, Evelyn and Walter Haas Jr. Fund, Marin Community Foundation, Peninsula Community Foundation, The San Francisco Foundation, and Charles and Helen Schwab Foundation. The community partners include the Institute for Local Self-Government, Greenbelt Alliance, the California Affordable Housing Law Project, the Nine County Housing Advocacy Network, and the Western Center on Law and Poverty.

Linking People to Regional Opportunities

While new development should equitably distribute housing choices across the region as a mechanism for reducing isolation and concentrated poverty, it is equally important to improve options and accessibility for low-income and working families where they currently live. Regional equity advocates actively pursue strategies and policy changes that connect low-income people to employment and other opportunities through improved transportation options.

In 1996, only 16 percent of jobs were within three miles of the central business district.[10] Given the decentralized nature of employment patterns, transportation systems consciously designed to link low-income communities to economic corridors and jobs are fundamental to regional equity. Transportation advocates are working on multiple fronts to promote more equitable transportation policies. Here we review two arenas: policies that support immigrant access to jobs, and promoting transit-oriented development in low-income neighborhoods.

Immigrants: The New Dimension of Regional Equity

One of the big stories emerging from Census 2000 is that immigration was responsible for much of the nation's growth—and that this trend shows no sign of slowing. There are interesting shifts happening in settlement patterns: immigrants who first settled in central cities are moving to the suburbs, but more recent immigrants are bypassing urban areas altogether and heading directly for suburbia. This shift is due in large part to sprawl-related job growth patterns. If immigrants are to acquire new jobs that are increasingly located far from city centers, they must either live where the jobs are, though affordable housing is scarce, or utilize public transit, which is limited or lacking in many metro areas. This is a new dimension of a fundamental regional equity challenge known as "spatial mismatch" between jobs and housing and is most evident in long commutes and regionwide traffic jams.

Against this backdrop, in September 2003, California Governor Gray Davis signed Senate Bill 60. The legislation, allowing undocumented immigrants to obtain a driver's license in California, was a pragmatic decision to respond to the realities of California's labor markets. It was repealed by Governor Arnold Schwarzenegger less than a month after he took office in November of the same year. As Michael Fix of the Urban Institute pointed out (in a PolicyLink interview in March 2004): "The driver's license debate in California was framed as an issue of equal rights for immigrants. Yet, at its heart it is a workforce supply issue. It would have had more universal appeal if it had been advocated for in terms of employer needs." Hope, and a chance to reframe the issue, still exists. Reborn as Senate Bill 1160, the driver's license legislation was recently approved by the California State Senate Transportation Committee and is winding its way through the legislative process.

Promoting Development and Investment around Transit Stations

Transit-oriented development (TOD) is development centered around transit stations as a way to improve transit accessibility and the surrounding community. In disinvested neighborhoods, TOD can be a major driver for revitalization, connecting the area to jobs and creating, or re-creating, a vital commercial center. Once the purview of planning agencies and private developers, transit-oriented development projects are increasingly being led by equity advocates, most notably community development corporations. While building economic development projects around transit stops in low-income communities provides a lifeline to opportunities across the region, such development can also fuel gentrification. The work of Chicago's Bethel New Life and Oakland's Spanish Speaking Unity Council are recognized national models of how to strike the balance between revitalization and preservation of affordability.[11]

While TOD projects have historically been planned around existing stations, regional equity advocates are also engaging in the planning and decision making about where new transit lines and stations should be located and using the opportunity to anticipate needed equitable development requirements. During regional planning for the Interstate Avenue light rail line in Portland, Oregon, a detailed redevelopment plan was created. As a result of community organizing and involvement, the redevelopment plan cites "benefit the existing community" and "outreach" as two of twelve guiding principles and statements about preventing resident displacement included in both the housing and economic development sections. Inclusion of such language is a notable shift—from a focus on regional planning to regional equity.

Promoting Equitable Public Investment

Equity advocates are gaining significant traction from the community benefits movement, which seeks to promote more equitable outcomes from large-scale economic development projects that are viewed as regional destinations—sport stadiums, entertainment arenas, hotels, office parks, and "big box" retail services. These economic development projects benefit from public subsidy (e.g., taxpayer support) and should therefore guarantee community benefits like good jobs, affordable housing, and child care. The movement is being driven by broad and diverse coalitions that include labor unions, community builders, housing developers, neighborhood advocates, and environmentalists.

A recent fifty state survey of economic development subsidy programs (e.g., loans, grants, and tax incentives) conducted by Good Jobs First revealed that not one state effectively coordinates its economic development spending with public transportation planning. The survey also found that only four states—Ohio, Minnesota, Maine, and Connecticut—have any kind of system to collect even fragmentary data on corporate relocations that receive economic development incentives. In other words, only four states collect data that could help them determine if their economic development programs are reducing or increasing access to jobs for workers who cannot afford a car, or if they are harming or improving commuter choice when jobs get relocated. These are troubling findings given that in virtually all major metropolitan areas there is a mismatch between low-income and working families living in urban and inner-ring areas and jobs in newly developing, suburban communities. The study recommends that economic development subsidies should be granted in a manner that is "location efficient" by restricting subsidies to projects that have access to public transit. (source: Missing the Bus: How States Fail to Connect Economic Development with Public Transit, Good Jobs First).

The community benefits movement began in California when organizations in Los Angeles, San Diego, San Jose, and the East Bay began leveraging the potential of large economic development projects to benefit low-income communities. Perhaps the most comprehensive community benefits agreement is the one negotiated by the Figueroa Corridor Coalition for Economic Justice around the development of the downtown Los Angeles Sports and Entertainment District (Staples Center), which featured living-wage jobs, local hiring requirements, job training, a 20 percent set-aside of affordable housing, and a commitment of $1 million for community parks and recreation. Since this victory, one of the coalition members—the Los Angeles Alliance for New Economy—has been tracking development in the broader Los Angeles region to determine when community benefits should be part of the project. And groups in Los Angeles and San Jose are pushing for policy changes to require public agencies to measure and ensure that community benefits accrue from large public investments.

The idea of community benefits is spreading rapidly, taking hold in metro regions across the country, including Milwaukee, Atlanta, Boston, Seattle, New York, and Washington, D.C.[12] A community benefits agreement was negotiated in 2004 for developments in the former Park East Freeway area of downtown Milwaukee. The Institute for Wisconsin's Future was a key advocate in this effort; affordable housing and union-level wages for construction workers are among the components of the agreement that will apply to all projects receiving public subsidies or built on public land.

Influencing Public Infrastructure Investments

Equity advocates are exerting increased influence on state public infrastructure investments. Infrastructure dollars account for a large percentage of state spending and affect virtually every aspect of neighborhoods, cities, and regions, including, for example, where housing is located and the kind of housing that can be built, if and how people can get to jobs, the quality of education in the community, and maintenance of basic public health and safety. In the absence of equitable public infrastructure policy, there can be little social and economic equity in communities.

Despite the importance of infrastructure issues, which involve complex, highly technical (and often convoluted) discussions, these issues are rarely the focus of public debate. This, however, is likely to change, given the power of infrastructure investment in shaping regions and the growing number of states, like California, that are facing "infrastructure crises"— long-term inattention to needed infrastructure improvements and advancements. Advocates for social and economic justice are focusing greater attention on these important regional equity issues.

School construction financing is an area of infrastructure investment that is uniting civil rights advocates and smart-growth proponents around the issue of regional equity. Most state funding formulas for school construction promote sprawl by favoring construction of new schools in growing suburban areas over rehabilitation of older schools in the central city and closer-in suburbs. In California, the Mexican American Legal Defense and Educational Fund and PolicyLink are working with a range of equity advocates and smart-growth leaders to push for the redistribution of school construction funds so that overcrowded schools in low-income communities become more of a priority for state spending than "greenfield" (i.e., suburban) school development. A new program begun in 2002 and re-funded in 2004 set aside $4.14 billion for new construction of critically overcrowded schools.

In 1997, a state supreme court legal decision found Ohio's K–12 school system to be unconstitutional because students were not receiving a "thorough and efficient" education. The deficient physical state of the schools was cited as a major factor in the decision. As a result, Ohio has revamped its funding for school facilities so that schools in need are priorities, and the state has become a national model of how to more equitably distribute school construction dollars. The litigation behind this action was spearheaded by the Ohio Coalition for Equity and Adequacy of School Funding.

Maryland's constitution contains a similar provision, requiring the state to provide a "thorough and efficient" education. Maryland assessed all of its schools for health and safety standards as well as the ability to support educational programming; this survey covered approximately 121,046,176 square feet of school space. The resulting facilities inventory helped to establish minimum facilities standards, determine the level of need, and target resources to where they are most needed. Lastly, the state encourages schools to be the focal point of a neighborhood or community, serving educational, social, recreational, and other needs.

Making All Neighborhoods Stable, Healthy, and Livable

Regional equity also means that all people in the region live in neighborhoods that have the essentials for healthy, productive living and are connected to opportunities throughout the region. One way to achieve this goal is to work to establish a minimum standard of livability that no communities fall below. Thus, the work of building strong, stable neighborhoods of choice across metropolitan communities is a key arena for regional equity action.

According to the 2000 Census, approximately one-quarter of all large cities (population more than 100,000) continue to face significant population decline and the attendant disinvestment that follows. These cities are primarily located in the northeast and Midwest and include Philadelphia, Cleveland, Detroit, and Pittsburgh.[13] PolicyLink is working to bring greater attention to the challenges that these "weak market" cities face, such as declining home values and equity, diminishing tax bases that lead to fewer public amenities, abundant vacant and abandoned property (including "brownfields," formerly industrial sites whose redevelopment is complicated by environmental and hazardous material cleanup concerns), racial concentration of poverty, loss of social networks, and lower median incomes.[14]

Rebuilding neighborhoods in weak market cities so that they become vibrant, supportive communities is a fundamental regional equity challenge. All communities in a region should be "places of choice," with the services and supports that individuals and families need to be economically and socially stable. Distressed communities lack the basic amenities (e.g., banks, grocery stores, neighborhood parks, and cultural centers) that families need to lead healthy, productive lives. Transforming distressed communities requires understanding the competitive advantage of these places relative to the region, then tailoring strategies to attract reinvestment, while connecting existing residents to the benefits of future revitalization.

A promising example of such transformation is the Healthy Neighborhoods Initiative (HNI) in Baltimore, Maryland. HNI recognizes the critical role that healthy, attractive neighborhoods play in making the city and region thrive. The initiative focuses on "in the middle" neighborhoods that usually do not have compelling enough problems to attract headlines yet also fail to attract investment dollars because of troubled properties. The Healthy Neighborhoods Initiative builds from neighborhood strength, harnessing assets and utilizing market forces to reinvigorate neighborhoods in the middle. Housing investments that build home equity and appreciation are coupled with civic engagement activities that strengthen the social fabric of the neighborhood.

In the Belair-Edison neighborhood, for instance, median sale prices for homes on target blocks increased over 9 percent from 2002 to 2003; long-term, existing residents are benefiting from this revitalization. Foundations such as the Goldseker Foundation and the Baltimore Community Foundation have made strategic investments in the Healthy Neighborhoods Initiative, recognizing the importance of this approach to building thriving neighborhoods that are connected to the broader region.

There are also distressed neighborhoods within economically vibrant regions that face similar challenges to reinvestment. Strategies to rebuild such places and create vital, stable, and supportive neighborhoods that are regional destinations—such as the Diamond Neighborhoods that are home to Market Creek Plaza in San Diego, are a critical arena for regional equity action.

Grocery Stores: Ensuring Neighborhood Livability

The neighborhood-region link is exemplified at Market Creek Plaza. Located in the low-income, diverse Diamond Neighborhoods in San Diego,

Market Creek Plaza extends over nine acres on a property that once housed a munitions factory. Both a commercial and cultural center, it includes a large supermarket—its anchor, ethnic restaurants, a fitness center, and an open-air community amphitheater. An outdoor public art collection—mosaics, totems, and murals—in combination with the design of the plaza's buildings reflects the artistic traditions of the diverse ethnic and cultural groups in the neighborhoods.

Spearheaded by the Jacobs Family Foundation, Market Creek Plaza is anticipating the success of its efforts by implementing mechanisms—such as minority contracting, local hiring, and resident ownership of the development—that benefit low-income and working families. A trolley stop located at Market Creek Plaza connects neighborhood residents to other locales across the region and also helps make this cultural and commercial center in the heart of the Diamond Neighborhoods a regional destination.

The state of Pennsylvania adopted groundbreaking legislation to spur the development and improvement of grocery stores in underserved areas. This is crucial, since Pennsylvania has the second-lowest number of supermarkets per capita of any state in the nation. State Representative Dwight Evans's supermarket initiative—a major part of Governor Edward Rendell's $1.1 billion comprehensive economic stimulus package—will provide financial assistance to urban and rural supermarkets in underserved areas of Pennsylvania. The supermarket development initiative falls under the $150 million First Industries (agriculture and tourism) section of the overall stimulus package and allows supermarkets to request planning grants or low-interest loans.

As communities begin to make comebacks and become attractive, connected places with amenities and services, it is important to guarantee that residents who stayed during difficult times can remain if they choose. Ironically, when a metropolitan region experiences a strong economy, it can threaten, rather than enhance, the stability of low-income communities and the livelihood of residents. When neighborhoods are transformed, tenured residents are often replaced—a process usually referred to as gentrification. Preventing displacement and securing low-income communities when revitalization begins is central to building equitable and inclusive regions. Strategies that allow long-term residents to remain in their neighborhoods to enjoy the long-awaited reinvestment are at the heart of advancing regional equity.

THE WAY FORWARD

There has been notable progress toward regional equity in the past several years; examples cited in this chapter are illustrative of dynamic and promising efforts under way around the country. The diversity of issue areas in which regional equity is being advanced and the breadth of actors who are leading this work are exciting and inspiring. While there is much progress to celebrate, the road to building more equitable and inclusive regions is a long one. Some important areas of investment that are needed to sustain and bring to scale the promising efforts discussed in this chapter include:

> *More resources.* Community and social justice advocates understand the importance of regional analysis and action, but for the most part they are positioned to work only in low-income, inner-city communities. There is usually no funding support for work that reaches outside those boundaries. For example, many community development corporations are totally dependent on low-income housing tax credits to develop their housing, and these credits are often restricted to housing built in inner cities. Redirected and new public, private, and philanthropic revenue sources are needed to support the innovative initiatives needed to realize the vision of regional equity. Additionally, the issue of more public resources aimed at reducing regional inequity need not pit those in favor of leaner government against those who feel that government should play a larger role. Investments that promote regional equity (public and private) in the long run should reduce the need to support those who can work but do not because of the physical inaccessibility of work. Also, promoting greater educational equity will strengthen the economic vitality of the region by allowing more people to contribute, and improving the environmental factors that contribute to poor health will reduce health-care expenditures.
>
> *New capacities.* Working regionally requires a different set of skills and knowledge than working at the neighborhood or city level. Finding the means to build the capacity of individuals and organizations to be regional equity actors is critical. For example, regional equity action often requires an understanding of planning, land use, and fiscal issues, which are not found in the traditional knowledge base of social justice advocates. Some of the skills and techniques that need to be built include: using data, mapping, and information to support policy change and inform campaigns; crafting compelling messages that make the case for regional equity; engaging diverse stakeholders; and organizing urban-core/inner-ring alliances. Sometimes this requires action in one jurisdiction, sometimes multiple ones. Other times action must move to the state level to reach the desired impact. Training, technical assistance, and translating existing research on regionalism into practical, on-the-ground solutions is an important area in need of continued and enhanced investment.
>
> *New collaborations and new venues for conversation and action.* Collaborations across sectors, across neighborhoods, and across jurisdictions are

essential for moving the regional equity agenda. Examples of collaborations between smart growth and social justice advocates highlighted in this chapter are promising, but such efforts need to be stronger, more inclusive, and more frequent. Moreover, regional discussions must move from talk to action to ensure that needed changes are enacted and implemented. There are a growing number of urban-suburban alliances and inner-ring suburban coalitions that need to be supported and strengthened. Regional equity requires analyzing and tackling deep-rooted issues of inequity in America—something that cannot be accomplished without honest and frank conversations about race. Venues for having these kinds of tough conversations in a focused, productive way are needed, as well as diverse strategies and leaders for change.

A *supportive infrastructure.* Given the new alliances, strategies, and analyses that are needed, an important area for investment is to build an organizational infrastructure that deepens and sustains regional equity action. It is very challenging for social justice advocates to enter regional conversations; anchor institutions that can serve as intermediaries that broadly engage a range of stakeholders on regional equity action are critical for fostering relationships and supporting change. For example, the Massachusetts Association of CDCs represents nonprofit housing developers at smart-growth and regional equity discussions and strategic venues and requires new resources to support its work. The emergence and growth of the regional equity movement as a promising vehicle for reinvigorating the quest for full inclusion and participation is exciting and timely. In the United States at least half the development needed to accommodate projected population growth has yet to be built, and as much as one-third of the built environment will need to be renovated or replaced between 2002 and 2025.[15] How government and the private sector respond to these needs will shape the country's future. Applying the values and policies of regional equity will help ensure a nation of inclusion and broad opportunity.

Getting a Seat at the Table

For equitable development to work, effective leadership is requisite, especially leadership by those who have a personal stake in their own community's future.

As the preceding examples attest, policy makers must take advantage of the wisdom, voice, and experience found in local constituencies throughout the United States. The failure to incorporate their knowledge deprives the nation of valuable input for policy formation. The solutions these communities could share are sources of inspiration and instruction in addressing perplexing problems that plague America's neighborhoods and regions.

The recognition that people experiencing problems should be integrally involved in proposing solutions is the source of the PolicyLink commitment to "lifting up what works"—through media outreach, presentations, and publications highlighting policies to achieve economic opportunity—so that the nation can use this wisdom, voice, and experience to address seemingly intractable problems and to make policy change and equitable progress.

A new generation of leadership is necessary to harness constituency knowledge and use it to advocate for a fully inclusive policy framework for the twenty-first century. Yet there are few avenues to policy making available to leaders who are truly representative of low-income communities and communities of color. In 2003, PolicyLink conducted research about leaders of color and policy development and published its findings in a report called *Leadership for Policy Change: Strengthening Communities of Color Through Leadership Development*. Drawing on interviews with more than a hundred leaders of nonprofit organizations and foundations, an analysis of seventy-two leadership development programs, and an extensive review of current leadership development literature, the report concluded that there is a need for more leaders of color who can be effective in developing and implementing economic and social policies; that barriers exist to their full participation; and strategies exist for removing these barriers and enabling leaders of color to use their expertise to benefit low-income communities of color *and* the nation.[16]

Involvement in policy making is critical. Public and private policies impact everyday life: jobs and education; health care and well-being; environmental preservation and neighborhood services; and transportation, recreation, and housing are all guided by local, state, and federal policies often formulated with little input from the many different residents who will be directly affected by those policies. Policies determine how and how long people will travel to get to work, result in disproportionate funding for inner-city and suburban schools, influence the quality of the air, and can be the means to affordable housing. Residents led by effective leaders can guide efforts to achieve policies to overcome neighborhood and community-wide challenges. Legislators, advocates, and the business community should engage these communities in advancing policy solutions that can address economic and social inequities based on race, class, gender, and geography.

Leadership for Policy Change makes clear that engaging more leaders of color in policy making requires a shift in resources, priorities, and power. When leaders who are directly connected to community concerns are engaged, new priorities emerge.

Successfully advancing economic and social equity agendas requires vigorous leadership to guide efforts to develop policy solutions that can ultimately benefit residents throughout the United States. These efforts must be led by leaders of color—and leaders who are not of color but who share a belief in the power of community, collaboration, and coalition building—who are fully prepared to engage the policy arena. Foundations can provide the support for skills development, training, and mentorship opportunities that leaders need.

Leadership for policy change is critical to the success of equitable development efforts and to making sure that practices that serve communities well are maintained and expanded for the greatest impact. This is the kind of leadership that must be actively encouraged and diligently supported so that everyone has the opportunity to participate and prosper in society.

NOTES

1. "America's Population to Hit 300 Million This Fall," *USA Today*, June 25, 2006.

2. Angela Glover Blackwell, Stewart Kwoh, and Manuel Pastor, *Searching for the Uncommon Common Ground: New Dimensions on Race in America* (W. W. Norton, 2002), 22.

3. Xavier de Souza Briggs, "A Piece of the Action: Community Equity in the New Economy," a paper prepared for the Social Venture Network Annual Meeting, New York, 2000.

4. PolicyLink has been in the forefront of one such emerging movement—*equitable development*. "Community building assumes that associations within a geographic area are important for community well-being; that bringing together a broad spectrum of stakeholders will provide a better understanding of problems; that sustainable solutions are based on knowing the facts, building on assets, and having a shared vision of improvement; and that an independent community-based capacity for analysis, planning, and convening is essential for success." *Stories of Renewal: Community Building and the Future of Urban America*, a report from The Rockefeller Foundation, January 1997, foreword, ii.

5. PolicyLink and the Funders' Network for Smart Growth and Livable Communities, *Promoting Regional Equity: A Framing Paper*, November 2002.

6. Collaborating in large measure with the author on this section of "Achieving Equitable Development" was Radhika K. Fox, senior program associate at PolicyLink in Oakland, CA.

7. Millennial Housing Commission, *Meeting Our Nation's Housing Challenges*, report of the Bipartisan Millennial Housing Commission Appointed by the Congress of the United States (Washington, DC: U.S. Government Printing Office, May 30, 2002).

8. Rolf Pendall, "Local Land Use Regulations and the Chain of Exclusion," *Journal of the American Planning Association* 66, no. 2 (Spring 2000): 125–43.

9. PolicyLink and the Pratt Institute Center for Community and Environmental Development (PICCED), *Increasing Housing Opportunity in New York City: The Case for Inclusionary Zoning* (Oakland, CA: PolicyLink and PICCED, September 2004).

10. Edward L. Glaeser and Matthew E. Kahn, "Decentralized Employment and the Transformation of the American City," National Bureau of Economic Research Working Paper Series, March 2001.

11. See PolicyLink, Equitable Development Toolkit: Equity in Transit-Oriented Development Tool for a more comprehensive discussion, at http://www.policylink .org/EquitableDevelopment/ (accessed August 2, 2004); Hank Dittmar and Gloria Ohland, *The New Transit Town: Best Practices in Transit Oriented Development* (Washington, DC: Island Press, 2003); Robert D. Bullard, Glenn S. Johnson, and Angel O. Torres, eds., *Highway Robbery: Transportation Racism and New Routes to Equity* (Boston: South End Press, 2004).

12. The California Partnership for Working Families, *Lifting Cities Out of Poverty: Opportunities and Challenges for the Emerging Community Benefits Movement*, 2004.

13. Edward L. Glaeser and Jesse Shapiro, *City Growth and the 2000 Census: Which Places Grew, and Why* (Washington, DC: Brookings Institution Center on Urban and Metropolitan Policy, 2001).

14. Paul Brophy and Kim Burnett, *Building a New Framework for Community Development in Weak Market Cities*, The Community Development Partnership Network, 2003.

15. The Funders' Network for Smart Growth and Livable Communities, *One Step Forward, Two Steps Back: Research on the Prospects for the Smart Growth and Livable Communities Movement* (Miami: The Funders' Network for Smart Growth and Livable Communities, 2004).

16. PolicyLink, *Leadership for Policy Change: Strengthening Communities of Color through Leadership Development* (Oakland, CA: PolicyLink, 2003).

Selected Bibliography

Anderson, Elijah, and Douglas S. Massey. *Problem of the Century: Racial Stratification in the United States at Century's End.* New York: Russell Sage Foundation, 2001.

Barnett, Jonathan. *Planning for a New Century: The Regional Agenda.* Washington, DC: Island Press, 2001.

Bell, Derek A. *Race, Racism, and American Law.* New York: Aspen Law and Business, 2000.

Benfield, F. Kaid, Jutka Terris, and Nancy Vorsanger. *Solving Sprawl: Models of Smart Growth in Communities Across America.* Washington, DC: Island Press, 2002.

Benfield, F. Kaid, Matthew D. Rami, and Donald D. T. Chen. *Once There Were Greenfields: How Urban Sprawl Is Undermining America's Environment, Economy and Social Fabric.* Washington, DC: Natural Resources Defense Council and Surface Transportation Project, 1999.

Blackwell, Angela Glover, Stewart Kwoh, and Manuel Pastor. *Searching for the Uncommon Ground: New Dimensions on Race in America.* New York: W. W. Norton, 2002.

Blakely, Edward J., and Mary G. Snyder. *Fortress America: Gated Communities in the United States.* Washington, DC: Brookings Institution Press, 1999.

Bluestone, Barry, and Mary Huff Stevenson. *The Boston Renaissance: Race, Space, and Economic Change in an American Metropolis.* New York: Russell Sage Foundation, 2000.

Bobo, Lawrence D., Melvin L. Oliver, James H. Johnson Jr., and Abel Valenzuela Jr., eds. *Prismatic Metropolis: Inequality in Los Angeles.* New York: Russell Sage Foundation, 2000.

Bonilla-Silva, Eduardo. *Racism Without Racists: Color-Blind Racism and the Persistence of Racial Inequality in the United States.* Lanham, MD: Rowman & Littlefield, 2003.

Bositis, David A. *The Political Perspectives of Young African Americans: A National Opinion Poll Special Report.* Washington, DC: Joint Center for Political and Economic Studies, 2001.

————. *Black Elected Officials: A Statistical Summary 2001*. Washington, DC: Joint Center for Political and Economic Studies, 2001.

Brinkley, Douglas. *The Great Deluge: Hurricane Katrina, New Orleans, and the Mississippi Gulf Coast*. New York: William Morrow, 2006.

Brown, Carolyn M., and David A. Padgett. "Top Cities for African Americans," *Black Enterprise* 34, no. 12 (July 2004): 1–13.

Bullard, Robert D., ed. *In Search of the New South: The Black Urban Experiences in the 1970s and 1980s*. Tuscaloosa: University of Alabama Press, 1991.

Bullard, Robert D., J. Eugene Grigsby III, and Charles Lee. *Residential Apartheid: The American Legacy*. Los Angeles: UCLA Center for African Studies, 1994.

Bullard, Robert D., and Glenn S. Johnson. *Just Transportation: Dismantling Race and Class Barriers to Mobility*. Gabriola Island, BC: New Society Publishers, 1997.

Bullard, Robert D., Glenn S. Johnson, and Angel O. Torres. *Highway Robbery: Transportation Racism and New Routes to Equity*. Cambridge, MA: South End Press, 2004.

————. *Sprawl City: Race, Politics, and Planning in Atlanta*. Washington, DC: Island Press, 2000.

Calthorpe, Peter, and William Fulton. *The Regional City: Planning for the End of Sprawl*. Washington, DC: Island Press, 2001.

Cashin, Sheryll. *The Failures of Integration: How Race and Class Are Undermining the American Dream*. New York: Public Affairs, 2004.

Conley, Dalton. *Being Black, Living in the Red: Race, Wealth, and Social Policy in America*. Berkeley: University of California Press, 1999.

Cutter, Susan. *Hazards, Vulnerability and Environmental Justice*. New York: Earthscan, 2006.

Darden, Joe T. *The Significance of White Supremacy in the Canadian Metropolis of Toronto*. Lewiston, NY: The Edwin Mellen Press, 2004.

————. "Residential Segregation: The Causes and Social and Economic Consequences." In *Racial Liberalism and the Politics of Urban America*, edited by Curtis Stokes and Theresa Melendez, 321–44. East Lansing: Michigan State University Press, 2003.

Darity, William A. Jr., and Samuel L. Myers Jr. *Persistent Disparity: Race and Inequality in the U.S. since 1945*. Northampton, MA: Edward Elgar Publishing, 1998.

Dreier, Peter, John Mollenkoph, and Todd Swanstrom. *Place Matters: Metropolitics for the Twenty-First Century*. Lawrence: University Press of Kansas, 2001.

Dyson, Michael Eric. *Come Hell or High Water: Hurricane Katrina and the Color of Disaster*. New York: Basic Books, 2006.

Farley, Reynolds, Sheldon Danziger, and Harry J. Holzer. *Detroit Divided*. New York: Russell Sage Foundation, 2002.

Feagin, Joe. *Racist America*. New York: Routledge, 2000.

Florida, Richard. *The Rise of the Creative Class: And How It's Transforming Work, Leisure, Community and Everyday Life*. New York: Basic Books, 2002.

Frankenberg, Erica, and Chungmei Lee. *Race in American Public Schools: Rapidly Resegregating School Districts*. Cambridge, MA: Harvard Civil Rights Project, August 2002.

Frazier, John W., Florence M. Margai, and Eugene Tettey-Fio. *Race and Place*. Boulder, CO: Westview Press, 2003.

Frey, William H. *Census 2000 Shows Large Black Return to the South, Reinforcing the Region's "White-Black" Demographic Profile.* PSC Research Report No. 01-473. Ann Arbor: University of Michigan, May 2001.

Gallagher, Charles A. *Rethinking the Color Line: Readings in Race and Ethnicity.* New York: McGraw-Hill, 2004.

George, Cardinal Francis, OMI. *Dwell in My Love: A Pastoral Letter on Racism.* Chicago: Archdiocese of Chicago, 2001.

Gillham, Oliver. *The Limitless City: A Primer on the Urban Sprawl Debate.* Washington, DC: Island Press, 2002.

Glaeser, Edward, and Jacob Vigdor. *Recent Segregation in the 2000 Census: Promising News.* Washington, DC: The Brookings Institution, 2001.

Gottlieb, Paul D. "Residential Amenities, Firm Location and Economic Development," *Urban Studies* 32 (1995): 1413–36.

Hacker, Andrew. *Two Nations: Black and White, Separate, Hostile, Unequal.* New York: Scribner, 2003.

Hartman, Chester, and Gregory Squires. *There Is No Such Thing as a Natural Disaster.* New York: Routledge, 2006.

Hochschild, Jennifer, and Nathan Scovronick. *The American Dream and the Public Schools.* New York: Oxford University Press, 2003.

Horn, Jed. *Breach of Faith: Hurricane Katrina and the Near Death of a Great American City.* New York: Random House, 2006.

Iceland, John, Daniel Weinberg, and Erika Steinmetz. *Racial and Ethnic Residential Segregation in the United States: 1980–2000.* Washington, DC: U.S. Bureau of the Census, 2002.

Institute on Race and Poverty. *Racism and Metropolitan Dynamics: The Civil Rights Challenge of the 21st Century.* Minneapolis: Commissioned for the Ford Foundation, 2002. http://www1.umn.edu/irp/fordinfo.html.

Jargowsky, Paul A. *Poverty and Place: Ghettos, Barrios, and the American City.* New York: Russell Sage Foundation, 1997.

Johnson, Valerie C. *Black Power in the Suburbs: The Myth or Reality of African-American Suburban Political Incorporation.* Albany: State University of New York Press, 2002.

Joint Center for Housing Studies. *The State of the Nation's Housing 2002.* Cambridge, MA: JCHD.

Joint Center for Political and Economic Studies, *Black Elected Officials: A Statistical Summary, 2001.* Washington, DC: Joint Center for Political and Economic Studies, 2003.

Katz, Bruce. *Reflections on Regionalism.* Washington, DC: The Brookings Institution, 2000.

Keister, Lisa. *Wealth in America.* New York: Cambridge University Press, 2000.

Lang, Robert E. *Office Sprawl: The Evolving Geography of Business.* Washington, DC: The Brookings Institution, 2000.

Levitan, Mark. *A Crisis of Black Male Employment: Unemployment and Joblessness in New York City, 2003.* New York: Community Service Society, February 2004.

Lipsitz, George. *The Possessive Investment in Whiteness.* Philadelphia: Temple University Press, 1998.

Loury, Glenn C. *The Anatomy of Racial Inequality.* Cambridge, MA: Harvard University Press, 2002.

Miller-Adams, Michelle. *Owning Up: Poverty, Assets, and the American Dream.* Washington, DC: Brookings Institution Press, 2002.

Muhammad, Dedrick, Attieno Davis, Meizhu Lui, and Betsy Leonard-Wright. *State of the Dream 2004: Enduring Disparities in Black and White.* Boston: United for a Fair Economy, 2004.

National Housing Law Project. *False HOPE: A Critical Assessment of the HOPE VI Public Housing Redevelopment Program.* Washington, DC: Center for Community Change, 2002.

National Urban League. *The State of Black America 2004.* New York: National Urban League, 2004.

O'Connor, Alice, Chris Tilly, and Lawrence D. Bobo, eds. *Urban Inequality: Evidence from Four Cities.* New York: Russell Sage Foundation, 2003.

Oliver, Melvin L., and Thomas M. Shapiro. *Black Wealth/White Wealth: A New Perspective on Racial Inequality.* New York: Routledge, 1996.

O'Neill, David, *The Smart Growth Tool Kit: Community Profiles and Case Studies to Help Advance Smart Growth Initiatives.* Washington, DC: Urban Land Institute, 2000.

Orfield, Myron. *American Metropolitics: The New Suburban Reality.* Washington, DC: Brookings Institution Press, 2002.

———. *Metropolitics: A Regional Agenda for Community and Stability.* Washington, DC: Brookings Institution Press, 1997.

Pastor, Manuel, Jr., Peter Dreier, J. Eugene Grigsby III, and Marta Lopez-Garza. *Regions That Work: How Cities and Suburbs Can Grow Together.* Minneapolis: University of Minnesota Press, 2000.

Pastor, Manuel, Jr., Robert D. Bullard, James Boyce, Alice Fothergill, Rachel Morello-Frosch, and Beverly Wright. *In the Wake of the Storm: Environment, Disaster, and Race after Katrina.* New York: The Russell Sage Foundation, 2006.

Pattillo-McCoy, Mary. *Black Picket Fences.* Chicago: University of Chicago Press, 1999.

PolicyLink. *Promoting Regional Equity: A Framing Paper.* Miami: The Funder's Network for Smart Growth, November 2002.

Popkin, Susan, Diane K. Levy, Laura Harris, Jennifer Comey, Mary Cunningham, and Larry Buron. *HOPE VI Panel Study: Baseline Report.* Washington, DC: Urban Institute, 2000.

powell, john a. *Racism and Metropolitan Dynamics: The Civil Rights Challenge of the 21st Century.* Minneapolis: Institute on Race & Poverty, University of Minnesota, August 2002.

Raphael, Steven, and Michael Stoll. *Moderate Progress in Narrowing Spatial Mismatch Between Blacks and Jobs in the 1990s.* Washington, DC: The Brookings Institution, 2002.

Ross, Stephen, and John Yinger. *The Color of Credit: Mortgage Discrimination, Research Methodology, and Fair-Lending Enforcement.* Cambridge, MA: MIT Press, 2002.

Rothenberg, Paula S. *White Privilege: Essential Readings on the Other Side of Racism.* 2nd ed. New York: Worth Publishers, 2005.

Rubinowitz, Leonard, and James Rosenbaum. *Crossing the Class and Color Lines.* Chicago: University of Chicago Press, 2000.

Rusk, David. *The Segregation Tax: The Cost of Racial Segregation on Black Homeowners.* Washington, DC: Brookings Institution Center on Urban and Metropolitan Policy, 2001.

———. *Inside Game/Outside Game: Winning Strategies for Saving Urban America.* Washington, DC: Brookings Institution Press, 1999.

Sanchez, Thomas W., and Robert E. Lang. *Security versus Status: The Two Worlds of Gated Communities.* Census Note. Metropolitan Institute, Virginia Tech, 2003.

Sen, Amartya. *Development as Freedom.* New York: Anchor Books, 1999.

Shapiro, Thomas M. *The Hidden Cost of Being African American: How Wealth Perpetuates Inequality.* New York: Oxford, 2004.

Shapiro, Thomas, and Edward Wolff. *Assets for the Poor.* New York: Russell Sage Foundation, 2001.

Sierra Club. *The Dark Side of the American Dream: The Cost and Consequences of Suburban Sprawl.* College Park, MD: Sierra Club, August 1998.

Simmons, Patrick. *Changes in Minority Homeownership during the 1990s.* Washington, DC: The Fannie Mae Foundation, 2001.

Sjoquist, David L. *The Atlanta Paradox.* New York: Russell Sage Foundation, 2000.

Squires, Gregory D. *Urban Sprawl: Causes, Consequences, and Policy Responses.* Washington, DC: Urban Institute Press, 2002.

Stack, Carol B. *Call to Home: African Americans Reclaim the Rural South.* New York: Basic Books, 1997.

Stoll, Michael A. *African Americans and the Color Line.* New York: Russell Sage Foundation and Population Reference Bureau, 2004.

Stuart, Guy. *Discriminating Risk: The U.S. Mortgage Lending Industry in the Twentieth Century.* Ithaca, NY: Cornell University Press, 2003.

Sugrue, Thomas J. *The Origins of the Urban Crisis: Race and Inequality in Postwar Detroit.* Princeton, NJ: Princeton University Press, 1996.

Thomas, June M., and Marsha Ritzdorf. *Urban Planning and the African American Community: In the Shadows.* Thousand Oaks, CA: Sage Publications, 1997.

Tilly, Charles. *Durable Inequality.* Berkeley: University of California Press, 1998.

Van Heerden, Ivor. *The Storm: What Went Wrong and Why during Hurricane Katrina.* New York: Viking, 2006.

Wilson, William J. *When Work Disappears: The World of the New Urban Poor.* New York: Vintage Books, 1997.

Winant, Howard. *The World Is a Ghetto.* New York: Basic Books, 2001.

Wolch, Jennifer, Manuel Pastor Jr., and Peter Dreier, eds. *Up Against Sprawl: Public Policy and the Making of Southern California.* Minneapolis: University of Minnesota Press, 2004.

Index

About the Editor and Contributors

Carl Anthony is the program director of the Sustainable Metropolitan Communities Initiative at the Ford Foundation. Prior to joining Ford, he was founder and executive director of the Urban Habitat Program in San Francisco, a founder and editor of the *Race, Poverty and Environment Journal*, president of Earth Island Institute, and a convener of the Bay Area Alliance for Sustainable Development. He has taught architecture and urban planning at University of California, Berkeley, and Columbia University.

Angela Glover Blackwell is president of PolicyLink, a national nonprofit research, communications, capacity-building, and advocacy organization. For a decade, beginning in 1977, Blackwell served as a partner with Public Advocates, a nationally known public interest law firm. Blackwell is a coauthor of *Searching for the Uncommon Common Ground: New Dimensions on Race in America* (2002).

Edward J. Blakely was appointed the New Orleans "Recovery Czar" in 2006. He is a former professor of urban and regional planning at the University of Sydney. Dr. Blakely is an internationally recognized scholar in urban community development, and has also been a successful practitioner in strategic planning, financing, real estate development, and project management. His books include *Economic Development Finance* (with Susan Giles, 2001), *Fortress America: Gated Communities in the United States* (1997), *Separate Societies: Poverty and Inequality in U.S. Cities* (1992, coauthored with William Goldsmith), *Planning Local Economic Development* (1989), *Taking Development Initiatives: Local Government's Role in Economic Development* (1986), and *Rural Communities in Advanced Industrial Society* (1980).

David A. Bositis is the author or coauthor of five books, nine monographs, and numerous scholarly articles, analyses, and reports. Prior to working at the Joint Center for Political and Economic Studies, he taught political science at the George Washington University and at SUNY-Potsdam. Since 1992, Dr. Bositis has designed and managed sixteen national surveys for the Joint Center, which have included more than 20,000 respondents. Since 1997, Dr. Bositis has also been the author of the yearly Joint Center series on black elected officials titled: *Black Elected Officials: A Statistical Analysis*.

Robert D. Bullard is the Ware Distinguished Professor of Sociology and director of the Environmental Justice Resource Center at Clark Atlanta University. His most recent books include *Dumping in Dixie: Race, Class and Environmental Quality* (2000), *Sprawl City: Race, Politics and Planning in Atlanta* (2000), *Just Sustainabilities: Development in an Unequal World* (2003), *Highway Robbery: Transportation Racism and New Routes to Equity* (2004), and *The Quest for Environmental Justice: Human Rights and the Politics of Pollution* (2005).

Sheryll Cashin is a professor at Georgetown Law Center. Prior to joining the faculty, Professor Cashin was the staff director for the Community Empowerment Board in the Office of the Vice President at the White House, an associate counsel for the Office of Transition Counsel, and an associate at Sirote & Permutt law firm. She was law clerk to U.S. Supreme Court Justice Thurgood Marshall and Judge Abner Mikva of the U.S. Court of Appeals for the District of Columbia Circuit. She is the author of *The Failures of Integration: How Race and Class Are Undermining the American Dream* (2004).

Joe T. Darden is professor of geography at Michigan State University. He is also a former Fulbright Scholar, Department of Geography, University of Toronto, 1997 to 1998. Dr. Darden's research interests are urban social geography, residential segregation, and socioeconomic neighborhood inequality in multiracial societies. His books include *Afro-Americans in Pittsburgh: The Residential Segregation of a People* (1973), *The Ghetto: Readings with Interpretations* (1981), *Detroit: Race and Uneven Development* (1987), and *The Significance of White Supremacy in the Canadian Metropolis of Toronto* (2004).

J. Eugene Grigsby III is the president and CEO of the National Health Education Foundation. His research has focused on urban housing, land use, and economic development strategies. An internationally recognized expert in urban development strategies, he is the coauthor of *Residential Apartheid: The American Legacy*, which received the 1996 Gustavus Myers Center Outstanding Book Award, and *Regions That Work: How Cities and Suburbs Can Grow Together* (2000). As director of the Advanced Policy Institute, he works to improve the performance of public agencies, nonprofit organizations, and private firms through training programs, technical assistance, and strategic policy conferences.

Glenn S. Johnson is a research associate in the Environmental Justice Resource Center and associate professor in the Department of Sociology and Criminal Justice at Clark Atlanta University. He is coeditor of *Just Transportation: Dismantling Race and Class Barriers to Mobility* (1997), *Sprawl City: Race, Politics, and Planning in Atlanta* (2000), and *Highway Robbery: Transportation Racism and New Routes* (2004).

john a. powell is a nationally recognized authority in the areas of civil rights; civil liberties; and issues relating to race, poverty, and the law. He teaches civil rights law, property law, and jurisprudence and was recently appointed the Gregory Williams Chair of Civil Rights and Civil Liberties Law at the Ohio State University Moritz College of Law. He is also the director of the Kirwan Institute on Race and Ethnicity at Ohio State University and the founder and former executive director of the Institute on Race and Poverty (IRP), which is located at the University of Minnesota Law School. The institute was created in 1993 to focus on dynamics created by the intersections of race and poverty.

Thomas W. Sanchez is an associate professor in the Department of Urban Affairs and Planning at Virginia Polytechnic Institute and State University. He holds a Ph.D. in city planning from the Georgia Institute of Technology. His teaching areas include transportation, land use, and geographic information systems, with research focused on the social and spatial impacts of transportation activities.

Michael A. Stoll is an associate professor of policy studies in the School of Public Policy and Social Research, and interim director of the Center for the Study of Urban Poverty at the University of California, Los Angeles (UCLA). His main research interests include the study of urban poverty and inequality, specifically the interplay of labor markets, race/ethnicity, geography, and workforce development. Dr. Stoll's published work includes an examination of the labor market difficulties of African Americans and less-skilled workers, in particular the roles that racial residential segregation, job location patterns, employer discrimination, transportation, and job information play in limiting employment opportunities.

Angel O. Torres is a Geographic Information Systems (GIS) training specialist with the Environmental Justice Resource Center at Clark Atlanta University. He has a master's degree in city planning from the Georgia Institute of Technology, with a concentration in GIS. Mr. Torres previously worked for the Corporation for Olympic Development of Atlanta and the Atlanta Project, where he was the GIS specialist on several neighborhoods and housing redevelopment plans. He coedited *Sprawl City: Race, Politics, and Planning in Atlanta* (2000) and *Highway Robbery: Transportation Racism and New Routes* (2004).

Beverly Wright is a sociologist and the founding director of the Deep South Center for Environmental Justice (DSCEJ) at Dillard University (formerly at Xavier University of Louisiana) in New Orleans. She is a leading scholar, advocate, and activist in the environmental justice arena. She served on the U.S. Commission of Civil Rights for the state of Louisiana and on the city of New Orleans's Select Committee for the Sewerage and Water Board. She is cochair of the National Black Environmental Justice Network and the Environmental Justice Climate Change (EJCC) Initiative. She is a native of New Orleans, survivor of Hurricane Katrina, and coeditor of *In the Wake of the Storm: Environment, Disaster, and Race after Katrina* (2006).